The Liberal Mind
1914–1929

Cambridge Studies in the History and Theory of Politics

The Liberal Mind
1914–1929

MICHAEL BENTLEY
Lecturer in History, University of Sheffield

CAMBRIDGE UNIVERSITY PRESS
CAMBRIDGE
LONDON · NEW YORK · MELBOURNE

Published by the Syndics of the Cambridge University Press
The Pitt Building, Trumpington Street, Cambridge CB2 1RP
Bentley House, 200 Euston Road, London NW1 2DB
32 East 57th Street, New York, NY 10022, USA
296 Beaconsfield Parade, Middle Park, Melbourne 3206, Australia

First published 1977

Printed in Great Britain at the
University Press, Cambridge

Library of Congress Cataloguing in Publication Data
Bentley, Michael, 1948– .
The liberal mind, 1914–1929.
(Cambridge studies in the history and
theory of politics)
Bibliography: p.
Includes index.
1. Liberalism – Great Britain – History.
2. Liberal Party (Gt. Brit.) – History.
3. Great Britain – Politics and
government – 1910–1936. I. Title.
JN231.B45   320.5′1′0941   76-11072
ISBN 0 521 21243 X

Contents

To My Parents

Acknowledgements

Valuable help was received from the archivists and staff of numerous libraries – in particular from those of Birmingham University Library, the Bodleian Library, the British Library, Cambridge University Library, Colindale Newspaper Library, Flintshire County Record Office, Liverpool Central Library, the British Library of Political and Economic Science, the Library of the National Liberal Club, the National Library of Scotland and the Scottish Record Office, Newcastle University Library, the Public Record Office, Reading University Library and Sheffield University Library – and the author wishes to record his thanks for their guidance and co-operation. He wishes also to thank owners of copyright material for granting access to private papers, especially Mr Mark Bonham Carter, Lord Gainford, Mr John Grigg, Viscount Harcourt, Miss Anne Holt, Lord Kennet, Mr John MacCallum Scott and Lady Stansgate. Dr Cameron Hazlehurst was very helpful in making available certain sources. Financial assistance during various stages of research undertaken in connexion with this book was provided by the Department of Education and Science, the Political Science Research Fund of the University of Cambridge and the University Research Fund of the University of Sheffield.

The research thesis on which this book is based was helpfully criticized by Dr K. O. Morgan and Professor J. R. Vincent. The debt which the author owes to his former research supervisor, Mr Maurice Cowling, is profound and patent. Less apparent is the guidance of the staff of Cambridge University Press, who have, by their efficiency, smoothed the passage of the book. Jane Bentley, Bob Moore and Clyde Binfield gave generously of their time and eradicated many mistakes in typescript and proof; those remaining are the sole responsibility of the author.

September 1976   M.B.

Note on the text

Abbreviations within quotations have been retained (except where their meaning may be unclear) apart from those flashes of the pen that have been taken to represent ampersands: these have been transcribed as 'and'. Original punctuation has usually been followed unless the clarity of a given passage was likely to be obscured, in which case punctuation has been inserted without comment. Expansions and substitutions within quotations have been placed in square brackets.

All printed works cited in the endnotes or bibliography were published in London unless otherwise stated. All unprinted sources consisting of bound volumes of folios have been given detailed references, though this has not been thought worth while where classification is still temporary or unhelpful. Question marks preceding names or dates indicate illegibility or an omission in the original. Where nomenclature is confused by grant of peerage or change of name (e.g. Asquith/Oxford, Mond/Melchett), the usage in references follows the style of the document concerned.

Introduction

This is a short book which, arguably, ought to be a long one. Yet considerations beyond economic stringency suggest the usefulness of brevity. It is the point of the book to argue a case and not to exhaust an area of research. It is not the intention to examine Liberalism in all its facets but rather to explore the mind of its adherents as it is revealed in the activities of the Liberal elite. Neither is it intended to examine the psephological history of the Liberal party and its electorate. Attention will be directed instead at the more limited problems posed by the relationship between Liberals and their Liberalism and what they thought it meant. The book should be seen, that is to say, as a commentary on Liberal cosmology during a period when that cosmology was understood by its adherents to be under frontal attack.

Between 1914 and 1929 the custodians of traditional Liberalism lost almost everything they most valued in political life. Their loss of political power was most noticeably reflected in the performance of the Liberal party at the polls, and it has been this aspect of the Liberal decline which has attracted the attention of historians. But there are related and possibly more fundamental perspectives to be noticed. The war and its aftermath uprooted the political world that Liberals had understood and substituted something which seemed by comparison brash, cheap and contemptible. It is the frame of mind which formulated judgements such as this that is made the object of study here. The period of Liberal decline offers the best context in which to carry out this study because at no other time were the preconceptions and assumptions of the Liberal mind rendered so explicit by the pressure of events. What might have sufficed as a generally acceptable understanding of what 'true Liberalism' was and who 'good Liberals' were in 1906 would not have been acceptable in 1916: it would have been even less so in 1926. Nor does such a study merely monitor responses to change, for through its axioms and anxieties the Liberal mind was itself partly responsible for the failure of Liberalism to cope with change effectively. It is an

1

anaemic explanation of political activity which does not take account of contemporary conceptions of what was understood to be permissible or possible by the politicians concerned.

A language of analysis is required to convey that understanding adequately, and the choice of a suitable one is problematical. It has been thought right to speak of a Liberal 'mind', not in obedience to intellectual fashion and its cant language, but out of respect for what the material prescribes. Authenticity (should it be wanted) is not difficult to demonstrate. Before the First World War one finds Lord Alfred Douglas, in a bilious review, 'appalled that the Liberal mind [was] a sour, dour, superior affair, full of kinks and ill-disposed to mankind at large'.[1] But it was the coming of the war which did most to stimulate thoughts which had long been allowed to lie peacefully, and particularly stimulating were the attitudes and activities of Lloyd George and his circle. '[T]he Northcliffes,' one reads, 'the Milners, the Beaverbrooks, the Bottomleys, the Pankhursts...d[id] not appeal to the Liberal mind.'[2] When the time came to construct explanations for political failure after the war, moreover, that Liberal mind – 'the open and receptive mind, eager for new impressions, brave, poetic and illogical'[3] – was still to be found hoping for better things and lamenting lost virtues.

More telling than any formal validation, however, is the obser vation that 'mind' was a staple term of political discussion in the years to be considered here, regardless of which individual was speaking or which party he belonged to. Hence Arthur Acland was thought to be useful to Liberals because he was thought to be 'in touch with the Labour people and the Labour mind'.[4] On the Conservative side, there were aspects of Lord Robert Cecil's 'political positive mind' which disturbed Herbert Gladstone.[5] It was as important for Lloyd George to convince supporters that his foreign policy was 'Liberal-minded' as it was for him to convince opponents that his 'whole bent of mind' was democratic.[6] Violet Bonham-Carter, on the other hand, can be seen reacting against the League of Nations (which Lloyd George pretended to champion) because she did not, in her own phrase, have 'the League mind'.[7] And so one could go on. As the historian works his way through the primary material he is struck by the pervasiveness of an explanatory language of 'mind' and 'spirit' and 'outlook'. It is reflected in the printed word.[8] It is common in the private muse – whether Lord Salisbury is postponing activity until 'the public mind is more at ease' (1919), Gladstone hoping that the country is about to develop 'a fairly stable political mind' (1929) or Ernest Simon doubting that a Liberal renaissance is feasible 'with the world in its present frame of mind' (1939).[9] There existed, that is to say, a language in which politics was debated, and within that language the vocabulary of 'mind' was an important constituent.

That Liberals believed this mode of explanation to be particularly relevant to their own situation after 1914 says a good deal about what Liberals thought their Liberalism ought to be about. It was not a series of readily applicable maxims which could be arranged in tidy order for the purpose of a political manifesto: it was in 'the very nature of such a creed that its articles, negative or positive, [could not] be engraved once for all upon tables of stone'.[10] In place of a view of Liberalism which implied a list of commandments, the vision was characterized by a metaphysical totality: 'Liberalism is more than a creed: it is a state of mind, a political religion. It has its saints and martyrs as well as its philosophers and teachers, and their numbers increase day by day.'[11] Mind and religion were in fact hard to separate and both tended to be subsumed in a politics of faith during a period when versions of the 'true' Liberalism became rapturous and urgent. Yet the language remained the same. Liberalism was 'the creed of open-minded men', 'a temper, an attitude, a state of mind', 'a temper, a spirit, a method of approach', 'a spirit, an attitude, an atmosphere'.[12] It was because the doctrine was unstated that its powers of comprehension were so great. It was able to explain all the world without needing to explain any one part of it. Indeed one reason why the Liberal mind manifested itself so plainly after 1914 was that this connected completeness was challenged for the first time. Contemporaries may have been in disagreement about what the Liberal mind ought to contain but no one could doubt that the content and values of the post-war political world had no part in it.

It would plainly be mistaken, however, to move from the statement that the Liberal mind entailed a comprehensive view of the world towards that which alleges that it was also a monolithic view among all 'Liberals'. In no sense is it the burden of this book to make the absurd suggestion that Liberals were 'of one mind' between 1914 and 1929. The overriding intention will be to depict and illustrate the various frames of mind through which Liberalism passed in those years. And despite this recourse to plurality, there is point in discussing 'the' Liberal mind in the singular because the doctrine and moods which Liberalism was believed by Liberals to embody were broadly identified and agreed. To think of oneself as a Liberal imposed some limitations on one's activities as a Liberal politician; it conditioned at the very least what could be said in public – which in turn conditioned what might later be said in private. If Liberals did not contemplate politics with a uniformity of outlook, neither did they do so with more diversity of outlook than might be thought appropriate to members of a political party. The requirements of what were understood to be distinctively Liberal ideals – thought, doctrine, policy, taste, tone – imposed restrictions on what might legitimately be done. They helped form a politician's conception of what his function was within the political system and of what he could hope to achieve.

But the history of the Liberal mind is not the history of an ideology. It is the outcome of an interconnexion between world and thought-world and it is to be discerned as much in practice as in theory. What is most frequently observed in the relationship between the two is not a body of theory prescribing and controlling activity so much as modes of activity (in which the variations are bounded by experience and institutional limitations) generating doctrines of explanation and benediction.[13] Successful politicians are seen to be successful, not because they apply doctrine to their politics, but because they recognize that their politics will produce as a necessary consequence doctrine which will need to be controlled and manipulated. Yet if the role of practice needs stressing it should not be assumed that doctrine can be ignored or reduced to something more elemental. The notion of an 'empirical' politics is in any case misleading. The judgement which politicians use in deciding what will work best or provoke least resistance is itself affected by considerations which are not empirical, since any conception of how the political world operates is as much a function of an observer's position as his conception of how it ought to operate. Doctrine plays a double role, therefore, as a conditioner of how the political world will be conceived and as a predictable and serious consequence of action within that world.

This circular relationship between theory and practice cannot be elucidated in the 'higher-flown think-pieces' disliked by Professor Elton.[14] The examination must anchor itself in the day-to-day milieu of political action of its portrait of a political mind is to be plausible.

That is not to say that an inquiry of this kind can concern itself only with the explicit. The search for contours which may have been blurred in contemporary eyes is a pressing one for the intellectual historian. He tries to silhouette what may have previously lain in shadow in order to lend to the period's image a definition beyond the experience of contemporaries. Doing so, moreover, need not imply that the process is an arbitrary one[15] nor that it is reducible to a search for controlling 'paradigms' within the political language of the period.[16] What one is doing is making a series of developments intelligible by responding to those aspects of the period which surviving material suggests were important to contemporaries. In this sense the Liberal mind is at once an historical contruction and a transmitted relic. The argument in these chapters begins with the thought that the idea of a Liberal mind helps to make sense of what is known to have happened and performs much the same function as Bacon's 'causes and axioms'. That axioms may be seen here to receive as much attention as causes may leave the impression that what follows is designed primarily to offer an illustration of the relationship between theory and practice in the history of politics. It is perhaps better seen, however, as a more restricted statement about the political world which Liberals believed they were living in between 1914 and 1929 and the frame of mind through which their vision found its focus.

I. The party spirit

1. Exhumation

The great recompense is that we have done with party politics for a while.
But how long the politician will be content to forego his morbid diet I
cannot tell.

    Rosebery to Spender, 23 January 1915, Spender MSS, 46387 fols.
87–8.

He is the only person I know who is not obsessed with ghosts, and there
are so many people who get obsessed with the ghosts of John Stuart Mill
or Adam Smith.

    Lord Riddell on Lloyd George, *c.* 1913, quoted in Lucy Masterman,
C. F. G. Masterman (1939), 257.

I

The Liberalism which observers were soon to call 'historic', the
doctrine which Mill announced, Gladstone embodied and 'which
Lord Morley define[d] in his beautiful "Recollections"',[1] was
neither completely dead nor yet very much alive in 1914. That
perspective of Liberal history which once led posterity to believe
that the doctrine and the party representing it had been doomed
in the face of intractable pre-war problems or 'rotting at its roots'
in the constituencies is one which has rightly been challenged. A
more plausible interpretation of the years before 1914 is one in
which the difficulties of the Liberals are seen to be severe but not
insuperable. The problems posed by the constitutional crisis,
Ireland, the suffragettes, industrial unrest and a trembling international situation were not problems with which Liberalism, as
understood by those who professed to practise it, was unfitted to
cope. For eight years Liberals had been running away (sensibly)
from contentious issues, and there was nothing in the discernible
context of Asquith's government after 1910 to prevent them from
running and trimming as they had done in the past. There was
always the prospect of fighting another day and fighting effectively
in the general election which was due in 1915. The material which
has survived provides no convincing demonstration that Liberalism was exhausted or that Liberals believed that it was, apart

from isolated moments of crisis or temper. Viewed from 1914, the years since 1906 did not present themselves to Liberals as a linear decline in political fortune. The party had often in the past revived after surviving a difficult period. There was every reason to hope that it would do so again.

Not that the years after 1910 had been pleasant ones for the Liberal government. Asquith's prediction that the elections of 1910 would 'clear the air and make the way fairly plain if not exactly smooth'[2] and Esher's belief that the political barometer was now 'set fair'[3] typified a confidence which was soon to be eroded. Legacies of earlier struggles with Home Rule, Welsh Disestablishment and the House of Lords remained to be confronted. As early as September 1911 Asquith expressed to Bryce his anxieties about these problems. '[W]hat with Home Rule and (still more) the reconstruction of the Second Chamber', he wrote, 'it will not be by any means plain sailing.'[4] Ireland was an oppressive weight, and among an apathetic electorate there was nowhere effectively to dump it.[5] Much dissension revealed itself over Disestablishment, which Holt believed would cause more trouble than Home Rule, and the suffragette campaigns.[6] The radical policies of 1911–14, moreover, brought as much irritation as inspiration in their train. Through the inauguration of his land scheme, Lloyd George incurred abuse 'owing to his attitude in having a private land system inquiry, and running a land question campaign through satellites at the bye elections'[7] – a resentment which was to be heard again after the war. National Insurance was an equally divisive issue and, together with the Cabinet ruction of 23 August 1911 and the banishing of McKenna from the Admiralty, it combined with Lloyd George's burgeoning radicalism to convince Grey that if the party were to be defeated in parliament (and by 1912 there were those who were looking towards an election)[8] there would be 'a distinct cleavage between Lloyd George who ha[d] wild schemes about the land, etc., and the more moderate section of the Party; again between those who ha[d] followed him [Grey] in foreign affairs and those who t[ook] the view of Massingham and the Nation'.[9]

Foreign affairs were taken to represent an area of unusual political delicacy during a period when small events constantly threatened to trigger large ones.[10] Just how violently this atmosphere could escalate internal party squabbles was demonstrated in the notorious quarrel between Lloyd George and Churchill over naval estimates in 1914 when enough of the Liberal elite associated themselves with Lloyd George's stand to lend weight to Maxse's castigation of pre-war Liberals as 'morbid lovers of peace'.[11] It would be a mistake to see in the Germanophil radicalism of these years an authentic emblem of the Liberal mind, but it would be far more damaging to ignore the path which such sentiment was to follow after 1914. It is important to recognize at the outset that there existed a section of Liberal thought which could see in the coming of the war only a tragic vindication of radical attacks on Grey's secret diplomacy and the end of 'pure' Liberalism as Gladstone wanted to project it.[12]

But did the challenges posed by these dilemmas assume a character which Liberals themselves conceived to be fundamental? Seemingly they did not. The problem of Home Rule, after all, would have bewildered any political party; the failure to deal with it was not viewed as a failure of Liberalism as such. And while Insurance and land reform incited hot criticism, the volume of it was declining rather than increasing as 1914 approached. By April 1913, for example, Samuel had come to believe that Insurance was a far less unpopular catchcry than the rival one of Tariff Reform.[13] Policies might flounder in the face of opposition but Holt was almost triumphant in his conviction that the passing of the Parliament Bill inaugurated a new era when 'things [would be] different' since the Liberals would 'have only to wait patiently and loyally for another 12 or 15 months to secure [their] objects'.[14] A disappointing by-election record might strike Churchill as 'a source of great peril and vexation',[15] but as well as having the capacity to kick back, Liberals could also count on enough luck to muddle through. Liberals had no monopoly of crises and disappointments and although the Conservative resurgence had begun, it was not to find its real momentum until during the war. If Liberals prayed in 1911 that Balfour be allowed to lead the Conservative party forever,[16] there was no reason to mope when he resigned. If it had been deep in the Conservative penumbra when Esher had seen the strength of the government lying in the weakness of the opposition,[17] that insight was to remain valid in less obvious moments.

Skirmishes between individuals and factions within the Liberal party were inevitable during a period of tension, but it is noteworthy that Grey believed personal relations within the government to be generally good.[18] That this was so was largely a product of Asquith's astute management; he was in his golden period, holding his Cabinet together 'under circumstances that would have baffled most of his predecessors' and taking it virtually united into the war.[19] His influence was extended through his *ménage* and particularly through the warnings and exhortations of his wife, Margot, a heavy-booted butterfly who hovered protectively wherever the flame seemed closest to her husband: '*Don't* recommend the Referendum for Suffrage wh. is Winston's idea and the Westminsters'. . . Let him stick to what he said and try and stop any more stumping. Don't let Loulou [Harcourt] and McKenna speak in Albert Hall and add fuel to the flames.'[20] Few opinions were likely to be altered by her letters, but she helped to cushion Asquith by letting those who mattered know what his 'line' would be in advance. There evolved a certain ability to ride over trouble, 'do[ing] my best and hoping for the best'.[21] It was an attitude which opponents were to dub 'wait and see', yet it is important to see that the phrase (if ever it was used) was imperative rather than plaintive. It was also intelligent. 'Looked at as the means which may give Asquith a chance of success', the Unionist Dicey wrote during the Irish crisis, 'it is in my judgement as good a course of action, or inaction, as he could adopt. . . In the arts of balancing one party against another Asquith is sure to excel, it is the only art of which he is a real master.'[22]

After 1910 there was no single tone of drooping pessimism. Instead politicians blew hot or cold according to how they conceived their fortunes to be moving. If doom was upon them they were certainly unconscious of it. '[I]n great good spirits';[23] 'nearly out of the wood';[24] 'a new lease of life';[25] 'counting on a 1915 election';[26] 'time is on our side':[27] phrases such as these reflect minds unconvinced of their own senescence and looking to the future as much in hope as in fear. Perhaps the Liberals had been too long in office, as Grey told Dean Inge,[28] but in the first half of 1914 the party was not on the verge of collapse. The Lloyd George/Churchill quarrel was over by February when the Chancellor became 'Churchill's man'.[29] For the rest, there was the full spectrum of success and failure, rising and falling:

How is the stock of our colleagues? I can almost hear you ask. What I can tell you is already known to you. The P.M. is at the top of his fame and popularity, Grey strong, Crewe's health is unreliable, otherwise he wears well, Reggie [McKenna] is distinctly up, L-G down, Samuel most unpopular with everyone, poor soul . . . Haldane down, Masterman deserted by his friends, Morley feeble, Winston distrusted by everyone.[30]

Up or down, Liberal politicians were exercised during July 1914 by two great matters, Ireland and the possibility of an autumn session – the latter being thought necessary because of the time-consuming nature of the former. Against this background the party leadership was engaged in trying to save its own skin from the teeth of the Opposition, from Northcliffe, from radicals obsessed with thoughts of the working class and, perhaps most of all, from 'the ordinary Liberals in the House like Ryland Adkins, Sir William Byles, T. C. Taylor and all the rest of that kind' who seemed willing to sit forever at Westminster in order to pass the Home Rule Bill.[31]

Asquith and his ministers sat at the top of a pyramid, suffering their coat-tails to be pulled by the minority interests and 'fads' which surrounded them. In that sense the years since 1906 had seen a simple continuation of conditions common in Gladstonian politics.[32] It was a continuity which could be seen in other directions also. Possibly there was a new strain in Liberal politics after 1906, 'a coherent ideology which lay behind the rhetoric of the 1910 elections'.[33] But despite the programmes of state intervention which had swung into action since 1908, the Liberal government had been elected on a virtually Gladstonian programme, 'no constructive ideas, merely objections to other people's ideas'.[34] An assured parliamentary majority had obviated any need for restraint among the various factions and reinforced H. G. Wells' prejudice that the Liberals could only be 'a diversified crowd'.[35] Similarly, J. A. Hobson dropped into Hobbesian metre to describe the Liberalism of his day as 'halting, weak, vacillating, divided and concessive'.[36] The Liberal government might later be remembered as a reformist administration but it would also be recalled that the reforms were pressed on harassed ministers by certain centres of tetchy and persistent energy. As Charles Trevelyan complained after the war, the government had had to find out what to do;[37] and it had sought answers in the expedient and the immediate rather than the distant canons of ideology.

Doctrine, however, can be dispensed with all too easily as a category of explanation, especially when its relationship to poli-

tical action is confused. Professor Vincent and Dr Clarke have
demonstrated the futility of searching for the roots of Liberal
practice in prescriptive doctrine. But if doctrine is conceived in
a non-prescriptive sense – as a nexus of assumptions, prejudices
and maxims understood to be something separate from attitudes
determining what was to take place in day-to-day political practice
– then neglect of doctrine can present the danger of throwing away
both baby and bathwater. Liberalism was far more complicated
in its doctrinal make-up than political theorists have allowed. That
part of it which was a rationalization of a given economic climate
or phase of political development was trivial, if indeed it ever
existed at all. For Liberalism was never an effective statement of
the intellectual, spiritual or economic requirements of a single
epoch: it never caught up with itself in time to be relevant.
Liberalism always involved, and sometimes amounted to, an
implicit language about the past and how the present had grown
out of it. To the early Victorians it was a language of Revolution
and Connexion; to the later ones it was a language of 1832 and
1867, of the secret ballot, free trade, religious toleration and the
Grand Old Man; to the Edwardians it was all these things (by now
ecstatically distorted) plus Campbell-Bannerman and, occasionally, Asquith. After the war 'C-B' moved to a higher level
in Liberal memory and Asquith took his place, bringing with him
Truth, Decency and a Manner which Liberals could trust, as the
representative of all that was best and which Lloyd George had
desecrated. In the strict sense of the word, Liberalism was a myth:
a story with a veiled meaning. It was a bizarre conception of
British constitutional development which took as its keystones
'big' men and 'true' principles. It was conscious of the need to
impregnate politics with a morality derived not so much from a
dogma as from an atmosphere breathed by the past. Liberalism
existed because it was believed to exist as the guiding force of
political progress, writ large between the lines of constitutional
lexicons since the coming of William of Orange.

If the Liberal party was still in 1914 'a coalition of convenience
and not the instrument of a creed'[38] the idea that the Liberal party
ought to be a credal instrument was one in which many Liberals
believed. What their creed ought to contain, however, few could
have said, except by reiterating 'old, stale shibboleths'.[39] Certainly the true Liberal identity was left to the eye of the beholder.

For some the radical movement after 1908 marked a return to 'real' Liberalism: 'We were being offered something which we wanted. Those who were Liberals felt that the heavy, stocky body of their party was about to grow wings and leave the ground.'[40] There were others who believed that the central task of Liberalism was located in arresting the very developments which Lowes Dickinson found so exciting. The so-called 'Holt Cave', for example, was described by Richard Holt as a 'combined remonstrance by business men and some survivors of the Cobden–Bright school of thought against the ill-considered and socialistic tendencies of the Government finance'.[41] Despite the confusions, however, the notion of there being some spiritual reservoir for rhetoric to tap was important in deciding the course of Liberalism after 1914. Indeed the confusions were themselves partly a consequence of the willingness of politicians to use spiritual appeal for their own ends on the platform and in their writings. Tactics and manoeuvre on the part of leaders, deference and mistaken beliefs on the part of followers, conspired to ensure that anything resembling a Liberal frame of mind was kept in control and thought the thoughts which the political context demanded. There is an odd sense of pettiness about pre-war Liberal debate in a retrospect clouded by knowledge of what was to come. Grey's seeing Massingham as his future opponent typifies the concealment in a contemporary mind of greater loyalties which the war was about to reveal.

The coming of the war substituted for a confused situation a more dangerous one in opening broader horizons of discussion and duty for Liberals. Recent anguish about Agadir or a prejudice against National Insurance would soon fade into insignificance before thoughts previously dormant because unchallenged – wider, more patent ideas such as the thought (appallingly trite, this, for a Liberal) that 'Character [was] after all the main thing in politics.'[42] It is on this not very ethereal level that the search for the Liberal mind must be carried out: on the level of the 'obvious' announced during a period when the 'obvious' needed to be stated more and more to justify attitudes adopted instinctively by all sane and decent-minded men. In no sense was good sense heightened by the war; but 'common sense' was made the more common as a network of assumptions and dull instincts was officially encouraged and other, less urgent ones suppressed by a program against extreme opinion. One of the strictures of a total war was the demand that Liberalism should be stifled together with other -isms and -ologies that went beyond simple patriotism. Some Liberals found this process absurd and said so. But it was nevertheless the case that although Liberals were quite capable of directing a war, they could do so only with principle, idealism, dignity, above all with aversion. Liberalism supplied a lens through which Lloyd George's 'doubting hand never struck firm blow'[43] appeared an image of amorality. Something subconsciously held as Liberal, Gentleman, Englishman, Christian, came into conflict with the realities of political life after 1914. A reaction was set in motion which cast the mind behind and above in search of a mainstay. What had previously been assumed (in some confused sense) to be woven into the fabric of British political life now became the object of a not quite conscious searching.

It is not the purpose of this study to document the thousands of points at which the war chafed the more sensitive areas of Liberalism. What is important to an understanding of the Liberal mind during the first two years of war is an appreciation of the weight of change which Liberals believed themselves to be supporting by the end of 1916, of what it meant and whom it involved. In the contemporary perception of that change three milestones loomed large: the formation of a coalition government in May 1915; the decision to impose conscription; and the splitting of the party in December 1916. In these contexts, therefore, the evolution of frames of mind within Liberal high politics is revealed to best advantage.

II

The war, when it came, came suddenly. The Sarajevo shootings aroused little interest in a country preoccupied with the Irish crisis, and it was not until the night of 23 July, with news of the Austrian ultimatum to Serbia, that alarm was awakened,[44] and even then there was little concern about potential escalation. When John Dillon forecast 'a most dangerous situation' on 25 July he still had the Irish problem in mind.[45] Indeed it was after the Cabinet of 24 July, which had been called to consider Ireland, that Grey's 'quiet grave tones...were heard reading a document', the Austrian ultimatum.[46] The Cabinet soon showed itself to be in favour of peace: Lloyd George later estimated that the anti-war party before the invasion of Belgium included between a third and a half of the Cabinet, and Temperley's researches suggested that this was an underestimate. He placed in this category Morley, Beauchamp, Burns, Simon, Hobhouse, Harcourt, Pease, McKinnon Wood, Lloyd George and Runciman, with Birrell and Aberdeen as possibles. Against them were ranged the more important names of Asquith and Grey, with Haldane and Churchill in support and Crewe, McKenna and Samuel forming an intermediate faction.[47]

The divisions in the Cabinet were reflected in the wider party. The precise character of party feeling is plainly beyond evaluation, but it will not do to argue that because only one Liberal voice was raised in support of the war in the famous debate of 3 August there was no bellicose faction in the party.[48] Many backbenchers were receptive to Grey's speech; nor should it be forgotten that the radical Pringle spoke in favour of intervention and persuaded others to his point of view. (It was Pringle rather than Grey, for example, who convinced Alexander MacCallum Scott.)[49] But it is clear enough that pacifist feeling in the party was worrying the leadership. On 2 August Asquith believed that three-quarters of his party wanted 'absolute non-interference at any price'.[50] A vociferous group whose views on foreign affairs had approximated to those of the Liberal Foreign Affairs Committee certainly found it impossible to believe that any Liberal government could drag them into such a war.[51] Among elder Liberal statesmen, Rosebery was claimed to be opposed to entry, though his official biographer later denied that he made statements to that effect either in public or in private.[52] Bryce was certainly in the anti-war camp until the violation of Belgian neutrality caused him to change his mind.[53] For most politicians, however, Belgium was used as a convenient opportunity to move their stance, once it became clear that Asquith was not going to fall.[54] To some the hypocrisy was overwhelming, especially to Morley, who was to remain convinced during the war that 'had not [Germany] begun to bully Belgium until three or four days later, the Cabinet would have broken to pieces on Aug. 3' and that Belgium had been no more than 'a convenient "let out"'.[55] Four members of the Cabinet – Morley, Burns, Simon and Beauchamp – resigned at once and the first two distinguished themselves by refusing to retract.

John Morley embodied a tradition at once living and dead, contemporary yet already classical. Some years after the war an

American academic wondered why he was 'the last survivor of a heroic age'[56] and the question still poses a problem. Perhaps it was because he was a manifestation of something broader than his own being and writing. He had outgrown his age and was saddened by its successor; it was he who begged the young to shun the 'exaggerated and misshapen rationalism that shuts out imagination, distrusts sentiment, despises tradition'.[57] He was anxious to prevent a certain upheaval of values (and these probably amounted to 'the pure milk of the Cobdenite word', as Laski thought).[58] Conceding war with barbarians to be a plausible act of Liberal policy seemed to him part of a violation, and its acceptance left nothing to do but mope.[59] His old age had less to do with 'patient gentleness'[60] than wet-eyed abdication. He turned his mind to where it was happiest, the age of classical Liberalism, its controversies and triumphs; to be in touch with him was to be in touch with a more spacious epoch.[61] He liked to feel that he was captain of an aged ship (a favourite image) which he would not desert despite wind and waves.[62] In 1914 the ship was facing a storm he knew it could not survive and he chose the captain's prerogative of going down with it.

Morley was everything that John Burns wished to be, believed himself to be, but never really became, a cultured *littérateur* frail of frame and feminine of mind. Burns shared with Morley at least 'common opinion and common action in a vital moment',[63] and they saw a good deal of one another during the war; the hero-worship which Burns felt for Morley (and occasionally for himself) expanded, and he was never happier than when Morley said something charming about his books[64] or when, gladiators both, they shook hands 'in the sunny porch [and] a cuckoo in a garden opposite gave forth his booming notes'.[65] He wanted to be deemed educated[66] but his attempts to seem so usually ended in pomposity. He wanted to appear detached but his anti-intellectualism and anti-semitism tied him down. Though sympathetic with the aims of the Lansdowne letter in 1917, for example, he was distracted by the thought that only a peer could command such an audience in a 'country of acquiescing snobs'.[67] There was too much vinegar in Burns to allow his hopes for himself to come to fruition.

Neither Morley nor Burns had the legal background of Sir John Simon, and it was this above all else that enabled Simon to remain inside the ministry until he was finally driven out by conscription in January 1916. His legalistic mind allowed him to enter subtle reservations where others resigned, though he remained unhappy at the prospect. 'He is', C. P. Scott wrote of him, '. . . an un-attached member of the Cabinet and sits very lightly.'[68] Before his resignation he was seen as a candidate for the leadership of the party should Asquith decide to relinquish it.[69] At no time, how-ever, did he fully settle whilst in the government, and FitzRoy probably described a predominant mood when he saw in Simon 'a man of anxious and troubled temper'.[70] It was this temper which reacted so violently against the decision to impose conscription – so violently, indeed, that the group of politicians in his circle (closest were McKenna, Runciman and Harcourt)[71] failed to follow him. When enjoined to keep an open mind on the subject, he admitted that he did not possess one; and it is worth recalling that when an opponent later accounted for his dislike of Simon, what he took exception to was 'his character and type of mind'.[72]

This 'type of mind' was by no means typical among Liberals during the first few months of the war, though it was to become more common as layers of illusion about the relationship between highly placed Liberals and their Liberalism were stripped away. The resigners did find support among rank-and-file members, especially among those on the Liberal Left such as C. P. Trevelyan (who himself resigned a Parliamentary Secretaryship), Ponsonby and Morel who were later to drift towards Labour through Morel's Union of Democratic Control.[73] Among Burns' papers dating from this period can be found traces of sympathy or admiration from Aneurin Williams, Percy Molteno, Joseph King, Harold Cox, G. P. Gooch, Massingham, Hobhouse, Hirst and Gulland as well as the predictable epistles from Labour prophets. But the significance of Liberal dissent from the policy of intervention can be overstressed. A balanced view requires that a moderate opinion such as that of Joseph Henry of Leeds be considered. The war, he said, was a 'dreadful thing'; those who had foisted it on the people were 'vermin'; everyone must expect great misery; but the decision had been made and it had to be seen through.[74] Liberals were as prone as anyone else to the propaganda of wartime, and a case for entry could readily be made out, even a case consonant with the demands of Liberal principle. '[I]n fighting against this outrage on Belgium', the argument might run, 'the Liberals of England have a right to claim that they have sincerely and honestly assented to the war on that account alone.'[75] Those politicians who had left the government lacked both the means and the inclination to broadcast their dissent and the thinking behind it; and they had caused little enough commotion even at the moment of crisis.[76] As events swirled, there was no opportunity for political matters to take more than shallow root in a world compared by Crewe to that in one of Wells' novels.[77] Stock could be taken of the domestic position only when the western front ground to a standstill. And by the end of the year the great questions in domestic politics were concerned with the so-called political truce which both parties had agreed to observe since the commencement of hostilities. What would happen when the truce began to wear thin? The answer disturbed MacCallum Scott as he tried to decide whether or not to join the army: when the truce ended, he reasoned, 'every Liberal Member w[ould] be wanted at Westminster'.[78]

The war had annihilated not merely one aspect of Liberal politics but all aspects which authentically could claim the name; at stake was 'national' survival, and 'national' policies dedicated to 'national' ends would be required to effect it. Both parties were meant to suffer equally from this restriction of activity, but it was not lost on Liberals that one would suffer more equally than the other. As early as 10 August Gilbert Murray expressed the hope that Liberalism would 'not let patriotism get identified with Toryism or militarism'[79] and he was not alone in his anxiety. Liberals were notoriously ill-equipped to contest Tory claims of representing 'the country', for their aim had traditionally been to fight the Conservatives by denouncing their jingoism rather than by outbidding their militarism. That option had now been closed by the exigencies of wartime. The Liberal party would need to arrange itself on unfamiliar ground and fight on the terms of its rival. The thin end of the Tory wedge had already been inserted because the government had been drawing on the advice and co-operation of Law and Chamberlain since the beginning of the war.[80] Conservatives may have gained little from that particular arrangement, but by the end of the year it had become a cause for concern among Liberals.

As the new year opened, a strain of Conservative thinking began to appear which took account of Healy's point that 'the Tories ha[d] not got enough out of the Govt. and that the Offices shd . . .

be halved with them', a hope which Asquith had encouraged by making it plain that he did not wish to offend the Opposition.[81] Indicative of the thinking which was now taking place is an important letter from Hugh Cecil to his brother Robert:

It is obvious that a section of the Cabinet are very pleased at the opportunity of working with leaders of the Opposition; and coupled with other indications I think it may be regarded as pretty certain that they would be glad to take part in some kind of coalition, if circumstances made such a course feasible. In this section of the Cabinet must certainly be reckoned Grey, Asquith, Churchill and Haldane and possibly others ...I am disposed to feel that both on patriotic and personal grounds... we ought to take advantage of the rather sloppy sentiment (which I hate) about 'no party feeling' to begin the building of a golden bridge by which they may cross over to us.[82]

If it is clear that the coalition of May 1915 did not come about through immediate conspiracies on the part of either Conservatives or Liberals,[83] it is equally plain that the Conservatives were not blind to the opportunity the war had given them. Everyone knew that parliamentary power depended on a certain balance of forces. That these had changed since the coming of the war was a fact too important, because too patent, to ignore.

'Parliament muzzled, country chloroformed, Papers drugged' was Burns' portrait of February 1915,[84] and Liberalism shared the reluctance to come alive. The future seemed to hold little for Liberals as the truce degenerated into a catchcry used by everybody. 'If things go wrong', Runciman moaned, 'we shall be flayed. If they go right, the Tories will find their joy in national triumph splashed a little by their caucus men who cannot bear to see us governing during a war.'[85] The caucus men were indeed writhing at Asquith's indolence and lack of bite. They went further than Cecil in pressing for a coalition: they wanted to evict the 'dawdling buggers'.[86] Asquith tried to forestall such criticism with an oratory which was still effective, at least among his own supporters, and Jack Pease recorded two 'brilliant' performances at the beginning of March. But under the impact of the shell crisis and the resignation of Fisher, and with the nagging problem of how to persuade the Conservatives to accept an extension of the government's life, oratory was no longer enough. Asquith was compelled to sue for terms with the Opposition and drew from Bonar Law an ultimatum which he could wave under the nose of Liberal colleagues to show that he was acting under duress.[87] A coalition government – discounted by Burns at the end of March[88] – became a reality in May.

Moreover the reality was harsher for its being sudden. What appears in retrospect as a growing tension beneath the surface of party politics after January 1915 struck Liberals at the time as something less dangerous, a mere manifestation of factiousness in the opposite camp. The radical Pringle had come to feel by the beginning of May that the Conservatives might try to force a general election on the issue of a more vigorous prosecution of the war,[89] but the prospect of a coalition was not in his mind. Asquith consulted no one about the negotiations with the Opposition, though some talks, of unclear significance, took place between Law and Lloyd George.[90] Well-founded opinion was limited to a small section of the Conservative party which was pushing for a place in government and was willing if necessary to force Asquith's hand through threats of parliamentary attack over military and labour conscription.[91] Events in fact fell into place with a smoothness which few Conservatives could have expected. On 19 May Asquith called a party meeting and announced his decision to reconstruct the ministry in a speech which was surprisingly well received by the rank and file. There were those who found the speech 'impressive but not ultimately convincing' and suspected that the change was the product of a 'dirty intrigue', but many sympathized with Asquith's obvious embarrassment, 'his voice husky and his face twitching'.[92] The chairman closed the meeting quickly in order to stifle inconvenient questions. MacCallum Scott and Pringle ran after the hastily departing Asquith to try to secure certain assurances, but in the main Members were content to disperse, 'bright-eyed with emotion, to a murmured chorus of "Trust the P.M."'.[93] Asquith had succeeded in conjuring up the right atmosphere but it was debatable how long it would last. Possibly all that had happened was that men and positions had been changed around, but there were bound to be worries about whether principles were not also changing.

Given the course of events since January the suspicion was not unnatural. The birth of the coalition had been surrounded with secrecy and seemed to reflect a covert concession to Toryism. What assurances had been given to the Opposition? This was Runciman's central concern. 'If we are honoured with invitations to come in I feel that we must first know with whom we are asked to associate and then be told what demands were made or assurances given on *policy* to Bonar and his colleagues.' It was particularly important to him to know whether the Conservatives had been told that the Liberals had 'an open mind on compulsory service or taxation or trade policy'.[94] In this anxiety that Liberalism might no longer be deciding its own course can be seen the awakening of the kind of mind which it is the purpose of this study to consider. By its very nature coalition involved co-existence with the tainted. The threat of it had been a nightmare to Morley even before the war, and since then Simon had intoned that coalition would be a grave for Liberalism.[95] Yet it seems that if anything was buried in 1915 it was not Liberalism as such but the party which purported to practise it.[96] May 1915 marked the separation of a body from a collection of ghosts. Still more ties would be cut before the end of 1916. Perhaps principle was spared in the surgery of 1915, as Dr Hazlehurst believes,[97] but a more important question is whether it was thought to have been spared at the time. Joseph Henry was not alone in wanting to return to Campbell-Bannerman and sound sense:

I must say that I have allways [*sic*] found that wherever a compromise with the tories takes place the Liberals have allways to go very near to tory principles or the whole thing breaks down . . . In my opinion the great danger to the country at present is the Coalition government . . . [O]ur old leader Sir Henry said away with this fooling and it wants saying again.[98]

In a consciousness which dwelt on the past, the formation of the coalition would come to be seen in the mythology of the 1920s as a significant event in the Liberal collapse, a signal mistake and milestone. For radicals such as Pringle and Hogge it was the beginning of the end, a foolish act which allowed Toryism, 'until then dormant and defeated', to awake and take control of the fortunes of Liberalism.[99] Nor was this response limited to the fringe; one observes Sir John Brunner feeling compelled to vote Labour in 1918 because it had been Asquith who 'had first admitted the enemy to the Liberal citadel' in 1915.[100] No new doctrine had been promulgated by this mild upheaval at the summit of British politics; no programme of action had been outlined against which dissidents could rebel and agitate. The affair could be seen as a piece of Westminster politics turning on personnel and personality. Yet in a sense it might have been healthier for

Liberalism to have had a windmill at which to tilt rather than allowing itself to be consumed by doubts and suspicions which the empty oratory of the leadership would be unable to allay. The Liberal mind could not have given vent to all its anxieties in 1915. But it had begun its career. It would have been incensed that Walter Long believed the Conservative party to have made 'all the sacrifices'.[101]

III

First to fall within the 'Liberal citadel', then, was a conception of purity which allowed to Liberalism high thoughts as recompense for its government's having run into hard times. This Asquith government was not only in difficulties; it had so sullied itself with Toryism that even the sober minds behind the *Manchester Guardian* were offended:

> The arrangement is alien to our traditions and we cannot be surprised that it should provoke strong criticism and even bitter opposition...[I]t is inevitable that misgivings should arise in many minds as to the effect on domestic policy of this complete surrender by the Liberal government, elected as such and still dominated by at least the spirit and tradition of Liberalism, of its authority and its initiative. It will amount in many minds to something of a revolution.[102]

For the less articulate, 'doctrine' and 'principle' had their importance, but they were seen to be located in people – individuals whose 'character' and 'integrity' could be trusted. It should be stressed at once that to draw any harsh distinction between principle and personnel is to oversimplify a blurred but firmly held association. When an observer lamented the loss of certain individuals – 'Beauchamp, Lucas, Haldane, Pease, Samuel, Hobhouse...also Emmott, a very good man'[103] – he could be thinking of an individual's administrative capacity, but he could be thinking too of his stance, perhaps, on contentious issues in the past, the atmosphere he radiated, the cumulative impression of the man's politics. If Liberals such as MacCallum Scott put their faith in character before the war, they would do so *a fortiori* under the duress and secrecies of wartime. Later in 1915, for example, he returned to the subject: 'What I mean is that in a political situation such as the present, when we are so much in the dark as to the facts of the situation, when plan and policy are to a large extent concealed from us, when ministers are assailed from all directions, in judging these ministers we must be guided by the conception we have formed of their character.'[104]

'Character' and Liberalism were not co-extensive, but neither were they unrelated. MacCallum Scott was a Liberal who believed in political principles, as his diary constantly reiterates. If he were to place trust in the 'character' of a leader he would clearly demand of him some manifestation of allegiance to the same principles. It seems unreasonable to believe that other Liberals did not have recourse to similar thoughts in the context of May 1915. Men who had been trusted as Liberals were being thrown out in order that distrusted, even despised, Conservatives might take their places: and this for reasons which no leader could explain, save the Prime Minister himself, and no one could fully comprehend. 'Why the fact that Winston quarrelled with Fisher', Masterman wrote to Samuel, 'should mean your giving up the L[ocal] G[overnment] B[oard] is a *non-sequitur* which today and tomorrow will find it difficult to explain . . . No wonder Bottomley asks, have we all gone mad?'[105] Morley found himself in similar darkness, confessing to Burns that he failed to see why the new government should require 'the suicide of its predecessor'.[106]

Unknown to both commentators, some Liberals had sufficiently recovered from Asquith's shock announcement to press for the retention of certain key offices in Liberal hands.[107] What they lacked, however, was the Conservatives' power to dictate to the Prime Minister. For the Conservative party the formation of the coalition had been, if not a triumph, at least 'a great step in the right direction'.[108] Into the Cabinet came, pre-eminently, Law, Balfour, Chamberlain, Long, Curzon and Lansdowne, and they were prepared to take surprisingly minor offices, with the exception of Balfour who replaced Churchill at the Admiralty. But Conservative power was little diluted by the taking of such posts, since Asquith was well aware that a walk-out would bring the ministry (and his own career) to the ground. The right wing, it is true, had only Chamberlain in the Cabinet: Milner's inclusion, for which Chamberlain had pressed,[109] had been refused by the Conservative leadership, and the new Ministry of Munitions, for which Midleton had pressed,[110] was not placed in the hands of a Conservative. The Milner group could at least be pleased that the new ministry was occupied by the one Liberal in whom they had a smattering of faith as a 'pusher' – David Lloyd George.

No satisfactory study of Lloyd George's role in party politics in 1915/16 has yet appeared, but certain aspects of his relationship with other parties are clear. The Conservative leadership had high hopes of him from the beginning[111] and even the right wing saw some reason for encouragement. His energy in tackling the daunting problems raised by the establishment of a new ministry soon convinced even such a fire-eater as Frederick Oliver that he could be 'a great asset for winning this war'; by July 1915, more significantly, Oliver had developed a 'firm belief' that Lloyd George could 'prove himself the courageous and imaginative leader we need'.[112] By that time Lloyd George had become the leading light of 'win the war' Conservatives and the *bête noir* of those Liberals whose principles chafed. And both sentiments were really the product of a single cause, for in his capacity as Minister of Munitions Lloyd George could not escape responsibility for furthering or retarding the growing demand for military conscription.

Just as 'coalition' had been an unloved word among Liberals even before the war, 'conscription' was regarded with similar animus. The mere possibility of this ultimate power being granted to the state was enough to prod one of Gladstone's sons into preaching neutrality in 1914.[113] Once the war was under way, conscription was seen by Liberals of most schools as a paradigm of the very system they believed themselves to be fighting. 'My hope', MacCallum Scott had written on 26 August, 'is that this War will demonstrate the triumph of voluntary service over conscription.'[114] In May 1915 that hope seemed likely to be short-lived. There was a further danger. Would military conscription, once conceded, open the door to the introduction of conscription for labour? It was this latter anxiety which moved Burns to demand '*none of your damned conscription*' of an impassive Strachey.[115] Such fears were founded on more than mere hysteria, for after May 1915 the Conservative ultimatum about conscription stood, even though the document had never been sent. As Austen Chamberlain hastened to reassure Milner after the Conservatives had entered the government, they would now be in a position to enforce orally what had previously been written.[116] Hence the threat, the gestation and the final triumph of conscription formed the crucial background to the party politics of 1915/16 and took a prominent place among the concerns of Liberals.

Conscription had first been raised to the status of a problem requiring a decision in a House of Lords debate on 8 January 1915, when Haldane had been agnostic and refused to 'take up any attitude based on abstract principle' about it and Crewe had refused to reassure Grimthorpe that the Liberal government would not impose it.[117] The contingency was in any case remote enough and had an air of unreality. Yet by the end of May, Richard Cross (friend of and solicitor to the Rowntrees) was warning Lloyd George that 'such a step would break up both the Liberal and Labour parties and wreck progress for a generation'.[118] Under the strain of recent military reverses, attitudes were beginning to harden and camps to be established: Francis Hirst declaimed upon the folly of conscription; Dr Clifford denounced it; Lord Robert Cecil stiffened against it.[119] MacCallum Scott examined the matter coolly and decided that a general election would have to be held before an attempt could be made to impose it, so as to avoid the 'mad folly' of leaving the country unconvinced of its necessity;[120] and the *Manchester Guardian* echoed his pragmatic approach, conceding that the 'moral defeat of the British system' would be no argument against its introduction if the case in favour of conscription were to be proven.[121]

The defection of certain left-wing elements to the newly formed No Conscription Fellowship was soon to show that coolness and detachment no longer characterized the response of the all Liberals to the threat of conscription.[122] Indeed the Liberal pacifist group went so far as to ask Burns to form an opposition group on an anti-war platform.[123] By the beginning of June Hirst was convinced that Nonconformity (with the exception of the Wesleyans) was 'furiously' against conscription,[124] and a week later MacCallum Scott, who admittedly was not in a good position to know, believed that four of the Cabinet – Runciman, Grey, Crewe and McKinnon Wood – would oppose the policy to the point of resignation. Even if he was wrong about the individuals he named, there was something ominous in his determination to bide his time and 'wait till we can oppose on a clear and definite question of principle'.[125] That moment arrived in December when the Opposition came within an inch of smashing the government.

Closer to the heart of the Liberal party, meanwhile, there was mounting resentment of the decision to abandon Liberalism to Tory principles. Charles Hobhouse, who had done much to spread

the rumours of a Lloyd George/Churchill conspiracy against
the late government, grew more hysterical as the days passed. '
Nothing will persuade me', he wrote to Runciman, 'that this is
not the end of the Liberal party as we have known it: and that you
and others will not find yourselves made responsible for measures
you disapprove but cannot in the supposed "national" interest
reject.'[126] There was a widening rift between Liberal leaders and
their bewildered followers. Simon was content to say that everyone had made great sacrifices and Heaven knew where it all
would end.[127] The man to whom he addressed his stoic views,
Alick Murray, actively tried to alleviate the situation by attempting
to organize a party meeting 'to rekindle the personal touch
between the Prime Minister and his supporters'.[128] But such critical feeling as existed among Liberals was directed less against
Asquith than against Lloyd George, whose colloguing with the
Conservatives was thought dangerous. Not a few Liberals,
Robertson Nicoll believed, would be glad to see his career
stopped.[129]

Two paramount facts about Lloyd George seemed patent: that
his contacts with Conservatives were part of a conspiracy and that
the conspiracy was aimed at Asquith. This latter rumour came to
a head in June: 'People say that Lloyd George will oust Asquith.
It is possible. He has the ear of the groundlings, and the Tories
have taken him to their bosom as I always knew they would.'[130]
Amid the chaos of the Ministry of Munitions, Lloyd George had
other things to occupy him, as even his attackers had come to see
by the second half of the month. On 14 June MacCallum Scott
noted that the 'Campaign to exploit Lloyd George' had 'fallen
flat', while even Hirst conceded on the 17th that 'Lloyd George's
bid for the premiership seem[ed] to have failed for the time.'[131]
That Lloyd George's designs on the premiership were at this stage
non-existent in no way detracts from the significance of the
current convictions that they were real. The rumours helped to
promote the formation of two radical groups, one led by Pringle,
the other by Sir Charles Nicolson, dedicated to the achievement
of nothing in particular. The first was a mutual protection society
which hoped to act in concert in accepting the coalition, advancing
the win-the-war cause and protecting the interests of its members
in their constituencies.[132] The second, the so-called 'Seven Wise
Men', was a group more concerned with the anti-Liberal policies

of the hybrid administration to whose acts they aspired to give 'a Liberal pull whenever possible'.[133] Neither group was effective. On 9 June Lord Sandhurst recorded that 'a small section of radicals' had managed to 'make themselves tiresome' but nothing more.

Cliques of this kind nevertheless helped to stimulate the atmosphere of factiousness and crumbling which contemporaries felt very keenly. There was a certain nervousness about the constitution in the air; with one bastion already fallen after a year of war, how many more would have to follow? From his reaction to the proposal to suspend the quinquennial rule and avoid a wartime election it may be judged that such fears were in the mind of MacCallum Scott. 'The constitution is now in peril', he wrote. 'If we permit the life of Parliament to be extended we commit an act than which there could be no greater overriding of the sovereignty of the People. (See Dicey)...Let us keep the forms and safeguards and jealously preserve them.'[134] It was precisely such 'forms and safeguards' that the coalition government was apparently bent on violating, though not crudely or overtly. Dr Hazlehurst is right to comment on 'half-intimated fears rather than defined objectives' on the part of the dissident factions.[135] It was less a matter of conscious opposition that of sullen resentment such as MacCallum Scott found in Edmund Browne, who had 'the air of a very mortified man watching a fine scheme going all wrong and not knowing whom to blame'.[136] Yet however passive these attitudes appear in retrospect, they contained important seeds for the future. It misses the point to argue that 'so long as the principles of these groups remained traditionally Liberal Asquith had nothing to fear'.[137] Asquith had everything to fear if the pressures of war should lead him (as they were to lead him) to take up positions far from 'traditionally Liberal'. There was nascent revolt in the Liberal party in 1915 but it was not the revolt of radicals pushing an old-guard leadership in a direction it did not want to go. It was rather a revolt of traditional Liberalism against an old guard who were ostensibly abdicating their responsibilities by relinquishing their Liberalism. It was not a revolt of the young against the old but of the past against the present. And if the past had little point on its sword, neither could it be side-stepped with a few wise words and gestures.

In this fragile atmosphere the Conservative pressure for conscription became stronger through the summer. Richard Holt may have believed in June that such agitation had been abandoned,[138] but it was in that same month that Oliver was writing to Chamberlain that a million fresh troops must be recruited for the 1916 campaign.[139] Other members of the right-wing circle were equally active. Amery, for example, saw his main task to be the rousing of Milner, who had been very much the pillar of respectable militarism since the death of Lord Roberts. Amery was also clear that he would need allies in the struggle for 'getting rid of Asquith', and his list of possibles was interesting. Carson, he felt sure, would co-operate and '[s]o *might* Lloyd George, if he once felt certain that he had no chance of becoming Prime Minister, and can at best hope to be an effective mouthpiece for those who really know and can lead'.[140] On 5 August Lansdowne wrote to Asquith to raise the issue of applying 'some form of compulsion' but found the Prime Minister unreceptive; as Walter Long told his party leader a few days later, 'old ideas and theories' were being allowed to predominate over what he took to be sound sense and the clear requirements of war.[141] In the House of Commons Christopher Addison tried to persuade his fellow Liberals to keep an open mind about conscription,[142] whilst outside parliament Northcliffe's *Times* hammered home the demand for compulsion with such hysterical misery that John Galsworthy found his morning paper 'like a daily bath in depression and covert malice'.[143] It was eloquent testimony to Asquith's unrest about the matter that such pressure drew from him only a Cabinet committee to inquire into military requirements. People who knew him recognized a predictable expedient through which he hoped to defuse the situation.

The committee delayed the inevitable confrontation with Liberals in parliament and delayed it to the advantage of the Opposition. In the early summer the affair might have been forced through quickly, since most Liberals were in a mood of troubled idealism which would have been found malleable by good handling. Like MacCallum Scott, many felt unsure which way to turn. ('I am in doubt. I cannot decide. I hestitate. I do not know which is the right course.')[144] In the wake of Neuve Chapelle there was a feeling that military urgency ought to override all else. The die had been cast in the decision to enter the war at all: the Liberals, whose consciences now hurt, had acquiesced in that obscenity.

'The major complaisance made easy the minor', Stephen McKenna wrote in retrospect, 'and the party which had left its principles on the threshold before drifting into war drifted into conscription without realising it had any more principles to abandon.'[145] The debate on the National Registration Bill in July brought forth a few remarks about 'principle' from R. L. Lambert and edgier ones from the Labour fringe; but if an explosion had been intended, the squib turned out to be damp.

While the Cabinet committee deliberated, a top-level political crisis was in the process of gestation as conscription ceased to be the cause of the humble and began in earnest to occupy the minds of political leaders. At the beginning of August Burns noted that Beauchamp was becoming progressively more unhappy at the threat of compulsion,[146] and by 16 August Montagu was speaking of 'disintegrating forces': more important, he was speaking in the ear of the Prime Minister:

> I *know* that the compulsory service party mean mischief or business. They want the thing and they mean to have it. Kitchener will agree and join them. L.G. will be chief protagonist backed by Winston, Curzon, B. Law, Chamberlain, etc. . . . [I]t has come to my knowledge that this is to be made a test question.[147]

Members of both factions plied their colleagues with propaganda. Pringle was certain that he had roused the Glasgow Liberals against the proposal; Alick Murray and Lord Cowdray did their best to convince Spender that his friends should 'stiffen up' their attitudes, for the war's sake.[148] On 2 September both sides were quietened a little by the appearance of the committee's report, which appeased one side with its conclusion that men were available for an army of seventy divisions and the other by deciding that the men could not be raised by voluntary means.

Compulsionists of all kinds now proceeded to beat Asquith with the stick which he had gratuitously placed in their hands, and the way was open for the first Cabinet crisis in October. Already one embittered observer (to whom Asquith had promised a job) was bewailing a *coup* on the part of Lloyd George; and Richard Holt had heard rumours that the conscriptionists were 'supposed to be intriguing behind the scenes and . . . openly trying to push their most objectional policy'.[149] He was right: where Lansdowne had failed, the Conservatives were hoping that Balfour might succeed in convincing Asquith, in the face of the committee's report, that conscription was necessary. Asquith himself pleaded for time, pointing to the certainty of massive opposition from Labour and, closer to home, an equally massive reaction from his own party:

I have received during the last few days from the most trusted and representative men of the rank and file a number of apparently spontaneous communications and all in the sense of resolute and dogged opposition. It is no exaggeration to say that, at this moment, the two most unpopular and distrusted men in the party are Ll. George and W. Churchill...I sincerely believe that...if I were to announce myself tomorrow a reluctant but whole-hearted convert to Compulsion, I should still have to face the hostility of the best, and in the country some of the most powerful, elements in the Liberal party.[150]

Too much can easily be read into the argument which rests on the content of Asquith's postbag, and it is also worth recalling that Asquith was writing here to a Conservative politician. It remains clear, however, that Asquith was determined not to be rushed into a course of action which would require him to confront an opposition faction which seemed to him to be powerful. The fear of one backbench Liberal M.P. that his party was about to be stampeded into disaster[151] may not have been well founded, but it must have been clear to Asquith that he could not sit on the fence for very much longer in view of opinion in the country and in the Ministry of Munitions.

The rift between Asquith and Lloyd George was now serious enough to suggest to Alick Murray the need for some kind of reconciliation. Murray believed that the split had in any case been manufactured by others: when the two men were kept in touch with one another so that the press could not spread stories of intrigue, they were 'really vy. good friends indeed'.[152] Naive views of this sort were becoming rarer. In September Lloyd George was on the point of resignation because of Asquith's lack of direction, and though that immediate crisis was overcome he was still turning for support to the Conservative party.[153] There is no clear evidence that Lloyd George's behaviour was conspiratorial, but it was definitely believed to be so when matters came to a head at a 'critical'[154] Cabinet meeting in October. On the following day Edmund Talbot reported to Law that a Cabinet crisis was at hand, that the Prime Minister might resign and that Lloyd George would be his successor.[155] It is clear, however, that far from pressing for Asquith's resignation, Lloyd George offered his own. Frances Stevenson recorded in her diary on 19 October:

> When D. arrived [at Walton Heath] he announced that he and Churchill, and 6 of the Tories had made up their minds to resign...The P.M. however would not accept the position, and said that he would resign himself. He asked for 24 hours to consider the whole thing. The Tories were very anxious for him to resign, and for D. to become P.M. But D. will not hear of this: he says he would not think of taking the responsibility at this moment. We are in for a series of disasters, and D. thinks the P.M. should take the full responsibility for enterprises which he consented should be launched.[156]

What had happened, however, was less important than what misinformed politicians took to have happened, and there was about the affair a strong smell of plotting and conniving. Even Asquith himself, who was in a position to know better, read to his wife the story of Simon Peter's betrayal of Christ and announced that Peter was a Celt.[157]

No schematic 'model' can be constructed to depict the mind of Liberalism in 1915 but certain aspects of the situation seem clear. By October of that year the twofold resentment of Liberals – against the coalition and against conscription – had fused to form a single anxiety: compulsion was viewed as a product of coalition and both were seen to be evidence of what happened when Liberal statecraft was prostituted. Montagu was certainly not alone in seeing that conscription was a symptom rather than a cause and that the malaise derived from embarking on a coalition of parties without a coalition of policies.[158] Not that there was any consensus among Liberal politicians. There were those like J. M. Robertson whose only desire was to see the war through at whatever cost; there were those like Sir William Byles whose religion or Liberalism prevented them from allowing *raison d'état* to override ethics; and there were those, probably a majority, who felt the confusion and hesitation of MacCallum Scott, 'enveloped in thick fog' with regard to the political situation and what line to take.[159] A month later the problem would have been greater still. 'The thought haunts me, and is beginning to be insistent – supposing Asquith is not the man...If we are going to suspend the Constitution...there is no room for half-measures. Grasp the nettle boldly, act with vigour and certainty.'[160]

This reaction is instructive, for it shows how misguided can be an 'analysis' of Liberalism which depends on crude quantitative exercises with batches of M.P.s – those who followed Asquith, those who followed Lloyd George – and apportions to those quantities a share in the development of 'Liberalism'. MacCallum Scott was a Liberal who believed in Liberalism (defined in his own terms) and who was almost morbidly concerned with the fate of Liberal principle and constitutional government. Yet in the flood tide of war he had come to feel that his leader was simply not 'the man' to reach the farther shore; and that in a war of this nature a 'man' was required. Thus his decision about whether it was desirable for a Liberal government at all costs to preserve the germ of Liberalism in its actions was governed not by considerations of doctrine but by decisions about the character and probable length of the war. The point requiring emphasis, however, is that the second course need not demand an abandonment of the first, merely its postponement. Conscription could be defended on 'Liberal' grounds as being the most effective expedient available to bring to an end the war that was making Liberalism impossible. The major complaisance, to return to Stephen McKenna, made easy the minor.

Complaisance was made still easier once the Liberal section of the Cabinet had acquiesced in the necessity of some form of military service. Asquith's decision to forestall the agitation by launching the Derby scheme in November went someway towards allaying the agitation, though he probably knew then that it would fail. There was already discontent among Liberal Members about Asquith's handling of the problem,[161] and in the difficult period between the abandonment of the Derby scheme (Law began complaining about it to Asquith in the middle of November)[162] and the decision taken in December to introduce a Military Service Bill, dissonant voices were heard in higher echelons also. The 'troublesome little cliques' which had been 'always making mischief'[163] since the formation of the coalition threatened to make a good deal more in the month to come. With rumour rife that Lloyd George was going to leave the government and go into opposition with Law, there were reasons for feeling that Asquith had walked into a trap by allowing himself to be drawn into making pledges about conscription.[164] 'We shall do no good in this war', one Unionist M.P. rose to tell the House, 'until we get rid of the "wait and see" lawyer who at present occupies the position of Prime Minister of this country.'[165] Whether or not such pressure was responsible for the decision to introduce conscription, it seemed so at the time to men whose nerves were already overstretched.

The parliamentary debate of 5/6 January 1916 showed plainly enough that few Liberals agreed with Leo Amery's frustrated *éclat*: 'This is not a question of principle at all; it is a question of how to get the men.'[166] Of course the debate was used by different factions for differing ends. Pringle wanted 'to try to force Lloyd George into the open'[167] and was unsuccessful; Sir William Byles wished to reiterate his Quaker position and say again that 'this Bill denotes not only the failure of all my ideals, but the negation of all the ideals I have lived for';[168] further to the Left, Percy Alden was more interested in this world and therefore more dangerous: 'I believe this Bill is wrong on principle because it is contrary to everything I have ever believed. It is contrary to everything I have ever been taught to believe by the Prime Minister himself, and by all those whom I have supported faithfully for ten years.'[169] It was a muted and eclectic revolt. It was all done 'on a high level', as Sandhurst observed.[170] Yet it was the very appeal to what was held to be high – conscience, principle, tradition – that made the augury so disturbing for the future of Liberalism. At that level the revolt (perhaps, more accurately, the revulsion) was wider and more damaging than any voting list will ever reveal. The debate was quiet and dignified, since Asquith could count on the votes – if not the support – of the moderates: there is some evidence that Gulland in any case put pressure on Liberal Members to vote the right way.[171] But in retrospect the admission of conscription by Liberals marked an important stage in the loss of credibility of Liberalism's claim to represent something more than an electoral machine.

Different anxieties were predominant in the minds of Cabinet ministers. The revolt there, though serious for the Asquith government, was less ethereal, motivated partly by a conviction that the timing of the measure was wrong, partly by a growing fear that Asquith was 'a contemptible tool'[172] in the hands of the Conservative party. The problem was seen to be one aspect of an established difficulty, that of survival within the framework of a coalition. Certainly, there had been some objection to conscription on doctrinal grounds, such as when Whitehouse had broken

with the government in September because compulsion had
become 'the paramount issue in Parliament' and 'its adoption
would mean the ruin of the country'.[173] However, the Cabinet
crisis of December 1915 was based on more pragmatic considerations. Arch-conspirator seems to have been Runciman, who was
briefing Pringle about the line he ought to take against Asquith;[174]
his fellow rebels were Simon, McKenna and, surprisingly, Grey.
Their objections to the policy were diverse and need not be
pursued here; it suffices to recall that their collective dissent
spread a cloud over the Christmas holiday, immediately after
which Runciman and McKenna tendered their resignations to
Asquith because the attempt to raise sixty-seven divisions would
exhaust the resources of the country.[175] All four rebels received
pleading letters from their colleagues. Samuel begged Runciman
not to leave the government, since '[t]he only thing that would
justify resignation would be...a conviction that, on grounds of
fundamental principle, compulsory service ought never to be
established in this country, and that view you do not hold'.[176]
Montagu told Grey that his 'responsibility' was 'unique' and that
he would deal a dreadful blow if he went.[177] And Margot Asquith
painted for McKenna a picture of the problem coloured by personal, rather than doctrinal, loyalties:

> What will the country think when it hears that you, Runciman and Simon
> – all of the same school – all real Liberals – all heart and soul in agreement
> with Henry, have left him...Is this what you are going to do to show
> the man you love that you are loyal? Do you love your opinions more than
> you love him?[178]

In this emotional atmosphere only Simon's resignation was
found to be intractable. Pringle was disgusted,[179] everyone else
relieved. Much had depended on Grey, but he had been pulled
into the current without realizing how important he was to the
government, and when he found out the flattery subdued him.[180]
Without Grey, Runciman and McKenna knew they could achieve
little by resigning, so they accepted Asquith's revised formula
over conscription and stayed in the government. Simon caused
little more than a ruffle in his resignation speech on 5 January – it
was badly received by the House – and by 11 January MacCallum
Scott believed Asquith to be 'gaining in prestige'.[181] Occasional
tremors emanated from Runciman, who still 'decline[d] to
be swindled with [his] eyes open' and agreed with Hirst that

Asquith had 'persuaded scores of his followers in the House of Commons to vote against their convictions'.[182] It was just this 'swindling' that would have to become Asquith's stock-in-trade if he wanted to hold together the Liberal fragment of the coalition. Haldane was right to suggest that Asquith did this sort of thing very well;[183] but he had already, as he must have realized, escaped many crises by the skin of his teeth and he could not hope to do so forever. Still, there was some cause for optimism. He had on his side the sluggish war mentality which resulted, for example, in only one M.P.'s noticing Law's declaration during the Committee stage of the Military Service Bill that further powers might be needed in the future.[184] Above all, Asquith could draw some comfort from the incontestable observation that '[t]he 10 plagues of Egypt would be preferred by Liberals to a L[loyd] G[eorge] Administration'.[185]

IV

It would overstate the case to maintain that by January 1916 the real split in the Liberal party had already taken place; that the following months would merely heighten an already brittle atmosphere; that when the *coup* came in December it would do no more than complete a process long since begun. But it would understate the truth to relegate the crises over coalition and conscription to a category of localized difficulties within Liberalism. If at the beginning of 1916 there did not exist two 'camps', the positions which the factions would adopt eleven months later were already apparent. If there were no armies, it was not for want of standards under which to rally. One of them could be seen in the win-the-war position which demanded from its adherents unflinching prosecution of the fighting regardless of principles, traditions and old-fashioned loyalties; in 1916 it could count among its number almost the whole of the Conservative party and the type of Liberal who supported the Liberal War Committee which had been established in January. The other position insisted that the dilemma posed by the bellicose – 'abandon Liberalism or . . . abandon the war'[186] – was a false one since the war could only be won *through* the practice of Liberalism, or if it could not then it was not worth winning. Few Liberals stood openly beneath this flag at the beginning of the year, but their number increased as Asquith was driven into adopting something like this position in order to rationalize his inadequacies as a war leader. Even during the conscription crisis this identification of positions with men had begun to be announced. '[T]he people who want compulsory service', Maurice Hankey wrote in his diary, 'don't want Asquith while those who want Asquith don't want compulsory service.'[187] It was an attitude which the events of the spring would serve to amplify.

January saw the formation of factions to represent most sections of political feeling in the House of Commons. On the 13th the Liberal War Committee was announced by Handel Booth, Sir Arthur Markham and Sir Henry Dalziel, with Sir Frederick Cawley as Chairman, taking as its objective 'a national Policy for the vigorous prosecution of the war'.[188] On a less idealistic plane, the group intended to monitor the activities of Liberals who had opposed the Military Service Bill and to try to secure their defeat at the next election.[189] To help it in its policing, the Committee hoped to work with the Conservative War Group, which already numbered over one hundred and which had just gained an accretion of strength through its links with a new 'ginger group' which was dedicated to 'secur[ing] a change of government'.[190] On the Asquithian side (the label would not have seemed anomalous) those who had opposed conscription organized themselves into a permanent opposition group under a committee composed of Simon, Whitehouse, Leif Jones and Richard Holt with J. H. Thomas as Labour representative.[191] Meanwhile Asquith was drawing around himself what Lloyd George considered to be a 'clique' directed against him.[192] In the House of Commons through the spring there operated a fairly broad-based movement among Liberals to prevent the Conservative party from pushing Liberalism in a direction it did not want to go. Handel Booth complained of this unpatriotic sentiment among Members on 2 May:

Men have been going round in the Liberal Party from time to time in the last year whispering that they are opposing, first of all the Registration Bill, and, secondly, the Compulsion Bill, at the request of Liberal Members. They really want us to get up a good agitation, then it strengthens their hands against the Conservatives in the country. This is the kind of doctrine that is talked about in the smoke-room and lobbies, and even on these benches, and it is time it was exposed.[193]

Individuals could and did change sides in the coming months, but there is no doubt that positions were being assumed. Asquith, as seen by the backbencher, was playing off one faction against another and 'mov[ing] us all about like pawns'.[194]

Beyond the ken of the Prime Minister, however, there were certain elements within the Conservative party which were determined to push him into a further crisis by advocating the broadening of conscription legislation. Sandhurst confided to his diary in February that feeling 'in society so-called' was against Asquith and was growing 'strong and outspoken',[195] while within the Conservative party hopes were high in March that a general election might be forced and Asquith brought down. 'The mind of the Government', Milner decided, 'in so far as it has a mind, is averse from an election...The moral seems to be that our first duty is to prepare for [one].'[196] Oliver agreed and recalled an extra advantage. 'The Liberal party would be split and the Liberal machine would be pretty near a break down.'[197] The notion of a split was far from absurd, for the growing estrangement between Asquith and Lloyd George was part of common gossip; and even if it were merely a figment of the press agitation, a belief in its existence helped politicians to calculate which way they would jump if the rift were to become unbridgeable.

Liberals who thought their leader was being maligned drew attention to Lloyd George's supposed flirtation with Northcliffe and Milner. The allegations were not implausible: Lloyd George and Milner had met in March and were probably in regular touch through Arthur Lee, Parliamentary Secretary to Lloyd George, who lived a few doors away from Milner in Great College Street.[198] The latter was seen to be shedding his past and adopting a new political position, one which was very much at odds with Lloyd George's own past:

I grieve over this rift in the Liberal Party. Even the victories which have been half-won – Reform of the Lords, the Land Question, the Temperance Question – are now in peril...The men who are now supporting Lloyd George were, as a set, the men who opposed his great measures of reform...Why cannot Lloyd George...say something which will make it clear even to his detractors that his old ideals of social progress have not been shaken in the tumult of War?[199]

The line of division between this new stance of Lloyd George and what the current conception of Liberalism involved was not yet clear, nor would it be so for some years after 1916. Besides, even if a serious situation were to arise and Asquith to resign, it was

by no means clear that Lloyd George would succeed him: Carson
or Curzon or Balfour was just as likely a candidate.[200] But the
division was there.

The final crisis over conscription matured in April, and Asquith
contemplated his departure if the situation ('black as Erebus')[201]
got completely out of hand. In fact it did not, though the Lloyd
George/Conservative alliance was putatively strengthened –
'I always thought he'd end by leading the Tories', was Sandhurst's
comment[202] – and Balfour and Lansdowne were left to fight a
Conservative rearguard defence of the coalition. If any prediction
carried conviction in the summer of 1916 it was that if Lloyd
George were to quit the government the Conservative party would
leave with him and Asquith would fall. The latter, however, had
come too far to make crass mistakes now. Designedly he waited
and saw until the Cabinet could be persuaded that it had agreed
and then announced the decision as his own.[203] He had often done
it before. It is remarkable that he should have been allowed to
do it again. By his riding out of the storm he contributed to the
legend that Lloyd George had been a crook 'who let his nearest
colleagues down about conscription at the critical moment and
then took up the question again when he thought the audience
more favourable and the limelight more concentrated on
himself';[204] and he added to his own atmosphere of offended
innocence. He had not only introduced conscription, he had
'generally scored' over Lloyd George in doing so.[205] The prompt
formation of a 'We Stand For Asquith' movement is an eloquent
witness both to his unique instinct for Liberal pose and to his
shrewd recognition that it was a Liberal pose which the situation
required.

Poses were all that were left in the Asquithian repertoire by
1916, and they became more transparent in the crowded months
between May and December. Detailed consideration of those
months can be omitted here: it is enough to emphasize that the
events of these months sharpened and deepened the rifts which
had opened the year before. Thus the Paris Resolutions of July
were significant not because free trade was overthrown (that dam
had been breached in the McKenna Duties of the previous year)
but because the overthrow seemed part of the larger process of
apostasy. The Liberal historian G. P. Gooch might see in retrospect that 'Protection trod on the heels of Conscription'[206] but it

is more significant that Lord Farrer was able before the event to predict that it would do so.[207] Similarly the Irish settlement, while it was politically notable in precipitating the resignation of Selborne,[208] was more significant for Liberalism when seen as part of a wider chain of happenings:

All the old principles of the Liberal party have been virtually abandoned by its leader. Even Free Trade and the Home Rule settlement of Ireland ...was torn up at the last minute by the English Tories.

The betrayal has been cruel:– war seems to arouse so many bad passions that Liberalism cannot live in its atmosphere.[209]

One could wish that 'party fights' would return to dispel that atmosphere so that 'principles will once more have a meaning, and all this anti-parliamentary claptrap about "national" policies will find its level – in the gutter with the "National" Review'.[210] But depression and dull acceptance of what was said to be inevitable were more common than heroism in a House of Commons which Burns found 'dreary, uninteresting [and] almost moribund' by October.[211] What is important is not to mistake lack of fight for lack of scruple. Liberals were not congenitally incapable of aggression; they were merely not so good at it as were Carson, Milner, Amery, Oliver and their putative ally Lloyd George.

The latter must have been aware by the summer of 1916 that he was 'a great power in the State';[212] and others were by that time clear that he would be likely to succeed Asquith after his, Lloyd George's, move to the War Office – a move which struck the distant Haldane as another example of Lloyd Georgian 'cudgell[ing]'[213] – following the death of Kitchener on 5 June. That situation was indeed immediately threatened when Lloyd George offered his resignation after finding his new powers insufficient; and he told intimates that he was prepared to form a new party if Asquith were foolish enough to accept it.[214] It was another crisis for a government used to living by them. Again it was overcome, again more teeth were set on edge, especially those of Liberal editors who saw their duty in preaching revolt or obedience to the Liberal conscience. Gardiner of the *Daily News* had attacked Lloyd George on 22 April and hurt him with his mordant phrases;[215] Spender of the *Westminster Gazette* told Balfour shortly after the death of Kitchener that if Lloyd George took the War Office he would break the Cabinet;[216] and Donald of the *Chronicle* had been *persona non grata* to Lloyd George for some time, perhaps because, as one contemporary believed, he was 'blinded by Principles...[and b]ound hand and foot by past traditions and utterances of statesmen now happily dead but unfortunately not forgotten'.[217] As Lloyd George himself later put it, his advocacy of conscription had 'added a fresh edge to the bitterness of those who held that my determination to fight the War through without hesitation or reserve, was a most improper and, indeed, unholy attitude'.[218] Before the Nigeria debate, before the resignation and subsequent agitation of Carson, before the emergence of a demand for a small War Committee to supersede the overgrown administration over which Asquith ineffectually reigned, the important decisions had already been taken.

Indeed the importance of the Liberal split of December 1916 has been at once overstressed and misunderstood: the former because the trials of the previous two years have been given insufficient weight, the latter because the split has been seen to have involved little more than a clash of personalities, 'a palace revolution, where we have a kind of Praetorian Guard in the Press',[219] enacted by 'Pitt of Printing House Square', one of the titles Lloyd George took with him to Downing Street.[220] More than this was involved; and the involvement was not limited to those fringe Liberals like Lees Smith who wanted to '[g]o back to the old Liberal tradition' and revive the days when politicians placed their trust in 'decent, kindly, humane forces'.[221] One of the latter, C. P. Trevelyan, told the Commons during a debate on the expulsion of Bertrand Russell from Trinity College, Cambridge, that there were 'masses of men who do not agree with us about the war who do not like this sort of thing', while Pringle (not on the fringe; indeed by now an influential M.P.) spoke of 'methods of tyranny which are utterly unworthy of a Liberal Ministry'.[222] Ghosts were walking. The Liberal leadership had not wanted to exhume them, nor would it have done so had not the war removed all their best options and forced them in directions they were unfitted to go. There were limits to the trimming abilities even of Asquith's government, and the changed circumstances of wartime had revealed them. By 1916 the Liberal mind had arrived. It had been created by Adam Smith, John Bright, Mill, Gladstone, a legendary ministry, a European war and Bonar Law's Conservative party.

It was to be the deposition of Asquith and the substitution of

Lloyd George which set the seal on the process. For Liberals, the most significant aspect of the crisis was its secrecy and behind-the-scenes scheming. Whether Lloyd George can be shown by historians to have been innocent of chicanery is irrelevant to the task of explaining the frame of mind of those involved. What is important is that contemporaries believed that the affair had been manufactured by Lloyd George, Northcliffe and the Conservatives. Even Strachey, who had long been pressing for a change of government, felt that Asquith's removal 'was the right thing done in so wrong a way that one's gorge rises at it'.[223] The metaphor was the same in the Asquithian pronouncement of Vaughan Nash: 'I wish I could shake off the feeling of nausea, but I can't do it: the smell of bilewater strikes up through everything.'[224] And the Lloyd Georgian head-counter Christopher Addison, while he maintained in public that 'so far as [he] ever knew there was no question of intrigue or spite about it',[225] nevertheless confessed privately to MacCallum Scott in 1921 that the overthrow of Asquith had been clumsily achieved, 'and might have been done in a cleaner way'.[226] Apart from the 126 Liberals promised by Addison to Lloyd George as supporters of a government led by him,[227] the tone among Liberals was one of confused bitterness, amplified by the Asquithian press. 'Asquith must go, Grey must go, Balfour must go, Lansdowne must go – all, in fact, but the men whose ability is not conspicuous enough to invite criticism.'[228]

MacCallum Scott wrote in his diary that the conflict of December 1916 was 'personal and trivial', John Burns in his that no greater consequence would follow than that 'the Gentlemen of England [would now] serve under the greatest cad in Europe'.[229] Neither of these remarks was typical of the Liberal tone. The material suggests overwhelmingly that Liberalism mattered to most Liberals and that out of the splitting of the party there emerged à outrance two conceptions of what Liberalism was about. Lloyd George drew his support from that section of the party which Phillip Kerr would later label 'War Liberals':[230] it is significant that he carried with him thirty of the forty who had served on the Liberal War Committee since January; significant too that that Committee met on 7 December and insisted on passing a motion in support of Lloyd George's efforts to form a government.[231] Asquith took with him a different kind of man.

Naivety attends any interpretation of the Liberal split which does not take account of individual calculation and exception: but the Asquithians were different for all that. Mr A. J. P. Taylor, relying 'more on feel than on figures', has seen in the Asquithians 'men of almost excessive culture and refinement' and in the supporters of Lloyd George men 'lower-class in origin, in temperament, in position'.[232] Mr Edward David has shown that the sociological hypotheses of Mr Taylor do not stand up to scrutiny as far as Liberal M.P.s are concerned, though it is interesting that a supporter of Lloyd George after 1916 had in his mind an image of the premier's parliamentary following as one 'a little too much "over the shop"' in the sense that it contained 'an undue preponderance of a certain business type'.[233] (And is not imagery as important to political motivation as a possibly unknown reality?) But Mr David in any case bases his rebuttal on an anaemic assumption. 'It is the social and economic background of a party', he writes in justification of his approach, 'which will determine the directions in which it will apply...experience and the way it will respond to great challenges and new problems.'[234] As a generalization the point has some substance, but as an explanation of the state of mind of Liberalism in 1916 it will not do. What mattered to Liberals in that charged atmosphere was not which schools they went to or what their occupations were. More significant was their willingness to commit themselves to, or divorce themselves from, a pervasively moral political tradition. Mr David is right to see in the Asquithians 'a cadre of intellectual talent' superior to that of their opponents',[235] but wrong to leave the matter there. The intellectual gulf between the two camps was not a question of brain-power: it turned on the indispensability of Liberal statecraft – or its superfluity – during a period of national trial. At the centre of the Liberal mind in 1916 were notions about the characteristics of 'right government' and what it ought to consist in; and between the two factions in this respect the mind of each was foreign to the other.

The year 1914 had set in motion a process which could make Liberals actually glad to dissociate themselves from a government that had become sordid. After the December crisis was over, Richard Holt was 'overjoyed at finding the Liberal leaders almost to a man free from the coalition and the degrading compromises'.[236] Not only had Asquith and Lloyd George come to be seen as irreconcilable men: they were observed to be symbols of irreconcilable ways of thinking about political life. No Act of God was deemed to have caused the Liberal party to fall apart. If it had, then there would have been no one to blame and Liberals might have been happier with one another. If Liberals had been conscious of a 'prolonged crisis in Liberalism'[237] in which their faith had shown itself inadequate to the demands of war, their response might have been more stoical. But their faith seemed to them alive and mocking. To them their creed was not responsible for the failure – hence the continual doubts and allegations of betrayal. Liberalism, for those who believed in it, had not been in crisis, Liberals had. The latter had lost their direction, the former had become exalted, purified and purged. Lloyd George may not have believed in Liberal ghosts, but he had helped to stimulate their exhumation; and it is reasonable for the historian to wonder where those ghosts went and whom they haunted.

2. Ghosts in the machine

I believe in the barefoot friars and not in a Minister of Education. Fishermen – not Fisher!! No great thing in this world has ever been achieved by organized effort...When 'machinery' begins to work, you get the Catholic Church or the British Cabinet.

> Esher to L. B., 30 November 1919, *Journals and Letters of Reginald Viscount Esher*, IV, 249.

In democracies, particularly, the Leader sets the tone of the Party.

> Lord Robert Cecil to Gladstone, 11 April 1922, Cecil MSS, 51163 fol. 80.

I

Neil James Archibald Primrose, son of Lord Rosebery, son-in-law of the seventeenth Earl of Derby, brother-in-law to the Marquess of Crewe, went to war in 1917. By way of a send-off, Sir Alfred Mond organized a dinner in his honour; and one of those attending was Viscount Sandhurst, who found the occasion 'interesting' but evocative of certain sad memories since the house in which the party was held had once belonged to the late Lord Kimberley, with whom he had often dined in happier days. 'But what a different gathering', Sandhurst mused in his diary, 'Gladstone, Granville, Spencers, Kimberleys, Breadalbanes and so on. The old order with a vengeance has given place to the new.'[1] Strength had been lent to the conviction, perhaps, by Sandhurst's immediate neighbours at the Primrose dinner, Lord Cowdray and Sir Robert Munro. The first was Asquithian and wealthy, a Yorkshire industrialist who wrote blank cheques for Liberal party funds,[2] allowed Asquithian conclaves to meet at his house in Carlton House Terrace,[3] and who was known pre-eminently in Liberal circles in his role as 'the good angel of the W[estminster] G[azette]'.[4] The other was Lloyd George's Minister for Scotland, a man who by taking office had incurred the displeasure of his fellow Scottish Liberal M.P.s, none of whom would agree to serve as his Parliamentary Secretary.[5]

Through such social encounters the fears and prejudices and

perspectives of the Liberal mind were directly underlined, and they are part of the reason for not studying that mind disembodied. How one way of life and thought conflicts with another is not to be noticed in the continuum of a single thought-world: the mind is jolted by contact with people and events. Or perhaps by a book: 'I have now read Ripon's Life. It brings back many memories of a very good and lovable man – with a fine and generous public spirit...These are the things which help to sweeten the too frequent aridity of political life.'[6] But there is little point in discussing what Liberals 'thought' or 'believed' after the split of 1916 until one is clear about who the actors were and what they did. Only with the completion of that task can the delicate process of subtracting the realities of manoeuvre from the pretensions of rhetoric properly begin.

In one sense the task is easier when dealing with the period 1916–29 than with the years before the split. Two fairly distinct camps present themselves to the historian – the Asquithian and the Lloyd Georgian – and the Liberal history of these years centres on their dialogue. From 1916 till the fall of Lloyd George in 1922 the creatures smiled and spat at one another; there followed a period when they lived in sin, with increasing discomfort for both partners; and finally they separated for good. The tussles of 'that competent rhetorician HHA and...that more competent liar LG'[7] pulled apart the fabric of the Liberal party until, as one observer lamented, it resembled a tattered sheet.[8] But that was not all. The splitting of the party into two warring factions heralded also the end of historic Liberalism. 'Even the rout of the Liberal party', Stephen McKenna later reflected, '[was] inconsiderable by comparison with the death of liberalism which took place that day' in 1916.[9] Perhaps in studying these factions the historian takes trivial squabbles and accords to them an importance they never possessed in the minds of contemporaries. It is arguable that he ought to see in the choices made in 1916 something 'personal, political and petty' and to see in all Liberals what Burns saw in Asquith, 'nothing but the ethic of the kennel'.[10] Yet the surviving material compels one to believe that the division was taken in deadly earnest. The issue could hardly be avoided or ignored: from 1917 onwards the Liberal party was a party of dichotomy. The Liberal label served only to tie together men facing in opposite directions. It was no longer a question of Asquith's being a bad war minister or of Lloyd George's being untrustworthy. Behind and beyond these strictures lay larger instincts. 'Why think of the past?' asked Esher during his Lloyd Georgian phase. 'I don't approve. All that is morbid. The present always has been and always must be the test of manhood. The past holds no regrets for me, and is not even pathetic.'[11] How could a mind such as this attune to that of a man who was so steeped in continuity that when he 'saw Curzon and Milner clamber into autocratic control in alliance with Lloyd George and Northcliffe, [he] felt a bleak despair and wanted another planet to collide with and smash this stricken world'?[12]

II

Among supporters of Asquith the feeling was strong that something more than a particular combination of Liberal leaders had departed from the government at the end of 1916. Some sections of the press merely ruminated about the accession of Lloyd George with a suppressed virulence. 'If we do not recriminate about the manner of this change', Spender wrote in his *Westminster Gazette*, '. . . it must not be supposed that we fail to resent the manner in which Mr. Asquith has been treated. We do most deeply resent it.'[13] But despite the context of wartime some others were pointed in their allegations and, more significantly, metaphysical in their anxieties:

The late Premier who never spoke one word 'to the gallery'. . .kept alive in the minds of the majority that they were fighting for the ideal. Who is to preserve in the nation those feelings so long sustained, if no one stands forth as the embodiment of the national faith?. . .No nation, any more than any individual, can reach forward to great inspiring ideals without a soul.[14]

For political leaders, however, it was not a time to think about the soul and Asquith went back to the Wharf to brood.

He was sixty-four. Advancing years had brought to certain facets of his personality changes which intimates had come to notice. A note by Lord Haldane written in 1926 looks back on the younger lawyer of the 1880s as 'a serious person'. 'His photograph', Haldane wrote, 'makes him look like a stern Nonconformist.'[15] In the 1890s Asquith struck Sir John Brunner as 'hard' and 'unsympathetic', more like a policeman than a statesman.[16] Everyone knew that this was not the man of 1917.

For several years his family had cocooned him from the abrasions of political life until events after 1914 made them impossible to avoid. He had allowed his personal life to collapse inwards into a small group of female intimates, kindly advisers and bridge players; he had permitted his intellectual life to do the same until all that remained was an occasional canter over known ground, pleasantly punctuated by conversation and the bottle. His son records that he rarely heard his father discuss a philosophical problem: it was not a turn of mind which Asquith enjoyed.[17] If he was not 'a stoic carved in butter', as an Aberdonian journalist alleged,[18] he was certainly a man softened by the pressures of wartime politics. Above all he was a desperately tired man; six weeks after the crisis of 1916 McKenna told Runciman that Asquith was still listless and gave the impression of being a man 'who ha[d] lived his life'.[19]

Whatever the real state of Asquith's mind, its political importance lay in what it was able consistently to represent. Asquith managed to radiate an atmosphere of being distant from and superior to other politicians, a radiation to which the *Nation* was probably most sensitive in a post-war article: 'Compared with any of his opponents [*sic*], Mr. Asquith's mind is – let us call it different; his culture is different, and his temper and his standard of conduct. There is really no comparison. The public knows that, instinctively.'[20] Asquith achieved through classical grace and a half-assumed generosity of spirit what Balfour achieved through woolly disinterestedness and Baldwin through homeliness – a right to don the self-tailored garb of the constitutionally worthy. It was not an atmosphere which could be explained in terms of a 'Treasury mind':[21] there was little of that mentality in Asquith's make-up. It is more probable that all the central assumptions on which the Asquithian world-view was founded were located in a temperamentally suitable conception of what orderly progress involved. As Sir Willoughby Dickinson observed, Asquith did not like people who advocated causes before their time.[22]

In the immediate context of December 1916, however, causes were rooted in men and political discussion was concerned with individuals. On Christmas Eve, Asquith wrote to Runciman that he was content 'to let things take their course, tho' I confess that the weak personnel of the new War Committee, and Carson's utter incompetence to run the Admiralty, fill me with a good deal of misgiving'.[23] Doubtless it also filled him with a certain baby-faced joy since he had resisted that personnel to the end. Still, it was felt that Asquith would not remain content for long with the role of spectator. Burns recorded in his diary as early as 19 December that Asquith intended to fight; and a fortnight later he was mentioning a growing feeling at Westminster that Lloyd George had treated Asquith 'abominably' and that 'events w[ould] be stronger than advertising'.[24] Typically, Asquith did not wait on events as long as his opponents might have hoped; he called a meeting of Liberal M.P.s at the Reform Club on 8 December and there tuned his pulpit very cleverly, drawing admiration and sympathy from all quarters. A letter written later in the month shows the potential of his audience. 'Good luck for the new year', George Lambert wished the Liberal editor C. P. Scott, 'but how can one even hope or wish that when we have such a set of d....d fools to govern us. The Germans couldn't serve us worse.'[25] But of course Asquith could do nothing by himself: he would need to mobilize his friends.

All the important Liberal figures in Asquith's coalition government – Grey, McKenna, Samuel, Crewe, Buckmaster, Runciman, Harcourt – followed him into the wilderness. Two other former ministers could be relied on, for though both Simon and Haldane had left the government since 1914 there was no reason to believe that they had any wish to join Lloyd George; it was Asquith who helped to place Simon at the Air Board in 1917 by leaning on the head of Intelligence in France,[26] while Haldane did not begin to look seriously towards the Labour party until after the war. Augustine Birrell, after his Irish *débâcle*, dropped out of politics altogether to become a narrowly bookish, twisted man living a 'speedy, *risqué* old age' and given to swearing.[27] Two further men might be mentioned, since the names of Edwin Montagu and Winston Churchill were later to acquire a bad smell among Liberals. Both of them defected, and for treachery Asquithian punishment was harsh. Its tone was made plain when Violet Bonham-Carter compared the two men. 'His [Montagu's] *cant* and cringing dishonesty make me quite sick. Give me Winston's frank, candid cynicism any day.'[28]

Montagu's rise had been rapid. He had been Asquith's P.P.S. before the war and during it had occupied the posts of Financial Secretary to the Treasury and Chancellor of the Duchy of Lancaster before replacing Lloyd George as Minister of Munitions after the death of Kitchener in July 1916. He had become partially estranged from Asquith after his, Montagu's, engagement to Venetia Stanley; Asquith may have been 'just too noble and splendid for words',[29] but he had felt the blow severely at a time of deep political crisis. The move to Munitions had brought Montagu into closer contact with Lloyd George, whose enemies he came to suspect of prejudice and envy. By the end of 1916 his role had become one of conciliation[30] and, though he refused to join Lloyd George's government, he had come to feel by 9 December that he was in profound disagreement with many of the inner counsels of the party.[31] Fear of the consequences probably kept him out of the government, and this he overcame in July 1917 when Asquith received a soulful letter pleading that, 'from the point of view of reconstruction alone', he had decided to join.[32] Among Asquith's supporters the response was chilling, as Montagu complained to Lloyd George: 'One might have supposed that when a Liberal with a progressive policy took the place of a rather hide-bound Conservative in a very important office, they would have been pleased. But not at all. They regard me as a deserter and accuse me of ingratitude. They say that "Asquith made me..."'[33] But Montagu's bitterness was as nothing compared with that of his new enemies. There is no better insight into the Asquithian mind than to note the tone of satisfaction in McKenna's description of Montagu's return to the House of Commons as a supporter of the government:

He stood at the Bar fumbling with his hat and white with fear, evidently afraid of a hostile demonstration. When his moment came it was neither a walk nor a run but a quick sidelong shuffle up to the Table, so strange and noticeable that there was a burst of laughter followed by complete silence ... As he shook hands with the Speaker the faithful Book cheered. Freddy Guest and Beck introduced him. Last time it was Asquith and Gulland.[34]

It is hard to believe that Asquithians were not as 'jubilant' as their leader[35] at Montagu's embarrassment over his *faux pas* in Indian policy and subsequent resignation from Lloyd George's government in 1922.

The position of Churchill, on the other hand, was far more anomalous. Never a man to be dovetailed into the precise proportions of party politics, Churchill had ceased to be in any sense

an 'Asquithian' after his dismissal from the Admiralty in May
1915. By the beginning of 1916 he had decided that, if his career
could be retrieved at all, it must be followed apart from that of
Asquith.[36] No succour was offered by Lloyd George when he was
Cabinet-making in the following December; and Churchill's wife
had always preferred Asquith anyway. 'At this moment', she
wrote to Churchill when he was in France in 1915, 'although I hate
the PM, if he held out his hand I could take it (though I would
give it a nasty twist) but before taking Ll G's I would have to
safeguard myself with charms, touchwords, exorcisms and by
crossing myself.'[37] For the most part the Asquithians regarded
Churchill with a mixture of amusement and fear. Asquith had
himself 'in moments of private relaxation' confessed to finding
Churchill a disappointment at the Admiralty long before the erup-
tion of the Fisher crisis;[38] but few ever saw him in the perspective
of Burns as 'fat, stale and unprofitable'.[39] Even Violet Bonham-
Carter, who later came to despise all that Churchill represented,
wrote kind and encouraging letters to him after his dismissal.[40] But
1917 found him still frustrated at being kept out of government
'with whose aims and temper [he] was in the most complete
accord'.[41] He had been excluded through the pressure of certain
Conservatives and the Northcliffe press, but it was a paltry enough
opposition for one so determined, and in May 1917 he was taken
unofficially into the counsel of the government. Why that particular time was chosen is less than clear. Churchill himself wrote
in *The World Crisis* that the event which decided Lloyd George
was an effective secret session of the Commons instigated by
Churchill.[42] What he does not record is that five days after the
debate he was approached by 'an influential friend of Lloyd
George' and was later driven down to Walton Heath, where he
argued that Lloyd George should establish a rapprochement with
Asquith and that Smuts should be taken into the War Cabinet.

In agreeing to what Churchill said, Lloyd George was merely
assenting to a *démarche* he had already made. Churchill was not
the first to be suggested for inclusion; he was probably taken in
because others had refused the offer. Haldane, for example, had
dined with Lloyd George on 17 April, had been pressed to 'come
in',[43] but had agreed only to become Chairman of the Committee
on the Machinery of Government. More significantly, a rumour
was in the air that Asquith himself was to be asked to join the

government. The occasion of the new overture seems to have been the possibility of American entry into the war. Lord Hardinge had written on 3 April: 'I may tell you in strict confidence that there is a scheme that when America is at war with Germany to send over Asquith as special Ambassador charged with all our war interests in America.'[44] Nothing came of this notion; but a fortnight later Alick Murray wrote to Guest emphasizing the importance of reconstructing the government by including Asquith.[45] Accordingly Reading sought out Asquith whilst among his party at the Wharf over Whitsun and pointed out that, since McKenna had retired from politics – thus removing one great objection to a reunion of the two camps – and since it was clear that Law wanted to leave the Exchequer and that Balfour was tiring at the Foreign Office, Asquith could have any post he wished other than that of Prime Minister.[46] Asquith and Crewe took some comfort from the approach which, they believed, showed 'in what direction the wind [was] blowing'.[47]

Plausible 'occasions' apart, it is sensible to ask whether deeper reasons prompted Lloyd George to make this attempt to draw Asquith into his government. Dr Douglas has suggested that one reason may have lain in a desire to detach Asquith from his followers who, it is alleged, differed from their leader over the question of possible negotiation with Germany.[48] This interpretation is perhaps rather forced. Certainly it was a prominent issue and provoked some divisions, as Burns noticed: 'I told [Buckmaster] that the "machine", "the Party", the Caucus, the Clique, had given several evidences to Anti-War members of its intention to send them to Coventry.'[49] Yet Burns writes of the Asquithian group as a whole and not of Asquith alone holding such views. The only solid evidence Dr Douglas adduces for his view is a single letter from Guest, whose political perspicacity was never renowned among his colleagues. And if it is clear that other Asquithians were not asked to join the government, the reason is equally plain: Lloyd George knew that they would do nothing without consulting Asquith. To bring in Asquith was to bring in his colleagues. Perhaps a more effective argument than that of Dr Douglas is a less tortuous one.

Two considerations seem to have governed the move: the control of the House of Commons which Asquith still plainly possessed; and the perilous position produced there by the Cotton Duties debate in April 1917.

Politicians of all hues agreed that the bulk of the parliamentary party followed Asquith after the crisis of 1916. The cause of this Asquithian sympathy was rooted in what Liberals conceived Lloyd George had done to Asquith rather than in the way Asquith had acted towards them. Indeed the latter's attitude towards his parliamentary supporters had been at best olympian since the beginning of the war. 'Members of Parliament', he wrote to Crewe in 1915, '...wd be much better employed doing some form of duty in their homes and constituencies than in jabbering or listening to jabber at Westminster.'[50] Further, he had been and would continue to be mean-minded in the giving of 'bye-election benedictions' to Liberal candidates.[51] The parliamentary atmosphere at the end of 1916, however, was too heated for precise calculation, and what had been done was for the moment less important than what had been seen to be done. Sandhurst noted that the House of Commons was 'frightened, like an old woman with the influenza. The past week has been too much for their nerves, knots of excited busybodies and cranks talk themselves almost into hysterics.'[52]

At the beginning of the new year there was an air of bewilderment. The '*coup*' had passed Members by: one of them was left to reflect that everything would have been different if only a direct vote had been taken.[53] In December Sandhurst had been moved to recall the removal of Peel in 1846; by February he was reporting the general view that 'all that has happened politically is that the Prime Minister (Asquith) has crossed the House';[54] and by April this view had crystallized:

[I]t is perfectly clear to anybody who has any knowledge of the House of Commons that Asquith's popularity in that Assembly is undiminished while that of Lloyd George does not exist. Asquith has the House of Commons in the palm of his hand...[H]e is a standing danger to Lloyd George and his Cabinet and Lloyd George realises that the first serious mistake he makes he will be ousted by his predecessor.[55]

Arguably that first mistake had already been made in allowing the vote on Indian Cotton Duties to become almost a vote of confidence in the government. The revolt centred on Lancashire. Sir Frederick Cawley complained that neither he nor any other Lancastrian Member had been consulted about the proposal. 'The other Liberal members ', he warned, 'and probably most of the Unionists will of course vote what they will call "Lancashire ". The Asquith party are very bitter and will do all they can to induce him to try and defeat the Govt.'[56] Private discussions provoked by the coming debate on 10 March were less concerned with Liberal hostility from without the government, however, than with Lancastrian hostility from within it. The Asquithians did not latch onto the significance of the situation until the time for effective action was past; and they lost an able advocate on 10 March when Montagu told Crewe that he could not be 'a party to a resolution asking the Government to reverse its policy'.[57] Nevertheless the government was badly rattled. Two days before the debate, Derby had reversed his earlier position of minimizing the problem and wrote to the Conservative leader that the situation was far more serious than he had realized: unless there were assurances of reconsideration after the war, Lancashire M.P.s would vote against the government.[58] By the day of the debate Liberal hopes were running high and there were those who anticipated a crisis during the coming week.[59]

Asquith held back, however, and the debate was something of a damp squib. The government won comfortably, though Burns noted that not many Liberals had voted (Asquith himself had abstained) and that Lloyd George had done badly.[60] Perhaps the Asquithian reticence was partly produced by a feeling that Lloyd George was very much Prime Minister-in-toils whose Liberalism was being stifled through the actions of Conservative colleagues. Certainly Bryce felt 'sincerely sorry' for him;[61] and there is clear evidence that Lloyd George himself was conscious at precisely this time of his ministry's being a coalition only in name.[62] But a stronger reason was suggested by Hardinge. Asquith was far too clever, Hardinge believed, to allow Lloyd George to go to the country on such an issue in an election which could only produce defeat for those rocking the boat.[63] Either way it seemed plain enough that Lloyd George's place was secure for the moment only because Asquith appeared reluctant to assume it. It is hard to believe that no such consideration lay behind the clumsy approaches of May 1917.

Meanwhile the Asquithian court, once exiled, had chosen to remain so. Realities were becoming clear: it was no accident that the numbers of the faithful began to shrink. Grey had gone off

to Falloden to rest his eyes and was in any case happy to let the
new government have a chance.[64] Neither Simon nor Samuel was
very active. The important names were Asquith, McKenna (for
a time), Runciman, with Crewe and Buckmaster in the Lords.
Closest to Asquith was undoubtedly the Marquess of Crewe; he
remained faithful to Asquith until the latter's death and then
transferred his allegiance, properly in Asquithian eyes, to Grey.
In a note once pushed across the Cabinet table to Runciman,
Crewe had announced himself opposed to what he called 'senti-
mental politics',[65] yet his career before 1922 shows him to have
been bound by ties of established connexion. Like Grey he was
one of the last of a dying *genre* of Liberal gentlemen. His altars
were never obvious nor his worship other than private, but neither
was his Liberalism overshadowed by calculation. Even so rabid
a mahatma as Margot Asquith sent untutored Liberals to him for
guidance. 'He is the wisest man and *the* strongest Liberal I have
ever met', she told Simon in 1924.[66]

Central to contention in the Commons during the first part of
1917, as far as the Asquithians were concerned, was the problem
of deciding who should be second-in-command. It was to be made
plain that the leader had no desire to have one, but in the meantime the struggle concerned McKenna and Runciman. Seniority
pointed to the former but there were those in the elite who resented 'McKenna shoving himself forward'.[67] No one opinion
predominated about the worth of either candidate. '[G]ood fellow
that', was Esher's view of McKenna, and Burns agreed;[68] but
Midleton thought he did not satisfy the City, FitzRoy thought him
'a mere politician' and Bertrand Russell thought he ought to be
put in the zoo.[69] His lawyer's mind contained a financial brain
which tended towards dryness and pedantry, a failing he wrote
'sheets' to Hardinge trying to deny.[70] Montagu came to hate him,
though he was taken in by McKenna's pose of being a financial
wizard; apart from that he could see only 'great ambition, great
jealousy, and a very petty, mean mind'.[71] In May 1917 McKenna
drifted off into the commercial circle from which he never returned, though not for want of offers. Runciman, McKenna's
rival, had done well since the beginning of the war at the Board of
Trade (he had drawn favourable comment from both Crewe
and Hardinge)[72] and he seemed marked out for high office. Two
serious illnesses, however, and a failure to win a seat in the

Commons between 1918 and 1924 ruined his chances. A practising Wesleyan Methodist, he gave to the unsympathetic an impression of puritanism.[73] By 1917 he was a prohibitionist.

Amidst the bickering, Asquith himself continued the non-party social relationships, which fulfilled a personal need, and old political ties, which had their uses during a period of upheaval. He remained in touch, for example, with the Gladstones and some of the functionaries associated with the National Liberal Federation. By lending an atmosphere of received authority, the Gladstonian connexion was particularly valuable, though only two of the family, Herbert and Henry, had survived to be of political importance. W. G. C. Gladstone had been killed in France in 1915, yet even he had managed in his brief life to reinforce all the apposite mythology. 'He was not comfortable', MacCallum Scott decided. 'He was too good...He did not admire cleverness or trickery or levity.'[74] Henry was Herbert's elder brother and spent most of the war developing his profound hatred of Lloyd George and brooding about the financial plight of his class in general and of Herbert in particular.[75] After the war he concentrated on the problem of keeping his Liberalism unsullied.[76] The better-known Herbert became important to the Asquithian cause after 1922 when he returned to Abingdon Street to try to reassemble the shattered electoral machine.

Gladstonian mythology was deliberately cultured by the Asquithians. It provided first-rate ammunition, for example, for open letters in which Asquith could refer to the 'guiding principles laid down by your father'.[77] Such pronouncements were merely rhetorical instruments. Margot Asquith brushed aside the tradition with her usual contempt for cobwebs and told Bryce that 'Gladstone sd. be faithfully dealt with – he was born to my mind with a faintly crooked mind like Newman and the Cecils.'[79] But as long as the necessary public identification was made, it mattered not at all what politicians thought in private. The rhetoric was working when Frederic Harrison (still Positivist and crotchety) could come to see in the Asquithians what he suspected in Gladstone: 'I am coming to think the GOM legend as [*sic*] a sinister myth, and the GOM lot – especially the LOM (Lesser Old Man) as bad as the crew of Lord North in [the] 18th century...Even the HHA group are infected by the GOM traditions.' And what he suspected in the court he found glaring in the rank and file: 'It's the House of

Commons – the new "Rump" – which is our curse – with its idiots and prigs talking about the "immortal principles of the great Liberal Party"'.[79]

That Harrison should have written in this sense to Rosebery was understandable: their years and alienation from current politics reinforced an old friendship and made them almost similar men. Rosebery's complete withdrawal from politics dated from long before the war and had its origins partly in certain temperamental tendencies, partly in the stark fact that no one wanted him to come back. 'I agree with neither party', he wrote in 1912, 'and the result is that I am obnoxious to both.'[80] By 1914 he had convinced himself that he had left politics because public life had ceased to be worthy of his presence – a conviction that the coming of the war heightened until politics became for him 'only the shadows of a distant, disagreeable cinematograph' in a world where political life ('always dirty and debasing') had become even dirtier and more debased.[81] Perhaps the simple truth was that Rosebery had become a Tory, as Esher believed;[82] at any rate he was taken to be no part of Liberalism during the war, though curiously a suggestion was made in December 1916 that he be offered the post of Lord Privy Seal in Lloyd George's government.[83] His day was over; it had been over for ten years. Yet still the name persisted and was commented on for another ten. Rattling round Dalmeny in his carriage in 1923 he brought to the mind of one observer the image of a ruined tower.[84] A new generation was left unmoved[85] as Rosebery entered the imagery of Liberalism and quitted its reality.

Realities continued to demand after May 1917 that Asquithians should concern themselves with parliament and exercise a Liberal voice there. What C. P. Scott had seen in February as 'a great disruption' within Liberalism[86] had turned out to be something much worse. 'Repeatedly of late', MacCallum Scott noted at the end of the year, 'we have had divisions on what is strict party lines, the Liberals voting in a solid block against the Government, practically no Liberals, save those who hold office, supporting the Government.'[87] Wise parliamentarians loyal to Lloyd George had urged him to come to the House more often,[88] but by the time of the Henderson debate in August it was clear that he had alienated all the important sections of opinion there – 'the bulk of the Liberals last December, the bulk of the Tories by the appointment of Winston and other things, and now the central forces of the Labour movement'.[89] Nor could Members of Parliament escape this atmosphere of animosity when they left the House: the divisions polluted the air even in their clubs. Frederick Guest reported in December 1917 that feeling in the National Liberal Club was 'preponderatingly against the Prime Minister and with Mr. Asquith',[90] and Robertson Nicoll found a similar situation at the Reform:

I have moved down to the Reform Club since the year began and have had a dreadful time. Many of the important politicians are there, and are very communicative. They belong exclusively, so far as I can find, either to the Asquithians or the Pacifists. What unites them is a common hatred of Lloyd George, which is simply maniacal and for which it is not easy to account.[91]

It was not an atmosphere for which all Liberals were temperamentally well suited. Sir John Simon was upset by the clash of 'personalities' which he saw at the heart of the matter. 'I bear no personal grudge against Lloyd George', he told MacCallum Scott. '. . . I won't label myself an Asquith man or a Lloyd George man. I'm not in that quarrel. It does not concern me. What have I got to do with it? After all I'm 20 years younger than the one and 12 years younger than the other. I belong to a different generation.'[92] He was in any case making no impact on politics so he decided to join the Air Force. Friends believed he had done it 'from the purest and best of motives' though Pringle and Hogge enjoyed themselves circulating ugly (and false) innuendoes.[93] The explanation he gave to both friends and public centred on his conviction that no negotiated peace was yet possible – an explanation which struck a responsive chord in the whiggery of seventy-nine-year-old George Otto Trevelyan, who described Simon's resignation letter as 'a very noble document' and spoke of Smuts in the same breath.[94]

Among others, not least among members of the Conservative party, there was a realization that Asquith's growing power would have tangible consequences. Soon after the formation of Lloyd George's government, Oliver had warned Carson that unless an organization of 'loyal' Liberals was set up the Asquithians would 'recover gradually all the old members of the Party'.[95] By September the tone was more urgent. Long advised Law on 18 September that 'unless prompt and effective steps [were] taken all the hard work of the past 10 or 12 years w[ould] be undone and the greatest party in the Country smashed to atoms'. 'Asquith', he concluded, 'has gained and is gaining, v. slowly but surely.'[96] It seemed reasonable to assume that Asquith would not remain forever content with his position in the wings when his parliamentary superiority to Lloyd George was so patent. War may have acted as a wet blanket, but it could not dampen all enthusiasm for political advantage. A challenge had to come; and in retrospect it seems to have been set in motion by the publication of Lord Lansdowne's notorious letter advocating a negotiated peace.

Ostensibly directed towards considerations of foreign policy, Lansdowne's letter gave rise (and conceivably was intended to give rise) to certain movements within domestic politics. It was a kite around the strings of which diverse opposition groups could rally; it offered respectability for those with a policy they had been reluctant to reveal and a policy for those without one. Who was responsible for the letter is not clear. Lansdowne had held the views it contained for at least a year, though he kept them to himself and would only confide to his daughter when the publicity came that he had been feeling the need to say something 'for some time'.[97] Philip Kerr believed that Loreburn was the immediate sponsor of the letter,[98] and certainly the dismal peer's views on the desirability of an end to the war consorted closely with those of Lansdowne; it was Loreburn, for example, who presented the non-party Address of Thanks to Lansdowne in the following January.[99] On the letter's publication some politicians professed horror, some admiration. All professed surprise. Kerr alleged at the time that both Geoffrey Howard and McKenna had said that Asquith knew nothing about the letter before its publication, but not all were equally innocent. The Archbishop of Canterbury – a convinced advocate of the Lansdowne policy – was sure that Balfour and Hardinge had known of and agreed to the content of the letter before publication, though they preferred to remain silent afterwards.[100] As for the Liberals, thinking about what to say went on through December and over Christmas. Asquith probably thought much and decided little: as late as 1921 an observer doubted that Asquith had ever been a 'Lansdownite'.[101] Simon decided as usual to agree and quibble concurrently.[102] Rank-and-file centrist Liberals seem to have felt that the letter was significant in some unclear way. It was 'an event' for MacCallum

Scott, and he described its significance in phraseology which ought to be marked: 'It crystallises an attitude of mind which has long been in solution in many minds . . . It is a challenge and a threat.'[103]

Less neutral positions were occupied by Liberals belonging to the twilight regions between Liberalism and Labour: they were interested more in Lansdowne's threat than in his challenge. Francis Hirst launched a Lansdowne League,[104] roped in Beauchamp to preside and pushed the idea hard in his *Common Sense*. There was similar commitment from H. W. Massingham. Indeed determining the proper direction for Liberalism to follow was the consuming passion of the latter and, fully a year before Lansdowne's decision to publish, he had told Runciman what ought to happen: '[A]s each day must increase the desire for an end to the war (with honour and advantage) Liberalism must either lead this movement or expire of inanition and division. I can't find it in my heart to help a renaissance of the party if it has no mind or will of its own.'[105] Through 1917 the Liberal party had held no brief for pacifists, but now there was a possibility of an Asquith/Lansdowne coalition drawing support from moderate Liberalism and certain Lib/Lab elements which still persisted in the party; and if such a combination could be contrived, Lloyd George appeared to be doomed. Moreover the parliamentary context seemed ripe for some such move. By the beginning of December there was only the problem of franchise reform to be overcome before radicals could afford to voice open opposition to the Lloyd George regime. Talks were already under way between men like Holt, Brunner, Molteno and Leif Jones with a view to generating a movement in favour of 'intelligent, patriotic and active opposition'.[106] It would not be long before such a mood began to be reflected in the division lobbies, and as early as 5 December MacCallum Scott was writing in his diary that the Lloyd George coalition was crumbling.[107] Nor was Lloyd George blind to the point; he was clear that the Asquithians were intent on mischief.[108] The problem of declaring 'war aims' occupied him over Christmas, and on 3 January he saw Asquith and explained his position on the matter; two days later Asquith and Grey breakfasted with him at Downing Street before he made his famous declaration.[109] According to both Grey's and Lloyd George's account, the latter attempted to procure nothing more from these meetings than their assent to his proposed statement,[110] but it is clear that in the following few weeks the Asquithian leaders were unsure how to respond to the new policy.

February was the crucial month. By the 8th Asquith had come to favour Lansdowne's position over a negotiated peace. 'If you see anything I ought to do', he told Randall Davidson, 'or any direction in which I should be moving, tell me frankly.'[111] Plainly the Liberal leader was looking for encouragement in his nascent schemes, and there was some support for the notion, but not from the Archbishop. Ponsonby's response to the Lansdowne letter, for example, had been: 'How can we make him Prime Minister?'[112] But it was Hirst who actually set about it; he wrote to Lansdowne urging him on,[113] and by the end of January he had concocted a paper government which he announced to Courtney. To see it is to realize at once why the Lansdowne movement failed. Lansdowne was to lead a government which, in Hirst's formulation, was not to include Asquith and the centre Liberals at all. Ponsonby was to be at the Foreign Office, Holt at the Exchequer, Burns to be (of all things) Secretary for War, Loreburn was to get the Woolsack, and MacDonald and Snowden were to be brought in at the Home Office and Ministry of Labour respectively.[114] Probably Courtney was too steeped in a lifetime's unreality to laugh, but the list would have guaranteed hysterics to most others. Lansdowne was to provide a venerable statue on which the flies could settle.

Introduce the Asquithians into the picture, however, and the prospect is less laughable. Some of the Lib/Labs realized that Asquith was necessary to the success of the plot; and as early as November 1917 they had been warned by one of their number that they were being stupid in 'not trying to get at [him]'.[115] For his part, Asquith might have contemplated a coalition with Lansdowne though not with the Labour people. He conceived Lansdowne to be a cultured, literate man with a civilized world-view, more competent and more acceptable than other Unionist peers. (Even after the immediate crisis had passed, Henry Gladstone still believed that Asquith and Lansdowne were 'in pretty close touch and agreement'.)[116] The pair of unlikely conspirators discussed the situation at Lansdowne House in the second week of February, and it may be significant that Esher told Hankey (and through him Lloyd George) on the 13th that Asquith was spending 'hours' there.[117] It may also be significant that Balfour was summoned to dine there on the 5th.[118] Westminster was running with rumour and even Burns noticed by the 13th that Asquith seemed to have been 'restored or resurrected for [*sic*] his old position of authority and leadership'. On the 16th he heard 'all sorts of rumours about reconstruction of the Government, exchange of offices, transfer of men from one place to another'[119] and, three days earlier, Haldane had written to his sister that Margot Asquith was 'intriguing busily' for a coalition.[120] By the 20th the latter was rumoured to have told Robertson – and the sympathy between Robertson, Haig and the Asquithian Liberals is not one to ignore[121] – that if he stuck to his guns he would be Secretary for War within a week.[122]

One or both of the leaders refused ultimately to act. It would have been in character for Asquith to have pulled back at the last moment; perhaps the whole affair was no more than an intellectual exercise for him. But again, Lansdowne had done little enough to co-operate with the minnows on the Left and it was after dining with him on the 15th (probably before any final decision was made) that Esher took away the definite impression that Lansdowne wanted only to reconstruct and not to destroy the government,[123] though it has to be added that on the same day Hankey reported that both Asquith and Lansdowne shared this view.[124] Whoever was responsible for backing away, the coalition idea was promoted henceforth by those used to crying in the dark. Strachey thought the idea prefigured his pet scheme of making the Speaker Prime Minister;[125] Beauchamp, Loreburn, MacDonald and Snowden persisted in an obstinate conclave;[126] and radicals like Holt continued to cajole. However, even the perpetually optimistic Courtney realized that the Commons as a whole were not prepared to press for a new government and, just as important, no plausible collection of politicians was available to take office.[127] Some still thought, like Holt, that the government could be overthrown[128] but those with their feet on the ground knew that if any overthrowing was to be done it would be done at the top, where politicians who mattered were too nervous to offer a challenge. Asquith's behaviour during these months may have reflected 'excellent good sense',[129] but what is patent in retrospect is that by avoiding the responsibilities of government he soured the prospects of the Liberal party at the next election and allowed himself to fall into a mood of impotence from which, with the exception of a brief flourish in 1920, he never recovered during the life of Lloyd George's government.

For the moment, however, some of the rank and file still believed that Asquith would yet win his way back to power. Having had little success with Simon, the irrepressible Holt turned to Asquith himself in April, pressing for a vote of no confidence in the government.[130] But in general it seems true to say that such *élan* as the Asquithians had once possessed was gone by now. There was a small radical group which met at Runciman's house, but according to Beauchamp it was ineffectually led and in need of reinforcement.[131] When Leif Jones set down in May the parliamentary problems provoked by the party's dilatory leadership, the picture did not offer much ground for encouragement: 'We are sorely denuded: Asquith comes seldom and intervenes very little: McKenna only looks in for odd moments: McK[innon] Wood is there, but silent. Runciman has been ill: Samuel is the only one of [the] old Cabinet who is really taking an active part . . . [and] . . . there are seldom heights in his level excellence.'[132] The court, for its part, had little love for frustrated Liberal backbenchers. Indeed by April Gulland was 'tired and disgusted' with the 'miserable crowd' who were always 'asking what A[squith] was going to do'.[133] By acting in the olympian fashion of pre-war days, Asquith did nothing to convince his followers that he was still a competent parliamentary leader. 'Alas!' Harcourt intoned to Runciman, 'I agree with your diagnosis that the present H of C and the Country do not want H.A. as a *War* Prime Minister. I think they are wrong, but they will not be converted by any of us.'[134]

Some Liberal members of the Cabinet were nevertheless still worried by the government's situation at the beginning of May.[135] After the Liberal failure in the Maurice debate, however, Lloyd George must have been clear that his former chief could now be safely ignored. Asquith was left to lament the 'unscrupulous use' which Lloyd George had made of the incident, and the Maurice incident was added to the dossier of Lloyd Georgian vice, where it has remained ever since.[136] Even so, before the end of the year there was to be another attempt to bring Asquith into the government. From whom the initiative came it is hard to say: Lloyd George later said that it began when he met a delegation from Manchester Liberal Federation which pushed for Asquith's inclusion as Lord Chancellor, to which Lloyd George agreed after consulting Law.[137] A more likely stimulus was provided by Rothermere. Certainly it was he who telephoned the Master of Elibank on 24 September to tell him that Lloyd George wished to see him. Murray went on the following day and was briefed about what he might offer Asquith: the Woolsack and nomination to two principal Secretaryships and six Under-Secretaryships. Murray saw Asquith on 26 September, but the latter found Lloyd George's conditions (an immediate election, conscription for Ireland and Home Rule without Ulster) unacceptable. Negotiations about inclusion therefore came to an end, though some strategic talk may still have taken place.[138] But the attitudes of Lloyd George and Asquith seem to have depressed Elibank. 'Unless I am much mistaken', he wrote later, 'in these two conversations I have been present at the obsequies of the Liberal Party as I knew it.'[139]

Neither Asquith nor his colleagues would have agreed. In retrospect they would come to see those obsequies as having been delayed until Lloyd George revealed the true extent of his capacity for treachery at the general election in December. 'The disintegration of the Liberal Party began with the Coupon Election. It then received a blow from which it has never since recovered.'[140] Asquith's judgement of 1927 is typical of one kind of Liberal diagnosis of what went wrong after 1914: treachery in 1916 followed by the great betrayal two years later. Lloyd George and Bonar Law, in the reliably extreme view of Margot Asquith, stood 'for ever condemned for inviting Revolution, dishing Labour and downing Asquith'.[141]

The election itself came as something of a shock to Liberal opinion. At the end of August Hardinge had found the possibility of a November election implausible, and even at the beginning of October Asquith saw it as 'a pure question of gambling'.[142] An objective assessment, moreover, could harden into a rhetorical indictment: Lloyd George had not only gambled, he had 'gambled . . . on the graves of Gallipoli in order to rush an election'.[143] Never before had relations between the two groups been so bitter. Even men whose views about Lloyd George were not especially severe reserved a special space for this election in their memoirs:

The foul slanders that were insidiously invented and circulated by some of the 'National' Liberal staff hirelings against men of high honour who had fought loyally side by side with [Lloyd George] as Liberal colleagues years before Sir Henry Campbell-Bannerman came into power, and in his and Mr. Asquith's Government until its fall, made 1918 to 1922 one of the most debasing epochs of recent political history.[144]

Foul or not, the slanders had their effect. All the members of the Asquithian court who had seats in the Commons lost them in 1918 and, except in the case of Asquith himself, little sympathy was forthcoming from other parties or even from their own. Austen Chamberlain reflected that the Asquithians had fought 'on exactly the old party lines' and 'raised the old cries'; he regretted the loss of Asquith, but for Runciman, McKenna, Simon and the 'lesser fry' he felt more contempt than sympathy.[145] The Gladstones, significantly, analysed the electoral disaster in much the same way, arguing that although Liberal principles had been 'duly set forth' there had been little else to rouse the new electorate. 'Sunday parties at the Wharf and bridge went steadily on. . .The result [was] so wretched that it ought to have been anticipated.'[146] More important for the future was the Asquithian determination to refuse to work with those who 'took the ticket'[147] and to deny them readmission without full confession of sin.

The central consequence of the Asquithian failure to come to terms with politics during 1918 revealed itself in the changed character of the Asquithian court. Despite Asquith's return for Paisley in 1920 it was to become after 1918 an extra-parliamentary conclave of the elder venerated, meeting in spacious drawing-rooms to await the second coming. Some of the court escaped the election, of course, by virtue of their being peers. 'What Liberal cares twopence for the House of Lords?' Frederick Guest asked in 1922.[148] The answer was that the Asquithians cared a good deal, since that chamber now housed 'the only section of the Free Liberal Party showing signs of vitality'.[149] Crewe had spent the early months of 1919 trying to marshal the Liberal forces there.[150] It seemed a worthwhile exercise, because the Lords had demonstrated their influence by almost succeeding in inserting a Proportional Representation clause in the Franchise Bill the previous year;[151] they were to show it again in 1920 when they refused to pass unamended the government's illiberal Aliens Bill, thereby saving England in Buckmaster's eyes from 'an ineffaceable disgrace'.[152] Liberal peers, moreover, were still distinguished by an atmosphere of mature statesmanship. Before the war they had constituted the 'little band' to which Acton had been proud to belong;[153] and in 1919 the band still included Grey, Crewe, Glad-

stone, Morley, Bryce, Buxton, Lincolnshire, Harcourt, Beauchamp, Pentland, Gainford, Granard, Denman, Farrer, Cowdray
and Spencer.[154] Odd names, these – especially Spencer with its
associations of Gladstone's last ministry. Like Harcourt he was
a son: he hated Lloyd George soundly enough after 1918, but his
health prevented him from carrying his dislike far beyond
Althorp.[155] Despite attempts by Lloyd George's propaganda
machine to identify Liberal policy in the House of Lords with that
of Die-Hard Toryism,[156] the Second Chamber nevertheless offered
an image of principled governance which those who could be made
to recall the pre-war Liberal government might be ready to admire.

In the Commons, both before and after Asquith's return to the
House, the main burden of Asquithian parliamentary politics
devolved upon Donald Maclean. A virtually unknown lawyer,
Maclean was thrust into this position because no one else was
available, except possibly Lambert who was 'a little sore' at
Maclean's promotion.[157] The most likely man, Pringle, had established an enviable reputation during the war,[158] but had lost his
seat with the rest in 1918. Contrary to expectation, however,
Maclean acquitted himself well. He was joined by Commander
Kenworthy after the latter's victory at Central Hull in what was
taken to be an important by-election in March 1919, and the two
men, with William Wedgwood Benn, formed the main prong of
the Asquithian opposition. 'By all accounts', an unsympathetic
observer wrote in April, 'Maclean is doing wonderfully well. He
is [one of the] few men who are alive to the urgency of healthy
finance and economy.'[159] By 1922 Maclean had come to realize
that Asquith was mistrusted as a leader because of his mode of
life and his 'ladies';[160] and Asquith had for his part adopted by
that time the policy of 'turning up in the House once in a blue
moon, and of leaving all the hard work as Leader of the Opposition
to Donald Maclean', though one Lloyd Georgian commentator
thought that the effectiveness of the latter had declined since
Asquith came back.[161]

Yet despite their self-advertisement through sophisticated
media, the activities of parliament were not crucial in establishing
the atmosphere of British politics after the war. Direct Action held
the attention of the Left in 1919/20, and such argument as stemmed
from that source was stocked with the vocabulary of unfulfilled
revolution and not that of the debating chamber. If Guest believed

the House of Lords to be of little consequence, Sandhurst believed the Commons mattered little more.[162] Asquithians knew only the politics of Westminster; there could be no Liberal essay in direct action. Instead Liberal high politics amounted to little more than a clique discussing its own impotence and seeking importance in trivia. Asquith could no longer be taken seriously: there were no more proposals to bring him into the government apart from a half-hearted one from Montagu at the time of the Paisley by-election.[163] As 1920 opened, Asquith told Bryce that he could not remember any year beginning so badly for the country and the world. Nor, he might have added, for himself and his retinue. Worse was to come during the year when his wife, Margot – 'a wild duck among the cuckoos'[164] – published reminiscences which Beauchamp later judged the finish of her husband.[165] The radical Hogge thought that Margot's 'incessant rubbish'[166] would make Asquith's return to Downing Street impossible. The book became, as it had been intended to become, the talk of high society. The Court let it be known that it was 'aghast'.[167]

Indeed, through 1919 and 1920 Asquith's future had come to be questioned among all sections of Liberalism and not merely among radicals with their bleat that Asquith must go, even if the only alternative seemed to be 'an honest, sober fellow like Maclean'.[168] Criticism was now coming from areas which Asquith would have once thought sound. There were squirms when Margot and Elizabeth Asquith were allowed to go running after Lloyd George in Paris, presumably trying to solicit office for the Wee Free leader.[169] There were anxieties even in the mind of a stalwart like Pease about Asquith's seeming inability to initiate rather than merely to comment on the ideas of others: 'If only he had LG's resource, impulse and courage. . .'[170] Perhaps what was true of today, moreover, was true also of yesterday? It was a time for doubts about some aspects of Asquith's political life, which had previously been assumed to have survived inviolate into the age of cheap politics. Herbert Gladstone, for example, had come across some nasty smells:

The fact is that apart from personal adherents and of [*sic*] the men who hate LG and think he betrayed A., there is an overwhelming feeling against him [i.e. Asquith] as P.M. Much has come to my ears. The regime for 8 years at No. 10, the things that went on, the stories true, untrue or partly true had a disastrous effect. M[argot]'s book put fuel on the embers.[171]

Asquith was clearly beginning to be regarded as a figure who needed to be carried, and the carrying was growing more tiresome every day.

It was reasonable for Asquithians to look elsewhere for effective leadership, and some of them believed that they could find it in Viscount Grey. The idea was not ridiculous: Grey's health might soon improve and if his natural reticence could be overcome there was a possibility of his leading an anti-Lloyd George *bloc* which would include the Asquithians, 'sane' Labour and some moderate Conservatives. Two groups held hopes that this might come about. An 'intellectual' impetus came from Lord Robert Cecil and Gilbert Murray, who were looking to Grey's moral atmosphere and League stance; and a more earthy approach was made by representatives of the machine – the Gladstones, Hudson and Cowdray with help from Runciman and Arthur Murray – who wanted to harness Grey to a Liberal (rather than cross-party) operation. Both sides of the Grey 'movement' wanted to depose Asquith. Both came up against Asquith's resolve not to be deposed.

Intricate negotiations aimed at involving Grey in politics again and making him face the possibility of supplanting Asquith occupied the minds of numerous factions between the autumn of 1920 and the summer of 1921, when Grey finally agreed to announce his reappearance in a speech at Berwick during the autumn. Those negotiations and the calculations behind them were too involved to be considered here and have been made the object of a separate study.[172] What is important in the present context is to understand that ideas about Grey lurked in the penumbra of the Liberal mind in 1920/21 and to appreciate why the conspiracy to depose Asquith in favour of Grey came to nothing. Part of the explanation for the failure lay with Grey himself, who never fully understood what was required of him by those doing the pushing. But a more fundamental reason can be seen in the failure of those doing the pushing to agree about what they wanted Grey to do. Half the pressure was directed towards encouraging Grey to make the Liberal party great again, half towards enjoining him to help abolish party labels and form a new organization which would capture the centre of politics. This dissipation, Grey's personal perplexity, and Asquith's determination not to help others in their bid for the leadership ensured that the Berwick speech in October was not an event of massive proportions. There was almost no follow-up to the *démarche*, and by the summer of 1922 the Grey episode had been consigned to the now extensive collection of Liberal might-have-beens. After Crewe's departure for the Paris embassy, Grey took the Liberal lead in the House of Lords in a mood closer to relief than disappointment.

Because of the failure of the Grey adventure, Lloyd George's irritating 'solution' of the Irish problem and the passing of protectionist legislation, 1921 had been 'a horrible year' for Asquithians.[173] By-elections had provided a chink of light on the horizon, though Anti-Waste had stolen the headlines. Even when opportunities presented themselves, the Asquithian court was ill-equipped to seize them and turn them to Liberal advantage. Such qualities of leadership as Asquith had once possessed were now gone and the '*ménage*' was seen by its adherents as 'really beneath contempt'.[174] Indeed by the beginning of 1922 rumour had it that Asquith was about to take himself off to Balliol as Master and relinquish the leadership to 'harmless Herbert' Gladstone.[175] Events washed up against the Asquithians in parliament whilst they tried vainly to channel the tide. All they could do was to trim and side-step and face all directions at once, 'sink[ing] daily deeper and deeper into the bog'.[176]

There was some cause for hope in the new year. The election scare of January 1922 brought in some cash to the party fund,[177] which was looking fairly healthy anyway because Cowdray had been 'keen as mustard' about the Grey movement and had been expressing himself in his cheque-book.[178] One financial helper had been lost in that McKenna had by now become 'pretty useless' in levering money out of the City and had gone over to the Beaverbrook circle.[179] Money apart, the leadership seems to have undergone something of a renaissance. Certainly even the old guard impressed Wedgwood Benn in January:

A great meeting at the Central Hall. The Old Man was at his best, with a good deal of the note of personal reproach [suit?]able to an audience of devoted followers. Grey was a su[ccess]. He started so piano that we thought he was going to say very little, and then proceeded to punch hard. He is in striking contrast with other speakers, carrying a great impression of sincerity. Buckmaster was good but too long. Runciman adapted himself to his two minutes splendidly. The 'Platform party' did not include a single member of the Parliamentary Party, except of course Mr. Asquith and Donald Maclean. It was a most impressive mausoleum.[180]

Dubious flattery of this kind was short-lived. Grey alienated much of the support he had built up over the past year through his tactless and unilateral French policy[181] – thereby pleasing Simon, who had always thought it a mistake to treat Grey like 'a god'.[182] During the spring of 1922 the Asquithians sank back into the mire and strange ideas were born of despair. By May Asquith was so desperate for past glory as to ask Burns to stand for Hackney now that Bottomley was safely in prison.[183] Runciman had also lost too many elections to be optimistic; he decided that if he lost the next one he would go on an eleven-month cruise to Java.[184]

When the government finally fell in October 1922 the Asquithians were totally unprepared. Radicals of the Pringle–Hogge stamp had for months been urging the leadership to evolve contingency plans, and Herbert Gladstone had pleaded from Abingdon Street for money to be spent on electoral organization. But Asquith and the court had held that Lloyd George would not go to the country for fear of cutting his own throat, and the possibility of someone else's cutting it had not arisen.[185] At the beginning of September Gladstone had discounted the current rumours of an imminent election.[186] Garvin's *Observer* (as always the source of much rumour) was thought to be lashing the wind again. 'I don't really think the Little Man is in serious danger', Gilbert Murray told Cecil on 10 October.[187] Even on the 13th, under a week before the Carlton Club meeting, Henry Gladstone was still thinking that Lloyd George would 'wriggle on for a while yet'.[188] As for Asquith, he was still 'concentrat[ing] for the moment on digging a grave for the Coalition' on the day that Lloyd George resigned.[189] He and his colleagues had in fact dug graves for themselves. They had conspired to render themselves leaderless: they were vulnerable to an attack by a leader without a party. A week before the Conservatives met, Hogge had said to MacCallum Scott: 'I have never had any doubt that Lloyd George, if he came out of the Coalition and bid for the Liberal leadership, could have it. The others are only duds.'[190]

III

Exclusively to accord to the Asquithians the mantle of true Liberalism is a strong temptation, but it is one to be avoided. Both in parliament and in the country significant numbers of Liberals

followed Lloyd George after 1916 without, in their own estima-
tion, alienating their Liberalism. It is a story which requires
explanation and one which involves the Liberal mind quite as
much as does the Asquithian saga. Of course there are differences.
Many observers believed that Lloyd George had not got a mind.
Lord Courtney (when 'very old and blind') shouted at a Downing
Street reception that the bottom had fallen out of it.[191] Lloyd
George was 'thin-minded' according to Laski;[192] he was an
'illiterate with an untrained mind' according to Haldane;[193] he had
a 'weakened mind of a low order' according to Hewins.[194] This
kind of diagnosis flattered itself into believing that its objections
were based on an assessment of Lloyd George's intellectual
capacity. In fact what was found to be objectionable was not his
lack of a mind but the directions in which he allowed it to lead
him. It was an ungrooved mind. It was worked by Lloyd George
for Lloyd George. It was not attuned to high frequency – whether
of doctrine, or theory or even 'common decency'. Perhaps his
missing of university – a perpetual boast – helped the process by
permitting him to remain unanglicized. Just as Asquith could only
have been English, so Lloyd George could only have been something else: his 'speculative, free moving mind' struck Lowes
Dickinson as having a touch of Frenchness about it.[195]

Contemporary appraisals reveal less about Lloyd George, however, than about his observers. Had he been born thirty years later
he would have aroused less animosity because his patterns of
thought would have been more widespread in the political elite
in which he was compelled to move. As it was, he had to endure
the glare of Margot Asquith. 'He will talk about anything', she
was reported as saying, '. . . He is quite detached. But all the time
he is pulling away at the wires and strings, and seeing how he can
turn everything to advantage. He uses people. See how he uses
the press. He never misses a chance.'[196] Her response was confused through an inadequate appreciation of what Lloyd George
was clever at doing. It is an area beyond the reach of historical
'evidence', but there is an overwhelming retrospective impression
that Lloyd George was able instinctively to maintain a wide
remove between what he thought he believed in private and what
he knew he wanted to say in public. All politicians tried to do it:
Lloyd George did it better than any. Doing it, moreover, involved
more than some crude construction of half-truth and rhetoric.

There was a preparatory artificial construction in the study, in the car, on the golf course; then there was a certain intellectual commitment to a 'line'; and then, on the platform or in the drawing room there was an emotional commitment to what he had invented. What he said, he probably (for an hour) 'believed'. He was 'the Popular Mind'. When he was on the platform he was also 'down among the audience'.[197] Occasionally he would misjudge the moment and leave an observer to point to 'lemonade before it has lost its gaseous "fizz"'.[198] But he was never merely a manipulator, as Strachey believed;[199] indeed, if he had been, the Asquithians might have survived him. He was in fact more complicated than they wanted to believe. More than having a fortune to offer, he had a spirituality to sell.

When Liberal politicians made their decisions in 1916 their options, it is true, were determined by old affinities, a patriotic contempt for politicking or a calculation of the main chance. The Liberal composition of the new government was correspondingly anomalous and evoked an image which clashed sharply with accepted notions. Lloyd George had improved a little on his raw material. He bagged Balfour for ornamentation and made a *coup* in attracting Herbert Fisher – 'so frank and moderate and sensible'[200] – as a repository of culture and proof of Lloyd George's desire to work with the 'moderate Liberal opinion' which Fisher 'represented with such distinction'.[201] He tried to get Rosebery and failed. The support which the new Prime Minister received came primarily from those who had helped or sympathized during the manoeuvres of 1916. Sir Frederick Cawley, Chairman of the Liberal War Committee, went to the Duchy of Lancaster. Christopher Addison, the head-counter of recent months and 'a political weakling...whose qualification for office [was] sycophancy to L.G.',[202] went to Munitions. Lloyd George later found him tiresome and was glad to be rid of him in 1921. Macnamara, 'as timid as a mouse', according to MacCallum Scott,[203] found his way to the Ministry of Labour by 1920. Posts were found for Sutherland, Kellaway, Beck and Guest. The slick businessman Sutherland was held by some in grudging respect, others detested him; Kellaway foolishly pledged fealty to Lloyd George 'through thick and thin';[204] Beck was a failure, though Auckland Geddes suggested him for ministerial rank in 1918;[205] Guest, Churchill's cousin, lasted longer than any of them and was still thinking in terms of 'National Liberals' in the mid-twenties. Churchill himself and Montagu were important acquisitions after July 1917. Sir Gordon Hewart took the office of Attorney-General after refusing the Home Office which Lloyd George had hitherto been dangling before the noses of detachable Asquithians.[206]

Seen as a whole, the government was singular in that it brought to the heart of the administrative machine the related spectres of Industry and the North, a development which helped to create an image of the government as a 'very low class' administration.[207] To the Air Ministry (a concept Asquith had opposed to the end) Lloyd George appointed two industrialists and a newspaper magnate during the lifetime of the coalition government. To Shipping he sent (strange departure, this) a shipowner. The introduction of the North was reflected in three of the four Secretaries for Ireland. Edward Shortt was a graduate of Durham University, Recorder of Sunderland before the war and M.P. for Newcastle, 'a capable but obstinate man too much bound to preconceived opinions'[208] – qualities which may have helped him after 1929 when he became President of the British Board of Film Censors. Shortt was succeeded by Ian MacPherson, a graduate of Edinburgh University, M.P. for Ross and Cromarty. The final Secretary was Hamar Greenwood who, like Beaverbrook and Law, had a Canadian background. He had been a convinced Lloyd George man since the middle of 1916, possibly since the latter had been responsible for the offer of a baronetcy which Greenwood had received the previous year.[209] His large personality struck FitzRoy as 'robust' and the more puritanical C. P. Scott as 'vulgar and soapy'.[210] Between 1916 and 1922 Greenwood was M.P. for Sunderland, and after the fall of the coalition he drifted for a time as an 'anti-Socialist' before moving across to the Conservative party.

Yet despite the peculiar grouping of opposites in the ministry – Burns called it a 'counterpane Government'[211] – it had a *raison d'être* located in something more fundamental than parliamentary ambition. What Lloyd George had to offer was what some politicians had been advocating for eighteen months, 'something not unlike a Prussian organization for the period of the war'.[212] Esher spelled out the policy in a letter to Haig on 4 December 1916: 'The organising of our resources is the objective of Lloyd Georgism. If he gets the power into his hands and does not use it because of hide-bound tradition, you will remain stuck in our present line and we shall lose the war.'[213] Lloyd George quickly showed that he intended using his power, and his doctrine of organization was well received among his followers. He was grateful. 'They have treated me well', he later told Riddell. 'They gave me my chance to win the war.'[214] But it was clear in 1916 that difficulties would later arise, for, as Rowntree had seen in April, the people who supported Lloyd George were the very people who would fall away when the doctrine of organization became redundant after the war.[215] 'Lloyd Georgism' was a recognizable policy but an ephemeral one geared to the exigencies of wartime. Lloyd George was 'kill or cure'.[216]

From the projection of such a policy two important consequences derived. The first was constitutional and was noticed at once because the activity of decision-taking was immediately concentrated into the hands of a few in theory and Lloyd George in practice, since Milner and Law had problems of their own and Henderson was of little consequence.[217] And in being made subject to Lloyd George's power it became subject also to his temperament, as Harcourt reported to Munro Ferguson with acid pleasure:

The new Govt...which is something in the nature of a Directorate, the Cabinet having been scrapped along with the House of Commons, is a curious experiment, but not destined I think to be a long-lived one...You, with your old knowledge of the present Prime Minister, will realise that the conduct of the Government is not very business-like in its administration and there is nothing but chaos and confusion in the Civil Service.[218]

Moreover the tentacles of government had begun to spread. Hardinge quoted in a letter a popular rhyme,

> Wait and See, said the 23
> Give us Time, say the 89,[219]

a jingle with which Henry Gladstone seems to have been familiar at Hawarden. 'I am about sick of the Ministry of 87', he complained to his brother in March 1917, 'and long for the Cabinet of 23 again.'[220] The figures were rarely the same,[221] but it hardly mattered; the notion was plainly current that government was expanding, '[m]inisters and undersecretaries...grow[ing] like blackberries on a hedge, all around Whitehall'.[222] Nor was it merely expansion that observers noticed. There was a certain strangeness about new procedures and oddly named posts, from the instigation of Cabinet minutes to Philip Kerr being employed 'in a sort of Secretariate '[223] – the very word looked like a foreign invention. Bryce shared Hardinge's difficulty in understanding the new secretarial system. 'I have been thinking of writing to a private Secretary', he wrote to Willoughby Dickinson, 'but can't make out who the secretaries are now, except that there is a young lady who treats everybody very cavalierly.'[224]

A second development was harder to notice though it was to attract attention in the 1920s. It was the attempted formation of a long-term political strategy going beyond the considerations of wartime politics to those of the Reconstruction which must follow. It never in fact materialized: by about November 1917 Lloyd George was clear that there would be an election at the end of 1918[225] but he never fully grasped the point of the policy created by others during the war. The best exposition of this thinking occurs in a letter Montagu wrote to Lloyd George in February 1917:

There are in politics two great collections of people who I believe are ready to follow your lead. The one are the younger Liberals, who joined the Liberal Party because of its great name and because they believed it was the party of purpose. They have been discontented for some time because orthodox Liberalism has tended to become so conservative, so much the party of the middle class. Then there are the younger Conservatives, who joined the Conservative Party, despite its name, because they realised, or hoped, that it was more Liberal than the orthodox Liberal Party. These two, coupled with the best elements of Labour... ought to make a fine National Party under your leadership. Such a Party would not contain Massingham and McKenna; such a Party would not, I think, contain Curzon, Chamberlain and Salisbury. But such a party would contain all the people who want to get a move on.[226]

Doubtless Lloyd George agreed; but in 1917/18 he was to be so preoccupied with either the war or the parliamentary situation[227] that he devised no clear policy, though he must have thought about the centre-party idea. By July 1917 he had become, like Asquith, 'hedged round by a "court" which [shut] him out from the people' and had succumbed to 'venal plaudits [which] he mist[ook] for popular approbation'.[228] Through necessity the government hopped none too nimbly from one crisis to the next. In August Austen Chamberlain was expecting a general election;[229] in September Inchcape was predicting a financial crash;[230] in November Strachey had come to doubt the whole legend of

'Pushful George': all he had pushed was himself, Northcliffe, Churchill and Reading.[231]

Individual members of the Lloyd George court had learned to live together in a state of fitful tension. Their master was prepared, as incompetents such as Hayes Fisher learned, to be a butcher; but he was also ready to be flattered and coaxed. A surprising number of supporters were not mere sycophants, however. Herbert Fisher, for example, was replete with beliefs and principles, and he pretended not to see what was happening. To mild Liberals his appointment had been 'the one redeeming feature of a not very satisfactory government'.[232] His intentions were reflected in his conduct. He voted in the minority in the debate on Conscientious Objectors in November 1917, voted for the Lords' amendment on Proportional Representation in February 1918 and shared the discomfort of some of his colleagues at the proscription of Liberals in the coupon election.[233] On the other hand, he helped to frame the programme for that election, along with Dudley Ward, Frederick Guest, Caradoc Rees and Robert Munro in March 1918.[234]

The election proved Burns wrong in his belief that the 'bloom [was] coming off the L.G. peach', but right in his fear that a 'Tory party masquerading as a Coalition [would] win by a large majority'.[235] An indefinable lack of virtue seems to have been the prevailing contemporary objection to Lloyd George. Chief offender, of course, was the system of 'coupons'. Fisher thought it all 'a tremendous mistake' and was depressed to find the names of candidates in *The Times* 'all or nearly all quite meaningless and obscure'.[236] Hilton Young was similarly perplexed to find himself included in that list as a Coalition Liberal, despite his original intention of standing as an Asquithian.[237] Nevertheless Lloyd George was at his zenith. He may have taken his key, as Keynes alleged in a famous phrase, from 'the grosser effluxions of the atmosphere which momentarily surround[ed] him',[238] but he took it accurately and performed in a manner to which audiences could readily respond. He could do little wrong; he told them that he had won the war and they loved it. Even his parliamentary supporters were blinded by devotion. When Sir William Barton, M.P. for Oldham since 1910, found an Asquithian standing against him, he told MacCallum Scott that the latter 'counted for nothing. He was all for teaching [the local Liberal association] its place.

He was out to support Lloyd George and nothing else mattered.'[239] When the results were known it became clear that Wales had been faithful almost to a man: only one Asquithian came back to the House, and he had been unopposed at Merioneth.[240] For the rest of the country the returns were equally encouraging. Lloyd George had won on a grand scale by condemning himself to sit amid a sea of hard faces from northern towns.[241]

Why did Liberal politicians support Lloyd George? For some the question – and it was posed often enough – was a source of embarrassment which provoked nervously loud pronouncements about the need to win the Peace, to stem the tide of Socialism, to counter the threat of Direct Action and Revolution. Capital letters abounded. Behind the words were the 'same faces' which would turn up everywhere between 1919 and 1922 and make up a 'facade of gilded or gold bricks with no real fabric behind it'.[242] But it is important to see that some of the rhetoric was not disingenuous. In November 1918 many believed the tortured Liberal protestations of Lloyd George. Even when Harry Barnes went over to the Asquithians a year later, he did so believing that Lloyd George was 'a great Liberal in an impasse' who '[l]ike Coeur-de-Lion [had] been captured coming from a crusade'.[243] A supporter of Lloyd George who did not defect was Alexander MacCallum Scott, and his diary offers an unparalleled insight into the mind of a backbench Lloyd Georgian during the coalition period. In June 1919 he rationalized his position thus:

Lloyd George must be given his chance of formulating his domestic programme. It would be most unfair to attack him yet for the lack of a policy which he could not develop while his main preoccupation was the Peace Treaty. I am myself as much responsible by the support I have given him for the present state of affairs as he is. If one claims a free hand now it must not be to attack or embarrass but only to influence him along certain lines.[244]

Eighteen months later he is still 'in an indeterminate position' but there is now a definite impression that he is whistling to keep his courage up:

I have gravitated steadily to the Coalition. Its policy – makeshift though it was, and opportunist though it was – has been the only policy I could honestly support. The narrow and sectional policy of the Independent Liberals – their policy of excommunicating all Liberals who support the government – has repelled me . . .

I have not become a partisan coalitionist. I have not tied myself to the
chariot wheels of Lloyd George; I have not adopted coalition as an end
in itself.[245]

Tender conscience was probably not very widespread within the
ranks of Coalition Liberals; yet the very fact that it was possible
for a 'Lloyd George man' to reflect in this way reveals that it was
believed to be reasonable to try to reconcile the demands of
Liberalism with those of following Lloyd George. Sir Edward
Grigg held strongly to the notion that Lloyd George was a true
Liberal trying to hold back the forces of reaction. Grigg himself
recoiled from 'that sort of mind which believes that the religion
of business is an all-sufficient food for the human spirit and an
impeccable guide in human affairs'. He told Austen Chamberlain
that Lloyd George's struggle 'with this type of mind [was] extra-
ordinarily like the struggle which [Joseph Chamberlain] waged
with narrow, middle-class Liberalism throughout his political
career'.[246] For Grigg, Lloyd George was not a chained crusader
but one taking the message actively to the country. Language of
a lyricism more common in Asquithian correspondence can be
found in the letters of Grigg. 'I have never seen him so determined', he wrote of Lloyd George a week before the Carlton Club
meeting, 'to make the conscience of the country respond to the
policy of peace and humanity which he has endeavoured against
great odds to pursue. He reminded me of that delightful nigger
spiritual song "Singing with a sword in my hand"'.[247] Despite the
Asquithian sneers there existed a Lloyd Georgian frame of mind
which proclaimed itself to be devoted to Liberal principle.[248]

If spiritual simile could be found among the Coalition Liberals,
however, it could be found the more rarely as the months of the
coalition's life elapsed. Hilton Young had entered, like Grigg, into
support of the government with eyes open and conscience clear,
determined to 'consolidate the party of the right under [Lloyd
George's] leadership, and, under the shadow of his wing, to do
what [he] could to make [the Liberal party] a liberal and not a
reactionary party'. But by March 1922 he had come to feel that
his hopes had no chance of being realized: 'What has happened
in the last month? – the reactionary elements...have pushed the
moderate elements...right off the stage. The moderates are out-
rowed and outfaced, and have lost heart. I fear that that is so
in the country; I see that it is so in the House.' The only future

he saw for Coalition Liberalism was death by suffocation. He was not impressed by the argument that Liberals should try to leaven the lump of Conservatism. 'That is not good enough. We ought to be the lump.'[249] Fisher, Mond and Montagu expressed similar fears – Montagu over safeguarding, Mond over the 'intellectual dishonesty' of the coalition, Fisher over everything and nothing. 'The difference between Asquith and the Coalition', the latter wrote, 'does not lie in the programme – but in the policy.' The best hope was to bring in Labour and the Asquithian Liberals.[250]

Quibbles and crotchets can be overstressed of course. If it is important to recognize that Liberalism had its moral imperatives and its doctrinal conscience which affected coalitionists, it is equally important that the recognition should not reduce to a naive portrait of Lloyd George's followers as martyrs constantly wringing their hands over the sacrifices of integrity which their leader forced upon them. Fisher, Young, Mond, McCurdy, MacPherson, Greenwood, Montagu and Addison were professional politicians who were where they were as a result of luck, instinct, context and calculation, not because a particular flavour of Liberalism appealed to their collective palate. If they thought earnestly about their Liberalism, they were just as earnest about fusing their party with the Conservatives' in order to strengthen their grip on office. If they sensed that anti-Liberal legislation about, say, the House of Lords had best be avoided so as not to offend Liberal supporters of the coalition,[251] they were equally concerned not to make that support their only, perhaps even their most important, parliamentary base. Such Liberal doctrine as they professed in any case allowed plenty of latitude for unradical action. It need be no surprise to find Fisher in Cabinet (trees to right and left) untroubled by doctrine when discussing Ireland; or to find McCurdy apologizing to his colleagues for having to pay unemployment relief more frequently than he would like.[252]

In whatever light Coalition Liberals chose to see themselves, a sometimes more significant consideration in the parliamentary context would be the light in which others saw them. And that was not glowing. Liberalism as a whole had no time for the concept of coalition or for its proponents. Asquithian descriptions of Lloyd George's government used terms which were always hostile, often insanitary. It was a 'political abortion',[253] an 'evil thing', an 'immoral instrument', 'a LIE'.[254] The private treatment which followers of Lloyd George received at the hands of Asquithians, moreover, suggests that this language had real meaning for those who spoke it. The *Lloyd George Liberal Magazine*, which appeared monthly between October 1920 and December 1923, spent much space in attacking the National Liberal Club for its continued Asquithian partisanship – in particular for its refusal to hang portraits of Lloyd George and Churchill and to accept nominations for membership from Coalition Liberals. The creation of a separate '1920 Club' was one reaction to this treatment.[255]

In public the Asquithian attack was spearheaded by the Burkean notion that '[p]arties exist usefully only in so far as they embody certain principles' and the allegation that the coalition had none.[256] 'What is imperatively needed is principle', Sandhurst believed;[257] and even Esher had come to regard the Prime Minister's 'active mind' as having been 'corrupted by the war and the subtle poison of European politics'.[258] Henry Gladstone, on the other hand, decided that his objection to Lloyd George, like Fisher's, amounted to a matter of 'tone'.[259] Despite their protestations of indifference, moreover, the coalition men felt these attacks very keenly:

A persistent campaign is being directed against them in their constituencies and in their local Liberal associations. They are continually being represented as traitors to Liberalism... Their words and their actions are zealously [mis]represented. A vigorous propaganda is being carried on against them in the party by means of the press, by leaflets and pamphlets, and by the Liberal Magazine. The whole official machinery of the party is directed against them... They are themselves quite defenceless.[260]

Words like 'campaign', 'traitors' and 'propaganda' reveal the bitterness. It appeared in other directions also. Gordon Hewart was convinced that the meeting of the two wings at Leamington in May 1920 had been called by the Asquithians simply 'in order to give as little chance as possible to the Liberal ministers' over the issue of fusion with the Conservative party.[261] Certainly Leamington was to coagulate into a reference point for the Lloyd Georgian mind in the same way that the coupon election had for the Asquithian. Coalition Liberals left the meeting 'surfeited with the high-falutin references to Liberal principles' and convinced that the Asquithians could do nothing more than 'assume the attitude of political saints'.[262] It was their reception at Leamington which did much to convince those responsible for Coalition Liberal organization that a separate machine was necessary, one 'run on liberal, not on Leamington, lines'; this appeared in the shape of the National Liberal Council in January 1922.[263] It is worth adding that the ministry which had given advancement to Mond, Montagu and Reading was also likely to feel the backlash of anti-semitic opinion from all parts of the political spectrum. Liberals may not have gone as far as Strachey in seeing the coalition as 'a sink of iniquity tinged with the worst kind of Hebraism',[264] but MacCallum Scott certainly believed that 'anti-Jew feeling' was strong in the Commons and that, though it took the form of banter, 'there [was] real feeling behind it'.[265]

Between 1916 and 1922 Lloyd George had the opportunity to construct a policy. He chose not to do so for a variety of reasons, most of them not germane to this study. The consequences of his decision not to decide impinged directly on his parliamentary followers; it is reflected, for example, in a pathetic letter from Guest to Lloyd George in September 1920. 'I have seen a good many Members of Parlt who intend visiting their constituencies during the next two or three weeks and they seem rather in difficulties as to what to say.'[266] The comment says volumes about the coalitionist mood. Bursts of enthusiasm punctuated the gloom, as when Fisher could exalt at the beginning of 1922: 'Meeting of Liberal Ministers. Very successful. We squash the National Liberal Party. We are Liberals.'[267] But Stansgate was probably nearer the mark when he saw Coalition Liberals 'anxious to get out and in a miserable plight'.[268] By the beginning of October 1922 Lloyd George was clear that Liberalism was 'done for' and that his principal concern within the world of high politics must be to carry with him Austen Chamberlain, Birkenhead and Balfour.[269] Among other Liberal ministers feelings varied. Greenwood, Macnamara, Kellaway and Young were looking to fusion with the Conservative party since they were 'dependent on Tory votes', while Shortt and Macpherson were frightened of any election because of the Irish *débâcle*. Mond remained isolated in his call for a Liberal breakaway from the coalition.[270]

It is hard to see what good a breakaway could have done. The Asquithians would not have accepted the renegades, or at least the Coalition Liberals would have had to make considerable penance. The attitude of both groups was unchanged. Revealing are Grigg's reflections during the coming election campaign about the Asquithian Tudor Walters, who 'is said to be of Welsh extraction and makes speeches full of copy-book maxims. Beyond assuring us that he is honest and animated by the soundest tenets of Liberal philosophy he has not contributed much to the practical politics of the country at the present time.'[271] Perhaps there was more than empty rhetoric in Asquith's insistence that the difference between the two camps '[went] down to the very root, the very essence, of [their] political creed'.[272] Certainly two fairly clear images of Liberalism appear in contemporary eyes. The picture is naturally not monochromatic. There were those like Loreburn who found Asquith shifty and those like Grigg who believed that Lloyd George was a crusader. But the cumulative impression is one in which empirical-minded Lloyd Georgians combat quasi-religious Asquithians: where secular rhetoricians with fingers on the popular pulse confront starched political priests with altars all their own.

3. Exorcism

[Y]ou revive a record which should have made co-operation impossible – until it had been repented of in dust and ashes. Having lain down with the dog you get up with his fleas; and the present Controversy seems to me very like an attempt to shake off the fleas of the dog whose bite has given you the hydrophobia of which you are destined to die.

> Lawrence Housman to Gilbert Murray, 10 June 1926, Murray MSS, Box 59.

Lord Morley: There are some people who would say the man was a cad.
Mr G. P. Gooch: But, Lord Morley, surely *you* would never use a word like that! I have never heard you use that word before.
Morley (with some annoyance): But it is a very *useful* word.

> Conversation reported in J. H. Morgan to Strachey, 7 January 1925, Strachey MSS, S/20/1/1.

I

It is only as a postscript that the years after 1922 tend to be contemplated by historians of Liberalism: the crucial events had passed, the important decisions been taken. Yet despite the confident finalities of psephologists, the period rewards examination. Certainly these years are marked by little enough success for the Liberal party; and the failure is compounded by a sordid atmosphere of faction. For all that, the Liberal mind is revealed here in all its breadth of thought and bloodiness of spirit. Perhaps the very fact of division acts as a catalyst in the process; or perhaps the mind is revealed because one question filled it: would the Liberal party accept Lloyd George as its eventual leader? 'Till that question is put and answered', wrote one Asquithian propagandist, 'all talk of Liberal reunion is evasive, external and inconclusive.'[1] This and many other judgements were prompted by an article which Lloyd George had written and published in the *Daily Chronicle* on 23 November 1922, calling for an end to faction and a 'new spirit of letting bygones be bygones'. By indicating a desire to reunite the Coalition Liberals with the Asquithians, Lloyd George placed the issue of reunion uppermost

84

in Liberal debate, and there it was to remain until the idea was finally abandoned in 1925/26. Nor could the matter be approached gently, for it was charged with the greatest of all political urgencies – the need to fight a general election – and it would have to be achieved by 'complete immersion *preceding* conversion... holding [their] noses and shutting [their] mouths'.[2]

Some attempt at reunion had already been made through George Lambert's conciliation committee and the efforts of individuals such as Harold Spender, who had tried, for example, to detach Simon from the Asquithians by stressing the cause of harmony.[3] In the summer of 1921 Frances Stevenson had believed that only Asquith, Maclean, Wedgwood Benn and Thorne were intransigent against the idea of reuniting the party under the leadership of Lloyd George.[4] But it was never a popular movement, especially after the Leamington meeting of May 1920 had endorsed Asquithian exclusiveness; and even before then Churchill had had no success at all in trying to bring the Scottish Liberal Federation back to Coalition Liberalism, whilst the National Liberal Club had swept away much Lloyd Georgian impurity.[5] Coalition Liberals had been driven to the conclusion that Asquithians were in the grip of 'Extremists ruling without supervision or rebuke'.[6] It was foolish to expect that the two sides would rush to embrace one another. The bitterness went too deep and had been voiced too recently.

Lloyd George framed the problem for his public as one precipitated entirely by the attitude of the Asquithian leadership:

Our attitude towards them has always been determined by their own leaders. (Hear, hear.) They have met; they have proclaimed their decision. They have declared war on us. They say, 'We don't want either to unite, to associate or to co-operate'...Well, you cannot force your company on people who do not want you even if you wanted to. (Laughter.)[7]

Certainly the Asquithians had done nothing to help the cause of unity. During the election the Marquess of Lincolnshire had urged his fellow Liberals to 'vote straight': Lloyd George the '"back stabber" whining over what he call[ed] a miserable vendetta and denouncing Labour, [was] not only contemptible but ridiculous'.[8] Those who phrased their animus more cautiously were nevertheless convinced that Lloyd George was too high a price to pay for reunion.[9] Asquith enjoined Maclean not to take reunion too seriously and his wife was characteristically appalled. 'Don't believe a *word* about Reunion. [N]ever was a greater lie; we would rather be out for *ever*.'[10] On the Left, meanwhile, Masterman, Massingham and Gardiner were preparing to make the supreme sacrifice and join the Labour party if Lloyd George were to be allowed back into the fold. As usual, principle and piety jostled with pettiness and primitive joy at the annihilation of the Lloyd Georgians at the election. '[I]t was a pleasure that the rats of different complexions got it rather hot – Leslie Wilson, Griffith Boscawen (*real* name Cohen) and Montagu etc.'[11] Masterman was similarly undisturbed by the Conservative victory: 'the ... thing was to get rid of L.G. and his crapulous crew *at any cost* '.[12]

For Lloyd George 1923 was to be a year of 'suspended animation'.[13] His basic reference point was nothing so simple as a desire to reunite the Liberal party or even to become its leader. His main preoccupation after the fall of the coalition was the construction of another one with himself at its head. The Liberal party was important to him but only as a bargaining counter in the game of centre-party politics he had been playing since 1920, and for the moment he was happy to leave the running of the machine to his chief whip, Hilton Young, and the senior officers of the National Liberal Organization, Macnamara and Sir Alfred Cope. Several balls were in the air in 1922: eventually he was to drop all of them. But in the meantime Lloyd George would see his Liberalism as only one part (and that a small one) of a three-party context wherein advantage would go to the man who could reconcile the disturbing polarities of contemporary politics in a doctrine of stable progress. What Lloyd George was able to conceive, however, Baldwin was able to perform without conception or theory. By the time that Lloyd George realized that he needed a strong Liberal party in order to survive as a national statesman, the time was gone when his help could be effective. Possibly his help would have made little difference anyway. He was conjuring with a kind of mind he did not understand.

II

All this would not become clear for some years. In November 1922 Lloyd George wrote a benevolent letter to Lambert in which he made apposite noises about reunion; the *British Weekly* seized on it as coming from the heart[14] and the Coalition Liberal staff at Old Queen Street lapsed into depression about their uncertain future.[15] Sensibly Lloyd George refused to dilate on the subject until he saw some sympathetic signs from the Asquithians. Unsure of what their leader was thinking, his lieutenants invented some thoughts of their own: 'What we have to do is to consolidate the anti-Socialist forces throughout the country under Liberal and progressive leadership with sufficient imagination to give the people some solid and sufficient alternative to the Socialist mirage.'[16] And indeed Lloyd George may have been tempted to use this sort of rhetoric, since his eye was on the Conservative party. Such a policy would require a united front on the part of the Liberals, however, and Grigg knew well enough that, despite their pro-testations of good will and their determination to bring about reunion by 'rediscovering. . .principles held in common',[17] the Asquithians were still hysterical about what they believed Lloyd George to represent – a species of political villainy with 'its ill-gotten funds, its bought press, its Sutherlands and McCurdys'[18] – and if they were thinking of reunion at all they were thinking in terms of years and not of months.

Only the constituencies, in the view of Grigg, could put pressure on the leaders and drive them to action.[19] Events were to show in fact what experienced politicians ought to have expected, that the constituencies would do nothing of the kind. There were occasional instances of the two Liberal wings co-operating in a constituency during the campaign of 1922;[20] but more typical of the contemporary mood was the instance of an Asquithian official proposing to compel a Lloyd George candidate to pledge himself to the repeal of the Safeguarding of Industries Act and to take the Asquithian whip until reunion was accomplished.[21] Coalition Liberals in parliament were made aware of such feeling from the rank and file also; the following, for example, was received by Henry Fildes, M.P., in April 1923:

In my opinion, yourself, Sir Edward Grigg, Sir Wm. Edge and Sir Henry Norman are 'Mongrel Liberals'. You are 'Debauchers' of Liberalism . . .There is no room in the Liberal ranks for your sort, the whole lot of you are a disgrace to Liberalism. . .I am well over 60 years of age and have been a Liberal (a real true one) all my days, and have got no patience with your sort. If ever you return to the Liberal party, I leave it.[22]

Those who wanted to return had little reason to be optimistic
in the summer of 1923. Lloyd George had been spreading stories
that Asquith and Grey had promised support to Bonar Law for
the 1923 session.[23] Grigg had complained to one person that Grey
was coquetting with the Conservatives and to another that he,
Grigg, was being attacked for doing the same.[24] Asquith believed
that all the talk about reunion – '[a] lot of nonsense' – was being
put about by Lloyd George through the 'vain and credulous
Beauchamp'[25] who was energetically engaged in trying to organize
a National Liberal *coup* in the House of Lords. MacCallum Scott,
from the Lloyd Georgian side, blamed the Asquithians for being
'too busy preventing reunion to have any time to think about
policy'. All they could do was to 'put up ingenious dilemmas
which [would] put National Liberals in a difficulty'.[26] The *Lloyd
George Liberal Magazine* was therefore clutching at straws when
it announced that real co-operation between the two wings had
occurred at the Anglesey by-election in April. Even in August
Lloyd George found the Welsh Wee Frees still preoccupied with
their 'vendetta' which was 'absorbing and poisoning their thought
and energies . . . like a bad tooth'.[27]

In September, however, rumour was rife in London that a
protectionist campaign was about to be launched by the government. Baldwin's Plymouth speech on 25 October confirmed those
rumours, and reunion was obliged to hasten apace under the
threat of another election. Lloyd George was in America and his
collaboration in a free trade stand was by no means a foregone
conclusion. Earlier in the year he had himself been toying with
the idea of using protection as a potential reservoir for his
speeches and had told Sir Robert Horne before sailing 'that the
old laissez-faire Free Trade policy would no longer suffice' and
that 'active intervention' by the state might be necessary.[28]
Baldwin had now beaten him to that platform: Lloyd George
therefore rallied to the main chance. Some carefully chosen words
of welcome had already been offered by Asquith in a speech to
Liberal M.P.s and candidates on 27 September:

Are Liberals going to fetter their efforts by unreal division? Let all come
in – (cheers) – who are animated by the same principles and are prepared,
without compromise, qualification or reserve, to pursue the same purpose. I do not like the word reunion; I prefer to speak of Liberal union. It
cannot be maintained by the artifices of engineering and manipulation;

it must come by spontaneous and co-operative effort. It is coming. (Cheers.)[29]

On 15 November Lloyd George addressed jointly with Asquith a meeting presided over by Viscount Grey, who was compelled to offer thoughts about 'a union, not artificial but vital, not planned or arranged but inevitable, not founded upon compromise but upon a thorough and unanimous agreement'.[30] What followed was in the manner of high farce. Liberals of all colours appeared on the same platforms, providing a 'spectacle . . . to make the gods smile' with 'Margot sitting side by side with L.G. . . . the thoughts of both too deep for tears'[31] and Lloyd George 'cartwheeling round the country with his apparatus of loudspeakers, journalists, jokes etc., baiting the Tories and exchanging complimentary views with [Asquith]!!'[32]

Politicians at the top took the opportunity to practise supreme strategy. Churchill saw the way the wind was blowing for the Conservative party and deserted Lloyd George (with whom he had been in close touch) very loudly, perhaps in the hope of striking a pleasing note in Asquithian ears.[33] Simon meanwhile saw himself as heir apparent and was encouraged to do so by the press – he 'possesse[d] many of the same qualities of mind as the Liberal leader'[34] – and by friends such as Leif Jones and Francis Hirst, who thought he would 'soon be in the sort of position Gladstone was when Palmerston's sun was setting'.[35] The Grey idea came back into circulation, this time with a policy of 'L[eague] of N[ations] plus Free Trade plus co-partnership in Industry', though even Cecil found this far-fetched.[36] Further down the hierarchy it was the Coalition Liberals who were most embarrassed by the new intimacy. Captain Arthur Evans and Captain Moreing decided to join the Conservatives, though the latter changed his mind;[37] and where there was not outright defection there was much chafing, such as that experienced by Sir Edward Grigg during the election campaign when he had to entertain Simon in his constituency after exchanging highly peppered letters with him in May.[38] Grigg, indeed, had a jaundiced view of the whole idea of reunion: his constituency machinery fell to pieces when the size of every committee was doubled and decisions became impossible to extract.[39] For those outside the Westminster echelons, Lloyd George might be admitted to be a man of genius, but for Asquithians to associate with Greenwood, Kellaway,

Sutherland 'and the other jackals who frequented Downing Street during the Coalition regime' was not easy.[40] Reunion was seen as a reality only by those with no real grip on the situation. While the ever-optimistic C. P. Scott was complimenting everyone on his 'fine spirit of generosity',[41] Margot Asquith was still boasting that she had ' *no* illusions';[42] and the Asquithian head-counters at Abingdon Street were still calculating their own stock at the expense of Lloyd George's and still pleased when the sum came out right.[43]

Once the election results of December 1923 were known, Liberal arithmetic seemed vindicated by the return of 159 Liberals to Westminster. It was the long-awaited revival, the swing away from Labour and back to sanity. Sir Willoughby Dickinson was in a minority in holding that the election was no more than a 'fillip': 'The Liberal party is too old', he said.[44] The party had clearly done well; and the significance of the years 1923/24 for the development of British Liberalism was to lie in something other than simple electoral success or failure in any case. It was in this period that Liberalism was translated into a function of what Lloyd George wanted and not of what Asquithians believed.

Two developments underlay this translation. In the first place Asquith, probably under pressure from Lloyd George, reversed his original position of wanting to throw out first the Conservatives and then Labour in the hope of forming a minority Liberal government, and decided instead to put in Labour – presumably believing that a taste of Socialism for the electorate would turn out to be emetic.[45] But the policy was to appear in retrospect a misguided one. All that Asquith reaped from it was the detestation of the Conservative party to members of which the Liberals appeared 'to have gone quite mad' in failing to realize that 'sooner or later they w[ould] have to work with the Conservatives or disappear'.[46] Why Asquith acted as he did is unclear. Perhaps he was convinced by the counsel of Lloyd George (they had two conversations during December). Perhaps, and this seems more likely, he felt with Grey that in the context both of the present parliamentary situation and of the past five years of anti-Conservative rhetoric, any other course would be 'ignominious and futile'.[47] What is quite clear is that an important section of Liberal opinion never forgave him for 'putting in the Socialists'. This was the last thing the rank and file were looking for in 1924.

A provincial newspaper owner had pleaded with Simon after the election for:

no more Coalitions! A working arrangement with Labour may be productive of progressive legislation; but if they accept office let the responsibility be theirs, and in any case avoid any compromise with reaction. A sane, sensible and sound movement of Liberalism to the Left seems to be the need both for the country and the party. That at any rate is a ranker's view.[48]

Asquith was to gain the worst of both worlds: he put in Labour and then appeared to conspire against them in league with the Conservatives. The truth was that the Asquithians had no intention of moving to the Left or, indeed, in any other direction.

During the first months of the Labour government there settled on all parts of Liberalism a cloud of supreme depression. Asquith was ill and stayed away from the House; Lloyd George was plotting and stayed away from everyone.[49] Instead of treating reunion as a 'practical' matter as Scott had originally hoped they would,[50] the Asquithian elite became even more elevated and precious than before, self-consciously referring to the Wharf circle as the 'Holy Family'.[51] They had in any case become merely an atmosphere-creating motif for Liberalism; the actual work was done by Phillipps, Howard and Rea at Abingdon Street where they guarded the machine 'like dogs in the manger'.[52] By the spring of 1924 the farce of reunion was over. The speeches of the past few months were forgotten and the two sections returned to their stances of the previous year, 'further apart than any other two in the House – or very nearly so'.[53] Moreover, as Lloyd George began to come out of his shell Asquithians found new reasons to hate him.

Therein lies the second important development which lends to 1924 great significance in the changing pattern of post-war Liberal politics. At the beginning of the year Lloyd George had waited on events to see what MacDonald would do; but it was soon revealed that the sympathetic relationship he had intended to build up with the Labour leader and his party was not going to be forthcoming. 'His general tendency [was] to move towards the Left', MacCallum Scott observed, 'but it seem[ed] to be pretty clear that the Left d[id] not trust him',[54] and this despite his theatrical preparations for baptism, including the sudden dismissal of his staff at 18 Abingdon Street (which bewildered the

Asquithians) and the winding up of the National Liberal Party, leaving its members 'in the lurch . . . [and] . . . simply dropped like a sucked orange'.[55] Lloyd George himself went through a quiet period,[56] unsure quite what to do next – a frame of mind which lasted until about the time of the Abbey by-election, which he watched 'with great interest'.[57] He was impressed by the results of Churchill's enforced re-thinking of platform language after his defeat at the 1923 election and in particular by the idea that a 'Conservative and Liberal Union', promising a 'sound basis for National Govt.',[58] might constitute a useful rhetorical core. It was a kind of language to which Lloyd George could respond and make others respond; but, at the same time, it would be foolish to put all his eggs into one fusionist basket. He was operating, as Grigg noted, in a parliamentary situation 'full of cross-currents',[59] one requiring care and discretion.

One decision seems to have been taken. Whatever Lloyd George's plans were going to be, they would only come to fruition if he could at least have control of the Liberal party. He was sufficiently sure of his intentions at the end of March to tell Grigg that nothing could be done with the party whilst the Asquithians retained their grip on the machine.[60] To change that situation Lloyd George could make use of his political fund. An election was plainly imminent and during the summer of 1924 that contingency pressed hard on the Asquithians since they were close to bankruptcy.[61] In their lore the Lloyd George fund provided almost as great a source of bitterness as the coupon election. No one knew how much Lloyd George had got: 'millions' was the staple term and was certainly an exaggeration. Much of the money was in any case tied up with the *Daily Chronicle* which Lloyd George had bought in 1918. For all that, the sum must have been significant (Farquhar seems to have given £80,000 of Conservative party funds) and honours sales must have brought in sizeable sums.[62] Maclean made dogged attempts in January, July and September to persuade Lloyd George to pledge money for the election;[63] but the latter would put nothing in writing and in the end gave only £50,000 which came too late to do much good.

Nor was Lloyd George restricted to the tactics of the purse-strings. Through Beauchamp he conquered the House of Lords where the Asquithian leadership had been weak because Grey, who had succeeded Crewe in 1923, never really wanted the job and intended from the start to lead only in a formal way.[64] Beauchamp tried to detach Grey from the Liberal leadership as a whole and make current the idea that he, Beauchamp, would be a better spokesman[65] – a policy which succeeded in provoking Grey's resignation in September. Abingdon Street was furious but resigned itself to a Lloyd Georgian leader since the only alternative was Buckmaster, and he had made 'rather bitter enemies'.[66] Lloyd George also made inroads into the Asquithians' control of the National Liberal Federation and had a 'phenomenal' reception at the annual meeting at Brighton from an audience 'almost entirely bitter Wee Free'.[67] Within what remained of his own organization Lloyd George was also taking a renewed interest. He took pains in May 1924 to ensure that a sympathetic nonentity was elected Chairman of the 1920 Club – 'the last survivor of all the Lloyd George organizations'[68] – in order to thwart Guest, who wanted to capture it for Churchill's new imperial line. Not that Lloyd George had fallen out of sympathy with Churchill: he seems to have collaborated with him in a half-hearted attempt to bring down the government at the end of May.[69] He simply wanted to keep every plate spinning until he made up his mind what he wanted to do.

By August 1924 Lloyd George had recovered his sense of direction though it is not obvious what it was saying to him. He had decided at least that MacDonald had been given his chance and now ought to be deposed.[70] Possibly he felt that the current situation was bringing no succour to the Liberals, despite his hopes for some sort of alliance.[71] Possibly he wanted to alter the terms of his radicalism in a land campaign: he had threatened Maclean with one in January and Mond was pressing for something of the sort.[72] Or perhaps his thinking revolved, as MacCallum Scott believed, about the possibility that 'In the Election Asquith and Simon w[ould] probably lose their seats . . . [and] L.G. would then have the field to himself'.[73] Whatever his motive, Lloyd George's determination both to precipitate an election and to prevent the Liberal party from fighting it was decisive. At the election of 1924 the Liberal party returned only forty M.P.s. The Campbell case, the Russian treaty, the Zinoviev letter and Lloyd George's financial manipulation together conspired to make that election an unmitigated disaster and one which set the seal on the doom of Asquithian Liberalism.

II

The struggle between Asquithians and Lloyd Georgians for control of the Liberal party ceased effectively with the retirement of Asquith in October 1926. Lloyd George was to win and the Asquithians to slump into an effete whiggery, drawing encouragement from bitterness and leadership from the Liberal Council. Between the electoral defeat of 1924 and the retirement of Asquith, the policy which Lloyd George had been propagating in 1924 was taken to its logical conclusion, and the Asquithians were entirely eliminated from the machine, leaving only the country faithful with their tattered ghosts to protect Liberalism against 'falsehood, trickery and dishonour'.[74] It was a strange two years for those who thought they understood what Liberal politics was about. The opportunist Lloyd George who had taken shelter with the Conservatives after 1916 was now the leftward-moving radical, initiating 'inquiries' into the working of society and toying with the idea of 'going Labour'; the Asquithians, on the other hand, were drifting into a right-wing position, opposing Lloyd George's nascent schemes as 'Socialistic' attempts to undermine the British style of life and sympathizing with those who, like Mond, left Lloyd George for the Conservative party.[75] The confusion was reflected in a letter to the *Nation* in 1925:

Recent developments seem to make the present employment of the designations 'Left' and 'Right' Wings of the Liberal party increasingly inappropriate. The so-called Left wing, under the leadership of Mr. Runciman, is surely the Conservative [*sic*] Wing of the Party – harking back to the principles of 'laissez-faire' and with no kinship whatever to the ideas of the Labour party. The so-called Right Wing of the Party, on the other hand...is obviously becoming more and more sympathetic to Socialistic ideas.[76]

Confusion went beyond this vertical division into two camps; there was also a horizontal one, as Scott noticed, between leaders and followers. Lloyd George was still supported by the right wing, the 'bad Liberals', and Asquith ('who [was] really a Whig') was accepted as the leader of true Liberalism.[77]

This is not the place to discuss the complicated issues of these years; but it is important to be aware that as Liberal sentiment veered away from the Asquithian position and towards the radicalism of Lloyd George, the process produced a reluctant rearrangement of ideas in the mind of the average Liberal, or a violent refusal to rearrange in that of the Asquithian stonewaller. What is crucial to historical understanding is catching the flavour of distilled bitterness which suffuses all issues, creating in the Asquithian an amalgam of personal antagonism and intellectual judgement which could carry him to the point of agreeing with Phillipps that if Lloyd George were to 'offer [him] the Kingdom of the world and all the glories thereof and were to say "what more do you want?"...[he]...would have to say "We don't want you."'[78]

In 1924 the Asquithians were not alone in their aversion. Sir Edward Grigg had moved away from an uncommitted Lloyd George position in order to join 'a small group of Liberal Imperialists' which numbered about twelve by the time of the election, including Hilton Young, J. H. Edwards, McCurdy, Hutchinson, Hore-Belisha, Beddoe Rees and Ernest Evans.[79] The election reduced the group, and in 1925 the rump associated itself with a few ex-Coalition Liberals led by Guest, though how many could be mustered is not certain: Guest thought (wrongly) that he could induce 'about 10' to agree on a line over the Budget in May 1925[80] while Grigg calculated in the same month that the section came to about seven.[81] By the beginning of June 1926, however, in the context of the party split over the General Strike, Guest felt able to offer Lloyd George the support of twenty Liberals including some of Grigg's group which had left the party in 1925;[82] and although the validity of some of the names on Guest's list has been challenged by Dr Morgan[83] the Guest Liberals do seem to have acted as a nucleus of parliamentary support for Lloyd George.[84] Support came also from an Asquithian defector, Charles Masterman, who had been invited to serve on the Coal and Power inquiry and had succumbed there to the 'inverted affection'[85] he felt for Lloyd George. He was taken up by Beaverbrook and by 1926 had become Lloyd George's 'chief Lieutenant'; it was ironic that he had also become 'very bitter about Asquith'.[86]

Thus armed, Lloyd George continued his pogrom against the Asquithians. The electoral disaster had been the more cutting for the latter, since the Lloyd George men came back proportionately stronger in the small parliamentary band; it was therefore reasonable for Lloyd George to expect to be elected leader of the party, since Asquith had lost his seat again. A meeting was

convened at 44 Bedford Square on 5 November to discuss the
matter. The Lloyd Georgians present – Lloyd George himself,
McCurdy, Macnamara, Mond, Macpherson, Beauchamp – were
astounded to find that the Asquithians – Asquith, Simon, Runciman, Pringle, Phillipps, Maclean, Hudson – were brazen enough
to suggest that the leader should be chosen by *defeated* as well
as successful candidates, a proposal which Lloyd George naturally
opposed since 'such a joint meeting would turn into a pro-Asquith
Demonstration'.[87] The motion had been proposed by Pringle, who
well knew that some strong counter-action was necessary if a
take-over by Lloyd George was to be avoided. His calculations
went awry, however, because he had not taken sufficient account
of the constitutional mind of Asquith. The latter refused to support
the proposals of his own side and he put his weight behind Lloyd
George.[88]

Nevertheless Lloyd George was not elected leader, nor was he
ever to be; the post of Chairman was the most the party would
ever allow him. Even so, his new power was formidable. With
Asquith removed to the Lords all the indications agreed that '[a]
leaf ha[d] been turned in the history of the Liberal Party'.[89] He
may have meant it when he said that he preferred the red benches
to the green,[90] but in going to the Lords Asquith relinquished the
power even to be an incubus. The pedestal on which he was now
placed was wide enough only for his person and a few carefully
draped myths. Lloyd George was meanwhile more than ready to
occupy the vacuum and '[b]y providing money for candidates, for
meetings, for organization, and for printed propaganda...to
effect a gradual transference of the party machine from the Official
Headquarters to Old Queen Street...[and thus]...obtain
practical control of the party'.[91]

Chaos was the prevailing characteristic of the opposition he
confronted. A so-called 'Radical Group' had been formed in the
wake of the election by Wedgwood Benn 'and 8 or 9 others' with
the object of opposing Lloyd George in his bid to dominate the
party and 'voicing the opinions of many thousands of Liberals
throughout the country'.[92] Runciman had surprised himself by
winning a seat, his first since 1918. He realized at once that the
organization of the party was shattered: the new electorate required education, and the world was 'not yet virtuous enough' to
do without Liberals.[93] Wedgwood Benn was held by Runciman

to be a 'pure-blooded radical'; he was to have been the link man with Labour if the 1918 election had gone better for the Liberals.[94] He had gained in parliamentary standing by refusing Lloyd George's offer to make him Chief Whip in 1916[95] (and Herbert Fisher went so far as to think that Benn's ostentatious taking of the corner seat in the House in 1924 signified a bid for the leadership).[96] Rarely happy among Asquithians, he was finally to drift across to the Labour party on the path of least resistance for one caught, as Churchill put it, between the devil and the deep L.G.[97] In concert, Runciman and Wedgwood Benn struck an odd pose. What they attempted to lead was a disparate group of economists and dyed-in-the-wool Asquithians whose pretensions towards being 'radical' were markedly modest. Like most of their *confrères*, they were a collection of dinner-talkers – sensible enough as individuals but silly enough in one another's company to consider starting a third party.[98] The group failed to capture the imagination of either the party in general, who could not see where they were radical, or of Sir John Simon in particular, who believed that Runciman was pushing the faction in an uppety attempt to occupy his, Simon's, position as heir to Asquith.[99]

Not content with constructing their public image on the level of personal malice against Lloyd George, the Asquithians were coming to see all politics in the same personalized way. Principle was still the measuring rod, to be sure, but everyone was to be measured, friend and foe alike, and if inadequate purged. 'Yours is the only name which is ever mentioned without an "if" or a "but"', Ernest Benn wrote to his brother; 'L.G. (crook); Simon (shifty); Runci (cold); Masterman (booze) and so on.'[100] The tone was pervasively catty and set in large measure by Vivian Phillipps, Charterhouse and Caius, 'cheerless and bitter',[101] a man who dominated what was left of the Asquithian machine and spent his waking hours trying to circumvent Lloyd George.[102] The atmosphere in which Asquith referred stoically to 'monstrous seeds . . . in the womb of time' as an explanation of his predicament[103] was being replaced by that of his wife who had 'never thought it *possible* that 2 of [her] oldest friends . . . could join the band of howlers against Henry at a moment when his fortunes [were] not too good'.[104] Even when the appeal was to policy rather than abuse the tone was acrid and resentful of 'amateur and well-meaning reformers' who were apparently determined to enter into a com-

petition with Labour for the Centre/Left instead of carving out a
Centre/Right position in some way distinct from that of the Conservative party.[105] Asquithianism was fast degenerating into a
voice from the Right offering a rhetoric of the Left, a radicalism
with cold feet. 'Many of them', Wedgwood Benn believed, 'are
afraid publicly to defy Ll. G. and yet are constantly being collared
for policies in which they don't believe. Land is another case in
point.'[106]

This policy seems to have materialized in Lloyd George's mind
during 1924 and to have crystallized after the election. Grigg had
written to Sinclair that if the party was to survive at all it would
need to evolve some sort of policy before Christmas.[107] He hoped
it would be an imperial one; it was in fact to be based on a radical
reorganization of land policy, harking back to Lloyd George's
campaign before the war. Sinclair was pleased and replied that
a policy was required which would 'arouse the emotions as well
as appeal to the intellect' of the electorate.[108] Doubtless Lloyd
George was likewise interested in eliciting an electoral response,
but he was probably more interested in eliciting one from
the Labour party, to which his eye had now turned. The land
policy therefore had two useful facets: it might detach what
radicalism remained within Liberalism from Runciman and his
group and attach it to Lloyd George, along with the support
of Liberals in the country which he felt sure he had acquired;[109]
and it would light a beacon for the benefit of the Labour
party.[110]

It was not a consistent policy. Little that Lloyd George did
between 1924 and 1927 can be reduced to conformity with a single
system of thought. During August 1925, for example, Lloyd
George's intensely political mind realized the possibility, in the
context of imminent industrial unrest forecast by Red Friday, of
constructing with the Conservative party a coalition government
whose rhetoric would be tailored to face the coming challenge to
constitutional democracy. Dame Margaret Lloyd George received
a letter from her husband which strongly denied any such intention,[111] but the denial was aimed at his local Liberal contacts more
than at his wife. Garvin of the *Observer* (a notorious coalition-
monger for the past fifteen years) and Gwynne of the *Morning Post*
received very different letters from Lloyd George, full of rococo
language – Gwynne learning that democracy itself was on trial and

could not be said to have been 'a definite and unmistakeable success'[112] and Garvin that the country was

> like a barque which has had a rough shaking in a prolonged typhoon... The crew are disgruntled and inclined to be mutinous. The influence of the mutineers over the forecastle has grown perceptibly since the captain showed fear of them. The officers are not particularly adequate to the emergency, the captain is decidedly weak, and his chief officer is reckless and inclined to put on sail when he ought to be shortening... What is needed is that the ship should turn in at the first available port for a complete overhaul.[113]

Lloyd George was not to leave dry land, however. Garvin told Hudson about the plot, and he quickly informed Gladstone and Maclean.[114] What was more, the men who mattered in the Conservative party were not impressed. The scheme collapsed and Lloyd George returned to his leftward-looking pose with the land policy.

While the 'Socialistic' aspects of the land scheme alienated Asquithians,[115] the brunt of the resentment derived from another source, because land was yet another issue through which Lloyd George appeared to be dominating the party. 'Magna Churta', as the plan was styled, impelled Sir Charles Hobhouse to tell Asquith firmly that he would resign if the plan were adopted as party policy and that 'very large numbers of voters and workers' would go with him.[116] Asquith himself was mildly amused at the heat which the plan generated and particularly at the plight of 'poor Francis Acland' who had agreed to allow Lloyd George to open his campaign at Killerton, Acland's Devonshire home. 'I observed', Asquith reported to Maclean, 'that all the sackbuts and psalteries were being tuned up for the advertised descent of Moses from the Mount.'[117] Publication of Asquith's cool response to the plan, moreover, widened the breach between the two camps and accentuated the financial difficulties of the Asquithians. Subscriptions to the Million Fund declined – partly because of opposition to the plan, partly because of the prospect of another squabble – and left the party again 'on the dole' to Lloyd George.[118]

The rift was not only as wide as ever, its justifications were equally tired, one side wondering whether 'it [was] consistent with the dignity, or even the life, of a Party to go on as the pensioner of a single man',[119] the other being able to see in its Liberal critics only a 'group of small-minded narrow little wire-pullers... Tapers and Tadpoles who mist[ook] personalities for policy'.[120] Nevertheless Beauchamp wrote insistently to Lloyd George to try to persuade him to offer the Asquithians money, make himself 'master of the situation', assure himself of the support of country Liberals who looked upon the split as a disaster and thus 'draw the claws of the ante[sic]-unity party'.[121] In view of the approaching Land Convention due to take place in the following February when Lloyd George's scheme was to be submitted to the party for acceptance, the advice carried weight; but it was difficult for Lloyd George to make any credible approaches, especially since Beaverbrook was spreading stories about an alliance between Lloyd George and J. H. Thomas.[122] In any case Lloyd George was away in Italy at the vital moment, while Vivian Phillipps was excelling in his self-appointed task of turning the Convention into a bear-garden.[123] Since it was on the platform at that Convention that Hore-Belisha publicly slapped Pringle's face, he was presumably successful.

Just how serious Lloyd George's designs on the Labour party were in 1926 is impossible to evaluate, since it suited all concerned to deny such ambitions; and any attempt to show that Lloyd George wanted simply to become a member of the Labour party in these critical months would be bound to fail, for his motivation was neither so simple nor so sure. 'Labour' represented one of the balls with which Lloyd George was juggling, and to imply that he was uninterested in keeping others in the air would be as inaccurate as to deny that he focussed on this one with special care. Consideration of the relationship between Lloyd George and Labour at this time offers an important insight into the way his mind was moving, though surprisingly it is an aspect left largely unconsidered. Studies of Lloyd George in this period have miscarried, however, not so much because they have ignored the Labour dimension as because they have credited Lloyd George with a static political viewpoint through the months of industrial crisis – and this at precisely the time when his mind was veering from one expedient to another in his search for a way of reviving his credibility as a national statesman.

Given Lloyd George's strategic oscillations since 1924, a preoccupation with the Labour party was not unreasonable. He seems to have recovered quickly from his failure with the Conservative party in the autumn of 1925, and by the end of January 1926

Churchill had given him up for lost. 'It is perfectly certain', he wrote to Mond, 'that L.G. will move steadily to the Left.'[124] MacCallum Scott held the same view in May and his diary shows that others did also: he himself believed that Lloyd George would produce a solution to the General Strike 'and make a bid for Labour support': 'The situation is just the kind that suits his special genius. He is the man of a situation. He would of course still further split his own Party and make a bid for a place in the Labour party.'[125] Later in the strike period he came across Commander Kenworthy and took tea with him:

'What is L-G going to do?' I asked.
'Oh he's going Labour.'
'And you?'
'Oh I'll go with him.'[126]

On the following day he reported that informal conversations were already taking place with a view to Lloyd George's receiving a free hand from Labour in the rural constituencies if he decided to take an independent line and campaign on his land scheme. It would also appear that during the strike Lloyd George had tried to persuade the owners of the major Liberal newspapers to produce a paper of an independent line to be financed by his own fund and printed by the proprietors of the *Luton News*. Spokesmen for the papers involved agreed to the scheme at Churt on 9 May, but the Asquithian directors of the *Daily News* backed away when they realized that they were to have no control over the line adopted by the new journal.[127] It is possible that Lloyd George wanted no more than to secure control of a powerful organ for broadcasting a Liberal line; but if there was any continuity at all in Lloyd George's thinking he was probably hoping to pour fuel on beacons lit earlier.

On 20 May his position changed radically when he received by messenger from Asquith the famous letter accusing him of misconduct.[128] For one of the few moments in his career, Lloyd George actually floundered: he plainly had not expected any such response to his behaviour during the strike, or to his writing for the American press; otherwise why did he wait a day before acknowledging the letter and then rush to Manchester to consult C. P. Scott about a reply?[129] If his conduct had been intended to be a provocative prolegomenon to challenging Asquith, why was he not more prepared and polished when the ploy succeeded? The truth was that even the Asquithians were amazed at their leader's anger at the meeting he called at Bedford Square on 18 May to review the situation. Hudson, for example, found Asquith '*far more* indignant at L.G.'s behaviour than [he had] ever seen', and the meeting '[a]greed unanimously that HHA should write to L.G. and say flatly that his patience was exhausted'.[130] In absenting himself from this meeting Lloyd George had been hoping to register a position of contemptuous independence more than to throw down a gauntlet; and when Asquith retaliated, the shock produced thought and calculation before the dispatch of Lloyd George's reply on the 24th. His thinking must have made clear that Asquith had miscalculated the feeling of Liberals. It was likely that Asquith would not be supported in the country if Lloyd George could assume a high, responsible and unvindictive position. There might even be a chance of finishing the leadership dispute once and for all.

When the correspondence was published on 26 May both sides thought they had won. The Asquithians persuaded themselves that Lloyd George's stock was 'never lower' and that '*Liberalism* w[ould] win and Ll.G. w[ould] not'.[131] Margot Oxford's certainty was not shared by the rank and file, however, who (as even she later realized) followed Lloyd George and 'by doing this...lost all that was fine, true and moral, and *everything* that Liberalism meant to [her]'.[132] And others saw the point much sooner: Keynes drafted a stinging letter to Margot Oxford on the day the Asquith/Lloyd George correspondence was published and made it plain that her husband had forced a split 'in circumstances in which a large mass of Liberals, who distrust[ed] Ll.G.'s character, [were] bound to side with him'.[133] There were those who, like Pringle, refused to see reality and continued to believe that Lloyd George had no supporters except those on his payroll.[134] But the power situation was clear to most of the politically aware, and Lloyd George's view that he could be sure of the support of every important Liberal organization, apart from the National Liberal Federation (which was still 'in the hands of "old fogies"'), was probably right.[135] 'Labour' as a category of aspiration was now relegated to second place; his first aim must be to consolidate his surprising victory which had been won in an atmosphere charged, as everyone agreed, with a determination not to compromise.[136]

The next few months were to show that victory to be complete. Organs which had long been held to be Asquithian fell into enemy hands through a series of clever manoeuvres and happy accidents. He took the Liberal Candidates' Association by storm on 11 June and delivered a striking rebuff to its inventor and chairman, the irrepressible Pringle;[137] he made a great impression on the N.L.F. at Weston-super-Mare after Asquith had been obliged to withdraw through illness. In September he attempted to consolidate these gains by proffering a scheme for reunion, the inevitable failure of which he could pointedly blame on the Asquithians. Arthur Crosfield had initiated the suggestion, and the half-hearted assault was carried out by Beauchamp, Sinclair and Reading.[138] The latter had returned to England from India on 22 September, and it was hoped that his viceregal absence would have sterilized him in the eyes of the Asquithians. It had not: his letter to Asquith was of a tone unsuited to the prevailing hysteria, and the project collapsed leaving Lloyd George well martyred and Crosfield to go off to Italy in a sulk, complaining how new ideas were always left to 'beat in vain against the walls of Abingdon St.'[139] For all that, Asquithian resistance was in the nature of a last stand and a peculiarly pointless one; all Lloyd George need do was to wait for their finances to collapse and then they would have to eat out of his hand in order to live. That very September Phillipps had conceded in a secret memorandum that Liberal headquarters would have to close down in March 1927 unless some means of raising money could be devised.[140] By the first week of October he was confiding to Runciman that the till was 'practically empty'.[141] The atmosphere held nothing but gloom, and that was darkened further when Asquith announced his determination to retire after his coming public meeting at Greenock. Simon felt the loss 'as a son feels the loss of his father'[142] and waited for primogeniture to take its course.

For others, however, the future was less pregnant. Between the General Strike and Asquith's retirement in October, Liberals of the old school went through their blackest hour. Asquith had some sympathizers left, but even men like Cowdray could not but be privately anxious about the future.[143] Within the machine, Lloyd George men such as Hutchinson were leaving because they were 'in the colloquial phrase, fed up with the divisions in the party';[144] within the House of Commons the Lloyd Georgians had come to outnumber the Asquithians by two to one, and the latter consisted mostly of Runciman's dismal radicals;[145] within the constituencies such reports as the centre received merely reflected the discouragement of the leaders and condemned the re-emergence of 'recriminations and bickerings'.[146] So those journalists who sought a romantic revival of Liberalism 'not from the top downwards, but from the bottom upwards'[147] were echoing a cry not heard since the fevers and humours of coalition days and now inaudible. It was no good enjoining candidates to foment a new spirit: there were hardly any candidates anyway. Like Geoffrey Shakespeare, who had accepted the nomination for Warwick and Leamington and then withdrawn after the quarrel of May, most potential candidates were 'loth to hold aloft the tattered banner of Liberalism in such an atmosphere of party strife'.[148] All the Asquithians could do, Runciman said, was to tell the public that they existed, were vigilant and ready to give a lead; their dominating concern must be 'to keep Liberalism clean'.[149] There was a general conviction that much dirty linen remained to be washed, and the stringencies of the Liberal mind would ensure that the laundering was exhaustive and public.

III

With the extinction of Asquith's mediating role within Liberalism, the language available to Liberal politicians was one embodying a variety of extremes. It was the product not of an 'ideology' or an intellectual 'position' but of a certain unthinking dogma or codified prejudice. Not that positions were entirely static: they were taken up, attacked and defended in the name of morality, progress, democracy and decency as well as Liberalism. But if there was debate then the debate was a false one, and it is important to understand why. Argument between Liberals involved a curious paradox in the late 1920s because, while the character of the Liberal mind had played a large part in determining the framework of discussion – the goals, the fouls, the free kicks – the direct presence of that mind is less obvious than in the previous decade. Statements of attitude tend to be couched in a vocabulary of wounded offence, and there is a lack of evidence about why particular positions are assumed. Indeed if the period were studied in isolation it would make little sense: the task of

explanation requires that the debate be understood not necessarily in its own terms but in those which do most to make
intelligible the history of Liberalism since 1914. The material
insists that it is not enough to construct a record of dwindling
electoral support, crumbling organization and depressed finances.
One must also feel the heat and smell the charring.

An obvious example of this obliqueness of argument concerns
the debate over the Lloyd George fund. The financial dependence
of the party on a 'dole' from Lloyd George had been a contentious
issue since the nominal reunion of 1923 (in fact it had been
anticipated by Loreburn as early as 1919)[150] and had provoked sour
discussion about the morality of allowing Lloyd George his pecun-
iary position within the organization of the party. The argument
had been a genuine one in the sense that rational processes were
employed to explain the conflicting positions. Through 1924, as
we have seen, the Asquithians tried to avail themselves of Lloyd
George's money and made no secret of their intentions; a purse
which they had spent much of their time castigating suddenly
became respectable. The attempt failed and after the failure the
Asquithians returned to the bitterness of former years. Indeed
they went further and developed an outlook which might almost
be said to suggest mental imbalance. Simple hatred of Lloyd
George was too base a motivation for promulgation to the public;
it needed to be canalized into worthier channels. The process was
not so cynical as this implies and was not pursued merely to
establish a platform rhetoric, for in private as much as in public
Asquithians convinced themselves that their loathing for Lloyd
George, which had partly been conceived in 'principle', was still
determined by adherence to certain standards of political morality.
When an Asquithian referred to 'that d....d Fund'[151] and
'wish[ed] it were at the bottom of the sea',[152] he was finding one
answer to the most pressing question of which he was aware: why
was Liberalism dying? Lloyd George's money was 'd....d' because if he and it had not come along 'the Party would [have been]
in fine fettle'. His fund ought to be at the bottom of the sea
because it had 'corroded the life and heart of the Liberal Party'.

Views of this sort made bewilderment and failure easier to live
with. They prevented contemporaries from seeing broader horizons and have encouraged historians to see finance as the central
problem of Liberalism. The mistake is easily made when so much

comment is aimed at it. It is impossible to miss letters like that of David Davies to his constituency chairman on his resignation from the party, stressing that the fund had been one of the factors behind his decision to go, since there could be 'no hope of Liberal unity' while separate funds existed.[153] Or one might note Viscount Gladstone's preoccupation with the fund even after the 1929 election when the matter was seen by most to be academic.[154] What is vital, however, is to look behind such observations to understand the sense in which finance was seen as part of a manichean division which it was not only impossible to forget but which '*ought* never to be forgotten'.[155] Ostensibly objective statements were underpinned by a series of moral imperatives to which the quarrels of the past ten years had given rise. The fund was a blind-spot; and the next few years were to show that it was not the only one.

Liberal politics after 1926 involved Finance, Inquiries, Land, Labour and Lloyd George, with the Asquithians being not so much involved as excluded with the same degree of calculated determination which they had hitherto shown to their opponents. Intractable positions were encouraged by a financial situation which required expedients seen as necessary by some and obscene by others; by a land scheme which was either an attempt to apply Liberal principles to agriculture or an underhand plot designed to achieve back-door nationalization; and by an attitude to Labour which was Socialistic or sensible. It was a political atmosphere suffused with allegations of attaching more importance to cash than to principle,[156] of offering rhetoric that was no more than 'a conjuring delusion whirling with words'[157] and of participation by certain Liberals in conversations in the homes of Labour politicians.[158] Tolerance was not a feature of these years as Asquithians were pushed further into political fringe-areas and the stultifying sessions of Grey's Liberal Council. Rather, it was a time for 'a mixture of Die Hards and Nonconformists'[159] to come into their own and screw up the past until it showed that 'but for the fortunes of war, [Asquith] wd have led his Party in the House of Commons against [Baldwin] with all the intellect and *fairness* that [were] his'.[160] The past, indeed, was made to answer for innumerable sins, but however one construed it one fact was plain: the present, and in all likelihood the future, would be dominated by the political mind of Lloyd George.

The resignation of Asquith had changed the internal situation within the party. In September 1926 Lloyd George had offered to support Liberal candidates in rural areas through the Land and Nation League; but with the whole field now open to penetration he was quick to make an 'enlarged offer' to the Liberal Administrative Committee to provide financial aid to the party on condition that the (Asquithian) executive was restructured. Before the Committee had provisionally accepted the offer, Lloyd George had already set the wheels in motion by drafting a cutting letter to Godfrey Collins informing him that he ought to relinquish the position of Chief Whip. (Collins in fact resigned on the following day, probably of his own volition.)[161] There remained Vivian Phillipps who had fought a rearguard action against acceptance of the Lloyd George initiative in September and October[162] and worn himself out by trying to take on the ex-premier single-handed.[163] By the end of November it was clear even to Phillipps that the battle was lost; he offered to resign gracefully so long as he was not pushed.[164] Yet he was never to swerve from insisting that the Lloyd George offer had not been 'unconditional' and, together with Spender, Maclean, Violet Bonham-Carter and others, he refused to take any further part in the negotiations after Sir Charles Hobhouse had offered to chair a mediating committee. With Collins and Phillipps gone little resistance remained. Sir Robert Hudson resigned as Secretary of the Liberal Central Association[165] and Runciman left the Northern Liberal Federation. Still, the Asquithians felt their rigid stance worth retaining, despite their elimination from the machine. In a formal as much as in a spiritual sense the Liberal party was no longer their party, and such ghosts as had managed to cling to it had been all but lain. The exiles had nothing but their past; and even in one who had once admired Lloyd George, the exorcism left 'a bad taste in the mouth'.[166]

In charge of the Liberal machine was now an amalgam of talents from the intelligentsia and relics of the coalition period. The immediate entourage centred on McCurdy, Macnamara and Masterman. The first two were names with coalition associations: it had been McCurdy whom Younger thought responsible for the mismanagement of the election possibility in January 1922, and it had been Macnamara who had drafted the preamble to the Centre Party manifesto in 1920.[167] Masterman never really shook

off his doubts about Lloyd George;[168] he proved to be useful in
the Beaverbrook press for a time but could not be relied on and
in any case died in November 1927. Apart from these three, the
Lloyd George organization was represented at court by A. J.
Sylvester and Colonel T. F. Tweed, who became chief of staff and
political adviser to Lloyd George in 1926. Good relations with the
press were maintained through Tom Clarke of the *Daily News* and
Hubert Henderson of the *Nation and Athenaeum*, as well as with
his own *Daily Chronicle* through Stuart Hodgson. Moreover,
Lloyd George was now intellectually respectable: he had captured
the support of the Liberal Summer Schools organization and held
the sympathies, with various degrees of commitment, of Keynes,
Muir, L. T. Hobhouse, R. H. Brand and Arnold McNair.

The latter was an international lawyer with a radical outlook;[169]
and there was another legal accretion for the Lloyd George camp
which may have appeared strange to those who noticed. During
Asquith's last years, Sir John Simon had taken pains not to
associate himself too strongly with the party's fortunes, perhaps
because of a certain frailty of conviction (which Eden later
observed),[170] perhaps because he did not wish to remain on a ship
so patently sinking. As early as 1924 Haldane believed Lloyd
George had begun 'roping in' Simon for his own court,[171] and by
1928 he seems to have gone over to Lloyd George in all but name.
Tom Clarke records his dining at Lloyd George's table on 17 April
with Reading, Hutchinson, Henderson, Layton and Sylvester as
unholy company.[172] If one ignores the now-centrist Samuel, he
was the only Asquithian to sit on the Executive Committee of the
Liberal Industrial Inquiry. But again, Simon had never pretended
to be a dogmatic Asquithian; that part of his make-up had been
imposed from without by the functionaries of Abingdon Street
when they wanted someone to project a charming, white-haired,
safe, Christian radicalism. When he cast off that mantle, however,
Simon still had to suffer accusations of betrayal as hitherto
friendly voices began to mutter about what might have been
achieved if he had had 'an ounce of courage, and a few stray
ounces of blood and a heart that beat'.[173]

Pot was really calling kettle, for the Asquithians themselves had
little activity to show. No leader emerged after the departure of
Asquith, and only Runciman and Grey were of sufficient standing
to represent the old school with any authority. Runciman

reaffirmed his doctrinal purity by refusing to stand again for a Welsh seat because of the feud with Lloyd George.[174] But it was Grey who still seemed 'the Wee Frees' last hope',[175] and about even his qualities there was no consensus any more except among those who could remember Grey of the legend. Garvin still saw him doing 'what his feeling of duty compel[led]' and thought '[t]he type of mind he represented w[ould] have to be reckoned with one way or another';[176] but Lady Selborne, for one, got it into her head that Grey was in alliance with Lloyd George.[177] There was a generation talking about politics to whom Grey's name meant only Sarajevo. Besides he was old and infirm and the situation confronting the Liberal party was one which it was thought even a young man would find daunting.

Liberalism was flat and sulky. The National Liberal Club, never a hive of activity after the war, had become 'as depressing as a house with a corpse in it the night before the funeral',[178] and there were those who wondered whether the party it lent its name to was worth any more time and money being spent on it. Grey, Runciman and the rest were irrelevant to the new pattern of politics. The party was beyond Asquithian calculation; it had been bought, they said, by Lloyd George 'with Tory money to put himself in a position to sell it when he likes to Labour'.[179] What the Asquithians were left with was a collection of party managers without a party, a situation which Asquith had helped to create in his last years when he surrounded himself with representatives of his last political hope, the machine,

small and petty men who leaned upon his ability and who formed a kind of Praetorian guard. Their one idea was to hold the ring. They were intellectual and moral snobs...men like Mallet, Geoffrey Howard, Rea, Gulland, Vivian Phillipps, Donald Maclean &c &c &c...He kept within his own little circle of intellectual and social high browo, like a Sultan in his harem, surrounded by janissaries.[180]

With the passing of the sultan the harem lost its allure, and politicians found themselves in a situation which required the construction of a Liberal alternative to Lloyd George without a national party organization on which to build it. It was to this predicament that the Liberal Council was intended to be a response.

On 30 November 1926 *The Times* printed a letter from Sir Charles Mallet asking Grey and others to give 'some indication' that the old loyalties and values of Liberalism still stood for something. Grey reacted on 13 December at the Hotel Cecil dinner in honour of Vivian Phillipps by making it clear that Liberal unity was a failure and that some divisions could not be glossed over. As always he was quietly impressive and managed to convince the *Times* leader-writer that his remarks amounted to 'something much more than a requiem over the ashes of a party'.[181] The Liberal Council was actually formed at the end of 1926 and attracted almost no attention from a press preoccupied with the crisis over Chinese policy and the threat of repressive trade union legislation in the early months of 1927. The new body offered its presidency to Grey, who accepted it, and its chairmanship to Gladstone, who refused it on the ground that further faction would do no good to Liberalism.[182] Offices were taken at 11 Great George Street and a sedentary attempt begun to find candidates and money independent of Lloyd George. Yet although corrupt finance was one prong of the Council's offensive against Lloyd George, the objection went deeper because the Council had every intention of carrying on even if Lloyd George turned over his money to the party. Grey had told Samuel and Reading, when the latter pair were angling for terms, that the general distrust of Lloyd George was such that the agitation against him would continue so long as he remained leader.[183]

The Council took as its aim the extirpation of all that Lloyd George stood for. Its officers hoped to find support among men like Lord Emmott who felt 'so distrustful both of the Liberalism and the reliability of L.G.' that they were unable to 'owe any allegiance to a Party of which he was head'.[184] Its *raison d'être* was less to add something to Liberalism than to preserve those characteristics which fitted Liberal myth: 'to save the historic party of Lord John Russell, Gladstone, John Bright, John Morley, and Sir Henry Campbell-Bannerman from becoming the mere personal weapon of an ex-Prime Minister because he ha[d] gained control of a political fund'.[185] There was a vague Nonconformity of outlook in its assumptions concerning the nature of 'clean' politics. 'Clean hands' were the only asset Grey could offer Crewe in 1928; but he thought it enough to offset the more obvious liability of 'empty pockets'.[186] The executive of the Council was composed of men drawn from the old machine, from journalism and the universities – men who placed a premium on what they

called 'principle' but what tended in practice to approximate to
the idea of 'tone' or 'atmosphere' in political life. Because it
viewed politics through this refractory atmosphere, the contribution which the Council was able to make to a Liberal renaissance
was less than distinguished. Lloyd George seems to have believed
that the activities of Runciman and Grey cost the Liberals the
Westbury by-election,[187] and he continued seeing the 'state of
indiscipline' of the party in the following year as a 'source of
weakness'.[188] But there is no hard evidence to suggest that the
Council had much influence; it had neither the money nor the
personnel to make up for what it lacked in membership and
organization.

By no means all Asquithians joined it, moreover. A potentially
useful acquisition like Crewe could not be ensnared; he managed
to hedge in the face of embarrassed requests from Grey that he
should join after his return to England in 1928.[189] More radical
figures, such as E. D. Simon of Manchester, might be offended
by the 'really disgusting manner' of the Council's leadership in
being more motivated by a hatred for Lloyd George than by any
concern for Liberalism.[190] The prospects were clearly not good.
When the election arrived in 1929 the Council found itself without
a plan and 'in peculiar difficulty'.[191] Grey decided to give support
only to Council candidates, but even that limited activity would
demand an element of panache, and Grey had little left to give.
Manifest distaste and reluctance marked his few political interventions in these years and when he at last stirred himself to move,
as in a belated pressing of Crewe to contribute to Council funds,
he could still be preoccupied by a heavy frost at Falloden.[192] If
it had been the hope of the Council's inventors to contradict the
'stupid' suggestion that they were no more than a 'body of whigs'
or a 'second Conservative Party',[193] that rebuttal seemed clumsily
contrived by 1929.

Or it seems thus in retrospect: perhaps the contemporary perception was more blurred. To all appearances there had been an
upswing in Liberal fortunes in the by-elections of 1927/28, following the decision to make Herbert Samuel responsible for party
organization in February 1927, and this at a time when by-elections
were beginning to be followed with real interest.[194] In the year after
March 1927 three Conservative seats (Bosworth, Lancaster and
St Ives) and one Labour (Southwark North) fell to the Liberals,

and politicians starved of success could be forgiven for feeling sanguine about their electoral position. Here was the revival which had been promised in 1923, aborted in 1924 and rendered almost inconceivable by the events of 1926 – a resurgence of Liberalism 'in the country' among electors sick of Baldwin yet frightened by Socialism. E. A. Strauss, who won Southwark, was impatient of MacCallum Scott's attempt to suggest otherwise. 'I cannot allow you to cast any doubt on the reality of the Liberal revival', he wrote. 'The conservatives [sic] are undoubtedly on the down grade, and the feeling is growing that there ought to be some alternative to some of your awful friends.'[195] Some members of the Labour party would have agreed. In the spring of 1927 Sidney Webb felt that the Liberals had 'turned the corner, and started to improve'; and when Galton estimated the party's chances at a general election he decided that the Liberals would come back a hundred strong.[196] By October 1928, indeed, when the Liberal impetus had largely dissipated, MacDonald saw Labour's situation as 'undoubtedly unhappy' because the discontent with Baldwin's government was expressing itself in support for Liberalism.[197]

If there was praise from without and elation from within at this turn in Liberal fortunes, it is important to note that the praise was seldom unqualified nor the elation unbounded. Always there was the anxiety that by-elections were merely eddies within deeper and less favourable currents. MacCallum Scott's cynicism about them had been based on two features: the seats had been won through the influence of 'adventitious aids' such as only the Lloyd George fund could provide so that, secondly and consequently, the candidates returned were men of the Lloyd George camp like Strauss and Sir William Edge – men whose return the Asquithians would cheer 'with a somewhat wry face'.[198] Expressions of internecine feeling became more than wry after the Liberal win at Lancaster where Lloyd George used his position as 'personal' victor there to turn on the Asquithians and blame them for the Liberal defeat at Northampton (the only by-election to go sour in this run of contests). In a speech at the Manchester Reform Club Lloyd George attacked the Northampton campaign as one 'not fought on the whole programme, but on a programme which was that of a sectional organization that repudiates the official organization of the party'.[199] The reference to the Liberal Council was thinly veiled. But even if the factiousness and the lubricating effluvium of the fund are ignored, the Liberal renaissance of 1927/28 seems in retrospect to have been as far away as ever. Had not the Liberals been lucky in the kind of constituency which had happened to fall vacant? MacDonald certainly thought so.[200] It was a question which would become more urgent when Liberals tried to fight Labour in the boroughs in the general election.

Liberals believed that Liberal*ism* was alive in 1929 but the Liberal party, it was obvious even to the optimistic, was emaciated and senescent. A dismal alternative had had to be faced – 'starve or be bought '[201] – and had been faced only in a mood of double-think, in the hope that the party could afford not to be bought because of its moral worth and that it would not starve because of its spiritual food. Soul, the implication was, would have to replace bread; and certainly a façade could be erected to convince Irwin (far away from the popular pulse in India) that the 'political qualities, courage and money' of Lloyd George would 'make some biggish ripples' when the election came round.[202] Nearer home, the prospect reeked of falsity. Asquithians were beginning to see a point on the horizon 'not many years distant' at which 'the Liberal bridle-path peter[ed] out' because of the crumbling from beneath that was so pervasive a problem for the party activists.[203] Those who did not see it were mostly too unimportant to contribute to the reversal of the process. They were the 'little old gang' still haunting Abingdon Street 'in their antediluvian world pretending and believing that nothing ha[d] changed'.[204] The Lloyd Georgians were, for their part, equally unhappy. Their parliamentary group was split into factions, sober and plodding like E. D. Simon's[205] or lightweight and frivolous like the Frothblowers Club, organized by Henry Fildes and Edge and dedicated to 'unlimited hospitality and guzzling and drinking and humour'.[206] For the ordinary Liberal to swear by, there were only Lloyd George and the Yellow Book:

The mind of the man in the street simply refuses to digest this mass of dry intellectual chaff. Few even of the most hardened politicians will digest it. It is a mass of detailed proposals, comments and exhortations but absolutely no general idea of political principle emerges. It will not be a life-belt but a sodden sack of straw for the unfortunate Liberal candidates in the next Election.[207]

The election campaign was confused. The Liberals had a policy
which a substantial minority of them wanted to recant. Labour
had no policy at all and was claiming paternity for the Liberals '.
The Conservatives made a conscious attempt to eradicate all
traces of policy in order to appear stolid and silhouette Lloyd
George as a very dangerous thing. This subtle operation was
probably conceived by Bridgeman, who had advised Baldwin in
March not to panic. '[O]ur only safe course ', he said, 'is to depend
on our record and to make as few promises either as to what we
shall do, or what we shall not do as possible.'[208] Melchett agreed
and thought that Lloyd George could be made to look even sillier
by deferring the election until the autumn now that Lloyd George
had begun his campaign without waiting for the dissolution.[209]

Lloyd George was alive to unpleasant possibilities and was in
the market for a coalition. Labour were uninterested and had been
since an embarrassing liaison between Lloyd George and Snowden in 1926, but Churchill was keen on the idea of a centrist
coalition to keep MacDonald out in the event of Labour doing well
at the polls. Lloyd George met Churchill in the latter's room in
the House of Commons on 18 February and put to him the idea
that Liberals would support a Conservative government after the
election on three conditions. In the first place, the government
would have to introduce some electoral reform; second, no tariffs
could be tolerated for they would split the party; and finally the
ministry would have to be reconstructed.[210] Churchill thought
the terms reasonable and the plan was revived when the
election results were known.[211] Baldwin was firm, however, in
his determination not to be involved with the Goat again: he
was one politician coalition ghosts would never find difficulty in
haunting.

The general election of 1929 put an end to Lloyd George's dream
of facing the coming decade as an influential statesman and former
world figure occupying the radical centre of parliamentary politics
with a consequential following ready to do what he asked of them.
It was only a temporary setback, Garvin told him; all he had to
do was to take up his stance as 'man of the nation' and wait for
the Liberals to stop voting Labour.[212] Lloyd George knew about
the realities of power far better than did Garvin, and was
not to be encouraged by such slobber. For Liberals of the old sort,
on the other hand, the election was not so much a nail in the coffin

as a confirmation that resurrection was beyond hope. In a peculiarly Asquithian way the situation could almost be enjoyed. Those
who had lost most in the election were those who had 'backed
the wrong horse when they deserted Henry; and had [had] a rude
awakening'.[213] Vivian Phillipps was ecstatic about the disaster.
'I wonder what the rank and file are thinking now that it's all over',
he reflected. 'With all the money and the boasting and bragging,
twelve extra Liberals have been brought back to the new House!
If I had remained at Abingdon Street I could not have done much
worse.'[214] The Lloyd Georgians could not see the joke. Grey was
'a naughty little boy who want[ed] spanking',[215] and there were
those who wanted to wipe out the past and start a new party
altogether.[216]

By 1929 something old and hallowed had all but disappeared
from Liberalism. What the loss consisted in few could have said;
it was an intangible quality in public life – that was easily agreed
– but its nature was not obvious. Politics had become tainted and
not simply by the Lloyd George fund. There was an impression
current that the whole political world had become, gradually and
insidiously, a less clean place to inhabit. For many Liberals that
lost world was one which was part of the drapery around Asquith's
persona: 'My lord, he *did* understand things. I have never met
another such man. But his self-appointed political executors are
poor stuff. They never ever grasped their idol's magnanimity.'[217]
Even Laski was prepared to concede after Asquith's death that
there was no one 'quite of his type' left and to recognize that the
post-Asquithian world was one dominated by 'a stunt press and
a devotion to the slogans of the market place'.[218] The contrast
between a better, earlier age and a worse, later one was heightened
by the onset of Depression and another Labour government. In
1931 Blanche Dugdale came away from the House of Commons
and related that she had heard 'Simon advocating tariffs and
Winston demanding Food Taxes!'[219] Yet ghosts from the period
when her observation would have been shocking were now hard
to find. Appeals to cherished ikons were likely to meet at best with
suspicion in 1929. Matters were too pressing, problems too
'practical' to allow patience for metaphysics; and facing Liberals
was the choice of responding to the demands of practical politics
or of keeping the faith as a doctrinal relic. It was in a tone of
resignation and not of exultation that Donald Maclean told Glad-

stone that the only thing to do was to 'go on seeking to keep on a straight road – where it [was] difficult to get lost'.[220] But the gospel had become a whisper. Death and apathy had removed those who once might have been troubled by it all. The road was to see few of its disciples again.

II. The wider Liberalism

4. Upper and nether millstones

[I]n Europe, Liberalism ha[s] been crushed between the upper and nether millstones of privilege and revolt.
> C. F. G. Masterman, *The New Liberalism* (1920), 48.

We seem to have polled over three million votes, which is not bad for a dying party set between the upper and nether millstones.
> Asquith to Hilda Harrisson, 31 October 1924, quoted in H. H. Asquith, *Letters to a Friend*, II (1934), 107.

[I]t is going to fight against the view that the Liberal party is a middle party and for the view that it represents one of the angles of a triangle, each of which is quite definitely opposed to the other two, but at the same time has points of contact and sympathy with the other two.
> Ramsay Muir writing about the *Nation*, which he prematurely believed he was going to be allowed to edit. Muir to Fisher, 9 February 1923, Fisher MSS.

I

Images are not to be despised by those wanting to understand a frame of mind, and these two images of Liberalism – as grist to a Conservative/Labour mill, or as one angle of an ideological triangle – offer effective comment on two ways in which Liberals tended to view their position in the political spectrum of the 1920s. There were, naturally, other images such as Sir Geoffrey Shakespeare's tattered sheet mentioned in the first part of this study;[1] but the positions described in these quotations may be taken to symbolize the two most important moods which three-party politics created. The first image was possibly popularized by Masterman: certainly he was sufficiently taken with it himself to repeat it in a private letter to his wife during the time he was writing *The New Liberalism*,[2] and Asquith, whose memory for telling phrases was prodigious, may have taken it from him. In general the image reflected depression, a feeling that Liberalism was being crushed by the twin juggernauts of 'Unionism or Socialism', 'the Tory Die-Hards on the extreme Right, and the Red Flaggers on the extreme Left', both of which were invading the centre and 'get[ting] accretions from the middle things'.[3] The triangle metaphor, on the other hand, suggested a more optimistic view of Liberal prospects, one impatient with the notion that Liberalism lay 'between' the other parties and more concerned to encourage Liberals to 'fight for their own "ism"'[4] and to prove that it was 'as much a political faith as Conservatism or Socialism'.[5] Both of these attitudes will appear in different guises during this discussion of the impact which Conservatism and Socialism had on the Liberal mind.

When Lloyd George could describe his colleagues in the coalition as Conservatives who were 'Liberal minded men'[6] and when Ramsay MacDonald could wish that the Conservative St Loe Strachey 'understood the mind of Socialists better',[7] there must have been some concern among politicians about political mentalities and the difficulties which their existence predicated. Common sense in any case makes quotation trite; it is inconceivable that politicians in any period have not found their function conditioned by the view they held of their opponents as much as by their view of themselves. And if this is true of all periods, the thought has special urgency for a discussion of the 1920s. Not since the 1880s, after all, had party lines and party thinking been so blurred. It has already been seen here that it was a decade of confusion for those concerned with the internal affairs of Liberalism; it was at least equally so for those, often the same people, trying to make sense of the place of Liberalism in the wider world. What could such people see after 1918? There was a new, unknown electorate and a new party system confounding rational calculation and weakening confidence. There was the inescapable development of Socialism with its 'mongrel, Continental, lunatic drivel'.[8] There was a movement away from familiar party labels and towards a situation in which nomenclature became strange or impossible. Rothermere was told by 'an M.P. friend' that half of Baldwin's government were Socialists.[9] Liberals could similarly be seen to be everywhere or nowhere. Hewins, on the far Right, thought that the Webbs were 'really very "Liberal"' and Margaret Cole, on the far Left, thought MacDonald's government of 1929 'a good Liberal Government'.[10] Bryce gave in completely and equated a 'truly Liberal spirit' after the war with being 'non-partizan'.[11]

For anyone able to accommodate the changed conditions of the post-war world the new structure could be manipulated as easily as the old, as Baldwin was to show. But there were those who never managed it and among them Liberals bulked large. It was a plausible argument for Socialist propagandists that Liberalism and the Liberal party had now parted company and that the true Liberalism lay in supporting the Labour party and progress.[12] Men like Sir Alfred Pease, however, could not claim the mental *tabula rasa* on which proselytizing depended. 'To old-fashioned and plain people', Pease wrote in 1931, 'all this is very bewildering, and the old party lines having been obliterated, the very names of Liberal, Labour, Tory, Conservative and Unionist now appear to be meaningless.'[13] Rigidity of mind might be, as in this case, the product of old age and a certain animus against the Socialist view of the state's role in society. It might also be founded on the persuasion that all the things that the Asquithians had been saying since 1916 were true. Cyril Asquith, for example, saw British politics as a sick joke by 1931, given the language of the past decade, with 'Ramsay leading the Tories and people like Donald Maclean faced with the alternative of embracing tariffs or standing out against them *with L.G.* who has become a sort of Wee Free!'[14]

If political confusion was a developing feature of the post-war decade, its origins lay in the events of the war, the fears which these had aroused and the guesses politicians made about what the electorate wanted to hear being said about them. In simple party terms the central consequence of the coming of the war had been that of bringing the Conservative party to the fore after May 1915 and of giving the Labour party its first chance to enter the world of high politics in any significant sense. What was more significant for the future, however, was the emergence of a related debate at the top of British politics, one not so much between Conservatism and Socialism as between Capital and Labour. This view – that the war would serve 'to bring nearer the day when there w[ould] again be two parties – Labour *v.* the rest '[15] – was to become crucial to the calculations of politicians after 1918. These were the millstones of the contemporary image, though Henry Gladstone seems to have had Scylla and Charybdis in mind when he saw Liberalism 'sink[ing] between the Coalitionists and Labour – a deplorable situation'.[16] The time was coming, plainly, when Liberals would need to find something convincing to say about wealth, class and social stability.

5

Just how unstable English society might show itself to be was a question which the war years again had helped to ask. E. M. Forster was not alone in wondering where the war would leave everyone. 'There's bound to be some queer regrouping', he told Hilton Young,[17] and that was as much as could be said for the moment. Regrouping would be necessary because Labour-cum-Socialism had arrived: it could be seen in the Clydeside troubles and in the Leeds Congress of 1917 which so disturbed Lloyd George's industrial spies.[18] Most of all it could be seen in Soviet Bolshevism, 'that mad jumble of philosophic tags stolen from Rousseau and Fourier and Karl Marx...festering in the minds of an uneducated rabble',[19] and in the widespread fear of social disruption in England in 1918/19 which the immediacy of the Russian experience did much to accentuate. About revolution Liberals worried desperately. There may have been a few with Haldane's clinical mind who could face the possibility with something like equanimity,[20] but bitter revolution had no place in the Liberal scheme of things. At best it could but drive moderates into the arms of reaction.[21] At worst it could strike at the very heart of civilized society by violating the sanctity of property. 'When will it be over?' Richard Holt wondered on the last day of 1917. 'And what sort of a country will it be to live in? Things look bad for the class we belong to. [W]e are likely to see all sorts of queer economic experiments by the poorer classes in the name of social equality.' The tone requires no comment, but it is instructive to note how much more nervous it becomes in the following year. By November there is a new word in his vocabulary as he writes about 'unpleasant reports of Bolshevism underground in this country' and prays that England may 'escape any social convulsion'.[22]

Come the end of the war, the wheels of the mill seemed set. The image occurs in 1919 in an article by Aneurin Williams in which he tried to predict what would happen to Liberalism in the next few years. Moderates would be frightened into the Conservative party and radicals would go over to Labour. '[T]he tendency will be to squeeze out the middle Party. It will be attacked by the Conservatives as half revolutionary, and at the same time blamed by the Labour Party for the delay of reforms.'[23] The Liberals, it was clear, could not escape being examined in terms of the other two parties, perhaps to be chided for 'do[ing] Tory work better than the Conservatives', perhaps to be criticized for missing the central fact that Liberal politics ought not to be about 'LG versus Asquith' but rather about 'LG versus Ramsay MacDonald'.[24] The logic of the situation seemed to demand that Liberals recognized that they occupied the vacuum left by the other two parties. It demanded with equal insistence that they should remove themselves from that position by announcing lines of policy which would stamp them as something other than a compromise group. Liberalism should not 'rest merely on the defensive': it should be 'aggressive' and 'attacking'.[25] There were many obstacles in the way of doing this, not least the belief that the 'no-man's land in which the moderates of all three Parties [were] practically indistinguishable in practical policy'[26] might prove to be a profitable position to occupy in this new political context.

Whatever party a politician belonged to, after all, his overriding aim in 1920 had to be that of projecting an image which was the opposite of extreme, unless he was a Die-Hard pleading for a renewal of landed or intellectual Conservatism or a man of the Left more interested in virtue than appeal. Not only was this position electorally sensible, it could also be justified on a number of grounds. It could provide a base for the public argument that 'between the reactionaries of Toryism and the extremists of Labour the nation [was] not unlikely to choose the "via media" of Liberal policy' which had been 'tried and tested and found sufficient when other things failed'.[27] It could offer encouragement in private that a fluid party situation might make the centre so desirable that representatives of all sections of moderate opinion might co-ordinate their activities in order to capture it. The attempt to depose Asquith in favour of Grey in 1921 had its roots in precisely such thinking; and even in the very different conditions of 1925 Asquith was willing to assure Murray that he still took 'as an end worth working for' the attraction to Liberalism of the best parts of Toryism and the saner section of Labour.[28] Nor were the Asquithians the only Liberals to feel this way. In the uncertain days of January 1924, for example, Sir Edward Grigg looked forward to a three-party fusion as one way of bringing about a strong parliamentary majority out of the chaos precipitated by the recent election.[29]

It is tempting to reflect in retrospect about the plausibility of

thinking of this kind. It is clear at once that such plans cannot be
written off as the idle musings of a decaying party. Consider, for
example, the leadership of the other parties. Lord Inchcape's
observation that MacDonald was a whig is well known,[30] but it
is by no means the only comment on the Labour leader's modera-
tion, perhaps even his Liberalism. To Norman Angell his foreign
policy seemed that of a Victorian Liberal.[31] His domestic policy
was also seen to be moderate to a fault: it was he who resorted
to 'shouting...and banging the box with fury' to inject a semblance of radicalism into what he was saying.[32] His 'word
twisting and word spinning' seemed to Lansbury so advanced as
to rival that of Lloyd George himself.[33] Beneath the oratory there
was the author of *Socialism: Critical and Constructive* with its
exposed Liberal roots. He was seen to be a Liberal without a party,
'belong[ing] neither to the Right nor the Left...neither Tory nor
Jacobin, neither Constitutionalist nor revolutionist'.[34] Moreover,
if the relationship between MacDonald and the Liberal leadership
was never happy or consistent, the reasons had more to do with
personal aversions than with the doctrinal differences on which
MacDonald liked publicly to dwell. Even the aversions were
largely in the future in 1920; it would not have been absurd then
for Liberals to believe that a democratic liberal like MacDonald
was not beyond the pale of centre politics. A man who could
complain to Dalton in 1923 that the capital levy was costing the
party votes[35] leaves behind him the impression that he would have
been ready to stop bearing crosses if workable plans promised to
make the stopping feasible.

Other Labour leaders were occasionally seen in favourable
lights by Liberals. It was worth while for Liberals to recall that
many of their leading opponents on the Labour side were themselves ex-Liberals, men who, 'in spite of public utterances',[36] may
have been amenable to an understanding with the Liberal party.
J. H. Thomas, for example, was held in some regard for his
anti-class-war rhetoric. He professed in public to have a great
regard for Asquith and in private he consulted the latter about
whether he ought to resign as his party instructed him to do in
1919.[37] Clynes also disliked behaving 'like a boor' in proclaiming
his proletarian credentials;[38] he was more successful than Thomas,
and his stature was further increased by his sympathetic response
to the idea of Grey's return to public life. But the most hopeful

candidate for detachment from the Labour party was undoubtedly Philip Snowden. He had a Liberal background of which a free-trade crotchet was the most conspicuous remnant.[39] More promising still was his patent detestation of MacDonald, which was nurtured by Ethel Snowden in the early years of the decade and led Snowden himself to 'desert' in 1922, 'not in heart and mind', MacDonald hastened to assure one correspondent, but to desert nevertheless.[40] The remaining heavyweights in the Labour leadership in 1920, Henderson and the Webbs, seem never to have been the objects of Liberal calculation or aspiration, though Henderson may have been involved in some of the discussions about Grey.

It behoved Coalition Liberals to see in the post-war Conservative party 'statesmen of high rank...whose Liberalism [was] beyond question and beyond doubt',[41] especially in men like Balfour, who had had his name linked to those of 'Asquith, McKenna, Simon, *et hoc genus omne*'.[42] Baldwin could (in some moods) appear to display the temperamental sympathy, notwithstanding the protectionist campaign of 1923, of a 'cultured liberal Conservative'.[43] Law and Chamberlain were tainted with the atmosphere of commerce and reflected the 'hard-faced' capitalism which Liberals found unacceptable. They were able occasionally to read something likeable in Baldwin's considered ambiguity. At a time when Conservatives were unsure whether they wanted a better, 'new' Conservatism[44] or a return to a better, old one which could offer 'straight politics' and 'clean and honest dealing',[45] Baldwin was able to face both ways. Two assets helped him to do so. In the first place, he was as unlike Lloyd George as it was possible to be; he therefore took to himself the mantle of 'simple honest man' who 'look[ed] straight ahead, st[ood] upright and [was] not always listening at the ground level'.[46] In the second, he controlled a reservoir of charm – half bucolic, half synthetic – which washed over the most obvious skulduggery. The technique may be briefly illustrated by quoting an extract from a letter to Birkenhead in 1923 and placing the deleted parts in parenthesis: 'What is possible now (will) may be more easily accomplished (after the election) later and I (am quite certain) have every hope that we shall then be able to achieve the complete union of the Party (in a very short space ot time).'[47]

Foliage of this density prevented Liberals from seeing that

Baldwin was doing what Lloyd George did and doing it better. If Lloyd George realized it, the insight could not help him: there had arisen a strong private and overwhelming public enmity between the two, and the only ammunition left to Lloyd George in later years lay in words like 'fraud' and 'humbug'.[48] Yet even he was compelled to acknowledge that Baldwin had stolen the admiration of thousands of Liberals through the propagation of his cultivated persona. Baldwin liked to share Asquith's pedestal[49] and Liberals were proud to see him there. Grey and Esher were willing to use phrases like 'triumph of character', 'public honour' and 'personal qualities' when they spoke about and to Baldwin.[50] Maclean was ready to applaud his 'lofty character and purity of motive';[51] Runciman compared Baldwin's budget of 1923 favourably with that of Asquith in 1907;[52] and there must have been many less articulate Liberals who would echo the eulogium of one unknown: 'I am a Liberal...What you really are I don't know but you have done a lasting service to us all.'[53] Whatever the depth of his political ratiocination, Baldwin held an assured place in that part of the Liberal mind which associated being admirable with being (in some distilled sense) English.

Party leadership was important in setting the tone which the country was to hear. It was not, however, the only part of the political elite which reflected the fluidity of post-war politics. Lesser men also played a role. One could point to those who drifted away from Liberalism towards one of the other parties; or those who, like Esher and possibly Hankey, lacked any clear party commitment and yet spoke for the centre; or, most of all, those whose minds never really settled into the grooves of party politics – men like Garvin and Philip Kerr, who, though a nominal Liberal in the 1920s and an ex-member of Lloyd George's staff, combined a Christian Scientist idealism with a practical core, 'a sort of dead centre of sanity and common sense'.[54] Such men were also to be found at the top, none more prominently than Lord Robert Cecil, whose involvement in the Grey movement was a demonstration of centrality, and Viscount Haldane, who was still regarded as a Liberal hopeful, despite his Labour leanings, and who as late as 1923 would probably have preferred an Asquith administration to a MacDonald one and a Baldwin government to either.[55] 'It must ultimately turn on leadership', Grigg said in 1924,[56] and to the extent that the comment was true there was hope for the Liberals. Yet there were problems even about this limited view of what three-party politics was about. What was to be done with Lloyd George? Was anyone prepared to consider his brand of 'leadership' on its merits? The first part of this study has suggested that the Liberal mind was not able to do so: corrupter or crusader were the only roles allowed to him. Lloyd George also offered problems to the Conservative and Labour parties, and when one examines the reasons for the failure of Liberalism to construct a viable relationship with other parties, the name of Lloyd George can never for long be kept out of the reckoning.

But of course all did not turn on 'leadership'. Another crucial element in the situation was Liberal 'doctrine' and the degree to which it was malleable enough to mould itself to fluid alliances. Some contemporaries (mostly hostile) saw no problem here at all. 'The Liberal Party has no creed, no cause', MacCallum Scott wrote in 1927. 'Its ideal is essentially that of a centre party – a do-as-little-as-possible party – a carry-on party. It is a pis-aller – a kind of shelter for timid passengers in the middle of a busy street. It rouses no enthusiasm. It enlists no zeal.'[57] However, 1927 was not 1920, and the evidence makes clear that a body of Liberal doctrine was built up after the war which, whether or not Liberals happened to 'believe' in it, made it hard to convince others that they might be useful allies and to persuade themselves that allies might be worthy vehicles for the Liberal message.

Caution is immediately necessary, however, because it has been taken to be thematic here that Liberal doctrine should be seen as being created in parallel with, or even in the train of, ongoing parliamentary activity. What politicians professed publicly to stand for can never, the suggestion is, be taken to represent 'the core of the argument'.[58] Where it was part of real argument at all, the role of public rhetoric was that of projecting argument privately resolved; it was not a core but a facade designed to attract the attention and stir the emotion of those looking on. Haldane's 'beliefs' in some ways corresponded to those of Liberal progressives like Muir and E. D. Simon; so, to a lesser extent, did those of Sir Alfred Mond. But what did the Manchester Liberal find when he tried to move them to action? 'Haldane came and spent a week-end with us; talked for 17 hours; gave us a hearty blessing; and joined the Labour Party. Lord Melchett began to take an active and sympathetic interest; and joined the Tories.'[59]

Good history demands as much as good taste that politicians be regarded as human beings and as capable of conviction as anyone else. But it is equally imperative to recognize that such conviction can only be properly used by the historian as an explanatory instrument when it has been placed in its immediate political context, alongside all the other variables that influence political action.

II

Conservative fortunes after the coupon appeal of 1918 were plainly bound up with those of Lloyd George and that section of Liberalism whose support he commanded. Thoughts of co-operating with the Asquithians were therefore ruled out for the bulk of the Conservative party during the existence of the coalition; they were not worth the effort, in electoral terms, of winning over, nor the risk of offending Lloyd George by appearing to do so. Bad odour surrounded Asquith anyway because of right-wing views of his wartime failures. There may have been a few Tories able to admire his honest image, or at least to suspect that Lloyd George's 'real war record' was less praiseworthy than their colleagues believed;[60] there were certainly those who thought the latter 'a bit of a Bolshevik at heart', always 'giv[ing] way to extreme Labour and rotten socialists like Addison'.[61] For all that, there existed an undeniable animus against the kind of watery pinkness which Asquith was thought to represent. 'Squiff and Squiffery' were, in the mind of the far Right, 'dead-dead-dead' after a war which had left the Liberal leader 'a poor creature, vain, self-righteous and shallow'.[62] Besides, the Conservative party was evolving a distinctive approach to the new politics. 'Why dilute it', Amery was to ask, 'with the ditchwater of Liberalism?'[63] Not only were such questions being asked, they were being asked by the kind of Conservative who was increasingly to control the party as the decade progressed. They were the men Baldwin could be made to listen to; and the doctrine they were pressing was one which took to be crucial the crushing of Liberalism so that the anti-Socialist and protectionist stance which they wanted Conservatism to assume would not be jockeyed by Liberal compromise: 'We have only got to go straight ahead, stick to our own policy, refuse to have any truck with the Liberals, and the game is ours.

The Liberal party is 'bust', and nothing can save it from breaking up, except insanity on our part.'[64]

There was, to be sure, an 'Asquithian' aspect to Conservatism in the early 1920s among an important section of the party anxious to expel Lloyd George from office. Nor did the similarity of their roles end there, for these Conservatives also wanted 'credit, reputation, courage and a moral existence as a party'[65] and were looking back to an older world and the lessons they 'learnt as a child at [their] mother's knee';[66] they too rejected the post-war political atmosphere 'in which to speak of morality or principle in politics [was] regarded as an indelicacy, an amusing provincialism' as the country 'condemn[ed] its liberties to the discretion of an able, self-confident but very imperfect man'.[67] Winterton found Lloyd George as much of a 'super-stuntist'[68] as did any Asquithian; Salisbury was as delighted as the bitterest Wee Free that Lloyd George raised no cheers at the Conservative Party Conference in 1921.[69] Both Conservatives and Liberals had their 'pure' wings, that is to say. Yet to regard them as possible allies would be to miss the whole reality of their positions. They held one another in complete contempt. There was no desire for alliance and, from the Conservative point of view, no need for one.

If the Asquithians were to receive no help at the hands of dissident Conservatives (except, of course, from Cecil), there was one right-wing pressure group which showed interest in them. It was odd that the Harmsworth press should have done so after its violent attacks on Asquith during the war. It was no less strange for being the product of a number of post-war developments – Northcliffe's burgeoning megalomania, Rothermere's belief that he could make the Liberals sing his own song. To his death in 1922 Northcliffe maintained his personal aversion to the Asquithians 'only less than he loathe[d] L.G.',[70] but so long as the Independent Liberals were the lesser of two evils it was conceivable that Northcliffe would boost them in order to hit at Lloyd George. For a time such aid even seemed likely in view of Northcliffe's great regard for Grey. In the summer of 1921 Cowdray was sure that Northcliffe would be 'prepared to do everything he c[ould] to further Grey being the leader of the Liberal Party', providing he would not have to 'lift a finger for Asquith'.[71] By the beginning of 1922 Hudson was confident enough to tell Gladstone that he

'*could do business* with Northcliffe if the Grey adventure could
be made to succeed'.[72] These judgements were important to the
Asquithian frame of mind. They were also wrong. There is in fact
no evidence to suggest that Northcliffe gave any real help to the
Asquithians between 1918 and 1922.

Help was forthcoming, however, from Northcliffe's brother,
Harold Harmsworth, Lord Rothermere. Just after the Maurice
debate in 1918, Rothermere's son had written to Runciman that
he viewed the future of Liberalism with some concern:

No-body can safely predict what will happen at the next General Election
and, whatever ensues, a united Liberal party must always be an important consideration.
   I write to you because I am unwilling to see the Liberal party ship-
wrecked without scattering a word of protest. I am not a Liberal by birth
or training, religion or conviction but simply because I have believed in
Liberalism and still believe in it as a political force.[73]

What Rothermere and his camp wanted was the opportunity to
use Liberalism as a 'political force'. This did not become apparent
until after the coupon election, during which Rothermere publicly
supported Lloyd George and the coalition.[74] It was during the
summer of 1919, after Esmond Harmsworth had won the Thanet
by-election, that Rothermere changed course and began to articulate his own brand of anti-waste propaganda; and it was in December that Elibank received from him a crude overture to do
the same. The whole problem about the Liberals, Rothermere
said, was that their speeches were centred on Ireland and free
trade: they ought instead to be talking about expenditure and the
cost of living. 'Why do not you consult your friends and have the
whole thing properly stage-managed?'[75] It was clear enough that
Rothermere had himself in mind for the job of stage manager.

   Governmental waste did form one small prong of the public
attack on Lloyd George which the Asquithians mounted, but its
inclusion was more likely to have been a congenial hangover from
the old doctrine of Retrenchment than a response to private
proddings from Rothermere, though the latter was in touch with
the Asquithian leadership.[76] But it is true that during the years of
the coalition government, Asquithians had reason to be grateful
to Rothermere for his 'effective work for [them] in the crowd',
and no one more so than the organizer Gladstone, who seems to
have been capable at one point of envisaging an alliance between

Rothermere and Cecil.[77] During the election of 1922 Rothermere was particularly active, both at the national level – he instructed *Daily Mail* leader-writers to 'write up' the Asquithians[78] – and at the local level where, for example, he promised Simon that he would urge the *Leeds Mercury* to boost his campaign.[79] It was the last election, however, for which he cherished any real hopes for the Liberals, and after 1922 he retained only a mild interest in 'fram[ing] up some way of escape' for Lloyd George from his political impotence.[80] He was a political dilettante once his anti-waste campaign came to an end. Baldwin was his new target and he had little need of Liberal ammunition.

No Conservative had much use for the latter after 1922. The electoral situation of the Liberals, apart from a few months in 1923/24, was such that other parties need not be desperate for their help nor inclined to proffer their own with an eye to a future *quid pro quo*. More damaging still was Lloyd George's return to the Liberal fold. About the latter a painful paradox may have occurred to the Asquithians. Before 1922 Conservatives had been un-interested in them because they were outside the Lloyd Georgian stable; after 1922 Conservatives would have nothing to do with them because they could not escape from it. It seems clear that if any chance had ever existed of forming an alliance on the right of the party, it had lain with Lloyd George and his group in the period 1916–22. The theme of that relationship had been Lloyd George's attempt to effect a realignment of Conservative and Liberal politics through the fusion of the more moderate wings of both into a 'National' or 'Centre' party. Though the plan was ultimately to fail, it was of great importance in Lloyd George's thinking during these years and a conspicuous motif in Liberal politics until at least 1925.

The idea of a centre party was in no way new to Lloyd George's mind in 1918. It had been he who had done most to press upon the pre-war Liberal government the advisability of coalition in 1910, and the idea itself, with its accompanying rhetoric of putting an end to the vacillation encouraged by the party system, could be traced back at least as far as the 'Efficiency' movement and Rosebery's Chesterfield speech of 1901.[81] It must have been soon after the crisis of 1916 that Lloyd George began seriously to think about the possibility of constructing some permanent arrangement between the Conservatives and the Coalition Liberal rump for the purpose of fighting the next election. Certainly before the end of 1917 he worried some of his Labour colleagues by thinking aloud about the need for a 'national' party at Westminster and in the constituencies.[82] Nor was nervousness at the prospect limited to those who were left of centre. When, for example, Curzon heard rumours that circumstance might dictate a fusion of Conservatives and Liberals, he begged Law to squash the idea at once.[83] In the context of 1918, however, there was little need for Lloyd George to press for such a fusion when a simple coalition arrangement gave him all the electoral advantage he needed. It would be in the longer term, when the man-who-won-the-war posture began to look outmoded, that he would need to find something else.

Because it was a long-term objective (and one full of tactical complication) the centre-party project lay beneath the surface of party politics for much of the duration of the coalition. Only on three occasions did it break through to become the focus of political thinking for both Conservatives and Liberals. The first occasion was in the summer of 1919 when, although Lloyd George was distracted by the peace conference, the flag could be carried by Churchill and Birkenhead. The second was in March 1920 when the atmosphere seemed favourable to a possible anti-Labour 'Constitutional Reform Party'[84] which would capture moderate Conservative opinion, consolidate Lloyd George's hold over his Coalition Liberals and possibly detach a few Asquithians from the leadership of the old guard. The final attempt to restructure his support came at the beginning of 1922, only to be sabotaged by the Conservative cabin-boy, Sir George Younger. Each of these *démarches* took on a character wedded to the existing political contexts: each of them was therefore different. Support for them came from different people and from a variety of motive. Apart from Lloyd George and Churchill, support from Liberals for the fusion idea came most consistently from Frederick Guest and his less-well-known brother Montague Guest, from Addison before his expulsion in 1921, and from Lloyd George's political functionaries like Sutherland, Kellaway and McCurdy. Fisher expressed support at certain times but was against the idea, for example, in 1920.[85] Mond and Shortt held broadly similar views.[86] Hewart was only won round in 1920 by his leader's cajoling. Macnamara, on the other hand, approached the problem from exactly the opposite direction: he was in favour of it in 1920 but opposed it in 1922.[87]

Inconclusive evidence makes difficult any decision about the degree to which Lloyd George was responsible for instigating the centre-party movement in 1919 and the degree to which he was educated towards it by Guest and Churchill. In January 1919 he thought about reunifying the Liberal party. In February he worried about what the Conservatives would do if they caught him doing it. 'A Central party probable' was Fisher's prognosis.[88] Some time in the first half of the year Guest placed the fusion argument before Lloyd George and advised him that there was only

one alternative to the return of Labour to power should the Coalition fail. It is that the Prime Minister, having failed to obtain sufficient backing for Reform from the Unionist majority, should appeal to the country on the details of a social programme and consolidate under his Leadership a new Centre Party which would be made up of the bulk of the Liberal Party, together with the progressive wing of the Unionist Party and the moderate sections of Labour.[89]

There are clear similarities of language between this appeal and that made by some Asquithians about the possibility of a Cecil/Asquith/Clynes combination. The crucial difference was Lloyd George's presence and it is doubtful that he ever saw fusion in the same way as Guest. For him it was a method of cementing the relationship between his own Liberals and the Conservative party. Labour, far from being a part of the combination, was to be projected as the disease which made fusion necessary. It may have been in Lloyd George's mind to attract a few moderates for tactical reasons, but Barnes, for one, claimed as late as July 1919 that he had 'heard nothing about a Centre Party'.[90]

There may simply have been nothing to hear. Except for a flying visit to England in April, Lloyd George was in Paris between the end of February and the end of June. If he was to do any political thinking, in consonance with that of his colleagues, it would have to wait until his fortnight's holiday at Criccieth which began immediately after he returned to Britain.[91] But two developments suggest that such thinking took place. In the House of Commons the press began to notice the existence of a new 'Centre group' which had been formed under the chairmanship of Montague Guest. *The Times* revealed on 18 July that Coalition Liberals accounted for five of the executive committee of thirteen and that the new organization had promises of financial support. But of the fifty-two members of the group who were present at its first meeting on 15 July, only three were Liberals. The group was seen, therefore, to be a body of young Conservative M.P.s who wanted the coalition to be continued on a permanent basis.[92] The second development concerned Churchill, who went to stay with Lloyd George at Criccieth for the weekend 12/13 July. It was Churchill who, three days later, addressed the centre-group meeting.[93] What emerged from his speech, however, was by no means a clear call for fusion, though some interpreted it as such, but rather an appeal to continue the coalition in order to fight Bolshevism and support White Russia. The press was willing to read more into the speech, however; the parliamentary correspondent of *The Times* noted that certain 'acute observers' had seen in Churchill's 'carefully prepared remarks' an indication that he was 'exploring the ground with a view to the ultimate creation of a homogeneous party of moderate men on the ashes of the Coalition'.[94] Hewins, at least, was impressed by such argument and commenced bizarre speculations about a retaliatory alliance between the Die-Hards and Labour.[95]

Events were to demonstrate that responses of this kind were more dramatic than the facts warranted. The 'New Members' Coalition Committee', as it now styled itself, continued to operate but only as an occasional platform for Lloyd George's frothy platitudes or Lord Robert Cecil's internationalist ones.[96] The Prime Minister seems to have lost interest in strategy for the moment. He went off on a long holiday to Deauville in the summer (though he had some ministers in attendance)[97] and in the autumn was preoccupied by a serious railway strike and the prospect of further Continental conferences. It is significant that Frederick Guest – always an enthusiast for the centre party – saw 'great difficulties' in the way of bringing it about by September 1919.[98] There were rumours about approaches having been made to the Labour leaders[99] but these may have been put about by Northcliffe or arisen out of the speculation following Churchill's speech in July. Certainly it was plain that Churchill had not spoken for the government as a whole, despite the Criccieth weekend. Asquithians could be forgiven for seeing the speech as 'a feeler on the part of Winston to ascertain whether there [was] any body of opinion in Parliament that would be likely to support and follow him'.[100]

Regardless of who provided the impetus for the introduction of a centre-party perspective in 1919, it was obvious that Lloyd George and Churchill held divergent ideas about why it was desirable. For Lloyd George it was a promising electoral device for shoring up his personal administration by developing a vocabulary of resistance to burgeoning Labour. For Churchill it was an almost necessary deduction from his anti-Bolshevik position. The embarrassment caused to the government by Churchill's eagerness to commit support and money to further the efforts of Kolchak and Denikin is well known. By the summer of 1919 Lloyd George was tired of it; and a long memorandum from Churchill requesting yet more commitment brought a sharp retort from Deauville.[101] In justification of his attitude Churchill explained that he regarded anti-Bolshevism as a key aspect of the plans Lloyd George and he had discussed 'about party matters'.[102] Possibly he was doing no more than placing his own emphasis on one facet of an agreed policy; but to others it appeared that he was writing his own manifestos in order to tell centre-minded politicians 'that they need not lack leadership'.[103] When Churchill laughingly pretended to Lloyd George that he was a party all by himself, Lloyd George was stung into reminding him that he was one without followers.[104]

The quarrel was made up in January when Churchill admitted defeat.[105] Yet already the results of numerous calculations were suggesting that the fusion idea could be pressed again and harder than before. Masterman said that this new mood began after the rail strike had convinced Lloyd George that a consolidated anti-Labour organization would yield political rewards.[106] Churchill had returned to the theme at the end of 1919 and most blatantly at Sunderland on 3 January 1920. This time there was no need for strained divinings: the meaning was clear. There was no reason why Liberals and Conservatives should not combine; and those who agreed should 'bind themselves together...for any action as will best enable them to secure the permanent ascendency of their political principles and beliefs'.[107] Lloyd Greame (possibly inspired) followed up the speech with a letter to *The Times* to underline that the speech was not a call for continued coalition but a plea for a 'National Party'.[108] What Lloyd George wanted people to see in it is less than clear. Frances Stevenson records his mood as one of silence – which she took to be indicative of his not being able to see his way, especially with the Paisley by-election pending with its threat of reviving the spirits of the Asquithians.[109] Fusion would make their threat unimportant. But could the Conservatives be persuaded to accept it?

In the middle of February, Balfour received a tentative approach from Lloyd George calling for a 'concerted effort' to prevent Labour's gaining control of the lower-middle-class vote.[110] The idea appealed to Balfour and he elaborated on it in a letter to his constituency chairman. There remained Bonar Law, however, who would be more difficult to convince. He was sent a draft of the Balfour letter and for the moment agreed to accept what was in it.[111] Meanwhile Lloyd George was instructed to confer with his Coalition Liberal colleagues, whose reactions he found to be mixed. But was their reaction the cause of his failure ultimately to press on with the plan? Law alleged that it was and his biographer accepts the interpretation,[112] yet Lloyd George had been preparing the move in his own camp long before Balfour sent the letter to Law. On 23 February Macnamara had sent Lloyd George a draft preamble for a centre-party manifesto,[113] so wheels must have been set in motion before then. Lloyd George knew what the feeling was about fusion: it did not prevent him going on with it. And if some Coalition Liberal ministers were against fusion there were others like Addison strongly in favour.[114] The real problem lay with someone much more important, Law himself. When Lloyd George sat down at Cobham on 17 March to prepare his important speech to a Liberal meeting the following day, he did so against the background of an interview with Law the previous morning from which he had returned 'very bad-tempered' because Law was 'funking it'.[115]

The Liberal meeting on 18 March had been organized by George Lambert as part of his personal crusade to try to unite the Liberal factions, but its significance lay elsewhere. During the past week the press had been anticipating a major centre-party statement from Lloyd George; on the previous Sunday Garvin had dutifully been 'flying a kite for...fusion',[116] and the scene was set for a confrontation with Asquith at the Thursday meeting. This did not happen. In the first place Asquith did not turn up: he sent Lambert a prim letter announcing that he could see no point in the meeting. Secondly, Lloyd George had decided the previous day that the time was not ripe (in view of Law's position) to push for fusion but only for closer 'co-operation' between the two wings.[117] Instead of the new diet, therefore, the Liberals were fed the customary oats with all the usual stuff about 'restoring and enriching' the country and 'making the poor our common comrade'.[118] Even in this anti-climax it was possible to see 'the beginning of a new era in the development of political Parties',[119] but Lloyd George knew better. Too much had been made too public too soon. Already he had had to face criticism from colleagues at Westminster; it would not be long before the 'country' began to protest.

Reaction from the latter was quick to arrive. 'The current in the constituencies', FitzRoy observed on 22 March, 'runs strongly against fusion.'[120] Lloyd George tried to reassure disgruntled Liberals with a slashing attack on Asquith at the National Liberal Club on 26 March, but country opinion proved difficult to divert. MacCallum Scott even considered that if the secret negotiations which the whips of both parties had been conducting were to be made public, the Coalition Liberals might split and leave Lloyd George stranded.[121] The only full account of Liberal constituency feeling is a virulently Asquithian one by Harold Storey.[122] Yet it is inescapable that at the Leamington meeting of 7 May 1920 only four delegates from local Liberal associations failed to support a resolution against co-operation with the Conservatives.[123] In the face of such opposition and the reservations of the Conservative leadership, the plan miscarried. By the summer of 1920 discussion of it was carried out in the past tense. It had failed, not because it contradicted natural law and would have produced 'a mere bundle of sticks tied together by string',[124] but because the cat had been let out of the bag at the wrong moment and because Liberal opinion had made it impossible to put it back again once Law had baulked Lloyd George at just the instant when he might have been able to pick it up and make it mascot.

Once this attempt failed, moreover, all future attempts were made more dangerous, since the interests concerned now had their briefs ready. The substitution of Chamberlain for Law in March 1921 promised something in that Chamberlain was far more enthusiastic about fusion than Law had been.[125] But for the most part 1921 was a year for recalling past failure and lost opportunity.[126] The growing urgency of the Irish problem, however, and the fissiparous effect it was likely to have on the Conservative party suggested by the end of the year that Lloyd George might be in a position to gather together in the centre most of the Conservatives (reacting against the Die-Hards) and a substantial segment of Liberalism (applauding his statesmanlike solution of the Irish question). January 1922 marked for Guest, at least, the 'supreme opportunity' to establish at last the reign of the 'great triumvirate' of Lloyd George, Churchill and Birkenhead.[127]

A general election was the obvious means of capitalizing on the government's new popularity. It would also bring about conditions favourable to the formation of a centre party, as one backbench Coalition Liberal reflected toward the end of the month as he considered the events of the past few weeks:

The real issue which dominated everything else was the possibility of a split in the Conservative Party...Lloyd George was fully prepared to meet the challenge [of the Die-Hards] and he preferred to do it now. He was prepared to split the Tory Party and to use a general election for the purpose of wiping out the Diehards as a Parliamentary force. Having split both Liberals and Conservatives he would build up a central Party of his own.[128]

Younger's revelation of Lloyd George's electoral intentions made such a course impossible. All the opposition which fusion had provoked in 1920 was brought into play again, especially among the Conservatives who now rallied to their party machine. Mac-Callum Scott noted with satisfaction that a lunch given for Birkenhead in February attracted only thirty-odd Conservatives 'in spite of desperate efforts to collect more'.[129] The two lesser members of the great triumvirate, indeed, had proved a source of much embarrassment for Lloyd George – Birkenhead through his personal notoriety, Churchill through his willingness to run with Chamberlain as energetically as he hunted with Lloyd George.[130] It was doubtless as a result of pondering these difficulties that Lloyd George came to a decision in March that the immediate political future must lie with the coalition and not with any new alignment.[131]

Defeat in 1922 led Lloyd George to believe that the centre-party idea was dead, and others thought the same. 'Ll.G. and his intrigues' had been 'checkmated'; 'coalitionism' and 'fusionism' were at an end; the Conservative party had been restored to its proper place in British politics.[132] Austen Chamberlain even pretended that he had never wanted fusion in the first place but only

'to give a new meaning to Unionist' by converting that portion
of Liberalism which was not 'already Labour in all but name';
and, whatever his past record might suggest, he was now clear
that the most pressing task facing the party was that of 'smash[ing]
the Liberal party'.[133] It was unlikely that former opponents would
believe such apologies. Even now they were watching for Lloyd
George's Conservative cronies trying to undo the work done at
the Carlton Club. Die-Hards like Gretton never forgave the
'"Brains"', as they like[d] to think themselves' and felt sure that
some of them 'still hanker[ed] after a Centre Party'.[134] Rumours
of such plots ran among the Asquithians as they observed helplessly what Lloyd George was doing to them. After the election
of 1924, for example, Arthur Murray was ready to believe that
Lloyd George had spent the pre-election weeks conspiring to
depose Baldwin and become Foreign Secretary in a Horne
government.[135] For Lloyd George such manoeuvres may still have
seemed part of practical politics, but to most Conservatives they
did not. Leading the Conservative party were men who wanted
little to do with coalitions and nothing whatever to do with Lloyd
George.

For a few months during 1924 it seemed that Conservatives might
still have some use for the Liberals if their own performance at
the next election were to be indifferent and the Liberals' respectable. Chamberlain still wanted to proselytize: he was angry with
Baldwin in July for not seeking to detach likely converts.[136] It
could be argued at the time that Conservatives who were anxious
to launch a last onslaught on the Liberals were being premature.
It was still possible to contemplate circumstances in which alliances might be required – perhaps 'some compact with the Tories
to prevent the two parties tumbling over each other for the benefit
of Labour' at the coming election, perhaps a personal arrangement
at the top such as 'Baldwin falling back on a man like Grey' for
the Foreign Office.[137] Admittedly the contingency seemed remote
even then. But it is interesting that during the counting of votes
at the 1924 election it was thought worth while to inform Baldwin
that 'some Liberal developments' ought to be considered; the
advice was withdrawn when, in view of what was clearly going
to be a massive majority, 'Liberal moderates c[ould] be of no
earthly interest to [him]'.[138] Numbers played a significant role in

Conservative thinking. It was these, rather than considerations of ideology or the temperaments of the political leaders which rendered the Liberals 'of no earthly interest'. Conservative interest in the Liberals could not be revived, therefore, until the approach of the next election. Some interest had been shown over the Liberals' stolidly constitutionalist stand during the General Strike (Younger even wanted a renewal of Guest's electoral arrangement of 1918),[139] and there had been pressure on the leadership to consider alliances with the Liberals at constituency level.[140] But such pressure found little success. The Conservative position was rigid: there could be no alliance so long as Lloyd George, 'a national disaster and calamity' was the head of it; all the issues on which Liberalism had once thriven were now dead and had left it 'a mercenary force, putting itself up for auction and buying itself in'; and even if it did manage to return to power, Liberalism had allowed itself to become so tainted with impossible schemes and stunt politics that it could not be expected to offer constructive policies.[141]

The only charity Liberals might hope to find would come from Liberal defectors like Churchill, Mond and Hilton Young. But only Churchill tried to help by forcing his colleagues to admit that a strategy about the Liberals was necessary.[142] His conversations with Lloyd George in 1929 came to nothing, but the way his mind was moving is shown by some reflections after the election:

I am deeply impressed with the critical character of the present situation. Eight million Tories, eight million Labour, five million Liberals. Where will these five millions go? If Gretton, Amery and C° have their way and run Protection, or if the anti-Liberal resentments of others have their way, there can only be one result – very likely final for our life-time, namely a Lib–Lab block in some form or another and a Conservative Right hopelessly excluded from power.[143]

His fellow defectors did not want to help because they had come over to Conservatism for different reasons. It was not the failure of Liberalism as a political machine which was uppermost in their minds in 1926 but the failure of Lloyd George accurately to represent those things which they took it to be essential that Liberalism should represent. They had swallowed a great deal but they could not swallow a land campaign which denied Liberal conventions which for them were axiomatic. In particular it carried the imprint of that Socialism which they believed it was the task of the authentic Liberal to eradicate.

III

The relationship between Liberalism and Labour/Socialism provides an important context against which the failure of Liberals to survive the three-party situation must be set. Considerations of space militate against treating the problem in any depth here: it has in any case been examined elsewhere.[144] Necessary to this study is simply an understanding of how Liberal and Labour politicians viewed one another, a question different in nature from that posed by the Liberal/Conservative dialogue because of the presence of doctrinal ingredients which expediency could not always neutralize. Bertrand Russell was surely right to see in Liberalism and Conservatism a certain community of action if not of dogma.[145] For all the oratorical froth, there was nothing intrinsically absurd in the idea of Grey becoming Baldwin's Foreign Secretary. Labour was somehow different. Its argument with Liberalism (private almost as much as public) claimed to take place not at the level of policy but at a deeper one of creed and doctrine. 'Between the two', one supporter of Lloyd George wrote in 1921, 'there can honestly be no truce, for their differences are fundamental.'[146] Consequently the opportunity for liaison between Liberals and Labour was one hard for politicians to engineer. There were too many difficulties in the way.

Some elements in this complicated relationship can be observed at once. In so far as attempts were made to establish a working partnership in the parliamentary context, the crucial period was that between the accession of the Labour government in January 1924 and the General Strike of May 1926. Before 1924 Liberals were unclear in their own minds what Labour wanted and what character of threat it represented. After 1926 they knew some of the answers but had found them out too late. It ought to be added that whether one is examining Liberal/Labour relations in 1919 or 1924 or 1929 the feature most prominent and intractable in the situation is the role of Lloyd George.

At least two sections of Liberalism came out of the war with hopes that closer relations might be established with Labour. Both of them tended to be labelled 'radical', though in fact they

concerned themselves with different areas of policy. One obvious
source of radicalism was that which based its critique of Liberal
politics on tendentious views about international relations in
general and Grey's pre-war diplomacy in particular. It was a
radicalism typified by Arthur Ponsonby and C. P. Trevelyan in
the House of Commons and by intellectuals like Lowes Dickinson
outside. There were Liberals who believed even during the war
that 'the mantle of C[ampbell] B[annerman]' had now fallen to
men of the Ponsonby stamp and that around their ideals a new
party should be founded.[147] Secondly, there was a radicalism
symbolized by the 'Manchester School' which achieved some
importance after the war in connexion with industrial policy. Its
defining characteristics, in contradistinction to its forebear, was
a desire for increased state responsibility in the life of the community (to the point of nationalization in limited areas), control
of the land market and, possibly, co-operation with Labour in
parliament.[148] An embodiment of this school was E. D. Simon,
who toyed with the idea of joining the Labour party after the war
but thought he might be embarrassed by his £20,000-a-year salary
from the Simon Engineering Group.[149]

Open diplomacy and industrial democracy were two ideal cate-
gories in which Liberal sympathy for Labour policy could usually
be found after 1918 under the impetus of journalists like Massingham, who made it his central message of the later war years
that 'the Radical Left and the Labour mass must come together
and work out the salvation of progressive England',[150] and the
goading of radical-minded politicians anxious to come to terms
with a newly powerful parliamentary party. From the latter,
contemporaries tended to confuse rhetorical gestures with expressions of conviction that the evidence did not warrant. The most
effective 'radical' Liberals in parliament were Pringle and Hogge;
and they were believed by members of other parties to be pressing
for nationalization, a capital levy and an alliance with Labour.[151]
Yet the predominant partner, Pringle, had established a strong
reputation during the war as an Asquithian Liberal. It was common
knowledge that he was Asquith's man; it was lobby gossip that
he was Mrs Asquith's man, that she was 'running and encouraging
him'.[152] After the war, moreover, his career demonstrated clearly
that he regarded himself still as an Asquithian even if he did want
to move closer to Labour. The radical press exaggerated this latter

stance – disastrously so in the case of the Rusholme by-election in October 1919. Pringle came bottom of the poll there, and a contemporary observer blamed 'Scott of the Guardian' for his 'recommendation of poor Pringle to the electors as an excellent candidate in that "in Nine Tenths of his programme he was in agreement with the Labour people"'.[153] It is an effective warning against reading too much 'radicalism' into politicians doing their best to survive.

Radicals whose Labour sympathies were more pronounced than Pringle's were not as influential as they might have been, since the bulk of them had already gone over, or were about to go over, to the Labour party by 1919. Most of the impressive names – the Buxtons, E. G. Hemmerde, Hobson, E. T. John, Joseph King, Lees-Smith, Chiozza Money, Outhwaite, Ponsonby and Trevelyan – were now to be counted among the ranks of the Labour party or as sympathetic to it.[154] Those who stayed within Liberalism, however, enjoyed little leverage in the party as a whole. The industrial policy developed by the Manchester wing in 1919 did not find recognizable form in official party policy until the Yellow Book of 1928. Meanwhile their proposals for the nationalization of mines and railways frightened some Liberals into forming a 'Liberal Anti-Nationalization Committee' in 1920 under the chairmanship of the aged Frederic Harrison.[155] The latter part of the decade was admittedly kinder to the radicals, but in the early years they could hardly claim to speak for Liberalism as a whole.

Nor, of course, could anyone else. The internal feud implied that the two factions would use Labour as a counter in their own game, especially the Asquithians, for whom the problem of what to do about Labour came a very poor second to that of deciding what to do about Lloyd George. The coalition was for them the focus of the rhetorical attack until 1922: everything else would fall into place once that venal administration was removed. It was a myopic way in which to observe politics in those years; and what was more myopic was the belief that the Labour party ought to view politics in the same way. Thus Elibank thought in 1919 that Asquith would be able to rally 'sane' Labour and control the Bolshevik threat because he alone had never soiled himself with the 'unclean thing'.[156] Of course Labour had no need to worry about whether he had or not: what Asquith thought about anything after 1918 need not trouble them. Electorally it was Labour who now had the whip hand. It had been Asquith, not Labour, who had wanted an electoral pact at the election. It had been Labour, not Asquith, who had refused it.[157] There may have been moments when members of the Labour leadership envisaged a resurgence of Asquithian Liberalism,[158] but for the most part the Labour view was that of Maxton: the Liberal party was 'a mere political, scheming, expediency party', caring only about keeping afloat.[159]

Asquithians had no clear view of the currents around them. For some the threat from Labour was all about revolution and 'the tide of the "workers", headed by Smillie'.[160] Not everyone would have expressed the situation in this way, but there was a pervasive anxiety that all politics was 'being put on the footing of class'[161] and the national debate resolving itself into only two opinions – those in favour of capitalism and those against it. On the same morning that Liberals read in their *Times* about Lord Robert Cecil's faith in the non-revolutionary character of England, they would see on another page the programme of the 'Clyde Workers' Soviet Committee' whose demands included the removal of parliament, a six-hour day for a £7 minimum wage, total expropriation of property and a tribunal to try political crimes.[162] The response which such agitation provoked could be one of mild condescension with a language about 'well meaning, anxious men...with very little knowledge of the compass or the stars'; it could be one which stimulated comparisons of a civilized past when society was ordered and a barbaric present when 'everyone love[d] money ...and the scum [were] rich'.[163] Asquith himself saw that the constitutional parties were operating a bluff when he remarked to Fisher that Labour would one day find out that it had the power to do as it liked.[164] But this was the private argument. In public the Asquithians were content during the life of the coalition to let Lloyd George make the running in evolving an anti-Labour position. They would merely trip him up when the opportunity occurred.[165]

The imagery which Lloyd George used in confronting Labour was one designed to portray the Soviet Revolution, British communism and the parliamentary Labour party as different faces of the same un-English conspiracy. This was an effective location for the wicket because it silhouetted Labour as the enemy of sane men and suggested that the Asquithians, whose attempts to strike up an arrangement with Labour had been widely reported, had a 'muddled sympathy with Communism'[166] and no scruple about placing party above country. It could also be used as a foil against Liberal pieties:

The independent Liberals had attempted to get up a programme. In order to distinguish between themselves and the Coalition Liberals they were trying to pick up little tags of Socialist programmes and to stitch them together in order to make some sort of banner which they could follow. They won't get Liberalism to follow the rags of Socialism.[167]

For Lloyd George, as for Asquith, the language in which the Labour threat ought to be announced was conditioned by the wider context of Liberal politics.

Of course Lloyd George could be compelled by circumstance or pressure to say that the enemy was not Labour but Bolshevism, but he made sure that he conflated the two when he paraded revolution before the public as an imminent danger. 'He has proclaimed the class war', Labour propaganda asserted, 'and has definitely and irretrievably ranged himself on the wrong side.'[168] If it is easy to understand Lloyd George's rhetoric, however, it is far more difficult to judge how much of it he believed. Was 'the difference between bondage and freedom, Egypt and Canaan'[169] a distinction he genuinely had in mind when he observed the Labour party? Or did its public announcement merely fulfil a situational requirement?

There is plenty of evidence to suggest that Lloyd George took the threat of revolution seriously in private. Letters to his wife in 1919, conversations with Riddell and discussions reported by Tom Jones all indicate that Lloyd George was preoccupied with social instability and the Bolshevik challenge.[170] He wrote to Law in 1920 about '[t]he grave struggle which [was] to come' and to Balfour about threats to 'the whole order of society'.[171] Yet evidence of this nature can be misleading. The correspondence with Law and Balfour has to be placed in the context of Lloyd George's angling for a centre-party agreement: the point of the letters is to announce a need to close ranks. The other evidence is stronger but again there are difficulties. If Tom Jones heard Lloyd George expatiate on the dangers of revolution in 1919 he heard him in 1920 doing 'a lot of unsuspected leg-pulling as he d[id] not believe in the imminence of the revolution'.[172] If Lloyd George had scare-mongers like Horne in Paris and Kerr at home to contend with,[173] he also had Jones to reassure him about the texture of English soil. His mood probably reflected what the evidence itself reflects – a continuing tension between what he personally believed and what circumstance demanded that he should appear to believe. Either way there could be no possibility of persuading Labour that he was still a radical intent on reform.

Subsiding fears of revolution, Black Friday in 1921 and the increased Labour poll at the election of 1922 helped to convince Liberals that the Labour threat should be seen as an electoral one. During 1923 the Liberals were mostly concerned with their internal affairs while Labour looked on in the hope, perhaps, that an attempted reunion would push those who most hated Lloyd George into their own camp.[174] Reunion did not come. Lloyd George began instead to turn his mind to the possibility of an alliance with MacDonald. It is hard to believe that Harold Spender's letter to MacDonald in December 1923, inviting such an alliance, was not inspired from above. MacDonald was not interested and wrote a prissy reply couched in terms of 'principle', 'the people' and 'not lik[ing] parties or leaders to be dishonest'.[175] If Lloyd George thought that by putting Labour into power he would earn the gratitude of Labour politicians, he was to learn his lesson very quickly. From the outset the Labour leadership resented a situation in which Liberals expected to make the new government 'powerless for serious mischief'.[176] They resented Liberal expectation that legislation would appear through joint consultation with the Liberals.[177] They were determined that the one Liberal hope for the future, proportional representation, should in no circumstances be granted.[178] The atmosphere between the two parties was black with recrimination – against Liberals for their 'small mindedness of Little Bethel, with none of its fervour', against Labour for its 'arrogant blindness' and readiness to 'crucify Christian morality in politics'. '[P]uny Pharisees' was one Labour term of abuse for Liberals: 'Pharisees of Pharisees' was one Liberal opinion of Labour.[179] In such an atmosphere no objective assessment was likely. 'Why associate with your bitterest enemies?' one correspondent asked Maclean.[180]

Lloyd George nevertheless had his reasons for wanting to move closer to Labour. Already he had begun to see that his future looked brighter on the Left than with Conservatism now that the anti-coalitionists were in control. It has been shown here that he was determined in 1924 to take over the Liberal party but only to use it as a counter in a wider game. Hilton Young reflected uneasily about this determination in the second month of the Labour government. 'L.G. is throwing his whole weight into the left wing and the support of Labour', he wrote. 'But what possible prospects has the poor old L[iberal] P[arty] in such a course?'[181] Lloyd George knew that its prospects were slim, especially when faced with a Labour party which 'ha[d] a machine fitted for the times', was 'forging ahead in every part of the country' and deploying 'consummate' propaganda.[182] By June he was spending weekends with Snowden.[183] Indeed his difficulties lay not with Labour but with his own party which, though it wanted to keep Labour in office so as to avoid another ruinous election,[184] had no desire to cement any permanent alliance. The bulk of Liberals continued to harass MacDonald in parliament, and by October he was sick of it, as he told Gilbert Murray:

I would warn you . . . that all hope of co-operation with the Liberal Party, as a Party, has now been driven out of my mind. I declined for a long time to put that aside absolutely as an impossibility; but the tone of the Liberal press . . . and the leadership of the House of Commons, have convinced me finally that the only kind of co-operation which is possible is the co-operation of men and women who come over and join us.[185]

That Liberals were responsible for getting rid of the Labour government did little to mitigate the fact that it had been they who had put them in. And of course Conservative propaganda made full play of Liberal complicity in the Labour fiasco. 'WHEN YOU VOTED LIBERAL', one broadside began, '[d]id you forsee that the Liberal Party would regularly support the Socialist Government in the House of Commons?'[186] Never had the millwheel image been more apposite. Liberals had tried to appear moderate so as not to lose their progressive vote to Labour; but at the same time they had had to side-step the charge of following the Socialists: 'if the electors want[ed] that, they prefer[red] to take it at first hand from the Socialist Party',[187] and the bulk of Liberal electors did not want that anyway. Only a few individuals – Lloyd George among the leadership, Wedgwood Benn and Kenworthy among the rank and file – could countenance alliance with the Left. The latter pair joined the Labour party in 1926/27. There has been cause to note that Lloyd George may have considered doing the same before Asquith threw down his challenge after the General Strike.

Shared defeat at the polls helped to impose a sense of common predicament on the two parties after 1924, and the animosities soon began to fade. There arose conditions in which 'intellectual co-operation' was thought desirable and which produced by the end of 1925 actual co-operation in the day-to-day business of the Commons with the parties 'working...debating...and standing up for each other'.[188] Wedgwood Benn believed that comradeship was more pronounced at the rank-and-file level than among the leaders; but he also noted in his diary that MacDonald made some sort of offer to the Liberals.[189] Negotiation seems also to have taken place in February 1926 though both sides denied that it had.[190] It was even suggested by one Labour M.P. that Labour Members had been asked to give their views about the possibility of Lloyd George joining them. Again there were wounded denials from both sides.[191] Journalists were right to point out that much of this speculation was founded on nothing more substantial than gossip, but Margot Asquith was equally right that 'Labour wd. be done for if their discontents knew' about such negotiations and that Labour had as much reason to cover up as Lloyd George.[192] Beyond that judgement the material does not permit the historian to go.

What is quite clear is that Liberal fears and hopes about Lloyd George's ultimate aims did much to provoke the batch of defections at that time to the Labour and Conservative parties. Hilton Young, Mond, Inchcape and Kilbracken turned to Conservatism because the Liberal party did not take a firm enough stance against 'sedition, strife and the destruction of a country', because its land programme embraced 'the first article of the Socialist faith' and because it aligned itself with what was the 'negation of Liberalism as Mr. Gladstone understood it'.[193] Wedgwood Benn and Kenworthy, on the other hand, saw not enough of the social progress in party policy which they took to be central to Liberalism. Asquith was happy to face both sets of treachery with the same expression. 'Liberalism must not be content with being an antithesis', he wrote to Hilton Young after his defection, 'it must also provide an antidote.'[194] The letter which Benn received was strikingly similar in its dwelling on principle and righteousness: 'I remember well the emphasis which you laid in your speeches upon the clear-cut distinction between the root *principles* of Liberal and Labour policy. That distinction appears to me to be as real and indelible now as it seemed to you then.'[195]

What else could Liberals say in 1927? All that remained unsullied through the sordid squabbles of the decade thus far was some conception of 'principle'. It may not have been a strong rallying cry for the electorate, but it was all that Liberals of the old sort had to offer. '[C]ompeting with attractive programmes' was a form of electioneering for which Liberals were ill-equipped: they would always be 'overbid by the Socialists'.[196] Somehow Liberals needed to escape from the millstone milieu and represent their position as being somewhere else:

[W]hat Liberals need is the imagination to convince Labour that there is a way out for it from the prison disclosed to them by Karl Marx, Lenin and others . . . If [they] are to capture the Labour mind, it will be because they offer an alternative to that Socialist theory which is disclosing its illusory nature more and more to the thinking working man.[197]

At this level Liberals could not afford to admit defeat: here at least the triangular image of party politics had to be shown to be valid. Liberals themselves believed that they represented principles and ideals which were unique and could not be surrendered. It is important to try to illustrate the character of these principles, for they often provided the framework in which decisions were taken about what could and could not be allowed to Liberal politicians. It is also important to know the extent to which they inhabited the minds of the politicians themselves.

IV

The doctrinal dimension of Liberalism is discernible on two levels. In the first place there was a notion of 'policy', really a cumulative label for a number of individual approaches to limited problems such as foreign relations, industrial structure, land ownership, taxation and so on. Secondly, there was a more fundamental world-view from which Liberals demanded that policy be deduced. One aspect of the intellectual history of Liberalism in the 1920s concerns the growing tensions between these two levels under the impact of a changing society and, more particularly, Lloyd George's willingness to push the party in directions it did

not want to go. Contemporary rhetoricians tended in practice to
conflate policy and cosmology into a single statement about the
essence of 'Liberalism' as a 'permanent human principle' based
on 'a high view of the human race'.[198] It was the uniqueness of
the height that was supposed to lend to Liberalism its special
genius and confirm its character as something better than 'a middle
course between Conservatism and Socialism'. It was a 'positive
and progressive creed, equally distinct from both'.[199] If the thrust
of the message was changing, this was only because there was
'shaping...a definite and distinct Liberal philosophy of politics,
a continuation of the old doctrine yet a development and
modification of it, fitted to the changed conditions of the modern
world'.[200] So ran the public argument. An examination of this
argument of continuing development shows it to be at best a gross
over-simplification and at worst a lie. But if policy and principle
were used by politicians as one kind of weapon in their armoury,
it was also the case that Liberal principle was grasped with a
tenacity which politicians could not afford to ignore.

The most consistent, because least significant, part of Liberal
policy was that directed at foreign affairs. Statements about this
area of policy could be simply avowals of support for the League
of Nations, which was unobjectionable to almost everyone, or
professions of faith ('We proclaim our pride and belief in the
commonwealth of free peoples which constitute the British
Empire')[201] or pleas for peace. The League was a universal in-
gredient in moderate views of how to change the world. It was
the 'shining jewel' which the war had left behind and on which
the 'best hopes of the world' were centred; it was 'the pivot of
[Liberal] foreign policy'.[202] Behind this view lay a desire to say
something not only inspiring but different. Conservatives could
have little success in trying to present themselves as inter-
nationalists while Labour suffered from the Left's constant asser-
tion that the League was an imperialist instrument. Even the
Labour moderates were 'not to be relied upon', according to
Gilbert Murray, and as late as 1927 Noel-Baker was complaining
that Labour was still hostile to the League of Nations Union.[203]
As well as being distinctive, the Liberal stand on the League also
reflected Gladstonian preconceptions of international relations as
the intercourse of moral personalities which were potentially
conformable to moral law. One of Gladstone's sons saw the

League in 1920 as the only cause in contemporary politics which could inspire devotion.[204]

But although foreign policy was of compelling importance to certain sections of Liberal society, notably to the intelligentsia, it represented at the level of high politics a category of rhetoric which needed to be filled. Not everyone managed the filling as painlessly as Lloyd George who could describe the League as 'deceptive and dangerous' on Saturday and give a speech about 'a great beginning of a great idea' on the following Wednesday.[205] Yet the Asquithians were less committed than they liked to appear. Asquith himself had greeted the formation of the League with great caution and argued against its having any firm constitution, against its having the function of a court and against its doing anything except wield its 'authority' against aggressors.[206] Grey, it is true, was committed to the League; but his Foreign Office days left him with a persistent Francophilia which he defended as necessary to the working of the League but which caused his colleagues much embarrassment.[207] Morley remembered things which even Grey had forgotten: he was completely against the League and saw it as a gratuitous abandonment of British power.[208] Asquith declared himself as much a 'bag-and-baggage man' as Gladstone had been,[209] but in so far as he spoke about foreign affairs at all he did so in the familiar language of 'authority', 'confidence' and the national 'word'.[210]

One area of policy occupied the middle ground between internal and external affairs and also exemplified the preoccupation after the war with issues and debates from before it. Home Rule for Ireland had been a staple of Liberal politics in what was already being seen as a golden age before 1914. A familiar stance was easy for Asquithians to adopt when Lloyd George decided to crush rebellion with the Black and Tans. The country which in 1916 had been seen as 'the grave of HHA Liberalism'[211] now offered for a time platform material in which Liberals were well versed. Lloyd George had insisted, 'in spite of the warnings from Mr. Asquith and others',[212] on trying to force conscription on Ireland. He had sent British troops there to settle internal problems, despite Asquithian petitions to the contrary.[213] At every turn through the degenerating situation of 1920/21 Asquithian propaganda seemed to be vindicated. Coalition Liberals like Fisher and Harold Spender were not insensitive to Lloyd George's illiberalism over

Ireland.[214] Their former colleagues were publicly outraged, especially the rank and file whose strictures were as much part of private correspondence as public pose during years in which Lloyd George 'brought...disgrace to the English name' and allowed the government to 'stagger down the easy slope of logical militarism into the morass of German rule in Belgium'.[215] And if the Asquithians had moved little since 1914 on Irish policy, Rosebery had moved not at all since 1905: he believed any negotiations with 'rebels and assassins' to be degrading.[216]

'Ireland' did not last long, however. By 1922 it was allowed to recede somewhat in order not to give undue publicity to Lloyd George's 'solution' of the problem. Another catchcry, equally ancient and revered, was that of free trade; and unlike Ireland this was to prove of great relevance to the central issues of political debate throughout the decade in face of Conservative attempts to impose protection on British industry. Free trade could be argued to be one facet of Liberal external policy, an application of Wilsonian ideals to international trade and therefore of importance to a sound foreign policy in its role as 'Handmaiden of Peace, and the most powerful auxiliary of the League of Nations'.[217] It could also be depicted as a cleansing agent because of the free and open competition which it was supposed to stimulate, whereas its opposite might create situations in which illegitimate pressure could be exercised on politicians to 'protect' certain areas of the economy.[218] But both of these justifications paled before the simple fact that free trade was an engrained canon of Liberal dogma. Outsiders often failed to understand this. Lloyd George, it is significant, did not understand it: it was a part of that hide-bound mentality he most despised.[219] For Philip Kerr it was a 'practical' problem.[220] For Tom Clarke it was a 'business matter'.[221]

Lloyd Georgian Liberals could not be relied upon to feel this way, however. As with Home Rule, the 'lure of old battlegrounds and rallying cries'[222] was still strong. This was not obvious to the political public because Asquithians had control of the machine and directed its propaganda against the Coalition Liberals to indict them for placing on the statute book the Dyes Act of 1920 and, more seriously, the Safeguarding of Industries Act of 1921.[223] In fact both these measures had also disturbed the minds of a number of Coalition Liberals. The Dyes Bill threatened to provoke a revolt

at one stage, and on the Safeguarding Bill McCurdy told Lloyd
George that opposition from his own party had been 'very difficult
to overcome'.[224] Nor was such opposition restricted to backbench
opinion, for the Cabinet had also had a struggle with the Coalition
Liberal ministers.[225] The opposition was even prepared to act on
its convictions in the division lobby; a motion from Wedgwood
Benn to repeal the Safeguarding Act in 1922 drew sixteen Coalition
Liberals into the same lobby as the Asquithians.[226]

The commitment of the latter group to the policy of free trade
arose out of fundamental conviction – the evidence suggests
overwhelmingly that this was the case. Private letters testify to
the 'refreshing' effects of 'the pure milk of Free Trade' on 'jaded
and spoiled Coalition palate[s]' and to a genuine fear of protection
as a 'great Serbonian bog'.[227] Naturally there were politicians on
the Asquithian side who were prepared to play protection by ear,
make a 'beau geste' in public 'as a matter of form'[228] and then
do what seemed best; but in general it is accurate to say that
Asquithians saw an indissoluble link between being a Liberal and
being a free trader. In 1919 Elibank even wanted the Liberals to
become a Free Trade Parliamentary Party and make the issue
paramount ('Let the dividing line in future be TARIFF').[229] When
Grigg tried to convince his Oldham constituency party that Imperial Preference deserved their support, he ran immediately into
the dogged opposition of those whose world, like Rosebery's,
'ha[d] not changed since 1905'.[230] To some Liberals the very
suggestion needed to be treated as an insult to political integrity:

Dear Grigg,
  I am in receipt of your memorandum on Imperial Preference but I think
it must have been sent to me in error. I happen to be a Liberal.
                                    Yours faithfully,
                                        G. F. Darbyshire[231]

There were some strings, plainly, which Liberals could not allow
to be untuned.

Although the tariff issue lost some of its bite after the failure
of Baldwin's campaign in 1923, Liberals continued with their
propaganda, since the result of the election seemed to suggest that
the electorate was impressed by the free trade argument. A
fifteen-page pamphlet appeared in 1925 and was later reprinted,
with a few amendments.[232] The language was dispassionate
and intended to create an atmosphere of logic. Free trade was

'natural'; it was 'democratic'; it provided the most employment; it was not a trick; it was 'the ordinary common sense way in which civilised people carr[ied] on most of their business'. Conversely protection was 'a form of stupidity' which could not 'live for an hour in the clear light of common sense'. More significant than such claims was the link (in the private mind) which free trade offered with a time when Liberalism was as great as the country that had nourished it. No other party could claim that attachment. Take but free trade away, Inchcape said, and there would be nothing to choose between Conservatism and Liberalism.[233] But Inchcape was as wrong as Lloyd George in his belief that it *could* be taken away: as late as 1929 one section of Liberalism was still insisting that the prosecution of the free trade case must be the 'chief activity' of Liberals.[234] So long as this idea was rooted in the Liberal mind, most politicians must have been aware that any electoral arrangement with the Conservatives would be hard to sustain.

There were, of course, other policies which would stand in the way of that rapprochement also, but these belonged to the radical period after 1924 when Lloyd George had all but given up the idea of another coalition in the immediate future. In so far as these policies were aimed at other parties they were aimed at the Labour party. However there were many doctrinal objections to this connexion as well as personal and electoral ones. Though Liberal foreign policy, for example, might be made consonant with Labour demands, the way in which Liberals wanted to approach industrial policy would be hard to align with Labour's plans. The fundamental point of disagreement was the simple one that Liberalism took its central task to be the better development of capitalism and never its overthrow. Liberals did not apologize for the capitalist system; they did not merely tolerate its existence. They gloried in it – provided that it was as wholesome as man was able to make it. 'The magic of private property, the rivalry of business, the invigorating exertion required by fair and free competition, the love of independence' were qualities of life which a correctly structured capitalism was capable of supporting.[235] There were undeniable problems about the present working of the system – monopoly, exploitation and so on – but the government ought to be able to combat these by judicious legislation. Lloyd George spoke for Liberals for once when he pledged himself to see no worker starve 'so long as there was a crust in the national cupboard '.[236]

Suppose the national cupboard was bare, however? Would Lloyd George then rob the rich of their private crusts and distribute them to the workers? Here was the real test and Labour knew full well that Lloyd George and all Liberals would fail it. Liberals wanted to be generous to the lower classes but it was a regrettable fact of economic life that rules existed, 'damnable but inexorable economic laws', 'as unalterable as thunderstorms, or tidal waves, or the multiplication table ',[237] which placed ambition and possibility in perpetual tension. 'I don't want to be the one to down the working man', Lloyd George said in 1920, '... but of course we must have more output.'[238] Without production there would be nothing to share out; and production would not be possible unless individual enterprise was given full rein and the selfishness of human nature harnessed to the cause of society at large.[239] Not that stale economic thinking need necessarily be adhered to (Lloyd George had as much contempt as anyone for what he called 'theological banking principles '),[240] but it was an inalienable point of the Liberal approach to government that the individual must be venerated for himself, 'the man as a man and the woman as a woman, as individuals, not as mathematical atoms in a mighty State molecule'.[241] Capitalism was adventurous and colourful, Socialism uniform and grey. When people were compelled to work for the state, a 'curious paralysing influence' came over them and reduced them to 'a machine-made product and to a dead level of mediocrity'.[242] Socialism put human nature in a straight jacket.[243]

Some Liberal policies in the latter half of the decade were nevertheless seen as part of an insidious attempt to work towards Socialism by the back door, in particular through the so-called Green and Yellow Books with their proposals for the land and the reorganization of industry. There was little evidence to support these fears; indeed the only part of Liberal policy which could realistically be seen in any sense to be Socialistic was the provision in the land programme to transfer control over agricultural land to county committees. For the rest, all they were intended to do was to shore up the potential of capitalism. The industrial inquiry of 1927/28 came to conclusions which consorted well with those of the National Liberal Federation's industrial policy committee seven years before, and these were hardly revolutionary. Liberalism did not desire the abolition of privately owned capital, the report had said; nor did it wish such capital to be acquired by a state 'which in such circumstances would be bound to be tyrannous, probably often corrupt, and generally inefficient'. Capital must instead be spread among all citizens 'so as to encourage each to fresh enterprise by the knowledge that he will reap where he has sown'.[244] Nothing in *Britain's Industrial Future* went beyond this credo. Accusations of abandoning the individualist ethic were neatly side-stepped by calling the discussion obsolete. Ideology was deemed dangerous. All that Liberals need do was to work for a better world within the capitalist framework. '[T]here is no question of principle at stake', ran the report, 'but one of degree, of expediency, of method.'[245]

Discussion of the proposed methods is outside the scope of this study. What is important here is to note that they were based on the same *naïveté* of message which Liberals offered in their foreign policy. There was a classless rhetoric presenting a fair deal for all in a new society which was going to be revitalized by a spirit of co-operation which was at present lacking. 'Spirit' strikes up again and again out of the contemporary material: 'creating the League of Nations' spirit in industry';[246] 'hope for quiet and real friendliness in industry';[247] 'a real spirit of friendly co-operation';[248] '[a] new spirit...between masters and men'.[249] In the short term this spirit might be conjured up by simple exhortation. If it was true that trade unions were potential tyrants and that the working classes sometimes refused to work, they would surely be receptive to a plea 'in this supreme moment of national need [to] co-operate with other organized elements of the community in an attempt to save the Commonwealth'.[250] And if exhortation were to fail in the short term, there was hope for education over a longer one. Workers would learn that the 'terrible weight upon the back of Labour is only a temporary phenomenon, that will cease when Capital has learnt...that it is not wise or profitable to be selfish'.[251] Gradually there would appear an eventual 'formulation of principles' and a 'growing recognition of common interests'.[252] The spirit, that is to say, would emerge.

Such doctrine came closer to the ethic of the Mond–Turner conversations than to any part of the Labour industrial programme. In all the areas of policy in which Labour had a large stake, Liberals fell short of Labour ambitions – whatever their propaganda might say to the contrary. They had a fear of 'vast arm[ies] of bureaucrats'[253] invading the private sphere; as late as 1927 one finds Philip Kerr writing to the secretary of the Industrial Inquiry to remind him that its role should be 'to increase the amount available for every individual rather than to increase the amount which is done for the underpaid individual by a benevolent bureaucracy'.[254] Apart from the Keynesian projects of the late 1920s, Liberal economic policy was based on a determination to avoid 'anything outrageously unorthodox'[255] and to remember sound lessons from the past. Peace, Retrenchment and Reform was a new slogan to many after the war but though it may have been 'pure Gladstonianism', it was also 'prove[n]' and was held, in public and private, 'to contain the germ of success'.[256] Sidney Webb was right to observe that when Liberals were driven into a corner they could be made to concede that they did not want to tax the rich in order to lighten the burden on the masses ('yet their candidates often sa[id] so').[257] Asquith was equally right to observe that Liberalism and Socialism were, in principle, different. What Liberals wanted was an organic society, free from class bitterness and economic exploitation, in which employers were charitable and workers reasonable so that capitalism could be resuscitated and British society made wholesome.

In at least one sense, then, the Liberal attempt to carve out a distinctive position for itself in the three-party situation could be said to have succeeded. It was not true that Liberalism was held together by nothing more than 'the traditional loyalty of unreflecting adherents', nor that Liberals 'ha[d] nothing to think about'.[258] If there were those on the Left who saw in its anti-statist mentality the seed of the downfall of Liberalism,[259] there were also those who saw 'developing a body of doctrine to take the place of the obsolete Asquithian creed'.[260] In its public insistence that Conservatism constituted a 'drag on progress' and that Socialism was 'responsible for the deplorable increase in class hatred', Liberalism established rhetorically a recognizable role. The political effectiveness of such a position would depend, however, on the extent to which it could be made to sound plausible to the electorate. It was of little value Liberals convincing themselves that what they had to say was unique: they had also to convince others.

Their failure to do so can best be explained by placing it in two contexts – the inability of Liberals to conceal the fact that their new language was the product of political expediency and their inability, as the decade progressed, to conceal it from the people who most needed to be convinced, the Liberals themselves.

Whatever Liberals said or did the millstone image seemed to prevail. In 1925 the 'new' Liberalism (the third in forty years) was beginning to be announced, yet MacCallum Scott had no reason to feel that his decision to join the Labour party may have been premature. He was not impressed by the new oratory:

The Liberal Party has fallen between two stools. It has made the fatal mistake of trying to be a centre party. It has lost all initiative. It can define its position only by offering a negative to the policy put forward by other parties. It is against the Tory policy of Protection and it is against the Labour policy of Socialism. It represents itself as standing between two extremes of reaction on the one side and of revolution on the other side, and it appeals to all the timid people who are afraid of a move in any direction.[261]

It was untrue, but it seemed to be true. It seemed true to Conservatives who could see in Liberalism nothing more than an ability to 'queer the pitch'. ('What else can they do?' Churchill was to ask.)[262] What was worse was that there came a time when the Liberals began themselves to accept the millstones as a fact of life. It was this mentality which lay behind the appeal of the Liberal Council, it was also this which lay behind some of the policy statements of the Lloyd Georgian wing. In 1922 its propaganda had pointed, not to Maclean's straight road, but to 'a *via media* which liberal-minded men and women...anxiously desire[d] to pursue'. And in 1926, when Kerr was trying to work out a distinctively Liberal way of tackling post-war problems, he came up with 'a proposal for a middle way such as the Liberals ought to be able to make their own'.[263]

There seems no reason in retrospect why Liberalism need have been crushed between Conservatism and Socialism. No ineluctable mechanics operated. If the Conservatives had not found Baldwin, if the Liberals could have lost Lloyd George . . .: it is easy to invent conditions which could have altered the picture considerably. Yet all the characteristics which, log-jammed together, meant 'Liberalism' to Churchill's five million voters would always make so many roads impassable. The problem was too much Liberalism preached over too long a period to men with too much to remember. That is not to say that the content of the Liberal mind was stupid, or that it was incapable of being made relevant, or that it was innocent about a supposedly imminent class struggle. But it was there. Liberal politicians either shared it or knew that other important people did. This is why a view of high politics which takes no account of doctrine ignores a crucial element in the complex. The Liberal mind was important because through its imperatives it set out horizons of tolerance within which Liberal politicians knew they would have to do their politicking. In the representation of that mind to the political world, moreover, some Liberals were plainly more equal than others.

5. The Liberal intelligentsia

In this atmosphere great seed could be sown by the spiritual and intellectual leaders...
> Smuts to Murray (copy), 7 December 1917, Murray MSS, Box 47.

Asquith appeals only to intellectuals, a very small party in this blessed nation.
> Esher to L.B., 25 June 1923, *Journals and Letters*, IV, 289.

This weekend I have *14* professors at Churt.
> Lloyd George to Dame Margaret Lloyd George, 22 September 1926, in K. O. Morgan (ed.), *Lloyd George Family Letters*, 207.

I

The student of twentieth-century Liberalism must take as his focus the activities and aspirations of the Liberal party, since the selection of any other perspective would remove from the raw material such bones as it possesses. Yet if it is clear that the Liberal party stands at the centre of Liberalism it is clear also that the two phenomena are not co-extensive. Contemporary material presses very strongly on the historian the instinct that to examine the nature of Liberalism is to do more than to recount the doings of members of the Liberal party. It has already been seen here that Liberalism can be found in other sectors of the parliamentary scene, beyond the boundaries of the Liberal party. Similarly, there existed areas of Liberal 'society' which it is important to recognize when trying to frame an understanding of Liberal politics. One section of that society was of particular importance to politicians. High politics, after all, was conducted by an exclusive elite; it should be no surprise that its practitioners were most interested in the elite of Liberal society: the intellectuals, the journalists, the Churchmen. This chapter will therefore concern itself with the contours of the Liberal mind as it is revealed in these leaders of Liberal opinion.

Definition is immediately necessary in order to combat an implication that the Liberalism of the intelligentsia was of a different order from that of Liberal politicians. What is under consideration here is a social elite rather than a collection of intellectuals;[1] it must therefore be expected that a number of individuals under consideration will be members of the Liberal party and participate in party politics quite as much as those discussed in earlier chapters. The intention, that is to say, is not to identify a splinter-group within Liberalism but to study one area of its periphery. Behind such a study many questions can be seen to lie, but perhaps two of them are particularly searching. First there is the problem of assessing the character of the relationship which subsisted between the Liberal intelligentsia and the world of high politics. Secondly there is the more elusive problem connected with the continuing hold which Liberalism retained on the intelligentsia after 1914. At a time when the political fortunes of Liberalism were obviously waning, why was so much intellectual power still bound up with the Liberal tradition in British politics?

One thing is clear: intellectual regard for Liberalism was certainly not a response to Liberal regard for intellectuals. The politicians may have had their myths, traditions and sensitivities but they were (and conceived themselves to be) practical men looking for solutions to practical problems. There were reflective minds among them but the reflections took place within known horizons. 'Abstract intellectual argument is futile', observed the very reflective MacCallum Scott; 'it is only one of the factors which sway men's minds – and not the most important factor'.[2] People who followed the futile path were likely to be boring or downright irritating. Nor was the irritation confined to the sour-minded like Burns, though it might be predicted that he would despise 'learned asses' who had been granted opportunities denied to him, '[t]he riff raff of Eton, the scum of Harrow and the intellectual ?vapour men of Oxford and Cambridge'.[3] It is more surprising, for example, to hear Maclean recalling that a 'crowded audience of intelligentsia' at Oxford had given him 'the unmitigated pip'.[4] Anti-intellectualism can be found in the Liberal mind as frequently as it can be found in any other: the clever inspired no special regard.

Enough has been said about Liberals and the way they thought about themselves and their Liberalism to imply that any different conclusions would be out of place. Persons and principles were discussed in a language far removed from questions of brain-power though perhaps closer to those concerning culture and civilized behaviour. In the years of internal dissension after 1914 Liberals judged one another in accordance with certain ideas of 'character' which demanded 'straightness' and 'decency' as a premium, intelligence only as an option. There is no reason to believe that these notions dissipated when the attention of Liberals was turned elsewhere, to the universities or the Third Estate, not to mention the Fourth. It is a characteristic of axioms that they persist. Thus MacCallum Scott when toying with the idea of writing a short story: 'Idea of plot – to illustrate the ultimate superiority of instinct over intellect, of character over calculation, of honesty of soul over trickery'.[5] This classic Liberal position would be reinforced by the disputes following the split of 1916. During the 1920s, for example, a man like Keynes was an obvious target for this animus since his economic thought looked like a collection of tricks and dodges. When he threw in his hand with Lloyd George in 1928, Margot Asquith was ready with her confused but ultimate indictment. 'You'll smile at me', she wrote to him, 'but in the end character is better than intelligence – especially intelligence without *intellect*.'[6] In so far as they were involved in Liberal politics, intellectuals seem to have started at a disadvantage in their relations with Liberals. An explanation for their dogged allegiance to the Liberal cause has to be sought elsewhere.

Two themes may help to throw light on the problem. Association can be explained through strictly personal links and relationships; it would be useful to know how great a role these played in holding together the Liberal intelligentsia after 1914. A second element in cementing such relationships may be a body of political-cum-philosophical ideas to which both the Liberal party and the Liberal intelligentsia may have been committed. Whether either of these considerations would be effective would depend to a large extent on the character of the intelligentsia in 1914. It ought to be stressed at once that the elite under consideration here never amounted to an 'intellectual aristocracy' of the kind analysed by Lord Annan.[7] Not that connexion was unimportant in certain parts of the complex, but the connexion tended to be localized and to owe as much to college acquaintance or more distant university attachment than to familial bonds. It contained disparate groups and factions, united often in nothing more than that Liberalism was a better cause to support than Conservatism or Socialism.

Consider, for example, the Liberalism of the two old universities. Within the world of Oxford Liberalism there is plenty of evidence of 'connexion' as the backbone of Liberal continuity. Two generations of Liberals are spanned by the names of Bryce, Fisher and Gilbert Murray. Bryce had been tutored by Dicey, himself a Liberal until Home Rule appeared, and his early years were spent in the atmosphere of Old Mortality, Jowett and Green. His brother, John Annan Bryce, was Liberal M.P. for Inverness Burghs between 1906 and 1918: Bryce therefore had an immediate familial link with day-to-day Liberal politics. In passing to Fisher and Murray ('two of the best brains in England', according to Asquith)[8] one slides into a new generation, but the links are nevertheless there. Fisher wrote Bryce's Life. He married a daughter of Sir Courtney Ilbert, an acquaintance from Bryce's early years in Oxford; he thereby became enmeshed in the parliamentary world and acquired a distinguished relative in G. G. Coulton. When Fisher was run over by a lorry in 1940 it was Murray who contributed the valediction to the *Dictionary of National Biography*. He, Murray, was also Liberally connected. In 1889 he had married Lady Henrietta Howard, daughter of the ninth Earl of Carlisle, and thus made himself Geoffrey Howard's brother-in-law. One daughter of the marriage, Rosalind, was to marry Arnold Toynbee. And his connexion with the Hammonds involves the observer with another world, that of L. T. Hobhouse and the *Manchester Guardian*.[9]

Cambridge, however, presented a different picture. Here Liberalism thought itself vital and energetic: connexion mattered less, conviction more. Inevitably there were links with Liberals outside – between Keynes and London Liberalism, for example[10] – but the tone of Cambridge Liberalism was set, not by the pronouncements of a few individuals, but by a more general movement impelled by a view of 'progressive' economics and a contempt, in the wake of Moore and Russell, for the woolly Idealism which was still believed to shroud Oxford.[11] There can be no better illustration of a Cambridge 'advanced' Liberal's contempt for Idealist assumptions than Lowes Dickinson's pencilled notes in his personal copy of Green's *Lectures on the Principles of Political Obligation*. On the title page is scrawled:

This book isn't written at all. It's a long and tedious attempt to write, every idea being stated a great number of times, because it is never stated clearly: And this because it is not grasped clearly. The 'philosophy' is that of a tired Oxford whig, not of a good, solid English Liberalism.[12]

Those wanting to grow wings and leave the ground had no time for fudgery. Theirs was the Liberalism of the *Independent Review* and the ill-fated *Tribune*.

Pre-war Liberalism had been marked by Wells' 'multitudinousness' in its intellectual attachments as much as its parliamentary composition. Motivations seem to have ranged from passionate convictions about 'progress' or foreign policy to a subdued desire to support that party which civilized people ought to support. Just as it is possible to detect in working-class politics in this period a certain 'Labourism', 'which consisted in little more than the opinion that the Labour Party. . .was the party for working men to belong to',[13] so one might see in some Liberal intellectuals an equally undogmatic 'Liberal-ism' – a feeling that intelligent and sensitive people owed it to themselves and their country not to cleave to the party of reaction. There was no need to stretch conscience unduly. Now, as ten years before, intellectuals were likely to prefer the manner of Asquith and Balfour to that of extremists on either wing;[14] and although any precise evaluation is impossible it is likely that this kind of commitment was common among intellectuals. Progressivism and its enthusiasms took a heavy blow in 1910 with the publication of *The Party System* and *The Servile State*: the warnings contained therein and the spread of distributist ideas sapped the Liberalism which the younger intellectuals had nourished after the turn of the century. 'Intelligent men. . .had done with progressivism after 1910', Maurice Reckitt wrote in his memoirs; 'it was dead, even though it would not lie down, a full four years before August 1914.'[15] In this respect the coming of the war was not the first assault on intellectual Liberalism. Nevertheless its onset was crucial to the development of the Liberal intellectual connexion.

The effects of the war on Liberal politicians have been observed to have entailed a doctrinal narrowing and petrification in the face of something alien. To some extent the intelligentsia exhibited similar characteristics; there was a peeling off of those elements whose Liberalism had once been eccentric but tolerable in quieter times and the establishment of a firm Liberal orthodoxy in the light of which Liberals judged and expected judgement. Unlike the situation within the parliamentary party, however, the Liberalism of the intelligentsia did not stabilize itself until after the war. The political troubles of 1914 impinged less upon them than upon the politicians. The important question was not so much Asquith versus Lloyd George, nor even Free England versus Servile England, as what moral lessons were to be drawn from the war and Liberalism's part in causing it. It was a question which brought gloom to Common Rooms in Oxford and Cambridge. The public face was manfully maintained. '[N]owhere else', one patriotic Liberal wrote of the universities, 'is there greater cheerfulness or more examples of personal sacrifice for that cause which is at once the cause of the Army and of the nation.'[16] But the 'restless and miserable' condition of Fisher, the morbid musings of Bryce and Lowes Dickinson's view that Cambridge 'ha[d] something of the alleged repose of the tomb' gave propaganda the lie.[17]

Alienation brought its own lenses through which politics might be viewed, but party politics did not completely pass by the intellectuals. The very knowledge that Bryce was 'a staunch liberal of the old school' enables one almost to deduce that 'he thought the first coalition unnecessary and the second deleterious'.[18] The No Conscription Fellowship had its complement of Liberal intellectuals and it is no surprise to find among Keynes' papers a receipt for a £50 donation to the National Council Against Conscription.[19] When Asquith was ejected in 1916 Robertson Nicoll observed that 'men like' E. V. Lucas were 'quite confident that Asquith w[ould] be back at the head of affairs in three months'.[20] Or one might notice Herbert Fisher feeling, despite his decision to join Lloyd George's government, 'acute pain' at an 'act of treachery to the men one most admires in politics'.[21] No Liberal could isolate himself, even if he ate in his own rooms and refused to talk to anybody.[22] If newspapers were depressing or disgusting, that in itself was an issue which was giving rise to an attitude for private mulling or conversation on high table. A protest letter about the content and influence of Northcliffe's *Times*, for example, was signed by Gilbert Murray and Scott Holland and would have been signed by the Warden of All Souls had not the editor been a Fellow of his College.[23]

A distinction between politicians bothering their heads with narrow issues and intellectuals bothering theirs with wider ones would therefore be inadequate. The distinction lay rather in the perspective in which issues were seen. What is observed in intellectual Liberalism during the war is simply a way of looking at the world. For Bryce or Fisher or Murray or Lowes Dickinson to have affected one set of views about Liberalism and another, separate set of attitudes about the war would have been absurd. There is a ring of falsity in Toynbee's judgement of Murray and his *confrères* when he argues that '[f]or an aristocratic liberal in the United Kingdom, the virtual destruction of the great Liberal Party...was in some sense an even more portentous event than the war itself' and a 'still clearer signal of the approaching dissolution of the world in which Murray and his likeminded contemporaries in England had grown up'.[24] Liberal intellectuals did not possess the detachment which this comment implies. They observed the war not apart from their Liberalism but through it. In that perspective war came into focus as an international disease and one preventable by medicine. Social excesses (smoking, sex, bad language) could be resisted if one had a 'strong moral constitution',[25] and international excesses could be controlled by the same morality. Perhaps this was why Liberal intellectuals were so closely connected with the British attempt to forward the cause of a 'League of Nations'. Certainly the idea bulked large in their thinking between 1914 and 1918.

The dialogue between internal and external policy had caught the attention of intelligent Liberals during the intense debate over foreign policy in face of German rearmament before 1914, particularly under the stimulus of the Angell movement after 1912.[26] Angellism depended on a supposed incompatibility between war and the best interests of capitalism: the events of August 1914 therefore made it appear rather silly. The Angell movement nevertheless formed an important background to the preoccupation of Liberals with the problems which Angell claimed to have mastered, and its existence had made Liberals receptive to internationalist ideas. Just one month after the declaration of war Bryce received a proposal urging the desirability of an 'After the War League'.[27] Bryce's reservations about the war could not be kept secret and he became a target for peace-league organizations and propagandists who wanted to avoid the stigma of being associated with fringe-groups or cranks. Bryce was one of the few men who could stand at the centre of a league movement without incurring the opprobrium of moderate-minded men. Less neutral was Lowes Dickinson, who provided the energy in this strange hybrid of Oxbridge Liberalism. It was Dickinson who wrote a circular containing proposals aimed at 'directing international policy towards building up the machinery whereby all disputes shall be settled by judicial authority'. After a consultation with Loreburn this was sent to Bryce.[28] Other notes and memoranda went to the same address – J. A. Hobson sent one – but it was to be the partnership of Bryce and Lowes Dickinson as spearheads of the 'Bryce group' which was to be crucial in setting in motion the movement for a post-war League of Nations.

The group included Richard Cross, solicitor to the Rowntrees, Hobson, Ponsonby and Willoughby Dickinson. In some ways it was absorbed by the League of Nations Society in 1915, Lowes Dickinson acting as a link between the two. But the Society did not take its principal object to be the capture of the intelligentsia; it was more concerned to make 'steady progress among humble and unimportant folk'.[29] It is true that the list of its Vice-Presidents included in 1918 Gilbert Murray and the Warden of Keble, but the list is more impressive for its wider political connexions with names like Aneurin Williams, Willoughby Dickinson, Donald Maclean and Walter Rea, at whose house the Society held its first meeting on 10 March 1915.[30] At the end of 1918 the Society amalgamated with the League of Free Nations Association, which was distinctive in that it wanted a League to be formed before the end of hostilities. At the meeting designed to secure the fusion of the two bodies, the representatives of the Association were Gilbert Murray and Charles McCurdy. The meeting took place, as if to re-echo the theme, at the National Liberal Club.

Other organizations existed for the purpose of stimulating interest in a 'better' foreign policy, one of them the Union of Democratic Control. But the U.D.C. was more thoroughly tarred with the pacifist brush than most others and based more overtly on a renunciation of the 'secret diplomacy' operated by Grey.[31] It was this attitude which tended to mark off those whose sympathies would gravitate towards Labour after the war. The formation of the coalition, the arrival of conscription, the deposition of Asquith – all these were trivial once the initial barbarism had been admitted. This view was not offered by the U.D.C. alone. The

Garton Foundation, once a nursery for Liberals like Hubert Henderson and Philip Kerr, had become an organ of the left by 1916 and a vehicle for men like Cole, Greenwood, Hammond, Tawney and Zimmern.[32] Individuals displayed similar shifts of emphasis. Lowes Dickinson, for example, became disillusioned with Liberalism and moved towards Morel's position, or at least towards 'one which Grey would certainly regard as "bolshevist"', seeing no hope until Labour 'g[ot] into power, and someone like Brailsford [was] foreign minister'.[33]

Liberal intellectuals who remained faithful did not believe Grey's policy to be monstrous. Some may have wished to see him '*pinned* with the responsibility' for British intervention in the war,[34] but to Liberals of the stamp of Bryce, Murray and Fisher the atmosphere surrounding Grey during and after the war was entirely honourable. Nor was the contrary view held by all those on the left of Liberalism. Graham Wallas, for example, found much to criticize in orthodox Liberalism, but he did not join the U.D.C. because he 'd[idn't] hate Grey' and indeed could conceive of circumstances which might lead him to fight 'more or less on Grey's side'.[35] Similarly L. T. Hobhouse was prepared to defend Grey when C. P. Scott turned on him. 'I have no more respect than you for Asquith', he wrote to his chief during the leadership crisis in 1916, 'but Grey is another matter. He represents a negotiated peace – to wh. in my belief we shall ultimately be driven.'[36] Yet the animus against secret diplomacy was strong and Liberalism was unable to beat it off. Even if a League were to be established, sceptics might argue, could Liberal Imperialists like Asquith and Grey be trusted to participate in the right spirit? Those who shared the fears of Lowes Dickinson believed they could not.

Back in the Liberal centre, support for the League ideal had nevertheless become a salient point on the horizon; and the bringing about of that situation had caused intellectuals to meet and discuss their relationship with political stances which once they might have assumed out of habit. Revulsion from the war had prodded them into seeking 'some gesture of disinterestedness somewhere in politics – something to show that somebody ha[d] faith in something beyond force and the possession of material things'.[37] It was a reasonable claim that Liberalism could best supply this need. Conservatism seemed to know only the language of Hang the Kaiser and Make Germany Bleed. Socialism offered class selfishness at home and the dangerous myth of international brotherhood abroad. The League of Nations ideal, on the other hand, might be seen as a middle course (again) between anarchy and an arms race. This centrality appealed to those who were thinking about the posture Liberals ought to adopt after the war. '[T]he British Liberal view' was, in Spender's mind, reducible to 'decisive victory, League of Nations, "clean peace"', with no "war after war", *provided* the German military machine and its engineers are smashed.'[38]

Once the League idea had been inseminated into the minds of intellectuals it was hard to eradicate, though it was to lose its urgency for some of them as they watched the depressing manoeuvres in Paris and later at Geneva. It was natural that the end of the war should begin a process of reconcentration on domestic issues. Hugh Dalton tried to inject some sense of war's tragedy into Cambridge undergraduates in 1919, but the evening turned out 'rather a dead, dull thing'. 'Not dramatic enough to be painful', he wrote in his diary. 'A list of the dead read aloud. I quote Rupert's war sonnets and Pericles. They all sit and stare in front of them. I doubt how few Englishmen, or any one, realise the war losses at all.'[39] It was a new generation; and it was soon to become part of a new electorate. Political commitment to the League ideal was therefore less necessary than it might have been. Intellectual commitment could not be expressed through party machinery, and those who thought it could spent a miserable decade after 1918. In so far as the thinking of the intelligentsia found public expression in the 1920s it did so through the press, through pamphlets, lectures and books. None of these was more significant than *The Economic Consequences of the Peace*, published in 1919.

Keynes' book (the comment is a cliché) held powerful sway over an entire generation. Its impact was the greater for the hopes which had been built up before the peace conference that the settlement would be high-minded and the establishment of the League kept separate from the impositions of victors on vanquished. It was a pity, Bryce believed, that Lloyd George had not asked Asquith and Grey to attend the Paris conference;[40] yet there was no reason to think that he would act illiberally there. He seemed from the outset to be supporting Wilson's moral stance.[41]

But fears emerged as the talks progressed. By May 1919 Bryce was speaking of apprehensions.[42] Keynes was privately expressing doubts which went far beyond apprehension. 'This is hell', he wrote to one correspondent, '[b]ut they won't sign, I think – which is some consolation. The full text of the Treaty is much worse even than what they have printed.'[43] It is common knowledge that Keynes was soon to resign his post with the British delegation and turn immediately to the book which was to occupy him to the end of the year. Meanwhile the pith of the book was announced in private letters. At a time when Spender was trying to revive Bryce's spirits by conceding the possibility of international disaster only if the new Europe did not pay heed to the League,[44] Keynes was unwilling to affect similar optimism:

The Peace Conference was a dreadful business. The more you hear of it, the worse you will discover it to have been. There is nothing but sham behind us and disaster in front. I hung on until the last moment in the hope of being of assistance in bringing some change into so dishonourable and inexpedient a document. But the position was clearly hopeless.[45]

The thesis of the book requires no reiteration. The treaty was laid bare as humiliating, punitive and economically unworkable. Lloyd George was portrayed as a trimming demagogue – notwithstanding the excision of some of the harsher passages on the advice of Asquith[46] – whose only concern had been 'to do a deal and bring home something which would pass muster for a week'.[47] What is of interest is that different aspects of the book influenced intellectuals in different ways. Bryce thought Keynes' harsh treatment of the peace conference perfectly valid; he could 'remember few cases in history where negotiations might have done so much good and have done so much evil'.[48] Paish and Hobson were more influenced by the economic argument and agreed with Keynes' conclusions, though they would not have accepted Lowes Dickinson's dismal prophecy that the end of European civilization was at hand.[49] Herbert Fisher was as always moderate. 'The fact that Keynes' book should have been possible', he wrote in his diary, '[is] a great reflection on the Peace.'[50]

More significant for the future of Liberalism, however, was the response of Fisher's friend Murray, because his deductions from Keynes' work and the context which had given rise to it were to be of importance in forming his League policy. Not that Murray better represented the main current of Liberalism. He did once

profess to be 'the average non-ministerial Liberal',[51] but the label
is an odd one to attach to Murray. His mind was freakishly
individual and operated on wavelengths of conscience which
lesser minds were ill-equipped to receive. 'I find him oppressively
virtuous and intellectual', MacCallum Scott later wrote of him.
'He is too self-conscious about it. There is something feminine
in his conviction that he is right and that all who differ from [him]
have a touch of wickedness about them. He would make an
admirable Father Confessor to a Nunnery.'[52] Murray's importance did not lie in his being average but in being so committedly
eccentric that he could act as a focus of Liberal energy inside the
organization of the League of Nations. Between 1923 and 1936
he combined the posts of Regius Professor of Greek at Oxford
and Chairman of the League of Nations Union. From these
vantage points the influence he could wield was great; and the
way he wanted to use that influence was conditioned by the
events of 1918/19:

Have you read Keynes on the Economic Consequences of the Peace
Conference? I think it is important as giving in a clear and definite form
the criticism of a Liberal-minded man who saw the proceedings from the
inside . . . I can not help thinking that it really gives the scheme of a bold
Liberal policy in foreign affairs. Aim, the re-integration of Europe, both
political and economic. Method, the correction of the Versailles settlement by the L. of N. [I]t gives us a real fighting policy which has the
further advantage of being right.[53]

There has already been cause to observe that for the Liberal
party leadership, commitment to a League policy in the 1920s was
more a matter of rhetorical convenience than an act of faith. A
number of important Liberals never saw this or only saw it late
in the decade. Murray had convinced himself by 1924 that there
could not be 'the slightest doubt of the firm hold which the League
ha[d] on all Liberal feeling in the country'.[54] But how could such
an estimate be validated? It was likely to be no more than a
projection of observed opinion within the closed intellectual elite.
It was one thing to notice that the composition of and attendance
at the League of Nations Union's Executive Committee was pre-
dominantly Liberal, or that it was Liberal philanthropists like the
Cadburys who put up money for parties of workmen to go to
Geneva to see the League in action.[55] It was, but was not perceived
to be, another thing to maintain that Liberals in the country were

wedded to the internationalist ethic and held the ideals of the
League close to their heart.

The part of the political spectrum which was most affected by
this thinking and energy, indeed, was neither the world of high
politics nor that of the intelligentsia so much as the nebulous area
of internationalist activity which was bound up with the League
organizations during the 1920s. It was an area through which all
party boundaries ran and several national ones too. What could
be seen in Smuts and Nansen could be seen in Noel-Baker or Eric
Drummond as well as in the mind of Murray or Cecil. Liberal
intellectuals did not disagree with Murray; they were merely tepid
where he was hot. Stephen Gladstone's feeling that the League
was going to make the world a better place to live in but that it
was 'hard to think *how*'[56] better reflects the tenor of intellectual
support for the League than does the conviction of Murray.
Certainly the League did not provide cement for the nexus between intellectuals and Liberalism to the extent that Murray might
have wished. It had done much to hold them together in wartime,
but in the context of overriding concern with domestic matters
after 1918 it was plain enough that if cement was to be found it
would have to be found there.

The chasm dividing what intelligent Liberals believed politicians
ought to do from what the politicians were actually doing seemed
wide and deep in 1918. All the advice given to politicians had been
ignored, Bryce believed. 'What we indicated as the natural consequence of the policy followed abroad and in Ireland has come
to pass. We needed no prophetic gift to predict the inevitable.'[57]
Some on the other side of the chasm were not impressed. Sir
Charles Hardinge had spent many years pondering foreign policy;
he felt he did not require instruction from a Cambridge don and
much resented Keynes being treated 'as a sort of hero...
spend[ing] all his time in London feasting in the houses of our
friends'.[58] In domestic politics the gulf was equally wide as
Liberals watched helplessly the triumph of Lloyd George and the
disaster at the polls. These were the realities which occupied the
foreground of political debate.

The involvement of the intellectuals in that debate could not be
so complete as that of the politicians. University politics and its
congenial underworld was waiting when peace came. It is plainly

impossible to evaluate the extent to which the smaller world excluded the larger or to be clear what that smaller world was about. There was little need, after all, to commit to paper thoughts destined for someone down the corridor or in the next building. The evidence which has survived seems to be thin and inconclusive. Liberal contemporaries were convinced, for example, that there was an upswing in the fortunes of Liberalism in the universities in the immediate post-war years. A Liberal propagandist claimed in 1921: 'Liberalism has never, at any rate in its recent history, been so strong in all the Universities as it is to-day. I don't think it is an exaggeration to say that the majority of the able young men in all our seats of learning to-day are Liberals.'[59] About the same time Richard Holt also 'gather[ed] Liberalism [was] quite flourishing at the Universities',[60] though it is conceivable that the first remark served as source for the second. But hard evidence is scarce. Gilbert Murray found Oxford Liberalism 'very lively and interesting' in 1919; yet in 1922 a representative of the Oxford Liberal Club found it a matter for self-congratulation that he could still count on a few keen men 'in spite of the unaccountable but obvious lack of interest that young Oxford shows in political matters just now'.[61]

Equally inconclusive are contemporary indications of Senior Common Room views. Not a great deal can be learned from the parliamentary elections for the university seats because their electorates were wide enough to swamp the judgements of active members of the university concerned. There were twelve such seats: three representing the Combined Scottish Universities, two the Combined English (with a further two each for Oxford and Cambridge) and one each for the universities of London, Wales and Belfast. The last returned an unopposed Conservative throughout the period, the Scottish representation included one Liberal – D. M. Cowan – throughout; the University of Wales returned a Liberal at all elections but one; one of the seats for the Combined English Universities was held by Herbert Fisher until his resignation in 1926 when he was succeeded by Ramsay Muir.[62] But the Conservative party fared far better in the incidence of its university representation; and it has to be remembered that to talk of party labels at all in this context can be misleading.[63] Both of these reservations apply also to the Oxbridge seats, but in these 'constituencies' the position of the Liberals was interesting.

Between 1919 and 1929 Oxford University was in the Conservative grip of Lord Hugh Cecil and Sir Charles Oman, the former radiating high religiosity and eccentric principle, the latter the atmosphere of 'a jolly fox-hunting squire'.[64] There were six, and not five, elections between 1918 and 1929 because of R. E. Prothero's elevation to the peerage as Lord Ernle in 1919. Gilbert Murray fought each one for the Liberals, without ever winning. After his disastrous poll at the 1918 election, Bryce wrote a consolatory letter and told him that '[i]f Mr. Gladstone were living he would not have got more support'.[65] Murray's reply shows a certain stoicism in defeat. 'A University candidature', he wrote, 'gives very little trouble, especially to the Liberal, who knows that the even tenor of his life will not be disturbed by the result of the election.'[66] In 1923 he fared much better and came within a hundred votes of Cecil – 'a really marvellous achievement', Noel-Baker believed[67] – but Murray's comment on the position in 1918 may be taken as a realistic evaluation of the Liberal party's prospects in Oxford in the 1920s. Some hopes were raised by the formation in 1920 of the 'Oxford University Liberal Club', but its numbers seem to have remained small and its administrative personnel bizarrely maladjusted: J. B. S. Haldane was a founder member, R. F. Harrod was the Treasurer and Beverley Nichols the Secretary. The avowed aim of the club was 'to rally progressive members of the University to the support of Liberal principles', but that slogan would attract no one until it was made clear whose principles they meant. Violet Bonham-Carter instructed Murray that its Liberalism must be 'of quite a different character to that practised by [Lloyd George] and his Govt.'[68] The opposition was similarly determined; a representative was later to inform Murray that those 'with Lloyd George tendencies' had decided to leave the club and start one of their own, 'backed up by Downing Street'.[69]

It is worth while to recall in passing that another kind of election promised to offer some indication of Liberal sympathies in Oxford when, following the death of Milner in 1925, the university had a chance to recognize a lifetime's connexion and 'gracefully choose H.H.A. as Chancellor'.[70] The election, however, was contested. It was expected, rightly, that Viscount Cave would gather to himself much of the traditional Conservatism of Oxford, and his supporters were indeed to be accused of wanting to turn the contest into a party affair.[71] On paper Asquith had the advantage of his name, his learning and his impressive ranks of supporters who included the Master of Balliol, the Wardens of All Souls and New College, the Principal of King's College, London, the Lord Chief Justice, three bishops and distinguished dons such as Murray, Pollard and Quiller-Couch.[72] For all that, he faced weighty and predictable opposition from what he was himself to call 'Zadok the Priest and Abiathar the Priest – with their half-literate followers in the rural parsonages': if they could be enticed into Cave's camp they were judged strong enough to beat Asquith.[73] This may have been the reason for Asquith's defeat. Cave himself believed that it had been the science dons who had helped him in,[74] but it appears that at least one of them did not. It seems curious in retrospect that the largest single contribution to Asquith's election expenses should have come from Professor F. A. Lindemann.[75]

Turning to the example of Cambridge reveals little change in the pattern observed in the case of Oxford. Again there was a Conservative allegiance which gave J. P. P. Rawlinson a seat until his death in 1926 when he was succeeded unopposed. The Liberal interest was in the hands of J. R. M. Butler and, unlike Murray at Oxford, Butler did succeed in beating a Conservative at one election (1922), though the seat returned to its normal allegiance the following year. Butler's success was based on the weakness of the Conservative candidate; it is significant that when a strong candidate was selected in 1923 – Sir Geoffrey Butler, President of the University Conservative Association and later P.P.S. to Hoare at the Air Ministry – he came top of the poll. J. R. M. Butler fought three elections as an 'Independent Liberal' since he wished himself to be associated with neither wing of the party though he was closer to the Asquithian side.[76] Among a list of supporters in 1923 there is no apparent bias.[77]

The tone of Cambridge Liberalism is hard to gauge and although there are scattered indications in the material which survives, no coherent picture can be said to emerge. When Fisher addressed the Liberal and Eighty Club in March 1920 he deduced from the discussion about Liberalism, Ireland and nationalization that the predominant sentiment was Asquithian.[78] The young dons, on the other hand, were perceived by the Tory Will Spens to be 'for coalition and would be for a good centre party with a tendency to prefer the latter'.[79] Printed material does little to help since it is so often at pains to pretend that faction amounts to something else. Judging from the tone of the *Cambridge Liberal Policy* announced in 1920 there was an element of 'pure' Liberalism:

Liberalism stands for a faith in human nature, and a respect for its mystery. It believes that the fundamental test by which all institutions must be judged is that of how far they respond to the needs and aspirations of human beings. And it believes that the only persons who in the ultimate resort can be the judges of that, are the mass of men and women themselves.[80]

No obvious flavour comes out of watered pottage like this. There was an injunction to remember Campbell-Bannerman,[81] which suggests an Asquithian bent, but one finds elsewhere that Cambridge Liberals 'recognise[d] clearly and unmistakeably that industry [was] the corner stone of modern politics',[82] which is more in the manner of Lloyd Georgian rhetoric. Again, the 'new borough Liberal Association' invited the Asquithians Maclean and Spender as speakers at its inaugural dinner, and those present included Keynes, Glover and Cope Morgan.[83] But these judgements follow nothing but instinct.

No less frustrating is the wider problem of deciding what was the character of Liberalism in the universities generally, since if it is difficult to formulate a quantitative account of Liberal strength, it is far more so to pronounce upon Asquithian or Lloyd Georgian proclivities. It is a reasonable assumption that the Liberalism of a small community could be tinged by the colour of a single personality. Oxford Liberalism, for example, revolved to some degree around Murray and Fisher. The latter was an Asquithian who at one stage found himself in the Lloyd George camp through pressure of circumstance. The former was a confirmed Asquithian. 'It does seem to me', he wrote to Asquith in 1925, 'that, all through the worst fortunes of Liberalism and of all the nobler causes in public life, from 1916 onwards, you have shown the right road and said the thing that ought to be said... You have helped the remnant of us to think rightly and to hold out.'[84] All the political axioms that lay behind this eulogy would be passed on through Murray's contacts at the University. Thus even a man like J. L. Hammond could concede that although he regarded himself as a supporter of Labour, Murray had done more than anyone else to form his 'outlook and general habit of mind'.[85]

Asquithianism was less rife among the Cambridge *alumni*. Keynes was an Asquithian of sorts until the mid-twenties, but he had connexions in the other camp, particularly Hubert Henderson. Politically he might have been happier at the London School of Economics where Graham Wallas declared himself a progressive Liberal who wanted to develop the kind of Liberalism associated with names like C. P. Scott and E. D. Simon; or at Manchester University where the influence of Muir was strong. The Liberalism of the latter was of an intellectual brand dedicated to overcoming personal squabbles in order to reach deeper truths. 'I believe we have thought too much about leaders and organizations and enquired too little', was a typically Lloyd Georgian outburst.[86] It was a characteristic of his Liberalism to transfer the energies of Liberals from destructive debate to 'constructive' thought – a notion to draw smiles from Asquithians and satire from the ultras:

> Shall the Liberal Party die?
> 'Be Constructive' is his cry,
> Gladstone, Asquith, Grey, C–B,
> Put them all in class C3.
> None is fit to touch the hem
> Of the garment of R.M.
> Day by day he writes and preaches,
> Tells us how to make our speeches,
> Proves how voters will be bucked if
> We will only be 'constructive'.[87]

It is fair to add that the intellectuals were less prone to the usual Liberal animosities. Where there were personal aversions the cause was not likely to be a matter of political principle. The willingness of the intelligentsia to merge all Liberal talent is no mere hypothesis, moreover. It was put into action in the most extraordinary, and in some ways the most successful, institution of post-war Liberalism – the Summer School, which was to become an annual feature of politics in these years.

The Manchester of Muir and Simon provided the impetus for a movement to begin regular conferences at which Liberal policy might be discussed and revised.[88] The 'school' idea was hatched at a meeting of Muir, Simon, Philip Guedalla and Ted Scott (son of C. P. Scott) at Simon's Herefordshire farm in 1920 and led to invitations being sent to ninety-five Liberals to attend a week's conference at Grasmere in October 1921.[89] The success of this gathering suggested another one at Oxford in August 1922; this

lasted five days and was 'quite admirable', according to Masterman, because 'everyone c[ame] round to our programme despite
gloomy warnings from Runciman, Simon and Co.'[90] Though that
programme was progressive, the school was seen by some as
an Asquithian instrument until the split after the General Strike.
Keynes, for example, wrote at the time of Asquith's challenge
to Lloyd George in 1926, and 'quote[d] this just as an example of
Liberal opinion', that most of the committee of the Summer
School were against Asquith's decision. The implication was that
this judgement was damning since it was made by people 'who
ha[d] been in the past as far as possible from being Ll.G.ers'.[91]
A clearer perspective about the composition of the school, however, can be gleaned from the list of those invited to the initial
conferences. No bias is evident from the 1922 list;[92] the names
represent a fair balance of all the interests in the party, and
Cawleys, Hendersons, Hobhouses, Muirs, Scotts and Tweeds
were there in sufficient numbers to balance the Bretts, Cadburys,
Bonham-Carters, Gardiners and Murrays.

Individuals whose connexions with Liberalism might have remained at best formal and at worst remote were sucked into active
political involvement through the organization of the Summer
School. They remained, moreover, fairly faithful to it: if one
examines the membership of the School Council in 1930, many
of the original names recur. The differences in 1930 are a product
of a general change of emphasis in the party as a whole. The
Asquithians were, after all, in ill repair; a few loyal journalists –
Dodds, Gardiner, Spender – and weathered individuals like Sir
Frederick Maurice still carried the flag, but the overall tone was
now Lloyd Georgian. Muir and Layton were Directors, E. D.
Simon was Treasurer. Among the intellectuals only Murray remained. Keynes was now in the Lloyd George camp and he had an
ally in Arnold Toynbee. The position of the latter is not entirely
clear but he seems to have believed that Massingham was not
badly treated by the *Nation* in 1923, which fails to turn the litmus
paper an Asquithian colour. Only the politically intense would
read significance into his naming his son Lawrence Leif Toynbee
after J. L. Hammond and Leif Jones, M.P.[93]

Judgements about the political positions of individual intellectuals are hedged round with difficulties since evidence is scanty
and too much can be read into a single act or fragment of *obiter*

dicta. Often the 'evidence' amounts to little more than the expression of an inspired optimism. Thus one has Ramsay Muir after losing the Combined English Universities in 1926: 'The modern univs. ought to be Liberal strongholds, and feeding grounds for all the constituencies. That is why I should like to have them.'[94] The tense is sufficient index of the comment's usefulness. In the following year Muir spoke at the Cambridge Union for a motion condemning Baldwin's foreign policy. The motion was carried. Muir then wrote to Lloyd George the next day telling him about the debate and received the reply that '[i]t [was] very gratifying to know that the best young men at Cambridge [were] turning towards Liberalism'.[95] Non-sequiturs of this kind do nothing to strengthen the confidence of the historian in such judgements. Dissonances within the evidence are also disturbing. In 1921, according to Professor Joseph Jones, the staffs of the Welsh Colleges were 'almost to a man' opposed to Lloyd George.[96] Yet four years later Wedgwood Benn was surprised to be well received at Cardiff because 'most of the people [there] had been Lloyd Georgians in their time'.[97] The evidence is more convincing where it underlines observations which seem plausible *a priori*, as when Sutherland warned Lloyd George in 1920 that the intellectuals were being ignored by the coalition machine, which was presenting the coalition to them as a party of capitalists.[98] Again there are instances when unambiguous statements are made about an individual or an organization. There can be little doubt about the position of the 'Union of University Liberal Societies' (a brainchild of Violet Bonham-Carter) because the sense of a meeting of the provisional committee was reported to Gilbert Murray.[99]

But direct statements are rare. If conclusions were to be drawn from the material available then they would seem to point to a slight Asquithian predominance in the early years of the post-war decade followed by a swing round to Lloyd George, though of course the latter had had with him from the beginning some men of academic stamp such as Thomas Jones and W. G. S. Adams. Even if such a judgement were accurate, however, it would distort the mind of the intellectuals, for whom the Liberal split did not assume the centrality it has been shown to have assumed in the minds of politicians. The terms of reference and the tone of their language were different. The most frequent message they conveyed to politicians was to press for unity and prevent further feuding. Even an Asquithian like T. R. Glover was ready, despite his support for 'the real Liberals', to hope by 1927 that 'the danger of further division of the Liberal Party . . . may be averted'.[100] And if dons were remote from the feuds, how much more so were their students. 'There are masses of people here', Wedgwood Benn noticed on his visit to Cardiff, 'to [sic] know nothing about the war, or even about the Coalition. It is from such that the plea for unity comes.'[101] The academic mentality, like the provincial one, was both integral to the Liberal mind and yet ultimately on its periphery.

II

This diffuse intellectual Liberalism was not a monopoly of university dons. It extended into some sections of business and commerce and it pervaded the Third and Fourth Estates. Of these the Churches enjoyed some degree of isolation and may be considered separately, but the university, press and business worlds revolved closely around one another. The Adult Education movement in which Haldane was involved after the war drew much of its financial sustenance from Thomas Wall's sausage firm.[102] Business prosperity underpinned some Liberal newspapers. The role of Cowdray in producing the Asquithian *Westminster Gazette* provides one obvious example, Cadbury's ownership of the *Daily News* another; or, for a less imposing illustration, one might go to the continuing Colman interest in certain East Anglian papers.[103] The relationship between the intellectuals and the press can easily be exemplified. What need is there to go beyond Keynes himself? In 1923 he was part of the group which succeeded in wresting the *Nation* from the grip of H. W. Massingham, just as it was he who formed a company in 1931 to amalgamate that periodical with the *New Statesman* under the editorship of 'one Kingsley Martin'.[104] Organizations also played a role. The 'Rainbow Circle' had been an important 'point of contact' before the war, and it continued to meet at the house of Sir Richard Stapley who had entered the House of Commons as a Liberal M.P. in 1910.[105] Binding all three worlds together, finally, is the impeccably Liberal progression of Harry Sacher: London School of Economics, to the *Manchester Guardian*, to Marks and Spencer.[106]

The character of Liberal journalism was naturally as variegated as were the talents within it. That those talents together consti-tuted the most gifted congeries in the profession is not, however, open to dispute. Consider the names mentioned *en passant* in an invitation which Bryce received from Spender of the *Westminster Gazette* in 1918:

The circle of Liberal writers and journalists . . . commission me to ask you if you will dine with them privately at the Reform Club this day fortnight . . . The leading members of the circle, so far as I can remember them are Gardiner, Sidney Webb, Gilbert Murray, Massingham, Paish (of the Statist), Hartley Withers (Economist), Graham Wallas, Lowes Dickinson and one or two others.[107]

But few would have contested the claims of C. P. Scott, editor of the *Manchester Guardian* since 1872, to first place within the ranks of Liberal writers. Scott's interventions in politics – whether when 'saving L.G.'s soul' by giving him morally spiced advice, or when giving him concrete help as in drafting the reply to Asquith in June 1926 – were an essential part of Lloyd George's political base. Behind Scott's activities lay an uncommon staunch-ness of 'principle' married to a commitment to reason and good taste which his newspaper was meant to reflect. Inside the *Man-chester Guardian* readers, many of them Liberals, knew they would find the journalism of Conscience under the imprint of men like L. T. Hobhouse and W. P. Crozier. Hobhouse had become an apostle of moralized politics at the turn of the century; the coming of the war underlined its necessity for him and by 1916 the publisher Unwin thought that his writings – mostly wailings against the fall of reason – were the 'growlings of an uneasy conscience'.[108] Crozier may not have had the same consciousness of crisis but it was enough that he was a product of bleakest Nonconformity.[109] Party occupied a comparatively small part of their political perspective, and by the mid-twenties Scott and Hobhouse agreed that there was 'next to nothing to choose' between Liberalism and what they conceived to be the better section of Labour.[110] Their tolerance of Lloyd George was never-theless almost infinite: the *Manchester Guardian* far outlasted Riddell's *News of the World* in that respect.

Asquithian journalism was proud of its finer focus. At its centre until his resignation from the *Gazette* in 1922 was James Alfred Spender. The son of a novelist, he had arrived as assistant editor

of the 'Westminster' by way of Bath College, Balliol and Stead's
Pall Mall Gazette. Oxford was a particularly important influence,
since the Oxford he knew was that which Asquith had known and
impressed a few years before; he was connected with Asquith,
not only by 'the potent Balliol tie' but by a 'rich community of
mind'.[111] His Liberal line ran deep and it was no accident that he
was to write the lives of Campbell-Bannerman, Asquith, Cowdray
and Sir Robert Hudson. Unlike Scott and Hobhouse, he was
avowedly *parti pris* and resisted attempts to dilute what he took
to be central to the Liberal outlook.[112] Also unlike the 'Manchester' team, Spender was understood by politicians to be an
important influence on the Asquithian leadership. Lloyd George
much resented this. In 1914 he threatened to have Spender removed if he did not toe the line over the naval estimates; in 1917
he believed Spender to be responsible for sabotaging his attempt
to lure Asquith into the government.[113] Any power that Spender
had depended on his ability to reach a wide audience through his
newspaper. The decision to resign from the *Westminster Gazette*,
following its transformation from an evening into a morning paper,
was therefore a miscalculation. Margot Asquith saw Cowdray's
letting him go as a 'powerful and pathetic blunder',[114] but the
phrase might better have been applied to Spender's willingness
to go. After 1922 he was compelled to turn to professional biography: he became a 'political cypher'.

   Both sides of Liberalism were served by party organs, the Lloyd
Georgian section by the *Daily Chronicle* after 1918 and the
Asquithians by the *Daily News*. (The two merged into the *News
Chronicle* in 1931.) Before Lloyd George bought it, the *Chronicle*
was edited by Robert Donald who, despite his animus against
Lloyd George during the war, had been a supporter of radical
causes in the pre-war years.[115] Donald's ejection, like Spender's
resignation, ended his effective career as a journalist, though some
years later there was a whisper that he had tried to acquire shares
in the *New Statesman*.[116] It is worth mentioning that the political
correspondent of the *Chronicle* for five years during the twenties
was Geoffrey Shakespeare, between fighting elections as a Lloyd
George Liberal, and that one of the leader-writers was R. C. K.
Ensor, who had been trained on Scott's *Manchester Guardian*.[117]
Editor of the *Daily News* until 1919 was A. G. Gardiner, who had
been installed by George Cadbury after his acquisition of the paper

in 1900. Gardiner was a dour Asquithian about whose character MacCallum Scott noticed 'something mean and envious' and whose concept of truth was 'sometimes limited by the strength of his prejudices'.[118] He too went the way of the scholar and wrote lives of Cadbury and Sir William Harcourt. His successor, moreover, was an unfortunate choice from the Asquithian point of view, since Stuart Hodgson was to gravitate towards the Lloyd George camp while the assistant editor, A. J. Cummings, drifted in the direction of Labour.[119] By 1920 Bryce was dismissing the paper as 'worse than useless'.[120] MacCallum Scott later thought it reminiscent of a maiden aunt and wrote of the 'mean-spirited partisanship of this self-righteous paper'.[121] The staff included H. N. Brailsford for a time.

On the wider front of weekly and monthly journalism, Liberalism was well represented. Keynes thought that Clifford Sharp of the *New Statesman* was virtually an Asquithian Liberal,[122] and if that view is hard to substantiate it is certainly true that Sharp received an interdict from Passfield Corner 'as Sidney was displeased with his attitude to the Labour Party'[123] and that he never ruled out the possibility of a Liberal revival. G. P. Gooch of the *Contemporary Review* was described by Dalton as Asquithian, bitter and miserable.[124] There was a chance for a while that the Liberals might penetrate the *Spectator*, for in 1922 Strachey offered Runciman up to a third of the shares with nomination to one directorship and permission to print the journal on his own presses. The proposal fell through only for technical reasons: Runciman continued to revere Strachey's 'unique journal, the views and tone of which attract[ed him] intensely'.[125] Lloyd George, on the other hand, had supporters on the *Round Table* – among them Grigg, Brand and Kerr – who at least discussed the idea of forming a parliamentary group.[126] The journal concerned itself principally with India and Ireland, pressed a strong imperial line and was heavy reading, though Lloyd George thought it influential.[127] Its Lloyd Georgian proclivities are suggested by Massingham's asking God to deliver him from it.[128] Another ex-Lloyd Georgian, David Davies, was a director of the *Review of Reviews* but his main interest was in pushing the League of Nations idea.[129] Nevertheless the journal had a Lib/Lab editor in Mary Agnes Hamilton who had been assistant editor on Hirst's *Common Sense* during the war.

In Francis Hirst Liberalism found one of its most powerful journalists, second only to Massingham in his high period. Hirst was a primitive Liberal: he believed the things Cobden and Bright had believed.[130] An economic fundamentalism appeared in his political writing in the form of a perverse and antiquated individualism. The war changed the emphasis of his thought to some extent, however, since he became less concerned with the problem of how to keep the state at bay and more involved in the predominant intellectual concern with containing international aggression. By 1917 he was out of touch with his *Economist* readership after 'a deplorable exhibition of how not to carry on a newspaper in war'[131] and resigned his editorship in order to throw himself into the internationalist movement. The path which he wanted to follow was delineated in a letter to Hammond in 1924. He could not feel excited, he said, about the Socialist challenge: he was concerned instead about the arms race and the threat of war.[132] His new orientation led him to consult Loreburn; they led him, worse, into the Lansdowne movement and the radical attempt to oust Lloyd George at the beginning of 1918.

The economic aspect of his thinking had not been entirely dormant. Towards the end of 1916, whilst he was still editor of the *Economist*, he had begun to edit also a weekly journal of political economy. *Common Sense* (a good Liberal way of looking at the economy) was financed by a group of strictly orthodox Liberals including D. M. Mason, Sir Hugh Bell and Percy Molteno and it reflected Hirsts's passion for hard truth and unpalatable fact. MacCallum Scott had said this of Hirst a few months before the floating of *Common Sense:*

[H]e is convinced that everyone who differs from [him] is either a rogue, or a time-server or a weakling. His political ideal seems summed up in Peace and Retrenchment. If he adds 'Reform' it is only in the sense of constitutional reform – the extension of the franchise. His creed is intensely individualist and opposed to all State interference.[133]

Needless to say, the Left was not amused by *Common Sense*. Sidney Webb bought a copy of the first number and sent it to Beatrice with the verdict 'very poor indeed'.[134] What is more surprising is that the financial base of the journal soon crumbled. By 1920 Richard Holt, who was also involved, regarded its position as 'desperate', and at a meeting of interested parties in

February 1921 the decision came to wind it up.[135] Hirst never recovered real influence within Liberalism.

A bigger blow than this to most Liberal contemporaries and one more significant in retrospect was the defection of Massingham. His role had always been slightly anomalous. Views and influence were repeatedly ascribed to him which the man himself would have disputed. Massingham was never a committed Liberal: he accepted some of the principles of 'Liberalism' but had the wrong instincts in its world of personal loyalties. He was a radical of a type usually associated with an earlier period. When it seemed to him that Labour encapsulated this radicalism better than did Liberalism, he changed his position accordingly. The radicalism could be puerile fretting, as in his hysteria about the government's treatment of the media on the outbreak of war;[136] on the other hand, it could be considered and dangerous, as in his anti-conscription stand or the attacks on Lloyd George which provoked the latter into having export of the *Nation* banned in 1917. His Labour sympathies were discernible by 1918 among those who had been close to his previous work and he was criticized for 'be[ing] so pessimistic and faithless'.[137] He took his lack of faith over to Labour. In 1922 he supported the Grey conspiracy, for example, but even then Hammond was waiting for the next spark which would fire his imagination and take him off at a tangent again.[138]

Massingham's dismissal from the *Nation* in 1923 rekindled Asquithian sympathy for him and it became one of the more durable myths of the 1920s that he had been badly treated. In fact he had not. Massingham had been asked if he wanted to buy the journal but he had been unable to raise the capital. It was only after a year or so that the Rowntrees offered the *Nation* to the Summer School, and this after an attempt to merge it earlier in the year with the *New Statesman*.[139] The new style *Nation and Athenaeum* was not an Asquithian organ and some considered it an important loss. But what was more significant was what was believed to have happened to Massingham. The latter – 'ill, angry and aggrieved'[140] – was not one to conceal bitterness, and his version of the events of 1923 was to join the Maurice Debate, the treatment of party officials by Lloyd George in the late 1920s and other examples of second-class infamy in the Asquithian library of such things. The former editor's acid mind (its character can be seen in his wanting to see Beaverbrook 'exterminated like any

7   BLM

other plague-carrying vermin')[141] ensured that the myth was brought into frequent focus. But 1923 nevertheless marked the watershed of his political power.

Standing back from these journalists it is reasonable to ask how extensive their power could have been anyway. It is possible they had an inflated view of their own significance. Is it really helpful to report that Haldane felt that the *New Statesman* was 'taking increasing hold of the public mind'?[142] There is clearly no way of validating judgements of this kind or even of being sure what they mean. But there is no escaping the preoccupation of politicians with print and propaganda after 1914. This is not to ignore the Balfours who never saw newspapers; nor to forget that politicians held different views about the ideal role and utility of the press; nor to overlook the possibility of regional variations in reading habits and availability of material.[143]

Newspaper readership increased sharply in the context of an ever more yellow press and, more especially, the need to be acquainted in wartime with news of relatives and military operations. Politicians could not remain oblivious to the development, and contemporary material strongly indicates the importance which the press had come to assume for them. If Haldane could not know the public mind, Henry Gladstone was quite familiar with his own during the critical weeks of 1916. 'As usual', he wrote to his brother, 'the "Westminster" leader of last night expresses my views on the situation.'[144] Such influence needed to be courted. Thus one finds MacCallum Scott at the beginning of 1914 wondering how best to consolidate his position in the party and deciding that he must try to write for the *Glasgow Herald* or the *Contemporary Review* or (a significant inclusion) the *Daily Mail*.[145] One anti-conscription M.P., again, thought that newspapers would be crucial in the fight and wrote to McKenna to complain about their weakness there.[146] In this case the concern was with the national press, but the time had already arrived when the provincial press needed to be considered also. It was a cause for celebration that the *Guardian* line on conscription was 'excellent'.[147] It was a cause for concern within the Conservative party that sufficient attention was not being paid to papers like the *Scotsman*, the *Yorkshire Post* and the *Liverpool Post*.[148]

Scott, Spender, Massingham and the rest would influence politicians in the degree to which the politicians thought they ought to be influenced, could afford to be influenced, or wanted to convince others that they were influenced. These considerations in turn depended to some extent on the public persona which a politician deemed it desirable to project. In the case of the Liberal leader, for example, the projection consisted in persuading the audience that he, Asquith, made political judgements in a serene, recondite temper and recoiled from acting on whims attended by popular clamour and mass enthusiasms. This stance was useful rhetorically, especially after the press attacks of 1915/16. It could be used in debate to isolate himself from lesser men:

I had very great doubts myself whether to intervene in the Debate at all. I have never taken a very active line in this particular controversy, partly for reasons of a personal character, and also because I have not yet succeeded...in divesting myself of an old heresy of mine, which I have professed and believed during the whole of my political life – that there is a great disposition among politicians to exaggerate the power of the Press, not as a vehicle of information, but as an instrument for the dissemination and propagation of opinion.[149]

The image contained private truth as well as public drapery. But the private face was nevertheless different from the public: it was the same man who found one of Gardiner's articles in the *News* in 1912 'an object lesson in the necessity of suppressing or absorbing that pernicious rag' on the grounds that he had 'never come across a more mischievous farrago of quarter truths, downright lies and malignant insinuations'.[150] Nor did Asquith make objection to the 'salting' of the press in advance of Grey's Berwick speech in 1921.[151]

Still, Asquith's actions after 1914 are not fully intelligible without the recognition that his relations with the press were not cordial. In the feuds of 1914–16 and 1926 the press played for Asquith a dominant and unsavoury role. He was contemptuous of newspapers because it was their common aim to arouse the baser instincts of common, contemptible people. In his own words, the Liberal press was 'written by Boobies for Boobies'.[152] Not that the contempt was bitter or even serious: it was all part of an implied joke about democracy. For the 'masses' Asquith felt that benign contempt which the Latin tutor bestows on a pupil who cannot construe. Over the years the attitude hardened into a rhetorical plank and a guide to conduct. Mounting personal criticism after 1918 can have done nothing to weaken it, nor the treatment his wife received at the hands of the 'vile, vulgar British press'[153] after the publication of her autobiography in 1920.

Lloyd George thought differently. Metaphysics were considered by him irrelevant to a grasp of the importance of the press in public life. The grasp he had was less because he was a 'born demagogue' (a cant phrase) than because his developed sense of reality suggested the usefulness of the press as an agency for pose. Lloyd George was good copy: he tried to be so. His success led him to be stamped with the image of being a communicator with the people. '[H]e has lived by the press', epitaphed Esher, 'and by the press he shall die.'[154] He did not die by it; indeed he used his *Daily Chronicle* to buttress himself politically.[155] When an observer thought that the 'syndicated Press Gang' was using Lloyd George for its own ends[156] he was misunderstanding the victim. It was not because he was exploited that Lloyd George wanted in 1914 to start a London edition of the *Manchester Guardian*; nor was it because of the Prime Minister's subservience that the newly appointed editor of the *Glasgow Herald* received in 1917 a telegram of congratulation from Lloyd George.[157] Similarly his cultivation of friendships with Northcliffe, Riddell and Scott went beyond personal regard. So anxious was Lloyd George to gain a favourable press for himself that he was willing to spend money in the newspaper market, either in order to acquire a powerful organ for himself – as in his attempt to take over the *Westminster Gazette* in 1917 and later *The Times* – or to silence discomforting opposition.

Despite the close involvement of the Liberal press with the politicians, it never lost one singular characteristic after 1914 – its remarkable quality. Liberal editors offered their public a 'high' journalism which remained discernible even in the more rakish moments of the post-Gardiner *News* or Lloyd George's *Chronicle*. Undoubtedly the standards of these latter papers were less rigorous than those of Spender's *Gazette* or Scott's *Guardian*. But the *Daily News*, for example, had the Cadbury conscience to subvert before it could resort to the lower journalism (it was not until the 1920s that bookmakers' advertisements were accepted) and even when Cadbury became more interested in circulation than in politics, journalists still believed that there was 'a tone about the *Daily News* which made it distinct in Fleet Street'.[158] As for the *Chronicle*, the traditions established by Donald were slow to disperse, and even towards the end of the 1920s Lloyd George was in despair about the political management of the paper under McCurdy.[159] He need not have been had he consulted someone better tuned to the Liberal mind. Spender had noticed five years before that the Lloyd Georgians could make no impact through their press until they could 'be got to believe that quality counts for something in our kind of journalism'.[160]

There was after 1914 a fairly definite Liberal attitude towards the place of the press in society. The war did not produce it, though it may have acted as a catalyst. A more fundamental development was the growth of popular journalism and in particular its advance into areas which had previously been considered immune from the contagion. The most striking example of the latter possibility was of course Northcliffe's *Times*, which was regarded as having slipped consistently downhill since its sale by the Walter family in 1908. Northcliffe's abrasive war propaganda, his attacks directed as much against the government as against the Germans and his growing paranoia confirmed what had previously been feared. Those who remembered *The Times* as an outward and visible form of an unwritten constitution were wont to recall 'the days of Delane, when "The Times" was a newspaper'.[161] Liberals were particularly appalled. The man was a 'cad'.[162] He was not a misguided patriot but a self-seeking careerist unmoved by the deeper issues of the war. 'It must be a great satisfaction to him', Simon wrote, 'to feel that he has sold his country for ½d.'[163] Execration of him did not, moreover, cease with the armistice. The opposition of *The Times* to Lloyd George's coalition after Northcliffe had been refused a place at the peace conference offended even erstwhile supporters like former editor Geoffrey Dawson, whose 'blood boil[ed] at Northcliffe's pretensions about being above party politics'.[164] It also gave Lloyd George a golden opportunity to proclaim *The Times* an Asquithian organ,[165] leaving to others the tedious task of separating the various strands of opposition to the coalition.

One important corollary of the rise to political power of North-cliffe, Beaverbrook, Bottomley and Rothermere was a growing recognition that newspapers were tending to become mouthpieces for enterprising capitalists rather than talented editors – a situation which it was felt the great editors of the past would have refused to tolerate.[166] Not only was such a process taking place,

it was being accelerated by the consolidation of previously independent newspapers into journalistic blocs under the control of
single individuals or organizations.[167] The power, tone and gim-
mickry of the press were looked upon by Liberals sometimes with
resignation, sometimes with anger, always with dismay. Perhaps
most would not have agreed with Burns that half of 'the factious
blackguards of Carmelite Street' should be in jail and the other
half in an asylum,[168] but many would have sympathized with
A. H. D. Acland's commendation of Spender's stand against the
new journalism. 'Northcliffe's policy', he wrote to Spender,
'weakens any and every government just where Governments
must be strong, in order to replace it by the influence of what he
chooses to call "The Press"'. . . When circulation is equivalent to
being right we have reached a disastrous state of things.'[169]
Spender himself was not averse to private comment about the
power of the press proprietors, a development from which he
was to suffer greatly at the hands of Cowdray. It was in the
middle of one such battle that he wrote to Bryce that the press still
seemed to him to be 'one of the great unsolved problems of democracy' which was threatening to precipitate 'an irresponsible
tyranny'.[170]

The idea that the press had become a serious social problem
was an important trait in argument about the quality of British
political life after 1914. Only a few years before, that argument
would have been conducted in a different language about the
'mischievous' power of a particular paper or the 'tone', perhaps,
of a journal like Stead's *Pall Mall Gazette*. Now the target was
not a single person or newspaper but a collective idea. St Loe
Strachey may have tried to convince Herbert Asquith that '[t]hat
damnable abstraction of the Press (with a big P) and public opinion
(also with capitals) [were] fearful chimeras',[171] but whether chim-
erical or not the image of the press as a commercial and political
conspiracy was a pervasive one. Esher thought the 'pressmen'
the natural successors to the Jesuits.[172] Buckmaster, after seeing
what Northcliffe had done to Haldane in 1915, was afraid even
to speak when they were about: 'Public life unfortunately has few
attractions today for highminded men. [T]o consider that you must
either conciliate the press or be subject to its constant perversion
of your views and actions . . . and the ceaseless iteration of some
foolish unguarded phrase . . . is enough to deter the bravest

man.'[173] The involvement of the politicians with the press, that is to say, was no longer a question of a few Members of Parliament having links with newspapers or of hypersensitive men being incensed about what some journal might be saying about them. When an influential political organizer could believe that certain newspapers had become 'powerful unsettling forces among Liberals'[174] a significant extra-parliamentary element had become part of what was understood to be sensible strategy among politicians. After 1914 governments survived or crumbled in the context of a barrage of newspaper support or criticism. Newspaper magnates actually served in governments. The press had arrived as a pivotal political instrument. It had learned to be not merely a vehicle for dialogue but a crucial contributor to it.

III

Examination of editors and writers has been thought worth while because they had access to the minds of untold Liberals. It is for the same reason that the leaders of the Churches between 1914 and 1929 reward inquiry, especially in the context of the much-discussed relationship between Liberalism and Nonconformity. Yet it must be conceded at once that the study of the twentieth-century Church is almost as difficult to conduct as it is to ignore. In order to make discussion manageable here, the inquiry will be narrowed to the small group who formed the ecclesiastical elite. There will be little time to confront blanket statements about the relationship between Church and Liberal society as a whole, which must await its own study.

Some superficial conclusions may be quickly reported. The Church 'declined': the platitude has to be asserted somewhere as a background to inquiry. In reviewing the situation of contemporary religion in 1909, C. F. G. Masterman felt sure that 'belief in religion, as a conception of life dependent upon supernatural sanction or as a revelation of a purpose and meaning beyond the actual business of the day, [was] slowly but steadily fading from the modern city race'.[175] The statement has a finality which the evidence does not entirely support. In the following year, for example, Haldane addressed the Theological Society of Edinburgh and cheered his audience with the thought that church attendance 'probably d[id] not really diminish, however the outward semblance of habit may have changed'.[176] But Masterman's judgement seems close enough to the truth: it is noticeable that Haldane's 'probably' found its way into the sentence as a pencilled afterthought. It is clear that in working-class areas attendance was poor by the turn of the century; clear too that in industrial South Wales Nonconformist allegiance had reached its peak about 1880 and declined thereafter except for the exceptional revival of 1904/05.[177] If it is too sweeping to assume that the Nonconformist conscience did not survive the First World War, it seems to be true that it lost its edge as denominations declined, especially Wesleyanism, which 'suffered a more prolonged loss of members than at any time in its history'.[178]

Apart from the perennial problem of combating their depressed state, the Churches were concerned between 1914 and 1929 with argument over Welsh Church disestablishment, temperance, ecumenicism and revision of the Prayer Book, though for the Methodists the overriding concern was of course with reunion after 1918. Against this background the natural identity of interest between Nonconformity and Liberalism was believed by many contemporaries to have been strengthened, or at least to have persisted. In Lord Elton's memory, for example, the post-war Liberal party 'appeared to be both moribund and increasingly corroded by the nonconformist conscience'.[179] That conscience was still there; it will not do to ignore it by intoning that old controversies were dead.[180] Differences in the relationship from that of the pre-war period can be found, but they appear to be less the product of a dwindling Nonconformity than of changes of emphasis in the character of Nonconformist allegiance. With a fully fledged Labour party able to draw away parts of traditionally Liberal support, Nonconformity was not compelled to bind itself to one party. Nor did the events of the war help to strengthen the Liberal connexion. Dissent was infuriated by conscription,[181] depressed by the electoral failures when peace returned and shocked by the hysteria of the post-war feuding.[182]

An impression of tension in the relationship between Liberalism and Nonconformity is strongly sensed in a reading of the *British Weekly* during the 1920s. In an article about 'The Voter's Responsibility' at the general election of 1923 the tone is plainly less than certain:

It has been the tradition of English Nonconformity, intertwined with names such as HUGH PRICE HUGHES and JOHN CLIFFORD, that living religion and living politics cannot altogether be sundered. *Perhaps in the past that was too much translated into terms of allegiance to one party,* but the essential truth abides that . . . our politics must be one of the points of application of our religion.[183]

A fortnight later the point was pressed home by reminding readers that the Unitarians were represented in both the Conservative and Labour parliamentary groups.[184] Nor were they the only denomination to wander. Of the seven Primitive Methodist M.P.s returned in 1918, five represented the Labour party, a proportion which grew to seven out of nine by 1924.[185] In a provisional list of twenty-four Quaker candidates at the general election of 1929 only half a dozen were Liberals and all but one of the rest were standing in the Labour interest.[186] The impression, however, is not a monolithic one. The allegiance of some denominations – the Congregationalist is perhaps the most striking – remained strong through to 1929; and in the course of the latter campaign the *British Weekly* strongly urged support for the Liberals.[187] Certainly adherence does not appear to have been completely shaken by the electoral failure of the Liberal party. '[W]e quote again those words of Ibsen's, "Minorities govern the world".'[188]

Ecclesiastical leaders were important to politicians in their role as instruments of moral pressure. When, for example, Brailsford was championing the agitation to reduce the number of imprisoned conscientious objectors during the war, he was anxious to have on his side 'only weighty names and no badly compromised ones'; he therefore approached three bishops, John Clifford and R. F. Horton.[189] Similarly, when Bryce and Dickinson were looking for signatories to a letter advocating a League of Nations they approached Churchmen including the Archbishops of Canterbury and York, Cardinal Bourne, the Bishop of Winchester, J. H. Shakespeare and G. Campbell Morgan.[190] Mention of the last name recalls an interesting connexion between Nonconformity and Liberal politics, for sitting among Morgan's congregation on the outbreak of war, 'occup[ying] his usual place near the pulpit',[191] was Sir Albert Spicer, paper magnate and Liberal patron. Another kind of contact was established through individual politicians like Haldane who entertained clergy at home and helped conciliate the warring factions over the Enabling Bill of

1919.[192] There was also an important relationship between Church and press since any moral movement required printed support; strictures on the failure of the Liberal press in such matters are not hard to find.[193] If contact with the universities was slighter this was because the Churches had their own intelligentsia. Whatever their status as mass movements, the Churches contained at their apex an intellectual sub-group whose spiritual parameters were part of the Liberal mind.

In 1914 British Nonconformity contained few names which the *British Weekly* might want to print in capital letters. Hugh Price Hughes had died in 1902, John Clifford was seventy-eight – though he was to take part in the anti-conscription agitation[194] and live on till 1923. Senior Nonconformity was represented by four figures, all of one generation, all born in the 1850s. Eldest was William Robertson Nicoll, a Presbyterian who had wielded much influence within the Free Churches through his editorship of the *Expositor* and *British Weekly* after 1885/86. Nicoll was a Scot 'first and last and all the time' and, according to one observer, had 'the Highlander's memory of an offence'.[195] Politically he was a Liberal, and what was more significant for the development of Liberalism was that he was a Lloyd George Liberal. Nicoll believed in Lloyd George with a faith reminiscent of C. P. Scott's, one which setbacks and frustrations never really removed. '[Y]ou have ...developed a genius for statesmanship', he wrote to Lloyd George in 1920, 'such as has been rarely displayed.'[196] Through Lloyd George's blackest period Nicoll defended him before the Nonconformist conscience and continued to do so until his death in the same year as Clifford's. For his part Lloyd George was grateful. In conversation with Riddell after Nicoll's death he readily admitted that the Free Church leader had been 'a great person and had been a good friend to him and a great help at the time of the war. Had it not been for Nicoll's attitude, the Free Churches might have taken a different line, and the whole course of the war might have been altered.'[197]

The other three names of importance in the Nonconformist hierarchy were, in order of descending age, John Scott Lidgett, R. F. Horton and J. H. Shakespeare. None of them had the political importance of a Clifford or a Nicoll, but their presence cannot be ignored. Scott Lidgett was a Wesleyan ('quite the best type of Nonconformist ')[198] and exerted his greatest political influence in London where he was an alderman on the L.C.C. between 1922 and 1928 and leader of the expiring Progressive party after 1918. Since 1911 he had been a joint editor of the *Contemporary Review* (which had thrust him into the university Liberalism of G. P. Gooch) and after 1922 he was a member of Senate at London University (which thrust him deeper still). Horton was a Congregationalist distinguished more by academic brilliance than political influence. Two places are associated with him: Oxford, where he lectured in ancient and modern history in the earlier part of his career, and Lyndhurst Road, Hampstead, where he preached between 1884 and 1930 in the chapel built for him. He was a Liberal but his Liberalism (like his career) was steady rather than cataclysmic. 'In politics', he wrote to Dicey in 1911, 'as in religion, there is need of faith.'[199] Finally there was Shakespeare, Secretary of the Baptist Union until 1924. He too was a Liberal, a supporter of his fellow Baptist Lloyd George – at least at the beginning of the period under review here, when they collaborated in forcing Nonconformist chaplains on a sceptical Kitchener.[200] Unity of the Free Churches was Shakespeare's abiding passion, however, and his efforts in that direction, culminating in his controversial *The Churches at the Cross Roads* (1918), offended some sections of orthodox Nonconformity.[201] He died, depressed, in 1928.

To select four names in this way is plainly an arbitrary procedure. If the 1850s were to be taken as the breeding ground of the future ecclesiastical intelligentsia, then mention would need to be made of Sir Henry Lunn, born in 1859. He will be seen here mostly in the fracas surrounding the question of Welsh Disestablishment at the beginning of the war. He had been a Liberal since 1886 and had in the later period showed tendencies towards a central, Asquithian position. If the boundaries of recruitment were to be pushed back even further the Anglican name of W. A. Spooner would arise; between 1914 and 1924 he was still Warden of New College, Oxford, and presumably a Lloyd Georgian, since he told Grigg in 1922 that the Welshman would 'stand out as [his] great figure in history'.[202] Moving forward into the 1860s, on the other hand, three significant names are encountered in Alfred Garvie, G. Campbell Morgan and Dugald Macfadyen. The first was to become a pillar of English Congregationalism (his pastor had been R. F. Horton) and a firm Liberal, though he voted Labour in the 1918 election in the absence of a Liberal candidate at Hampstead.[203] Morgan, another Liberal, could also boast a connexion with the great, this time with Nicoll who took part in his recognition as minister of Westminster Chapel in 1904.[204] The politics of Macfadyen are unclear. He was to Highgate what Morgan was to Westminster; both men spent time in the United States after the war. Further forward in time are J. E. Rattenbury, who was to exert great influence on twentieth-century Wesleyanism, and Henry Carter, 'that brilliant exponent of young Methodism' who played an important part in the temperance movement during and after the war and brought with him, in Randall Davidson's evaluation, 'a new force which increasingly command[ed] the respect of friend and opponent alike'.[205]

An admixture of Anglicans like Spooner and Davidson may be taken as a reminder that it was not only the Free Churches which could offer a platform for a Liberal intelligentsia. To be sure, the historical identity between the Church of England and Conservatism was as much a feature of this period as of any other, but it would be a mistake to dismiss eddies of Liberalism in the wider stream. At a time when theologians were searching for a 'Liberal, even a politically Liberal, Christ'[206] there was at least one Liberal bishop to contradict the assumption of a uniform Conservatism. Percival of Hereford had been a headmaster of Rugby in earlier years and had caused a furore there through his generous treatment of Nonconformists.[207] As an Anglican bishop he was hardly less egregious in his broadcasting of Liberal principle: as Henson was later to recall, Percival was 'a Liberal who did not hide his political lamp under a bushel, but set it on the stand of a bold and even aggressive advocacy of his Party's programme'.[208]

Observations about the other members of the Anglican hierarchy are far less certain. Davidson himself was probably neutral politically: Haldane thought him 'on the whole a Georgite by necessity' in 1918.[209] There are occasional flashes of the Liberal mind: Henson's views on free trade, for example, or the Bishop of Lincoln's support for wartime temperance. But Henson also believed in conscription; and the Bishop of Lincoln's thinking about temperance was less than Liberal. ('Asquith will not give up his liquor: this is the bottom of it.')[210] Gore showed occasional flashes of political radicalism. He confessed to Gilbert Murray

– the recipient is interesting – that secret treaties between nations stuck in his gizzard; and Murray heard through Hammond after the war that Gore had been 'staggered' by the vote in the reprisals debate.[211] But it is possible also to find contemporaries shocked by Gore's illiberalism, one which could 'admit so fully the divine right of the State'.[212] For the most part the attitude of the established Church during the war had been of this kind. In the postwar years, moreover, the ecumenicism of Lambeth and Malines became the focus of discussion, and the Church of England did not touch significantly on Liberal politics, unless one counts as a Liberal Lord Robert Cecil who was 'My dear Bob' to Archbishop Lang.[213]

Nonconformist responses to the political events of 1914–29 are easier to observe (because more explicit) and more significant for the history of Liberalism. In the first place the reaction of the Free Churches to the coming of the war reflected the pacifist mood of the Liberal party. Hesitancies tended later to be disowned by denominations which quickly swung round to support of the war once it had begun. But the *British Weekly* admitted in 1916 that although Nonconformity had 'stood like a rock' it had to be said that 'frankly...there [had been] a danger'.[214] The lack of a united front in 1914 can be explained to some extent by simple accident since many of the Nonconformist leaders were attending a conference in Germany when the war broke out. However, it was also a reaction against popular jingoism; and though intervention was endorsed after the rape of Belgium, the endorsement was always linked to the justice of the cause or something even higher:

[P]atriotism can be redeemed by being subordinated to the Kingdom of GOD. For this sublime ideal, which is also a sublime reality, all nations have a calling, even those which are at war with one another. It is when they are false to it, as Germany has now proved false...and it is only as we are true to it...that we can believe GOD is on our side.[215]

The appeal of such sentiment could be compelling. Nicoll, for example, said in 1915 that he had 'no politics' and was interested only in seeing an end to the war.[216] Yet others saw political implications deriving from the high position which the Churchmen declared themselves to be assuming. One such was Clifford who, while he was prepared to accept that the war had been entered into 'with a clean conscience and clean hands', was concerned that Britain should emerge from it 'without stains on either hands or conscience'.[217] It was conviction of this kind which involved Churchmen in the fight against conscription and the harsh treatment of conscientious objectors. Some went further towards the pacifist camp: George Unwin found that many of the students at Mansfield College in 1915 were of an anti-war mentality, though the dons remained in a more orthodox frame of mind.[218] From pacifists and non-pacifists alike, demands were likely to be made of the politicians in whose hands the national conscience lay. Demands would also be made of the ecclesiastical leaders. For every Nonconformist who was willing to join Nicoll in the win-the-war position, after all, there would be another wanting 'to shake hands with Clifford again and to feel that the Free Churchmen do believe in freedom and conscience'.[219] Self-assertive Nonconformity certainly was not dormant in the war years. Its presence is amply demonstrated by the degree of bitterness and involvement associated with the most contentious areas of Nonconformist politics between 1914 and 1918, the disestablishment of the Welsh Church and the agitation for control of liquor by the state.

The first problem straddled the threshold established by the declaration of war because of the decision of the government to postpone disestablishment for the duration of the war, even though the Welsh Disestablishment Bill had already been passed by the Commons.[220] Over this issue, as over the desirability of intervention in the war, the politicians and the leadership of Nonconformity were out of tune with the feelings of the rank and file. For the politicians Nonconformity was simply a target at which to aim scented words; only Lloyd George saw the 'explosive' feeling in Wales and the 'almost morbid suspicion' in which Liberal politicians were viewed there.[221] And even he saw the matter in purely electoral terms.[222] More surprisingly Sir Henry Lunn saw the problem in much the same way. 'The situation in a sentence was this', he wrote in his memoirs. 'We Liberals were using our party machinery to carry through a measure for which there was no strong demand from any but the Welsh extremists, and which was directly contrary to the feeling of that large body of voters which represents the Church of England.'[223]

Lunn may have been correct in seeing the Welsh pressure as the product of a small minority, but the 'betrayal' over disestablishment was seen by some as part of a larger one. It was symbolic of a seeming disregard of cherished values on the part of the Nonconformist leadership. Clifford's position was plain; he would have nothing to do with Lunn's conciliatory *démarches*. Doubtless the positions of the other leaders were equally capable of definition, but they were not so easily explicable, and to some lowly Nonconformists the lack of explanation was a source of bitterness:

Sir H. Lunn quotes Drs. Selbie, Peake and Scott Lidgett, and even Rev. J. H. Shakespeare. Are these leaders supporters of the Establishment principle or not? What a weakening of our heritage and moral forces since the days of Edward Miall, Henry Richard, Dr. R. W. Dale, and Dr. Guinness Rogers! Under weak-kneed leaders will England ever see true religious equality?[224]

Gladstone and Campbell-Bannerman are not among the names exhumed for admiration but the ethic is the same, the contrast between past and present as strong. The distance between leaders and followers in Nonconformity was lengthening, just as was that between the politicians and their Welsh Nonconformist voters. It was not an issue which politicians could be brought to trouble themselves with unless their constituency happened to be in Wales. When he received a request for information about the current state of disestablishment plans in 1917, Asquith confessed to being 'a little hazy about the exact position' and hastily passed on his correspondent's request to Simon who, he was confident, would 'tell [him] all about it'.[225]

There was a sense in which the cause of temperance had a more important effect on Liberalism than did disestablishment, since the former was bound up with the name of Lloyd George once the latter had made in 1915 his famous pronouncement that Britain was fighting Germany, Austria and Drink. The agitation for state purchase of the liquor trade reached its height in the spring of 1915, though both Nonconformists and Liberals differed among themselves about whether it was wise (or moral) for the state to accept such a responsibility. Liberal employers bulked large among those in sympathy with the idea of reducing absenteeism in industry by attacking drunkenness; into this category fell Runciman, Macara and Richard Cadbury. Others were more worried by the obvious electoral unpopularity attending any party which could be accused of trying to deprive the worker of his glass of beer. The Nonconformist division was based on more credal considerations. There

were those who, like Denney, were 'much in favour of the
Government taking some drastic action about the use of liquor
during the war'.[226] There were those who, like Clifford, were
'rigidly against' any such idea[227] becuase it would tend towards
pickling the state in alcohol. '[I]f there is any party in the country ',
the *Manchester Guardian* commented, 'which has strenuously
opposed every proposal for public management of the liquor trade
it is the Temperance party.'[228] In the context of 1915 many
Nonconformists must have set aside former principle and acceded
to the notion of state control; and since the future of that scheme
was in the hands of Lloyd George such conversion could only do
him good.

The latter clearly lost some support among the Nonconformists
because of his 'surrender on the matter of Cons[cription] and his
acceptance of the Scheme of Purchase of the Liquor Trade '.[229]
It is likely, however, that he won more than he lost. Whatever
else he had done (George Cadbury pointed out to his son in 1916),
Lloyd George was 'still not ashamed to be a Free Churchman'
and 'attack England's greatest foe, the liquor traffic '.[230] Given that
Cadbury was at that time managing director of the *Daily News*
his opinion was perhaps more important than Clifford's. True,
in Cadbury Lloyd George had been preaching to the converted
But it is significant that even Nicoll, who had looked with some
distaste on the idea of state purchase, nevertheless pressed Lloyd
George's claims on the Nonconformist electorate during the unclear period in the first week of December 1916. 'We take it for
granted', he wrote in the *British Weekly*, 'that any possible Prime
Minister will seek the help of the great and brilliant statesman
who...is incomparably the chief force in the country'; and
this after a narrative calculated to show that Lloyd George never
wanted to be Prime Minister at all.[231] Nor, it seems, was Lloyd
George's Nonconformist support alienated by his political
manoeuvres as much as Clifford's fading judgement implies. His
own denomination held him in awe at the end of the war. An
address from the Council of the Baptist Union commented on
Lloyd George's 'strong faith in the great Disposer of events':
'You believed, as we believed, that the good hand of God was
upon us, that we were battling for the Kingdom of God and His
righteousness against the forces of darkness which were destroy-
ing the conscience of the world.'[232]

To what extent Lloyd George was able to retain the support of Nonconformists is conjectural. It is certainly not clear, as one historian has recently suggested, that he 'stood secure in their good graces'[233] after the war. Many Nonconformists were offended by Lloyd George's political and personal amorality during the coalition period, and it will not do to extrapolate from the war situation to that which Nonconformists observed from the outside after 1918. The evidence supplies firmer grounds for supposing simply that Lloyd George did what he could to promote himself and his own kind of Liberalism as forces in touch with the wants of the Free Churches. Promotion of this kind required techniques in which Lloyd George had had a lifetime's education. It required, in the first place, careful calculation within the context of high politics. Thus Lloyd George was 'most anxious' about how to apply Hewart's proposed Licensing Bill to Wales without alienating important parts of Nonconformity. His solution was ingenious: licensed premises should be closed on Sundays but clubs, with their clientele of working-class electors, should be allowed to open.[234] Radiation of the correct atmosphere would also involve propaganda geared to presenting Lloyd George as the embodiment of chapel propriety, one who 'ha[d] not abandoned a single Free Church or Liberal principle'.[235] Consequently he was not slow to invite Free Church leaders to breakfast, where he could announce 'his personal conviction that a religious revival was a necessary precedent to social reform', or the prominent Congregationalist Murray Hyslop to lunch, where he could be impressed by Lloyd George's concern with those moral problems 'very dear to [his] heart'.[236] Occasions like these would find their way into the *Lloyd George Liberal Magazine* or the *Daily Chronicle*; and of course Free Churchmen were ready to return the compliments publicly:

Mr. Lloyd George won the enthusiastic suffrages of the Free Churches to a degree which Mr. Gladstone, who disliked and misunderstood us, never did, first and foremost by his fearless identification of himself with nonconformity, and by his avowed purposes in politics to further ends and causes that were . . . essentially akin to the people's social and moral life. His humanisation of the arid world of politics and his infusion of his campaigns and programmes with the passion of moral and religious enthusiasm, explains his unique appeal to [those] who are not either of the Established Church or the morally or agnostically indifferent classes.[237]

Passages such as this underline the importance of acknowledging the ability of a man described by an intimate as 'essentially a pagan'[238] to create spiritual attraction at a time when he was calling the tune politically.

He was not of course alone in trying to create this aura. Their electoral situation after 1918 insisted that the Asquithians pay attention to the Nonconformist electorate. They did not have Lloyd George's advantages in this sphere. One of Lloyd George's M.P.s, for example, was the son of J. H. Shakespeare and could be used to manipulate Baptist support, or so the Asquithians believed.[239] But again, the latter could counter-attack through the Rev. G. Hooper, President of the Free Church Conference, 'a real stalwart'[240] who took his main duty to be that of extricating Nonconformity from the grip of Lloyd George. After the 1922 election had confirmed the electoral fears of both sides, rhetorical flares were sent up for the benefit of Churchmen. In 1923 Esher thought that a speech of Lloyd George's, ostensibly about Liberal reunion, was really an attempt to attract the Nonconformist conscience.[241] If, on the other hand, a Nonconformist elector picked up his *British Weekly* during the election campaign of that year, he would have found the following in bold type:

May I remind my countrymen of the Free Churches, many of whom have for years been my friends and fellow workers, that Liberalism is still following the paths of sanity and peace, and is opposing under any guise any encroachment upon freedom of trade, enterprise and opinion.

H. H. Asquith[242]

Dwindling fortunes within an expanding electorate made it necessary for politicians to make some attempt to harness the forces of Nonconformity.

But how were the politicians to pitch their appeal to the Nonconformist mind? What were they to talk about? After 1920 disestablishment was a dead letter. Temperance was still an issue but it was one which the Labour party – and even some sections of Conservatism[243] – could exploit as well as the Liberals. Indeed Labour used it more effectively. Thus while one can find Maclean saying the right things during the second reading of the Licensing Bill in 1921,[244] it is noteworthy that at a temperance conference held at Broxbourne in 1925 the presiding figure was Philip Snowden.[245] Recourse could be had to the League of Nations, but that call was hardly loud enough to sustain support over a wide field of policy. It was in any case unclear what Nonconformists thought about the League. At one meeting of the 'League of Nations people' in 1919, an observer (admittedly biassed) found the audience 'not enthusiastic' even though it was 'composed largely of Nonconformists of the lower middle class'; they had turned up, he believed, to see Clifford rather than to respond to his message.[246]

The post-war generation could not be expected to see a great deal to applaud in Liberalism. Its radical wing seemed to have collapsed: the Lloyd George who had once been able to make some pretence of radicalism was now tarred with the coalition brush. Violet Bonham-Carter was afraid in 1923 that Lloyd George might still be able to fool the Nonconformists by 'blow[ing] away Reprisals and Versailles' with a 'puff of pulpit gas',[247] but her fears were unfounded. Few Liberals had any very radical reappraisal to make of the issues which hit hardest at the post-war population. It has been seen here that the failure was resented among the progressive sections of the party; it was resented also within progressive Nonconformity. In the same breath that offered support to the Liberals in 1929, the *British Weekly* offered also a warning:

A policy of rest-and-be-thankful will never touch the imagination of the best minds in the country; certainly, it will lose the loyalty of the younger portion of the community. Our representatives...must give proof that they are as daring as are others of whom we are a little afraid; that they also have their dreams which they are willing to embody in some new public amenity. They also must give evidence that they are opposed to squalid homes and miserable streets.[248]

That the Labour party was still held in some fear could give little comfort to the Liberals. When an ex-Moderator of the Presbyterian Church Assembly could tell Sidney Webb that the Labour party held the future in its hands,[249] when Nonconformist ministers were willing to chair Labour meetings,[250] when a rabidly Catholic Conservative could make Liberal converts and bring 'some of the Nonconformist leaders...openly with' him,[251] the relationship between Liberalism and its religious base was undergoing tensions it had never known before.

Only when some extraordinary issue presented itself could the old harmony be restored. When revision of the Prayer Book was proposed in 1927/28, Hugh Dalton was depressed at the likely consequences. 'Prayer Book thrown out again', he wrote in his diary. 'Damn! I see a vision of religion coming back into British politics... and, perhaps, incidentally reviving the Liberals.'[252] It is conceivable that the fillip that this issue gave to the Liberals contributed to their revival in the constituencies. It is certain that the Prayer Book became something of a Liberal 'touchstone' for Nonconformists, as Dr J. D. Jones had predicted:

> I wrote to [Lloyd George] before the debate pointing out... that until Liberalism regained the confidence of Free Churchmen there was small chance for it in the Country... Congregationalists are an independent lot of folk and are rarely unanimous about anything. But they are practically unanimous about this and so are the Baptists and so are the Primitive and United Methodists and the vast majority of Wesleyan Methodists... You know what defections there have been from our Nonconformist ranks. I believe nothing could do more to win them back than a firm stand on this Prayer Book issue.[253]

Lloyd George made sure he voted in both important divisions.[254] The Asquithians, however, made little capital out of the situation, partly because Asquith was undergoing his last illness at the time, partly because he and Grey had been afraid throughout the controversy of saying anything definite for fear of alienating supporters of one persuasion or another.[255]

Beyond such fortuitous *causes* Liberalism did not involve Nonconformity in its day-to-day thinking to nearly the same degree that it involved the intelligentsia of the universities or the press. No Churchmen, for example, served on the Industrial Inquiry. Some contact did take place between leaders but it was likely to be in the context of pleasantries over the dinner table at Grillions. Erosion was happening quietly. Liberals were, many of them, prepared to believe that the Good Old Cause lived on and that Liberalism was still 'both the cause and the product of Nonconformity'.[256] But Liberalism was now part of the world of land campaigns, Keynesian economics and unemployment statistics. The Churches, for their part, were looking towards the future more in the perspective of the COPEC conference of 1924 than in one angled towards old connexions. The task of religious groups, as of political parties, was to stir the enthusiasm of people whom Mr Gladstone would have misunderstood and disliked.

Only a composite explanation of the persistence of the Liberal intellectual tradition seems possible. The intelligentsia operated within its own world, one which touched that of high politics at many points but which was a different world for all that: depictions of the mind of Asquithians and Lloyd Georgians are often inapposite when considering Gilbert Murray or J. A. Spender or J. H. Shakespeare. Nevertheless the intelligentsia had fathers and mothers and childhoods and upbringings; its formative years were spent in a context of personal contact and atmospheric steeping. Perhaps that context gave rise to at least three kinds of continuity. Familial, collegiate and organizational links – the potent Balliol tie, the League of Nations Union, the Summer Schools, the Rainbow circle, Grillions, Nonconformist conferences – helped to make old affiliations harder to dissolve and involvement in party activity harder to avoid. The activity which Liberalism demanded after 1914, secondly, seems to have changed little from that of pre-war years, except for the underpinning of Lloyd George's radicalism towards the end of the 1920s (and that probably lost more than it gained in intellectual sympathy). Those seeking reason and balance in politics would be likely to gravitate towards Liberalism as a stable median in the often violent debate between anarchy and property; and the willingness of the parliamentary party to commit itself to a 'middle way' allowed it to propagate an image as safe as that offered by Campbell-Bannerman and Asquith before the war.

More significant than these continuities, however, was the belief of the Liberal intelligentsia in continuity itself as a process whereby contact with what was true and venerable within Liberalism could be maintained. The temperament which confronted current problems as functions of bequeathed lessons was one which the intelligentsia largely shared with the politicians. There was a dissenting strand of opinion in the self-conscious radicalism of Muir and Wallas; and there was a still more radical departure, oddly, in the mind of much of Nonconformity whose spiritual horizons went far enough beyond Liberal tradition to enable it sometimes to ask bold questions and even to begin to think of looking elsewhere for the answers. But much the larger segment of opinion was that which sought 'to think rightly and to hold out', to count itself a clear-eyed observer of political morality as Mill and Morley were conceived to have been. Fisher's taking down of *Principia Ethica* from his shelf amounted to the same exercise as Acland's taking down a Life of Ripon from his, or a Liberal editor recalling the days when journalism was high and *The Times* was a newspaper. Like the party which looked to it for applause, the Liberal intelligentsia perceived its unpleasant present through the lens of a hallowed past.

Collect

The Corinthians erected an altar to the unknown God. The Liberals erect their altar to the unknown principle. They write prize poems to it, but they can't tell what it is. They are prepared to be martyrs for their principles if they only could find out what they are.

MacCallum Scott Diary, 11 January 1925.

Bishop Butler says in one of his sermons that it is as easy to close the eyes of the mind as of the body. But is it as easy to open them?

Asquith to Murray, 19 November 1926, Murray MSS, Box 3.

I remember New Year's eve the old days when we used to open the Gallery doors and listen to the bells across the snow. So many hopes and joys are associated with those days. I really don't think I could bear the contrast. All this, I suppose, would be thought 'soppy'. I only hope for their sakes that a few soppy-minded people are left in this jazzy world.

Esher to Maurice Brett, 13 January 1928, *Journals and Letters of Reginald Viscount Esher*, IV (1938), 301–2.

Perverse religiosity may be said to have been the theme of this study. Religiosity, because it has been seen to have been a recurring characteristic of the Liberal mind between 1914 and 1929 that it should dwell upon 'faith' and 'principle' and 'the straight road'. Perverse, because this concentration on political metaphysics lay at the heart of the Liberal failure to come to terms with the world as it was to be after 1914. That is not to say that the high politics of Liberalism did not contain calculation and compromise – indeed as the fortunes of the party dwindled, so was the need for such activity accentuated. But behind the small change of politics there was always the larger currency, a language of principle; and it was only by its 'unstinted and fearless application' that the world could be rebuilt after 1918 or perhaps even saved at all.[1] Liberals worthy of the name were obliged to 'go straight on – *straight*'.[2] There was no room for flexibility. 'Common sense and fair play w[ould] gradually emerge out of all this mud.' Liberalism would eventually make its return to the centre of national life because everyone must soon tire of what was 'sick and low' and yearn for what was 'clean and straight'.[3] Politicians in the House of Commons, intellectuals in the universities, sympathizers in the country: all Liberals agreed that morality-in-politics was the medium through which the country might be brought back to sanity after the madness of war. They were, quite simply, wrong. British society learned to live with itself and pushed politics to the edge of its consciousness. Liberals, on the other hand, never ceased to reiterate the slogans of their old thought-world. As late as 1932 Ramsay Muir was still looking for 'a re-statement of the meaning and aims of Liberalism' in order to put some life into his 'disheartened and reduced Party'.[4] Faith's perversities endured long after the corpse was cold.

It had been the war period which had thrown all into confusion and created situations in which politicians seemed unable to 'find their feet'.[5] Earlier periods had also witnessed important shifts in the political world, of course. In many areas of political life before the war there were fears that the character of politics was changing for the worse. Socialism and anarchism were mock-serious threats in the Liberal imagination, and some regarded the attempts of Asquith's government to divert such movements as portending a bastard Liberalism, a 'neo-Liberalism',[6] which, once created, would mean the end of Liberalism as its adherents wanted to know it. In any case the aristocratic grip on high politics was apparently declining, and it was natural for grooved minds to associate the development with political instability and distasteful scandal. It led Dicey to the conclusion that 'public life [was] undergoing a decline in character' by 1911, with statesmen less trustworthy than they used to be and 'unconcealed self-seeking' a common trait in high politics.[7] It led Esher to vow his detestation of democracy and his determination to prevent the diplomatic service from being sullied.[8] However, comments like these need to be placed in perspective. Neither Dicey nor Esher in their respective ways represented central Liberal thinking in the immediate pre-war years; and those who were better qualified to speak tended to do so in retrospect, like Haldane in his memorandum of 1926 or Sir Alfred Pease in memoirs published even later.

But both contemporary and retrospective opinion agreed that fundamental changes took place within Liberalism between 1914 and 1917. It has become a cliché of the undergraduate essay to say that war 'challenged Liberal principles', a way of expressing understanding without having any. It has been the point of this study to lend emphasis to the proportions of the war's impact on the Liberal mind and to stress that doing so involves more than a stale recitation of the difficulties raised by Defence of the Realm Acts, the Paris Resolutions and conscription. Rather, it involves the evocation of a sense in which the war did not so much challenge Liberal principle as create it. Principles were brought to the fore of the Liberal mind only when they seemed to be assaulted by the challenges which the war threw up. It was when the war was one year old, for example, that MacCallum Scott wrote in his diary the heading 'A Confession of Faith'.[9] What he wrote beneath this title was in no way revolutionary, merely his conception of the function of parliament in wartime and of how it should be trusted to do its work providing there existed adequate safeguards against tyranny. What is important, however, is less the content of the declaration than the fact that a Liberal M.P. thought it desirable to make one. As the war progressed, the argument became at once more public and more subtle: it was framed in deceptively personal terms but behind the quarrels and the personal slights often lay larger questions concerning the character of Liberalism.

Indeed, if the primary material yielded by the fifteen years after 1914 were to be piled together in one room and read in random order, without regard to personality or chronology, it is a reasonable hypothesis that this sense of a personal language camouflaging a larger world would nevertheless be conveyed. Insensitive readers might not be impressed; they could simply record that the Quaker conscience among those who 'seem[ed] too good for politics' had been crushed by the war, and it is conveniently explicit that a man like Gordon Harvey writes openly about his 'disappointments' and 'the toppling over of idols'.[10] Yet to leave the matter there is to court danger more than safety, for concern with ultimate Liberal values has been seen here to have been no monopoly of Nonconformist or Leftish Liberalism. Equally deep anxieties can be found elsewhere: it is only the language in which they are articulated that is different. When Morley wrote to Crewe, 'You stand for much and you understand it all',[11] he was making a statement about his Liberalism as well as a compliment to a friend. Lloyd George, similarly, made statements about his Liberalism when he refused to be guided by his 'connexion with [Gladstone] and Hawarden in decent fashion'.[12] Men like

'Winston, Ll.G., etc.' were 'men who dangle[d] a loose leg to hop down in every camp and believe[d] in *nothing*'.[13] Unlike Crewe, in Asquithian eyes, they stood for nothing and understood nothing. And both of these ideas sprang from the war years and what the Liberal mind had made of them. For one section (much the larger), Liberal high politics was characterized by the pressing into relief of principle and faith, whilst for the smaller section the war and its traumas only served to show that principle and faith were not enough. The tension between these standpoints has formed the tone of much that has been written here.

Wider Liberalism suffered attacks both at the level of public positioning and personal thought-world after 1914. The exigencies of war compelled politicians to construct new images of themselves. The mentality of the electorate was now as incalculable as its proportions were intimidating.[14] '[T]he vast new electorate',[15] 'such a vast mob',[16] was described in phrases which themselves suggested the necessity of gesture and pose for politicians who wanted to sound relevant. The kind of society which the latter best knew how to live with was one which had been compelled to undergo important transitions. One observation of these changes came from Beddington Behrens in 1919:

In the old days the landed nobility had its privileges...but it also had its duties...the moneyed oligarchy who [*sic*] has largely taken its place has taken over its privileges but has forgotten the sacred duty of caring for the people...[T]here is no moral force to unite and bind us any more in England. What is wanted is a new religion, what is wanted is a great moral force to unite us for a great purpose.[17]

This is the view from Christ Church; it is an image which intellectuals and Churchmen could hold at the core of their thinking. For politicians, images like this were harder to create. Such images as they had were necessarily more prosaic and were marked most consistently by a conception of pre-war 'political' questions becoming post-war 'economic' and 'social' ones.[18] It was too much to expect politicians to generate generous moral impulses within a political world which seemed to be suffering from 'mental and spiritual exhaustion',[19] one in which the ordinary intercourse of daily political life had become 'a dirty business',[20] a 'weltering pig's wash'.[21]

The depression associated with trying to project the faith forwards was one stimulus for the widespread disposition among

Liberals to project it backwards to an age more obviously moulded in their own image. It was a natural inclination for those who had 'passed middle life' to reflect that the world would never again be what it had been in the days of 'W.E.G., Dizzy...Derby, Salisbury, A.J.B.' – days of dignity when there were no cameramen at St Moritz to snap the Lord Chancellor in 'a jumper, knickerbockers and skates'.[22] But whilst it was natural for a Conservative to lament the passing of gentlemen, Liberals were more prone to mourn certain intangibles which their gentlemen had been believed once to encapsulate. The war had now made those things appear both urgent and inadequate. 'The physical world is the same', MacCallum Scott wrote at the end of 1917, 'but the mental habits have become demoralised – the brain has jumped the rails of the old fixed ideas and ideals.'[23] Elder statesmen, however, had been travelling one way for too long to be practised in jumping rails; and no Liberal disturbed by the war needed to go to Marx to learn about the traditions of the dead weighing on the minds of the living. As the very un-Marxist, ex-Liberal Melchett put it in 1930, one did not change when one grew old but merely became more so.[24]

Better times had of necessity to be observed from the perspective of the 'faded'[25] and 'dishevelled'[26] present. And Acland was right: 1895 *was* a long way away.[27] Yet the war seemed somehow to bring that era closer by making its recollection so much more pleasant. After all, the years of *fin-de-siècle* Liberalism were the years which most of the post-1914 leadership knew best: the shedding of the Whigs, the departure of Gladstone, the Rosebery/Harcourt feuds, the comings and goings of Campbell-Bannerman were all part of their familiar vocabulary when talking between themselves about the recent past. Once the subject of acrid dispute, these matters were now suitable for leisured reminiscence in a letter to a former combatant or perhaps in one's own thoughts over the pages of the political memoirs which were beginning to come in a trickle. Some of those involved in the golden age were now gone, leaving less sensitive heirs to regret that the 'Whig Tradition' was something 'one [was] inclined to forget' after the war.[28] But others survived and for them the parameters of the earlier world were still the ones that mattered:

I want to write to you about the Whigs. I used to dislike them, but in my years of loneliness I have come to the conclusion that they governed

England better than anybody else. They thought out their measures carefully, and adapted them to their time and generation. In modern days we see so much heroism of a kind, but little wisdom.[29]

Indeed for Crewe it was impossible to regard pre-war politics as being out of date. He looked forward to reading Spender's Life of Campbell-Bannerman, he told the author in 1923, and to Gardiner's Life of Harcourt.[30] So possessive were the rival Liberal factions about the stature of their heroes that even the authorship of such biographies was a matter for cogitation and quarrel. Why should Spender ('an Imperialist') be allowed to misrepresent the achievements of 'C–B'?[31] Why should the same author, having been offered the honour of writing a Life of Spencer, want to be paid for doing it?[32]

There was a dimension of Liberal change after 1914 which took its character from the process of old men becoming older and old ideas deepening in their familiarity. This says more than might be thought. The historian wanting to undestand Liberal politics after 1914 cannot ignore the mood – the mind – of politicians at the top; and in this sense Esher's bells across the snow are as relevant a constituent of historical explanation as are accounts of the financial difficulties of the party or statistics about the size of the Labour vote in Chorley and Chippenham. Truth to be told, they are more central to the explanatory exercise, because the latter considerations tell one which problems Liberals needed to face whilst the former yields one kind of reason why Liberals did not want to face them. Historians who like their history hard-boiled may dismiss as senile ramblings Rosebery's 'sorrowing over the departing world' in 1929,[33] but no proliferation of graphs or computation of 'swing' will contradict the conclusion that Liberal politicians believed that much which had been worth while in politics had disappeared. Nor is it necessary to remain within the confines of traditionalist Liberalism to illustrate the point. The radical-cum-pacifist mind of Loreburn, for example, was ready to concede that 'the old doctrines of Cobden' were still part of his 'mental equipment' in 1919.[34] Again, the Manchester School of Simon, Muir and Oliver pretended to be distant from orthodox Liberalism, but Tawney still liked to refer to them as the 1850 Club.[35]

The connexion between Liberals and their past was personal or organizational before it was 'ideological'. High politics was not, to be sure, a desiccated activity, but the ideals and metaphysics found there tended to follow calculation and trimming rather than precede them. Contact with the past was attained through individuals of great present stature, men who symbolized 'the best' of their generation. After 1914 there was a pervasive belief that such men had left the stage. The followers, however, remained, survivors of a past generation, 'approaching superannuation', 'old men who ha[d] not sufficient brains left to see the world as it [was]';[36] and if the leaders were gone or about to go, it was still possible to remember the character of political virtue and elevate it into habit. 'Within both these camps', one correspondent wrote to Murray about the Liberal split, 'there are large numbers of persons who feel compelled to remain where they are owing to the loyalty bred of association with persons and emphasized by traditions.'[37] Possibly it would have been more accurate to write about association with traditions emphasized by persons, but either way of looking at the political world was likely to produce that language of regret and recrimination which is such a feature of the Liberal mind after 1914. Those who wanted to move in new directions were frustrated by 'the dead hand of the past'.[38] Those who wanted to move back to old ones were left to savour the company of an ever-decreasing circle of stalwarts who shared their views. 'But, oh, how many of . . . my old friends are gone', Haldane was to muse in 1927. 'To talk now is like exploring a cemetery.'[39]

Many of the people who were eventually to populate Haldane's cemetery were responsible for the guidance of Liberalism after 1914. It was in the image of their minds that the party mind had been established. In the constituencies, where '[t]he bulk of the Associations, and practically all the agents [were] firmly Asquithian' (so much so that it was hard to persuade Coalition Liberal M.P.s to face them), power was in the hands of the 'old-time caucus men' like the 'senile and querulous' alderman of Dalton's acquaintance or men like 'old Thomas Parry, the timber-merchant of Mold, an old faithful Liberal'.[40] Such men took their politics from the cultivated tone of the Asquithian establishment and responded to its measured rhetoric and familiar argument, 'principles and traditions' which Asquith had 'embodied and interpreted' to a generation of 'middle-class puritans'.[41] If those principles and traditions seemed not to be answering in the post-war world, then that world must have been 'temporarily handed over to the Devil'.[42] The devil was usually identified in Lloyd George, of course, and the possibility of exorcizing him was to become a prime objective in the minds of the 'old men and Northcliffe' in whose hands the future of the country seemed to be held.[43] And it was seen in the first part of this study that this preoccupation attained a morbidity of outlook which militated against realistic evaluations of Liberal options.

Within what has been called here 'the wider Liberalism' divisions tended to be less virulent, but they took their toll in the way individuals formulated their views about what Liberalism ought to be offering to the post-war public. Intellectuals in the universities and spiritual leaders in the chapels could not escape the natural association of certain ideas with certain men. It was an undeniable if 'curious fact that Liberalism, which ha[d] taken as one of its war-cries "measures not men"', ha[d] known far more serious tensions and clashes arising out of questions and doubts with regard to persons than ha[d] been the case with Conservatism'.[44] Observers might argue about the causes of this inter-connexion, but its existence made itself felt in innumerable ways, some of them direct, some less so. Although Nicholas Murray Butler made no overt reference to Liberal divisions in writing to Asquith about the need to teach people 'what to read and what to pass by' and to extol 'the standard of genuine classic excellence and merit' which he associated with Asquith, it is hard to imagine him writing to Lloyd George in similar vein.[45] Equally, it is hard to imagine MacCallum Scott accusing Lloyd George of 'deducing a programme from some abstract first principle as to the rights of man'.[46] In this oblique way a vast number of statements about 'Liberalism' contained implications about one species of Liberalism which the observer had in mind. It has been argued here that these species were reducible ultimately to two.

Best to concede at once that reductionism of this kind invites crudity. Yet perhaps the vice is pardonable if its practice helps fix in the mind a focussed image of Liberalism during its last years as an 'historic' phenomenon. The events and opinions discussed here have made it necessary repeatedly to suggest that Asquithian Liberalism degenerated into an acidulated church whilst the Liberalism of Lloyd George and his followers became the home of the secular and the flexible and the expedient. Too often this statement lacks authority because of the nature of the material which has survived. It is therefore refreshing to find in MacCallum Scott's diary two superb vignettes which help to lend definition to the image. Both of them date from the middle period, 1919–22, when the ground-rules of politics had been redrawn, and this makes them especially interesting. Chronologically the first portrait is that of a Mancunian industrialist, a supporter of Lloyd George:

He is a sterling man, one of the best type of Manchester Liberals, firmly grounded in principle yet with a mind that does not run in a narrow groove – not a pedant, not a doctrinaire, not hidebound in theory. He is a shrewd and hard-headed business man, but his practical common sense is trans-fused with a sturdy and invincible idealism. He will not swerve from what he considers to be the course of right and justice. He is of the same stock from which John Bright sprang, but with a broader outlook and a more tolerant temperament.[47]

Important lessons may be gleaned from this quotation if it is left to stand alone, but these lessons are underlined when the picture is contrasted with that of a Glaswegian Asquithian described by MacCallum Scott in 1922:

[He] is very bitter about the Coalition and by constant brooding and concentration he has accumulated an overwhelming case against it. It is almost impossible for one who is not a trained political reasoner to stand up against it. In him the Scottish passion for theology has been diverted to politics. He adheres to dogmatic first principles with which he tends to confuse certain inherited or acquired prejudices. He instinctively hates and suspects 'practical politics', opportunism, realism in politics. All this savours of the doctrine of Works rather than of Faith. We Coalition Liberals have done the unforgivable thing – we have worshipped in another church. We are all destined to his political Hell.[48]

The character of Liberal thinking 'in the country' – the frame of mind of the society in which men like MacCallum Scott's two Liberals moved and talked – is for the present unclear and will remain so until it has been made the subject of a number of detailed, and probably regional, studies. But it will be recalled that this inquiry has concerned itself less with objective historical situations than with the view which contemporary politicians had of them: the lenses, and the distortions they produced, have been as much the centre of study as have the situations on which they were trained. From this point of view it can be said that the Liberal view of the wider world was one which tended to confirm impressions made current by the activities at Westminster. The idea that true Liberalism was waiting unuttered in the country, a Liberalism which '[s]omeday...w[ould] become articulate',[49] may have been a wrong idea for an Asquithian to believe in, but it was nevertheless the starting point for much political thinking.

It is clear that in a pre-psephological context the calculations which politicians could make about 'public opinion' were very limited and often the product of a personal (perhaps chance) encounter with individuals or organizations, or of hearing reports of such encounters from others. Judgement began with the particular and the singular. To hear the applause of 'little crowds of *white*-hot Liberal associations'[50] on platforms all along the line from Paisley was to form a view of potential Liberal vitality on a broader scale. To hear from a local activist that ' *Wm. Crozier*, the Clogmaker, [was] unfortunately still Coalition and L–G' but that Andrew Simpson was 'a very nice man and a strong backer of Ind. Liberalism' was one step towards instilling in the mind of an important Asquithian politician (Simon) that the thought-world of high politics was reflected also in the local context.[51] In this way random splashes of colour could be smudged outwards to form a blurred landscape.

If Liberals at the centre believed that Liberals in the country shared their preoccupations, the belief could not but affect the nature of the rhetoric which politicians thought it desirable to use. Granted that the war had soiled the decencies of public life and introduced into its conduct new and unpleasant elements, it was reasonable for Liberals to believe that their language about older and better times was as profitable as it was natural. If the war had had the 'sinister result' of bringing about 'a certain lowering of political standards', it made sense for Asquithians to argue that '[i]f English public life [was] to recover its old levels, it must be through the persistent adherence of Liberalism to *its* old standards, as exhibited in its choice of leaders'.[52] All that real Liberals valued most had been 'compassed about' with opposition and constraint; it would take 'courage and constant calm exposition of political principles and political truth' if the 'middle path of free and democratic government' was to be trodden.[53] However, such thinking did not take place in a doctrinal vacuum: it has been seen here that the gradual assumption of a central position was one which extraneous pressures encouraged. It was nevertheless the case that the Liberal conception of what supporters in the country were looking to their politicians for also impelled Liberals to take up the role of historic party offering established truth.

This truth is to be found beneath the oratory of the traditional wing of Liberalism during the 1920s. '[W]e shall have to teach the people what Liberalism is',[54] one Asquithian observed in 1924, and it is in this light that the rhetoric is to be seen. Witness, for example, Herbert Gladstone's private reflections about the Liberal platform which might be built in 1922. Lloyd Georgian methods at Downing Street would have to be eradicated; free trade ought to be revived and urged; the League of Nations ought to be pressed on the electorate as a good thing; the doctrine of Cabinet responsibility should be resuscitated; the best elements of Gladstonian finance ought to be preserved; Labour should be kept at arm's length and dialogue maintained only with its 'soundest' sections.[55] The programme takes as its starting point the demands of a political context which existed before the war and which might, Liberals hoped, be created again. In order to face forwards Liberalism needed first of all to go back to 'recover its moral and economic traditions and prove its identity with the Liberal party of Gladstone and Campbell-Bannerman'.[56] Once the country had been properly instructed the Liberal revival could surely not be long delayed, even if 'the waiting [was] wearisome' in the meantime.[57] The Liberal position, that is to say, was essentially static. There were platform pretences that Liberalism had a new world to offer but Liberals knew themselves to be more at home when offering an older world and waiting for the new one to recognize its sins and recant.

It ought not to be left unsaid that there were Liberals who wanted to change all this and move forward rather than back. This strand of Liberal thinking has been seen here in the activities of the wartime radicals, in the programme of the Manchester Group in the early 1920s and in the developing ideas of the Lloyd Georgian section of the party as it turned its mind to the problems associated with energy policy, industrial policy and land usage. It was not a strand, moreover, exclusive to the non-Asquithian sector: it was neither a radical nor a Lloyd Georgian, but Lord Robert Cecil, who wrote to Asquith in 1921 that he felt 'very strongly that there [was] a great current of disapproval of all the old parties because they represent[ed] the pre-war condition of

8

affairs' and saw 'in the minds of a large number of people...a
more or less conscious impression that the war was a proof that
there was something wrong in the old political organisation of
society'.[58] Liberals were sometimes as clear as anyone else that
promises of something new had to be made, even by such mani-
festly unradical organizations as the Liberal Council whose
manifesto saw the future of Liberalism 'hang[ing] largely on a
complete re-assessment of forces and values, and on fresh and
virile conceptions on national problems'.[59]

But thoughts like these tended to penetrate no further than the
level of oratory, or, when they did, the framework in which the
discussion was set gave the lie to radical noises. Runciman's
radical group, for example, stood for nothing more than the moral
and economic traditions eulogized by Hirst; and Grey's Liberal
Council spoke little other than the language of common sense and
personal integrity. As for the more genuinely radical segments,
the pacifist/anti-Grey/pro-Labour sections had lost most of their
important personnel to Labour by 1920. The Manchester Group
remained but its influence was hardly pivotal: indeed in so far as
its operations offer lessons about the character of Liberalism at
all, they show little more than the extent of the remove between
one element in the wider Liberalism and the ideas of the 'main-line'
Liberalism of the parliamentary party. It seems plain enough in
retrospect that the only kind of radicalism which was in any real
position to affect the course of parliamentary Liberalism was that
associated with Lloyd George during the last years of the post-war
decade.

Yet although this radicalism was to make important contributions to Liberal thought and to set the scene for much of what
Liberals would want to say in the 1930s, it failed to set its stamp
on Liberalism as a whole. That failure was rooted in the nature
of the Liberal mind and Lloyd George's inability to understand,
far less conquer, it. If Liberals had cause to regret that the new
world was 'in the hands of Mr. Hodges and Ll.G.' it was still a
matter for congratulation that Lloyd George had not been able to
kill Liberalism.[60] Time was to show, moreover, that he never
would be able to extinguish that element of Liberalism which he
most despised. He was to feel the edge of both Liberal and
Conservative antipathy to cranks and stunt-men.[61] He was to gain
control of the Liberal parliamentary party, but only after the

Liberals had failed in four general elections and when the usefulness of the Liberal machine was much reduced. Perhaps control
of that machine was all that mattered to Lloyd George. If so, his
thinking was misguided. Any new current in Liberalism, if it was
to have a chance of taking over the main stream, would need to
overcome things metaphysical, and in that sense Lloyd George
never fully realized what he was up against.

Liberalism will live. It cannot die. It is an immortal spirit.
    But the Liberal party machine is a mere temporary agent, or instrument.
It may fail or prove unworthy. It may break down and entirely disappear.
It will do so if [it] gets out of touch with the spirit, if it ceases to be
inspired . . .
    Liberalism is not a programme, a formula, a formal and dogmatic creed.
It is a spirit, a motive, an attitude towards the world.[62]

The lyricism comes from one of Lloyd George's own supporters,
but it is doubtful that he could have grasped its significance. If
he had, it is at least conceivable that the force of the Liberal split
would have been lessened.

    The split, however, concerned personality as well as principle
and the Liberal mind revealed itself there more than in any
coherent 'philosophy'. The context in which the mind operated
was often as important as the content of the mind itself. Certainly
Liberals believed they had in common an attitude towards the
world, but before the idea can have point for the historian it must
be placed in a complicated web of intention, calculation and
manoeuvre. When the mind is studied without reference to context
the study becomes dangerous (if it is done well) or silly (if it is
done badly). If, on the other hand, the mind is ignored then the
study is anaemic. However, when the inter-connexion between
these approaches is recognized, what it suggests about Liberal
history during and after the First World War is the presence of
a striking continuity of personnel and thought, a continuity easily
severed by those who take analysis ('the resolution of anything
complex into its simple elements') to be the only acceptable
vehicle for historical explanation. The pulling apart of Liberalism
has enabled much useful observation of its character to be made
but there is a sense in which the activity blurs as much as it defines.
There is value also in studying the contemporary perception of
the Liberal thought-world in all its totality.

    The insight which this perception offers is that the Liberals were

8-2

their own worst enemy. Not that the Liberal predicament after
1914 was other than difficult; but the cumulative impression
derived from what Liberals said to one another and to their
public is one which suggests that what was more important than
the predicament itself was the Liberal perception of it. The real
predicament of Liberalism was the nature of the Liberals who
championed it. Between the world and Liberal knowledge of it
there was the Liberal mind with its principles, its personal associations, its poisons; and whether Liberals were thinking about
the politics of the war, or the role of traditional values after it,
or the right attitude to adopt towards Lloyd George, the influence
of that strange epistemology could not be other than pervasive.
Perhaps an accurate evaluation could only be made from the
outside; it was certainly a Labour supporter who best assessed
the Liberal dilemma. 'I do not suppose that Liberalism is dead',
he wrote to Gilbert Murray in the mid-twenties, 'but I do say that
it is members of the Liberal party that will not let it live.'[63]
Nowhere in the political history of Liberalism between 1914 and
1929 is this paradox not apparent. Inside a rigid conception of the
politically moral there seemed no way either to end or ignore the
dichotomy between ghost and machine, and as the years passed
the paradox was to become too ultimate to be supportable.
Innumerable contextual problems dogged the Liberalism of
Asquith and Lloyd George, and it is right that they should attract
histories. But it was the lot of the Liberal mind to foster this more
fundamental truth: that Liberalism, to live, required Liberals to
die; and sufficient peace for the dead to bury their dead.

Notes

INTRODUCTION

1 Quoted in Samuel Hynes, *The Edwardian Turn of Mind* (Oxford, 1968), 77.
2 Letter to editor, *Westminster Gazette*, 6 November 1918.
3 Oliver Brett, *A Defence of Liberty* (1920), 44.
4 Morley, quoted in biography of A. H. D. Acland in *Dictionary of National Biography*. Ramsay MacDonald was himself to write of Labour's 'mind and spirit': to Ponsonby [1918], Ponsonby MSS.
5 Gladstone to Cecil, 5 June 1922, Cecil MSS, 51163 fol. 101.
6 *Lloyd George Liberal Magazine*, November 1922.
7 Violet Bonham-Carter to Murray, 6 July 1923, Murray MSS, Box 10.
8 E.g. Victoria de Bunsen, *The War and Men's Minds* (1919); Sir Reginald Mitchell Banks, *The Conservative Outlook* (1929).
9 Salisbury to Crewe, 4 October 1919, Crewe MSS, C/44; memo. by Maclean [1929], Maclean MSS, 468 fol. 108; Simon to Buchi (copy), 7 February 1939, E. D. Simon MSS, M11/16/14.
10 Asquith reported in *Liberal Magazine*, February 1918.
11 Zimmern, quoted in W. Watkin Davies, 'The New Liberalism', *Lloyd George Liberal Magazine*, October 1921.
12 *Nation*, 27 September 1919; Nicholas Murray Butler, *The Faith of a Liberal* (New York, 1924), 7; H. L. Nathan and H. H. Williams (eds.), *Liberal Points of View* (1927), 17; J. H. Shakespeare reported in *Lloyd George Liberal Magazine*, February 1922.
13 Cf. Michael Oakeshott, 'Political Education', in Peter Laslett (ed.), *Philosophy, Politics and Society* (Oxford, 1967), 5–11.
14 G. R. Elton, *Political History* (1970), 114.
15 Quentin Skinner, 'The Limits of Historical Explanations', *Philosophy*, XLI (1966), 206.
16 J. G. A. Pocock, *Politics, Language and Time: Essays on Political Thought and History* (1972), 33, 277.

CHAPTER I. EXHUMATION

1 Morel to Cadbury, 7 April 1918, quoted in Marvin Swartz, *The Union of Democratic Control in British Politics during the First World War* (Oxford, 1971), 211.
2 Asquith to Bryce, 17 January 1911, Bryce MSS, UB 1.
3 Esher to O.S.B., 10 April 1911, in Oliver, Viscount Esher (ed.), *The Journals and Letters of Reginald Viscount Esher*, III (1938), 47.
4 Asquith to Bryce, 8 September 1911, Bryce MSS, UB 1.

5 For Home Rule being 'neither popular nor unpopular', see Holt Diary, 5 February 1912, Holt MSS. For the Ulster problem, see Margot Asquith to Chamberlain and reply, 10/11 May 1914, Chamberlain MSS, AC 14/3/4–5.

6 Holt Diary, 14 January 1912, Holt MSS; cf. Scott Diary, 2 February 1911, in Trevor Wilson (ed.), *The Political Diaries of C. P. Scott, 1911–28* (1970), 37.

7 Pease Diary, August/October 1912, Pease MSS. Cf. *ibid.*, 11 April 1911, and H. V. Emy, *Liberals, Radicals and Social Politics, 1892–1914* (Cambridge, 1973), 218–19.

8 E.g. Donald to Murray, 12 March 1912, Elibank MSS, 8803 fol. 26.

9 Esher to Knollys, 29 September 1912, *Journals and Letters*, III, 109; for Massingham and foreign affairs, see Howard S. Weinroth, 'The British Radicals and the Balance of Power, 1902–14', *Historical Journal*, 13 (1970), esp. 677–80.

10 Raleigh to Sheppard, 24 June 1911, Sheppard MSS.

11 Pease Diary, 1 February 1914, Pease MSS; Hirst to Brunner, 15 July 1912, quoted in Stephen Koss, *Sir John Brunner* (1970), 254; L. J. Maxse, *Politicians on the War-Path* (1920), 35.

12 See Swartz, *op. cit.*, 11–45.

13 Samuel to Gladstone, 27 April 1913, Gladstone MSS, 45992 fol. 273.

14 Holt Diary, 16 February 1913, Holt MSS.

15 Churchill to Elibank, 9 April 1912, Elibank MSS, 8803 fol. 41. Asquith regarded South Manchester 'very seriously': Pease Diary, 6 March 1912. For Bethnal Green's having been 'given away', see McKenna to Runciman, 24 February 1914, Runciman MSS.

16 E.g. Ponsonby to Gladstone, 10 January 1911, Gladstone MSS, 46023 fol. 211.

17 Esher to Fisher, 31 December 1911, *Journals and Letters*, III, 77.

18 Grey to Lloyd George, 20 June 1913, Lloyd George MSS, C/4/14/9.

19 Esher to Fisher, 11 April 1912, *Journals and Letters*, III, 86; Cameron Hazlehurst, *Politicians at War* (1971), 121.

20 Margot Asquith to Elibank, 28 January 1912, Elibank MSS, 8803 fol. 12. Donald Maclean said after the war that her influence was small: Scott Diary, 18/20 January 1922, in Wilson (ed.), *Political Diaries*, 416 and n.

21 See Asquith to Bryce, 19 December 1912, Bryce MSS, UB 1.

22 Dicey to Strachey, 24 June 1914, Strachey MSS, S/5/7/3.

23 Holt Diary, 5 February 1912, Holt MSS.

24 Asquith to Elibank, 30 March 1912, Elibank MSS, 8803 fol. 39.

25 Lincolnshire to Gosse, 3 February 1913, Gosse MSS.

26 Rowntree to Lloyd George, 25 May 1912, quoted in H. V. Emy, 'The Land Campaign: Lloyd George as a Social Reformer', in A. J. P. Taylor (ed.), *Lloyd George: Twelve Essays* (1971), 65.

27 Goddard to Lloyd George, 29 May 1914, Lloyd George MSS, C/11/1/53.

28 Inge Diary, 2 April 1912, in W. R. Inge, *Diary of a Dean: St. Paul's 1911–34* (1949), 15.
29 See David Ayerst, *Guardian: Biography of a Newspaper* (1971), 371.
30 Runciman to Chalmers, 24 June 1914, Runciman MSS.
31 Mair to Scott, 22 July 1914, Scott MSS, 50908 fols. 18–19; cf. Harcourt to Ferguson, 2 July 1914, Harcourt MSS, and Burns Diary, 8 July 1914, Burns MSS, 46336 fol. 116. For the working-class preoccupation see C. P. Trevelyan to Runciman, 25 July 1914, Runciman MSS; and for Northcliffe, Tom Clarke, *My Northcliffe Diary* (1931), 58–9, and Norman Angell, *After All* (1951), 179.
32 See D. A. Hamer, *Liberal Politics in the Age of Gladstone and Rosebery* (Oxford, 1972), *passim*.
33 P. F. Clarke, *Lancashire and the New Liberalism* (Cambridge, 1971), 406–7. But see Dr Clarke's remarks about 'a coalition in a state of constant adjustment' in his unpub. doctoral dissertation, 'Elections and the Electorate in North-West England' (Cambridge, 1967), 32.
34 Haldane in 1907, quoted in Hamer, *op. cit.*, 323.
35 Quoted in Samuel Hynes, *The Edwardian Turn of Mind* (1968), 12.
36 J. A. Hobson, *The Crisis of Liberalism* (1909), viii.
37 See R. Lyman, *The First Labour Government* (1957), 278.
38 John Vincent, *The Formation of the Liberal Party, 1857–68* (1966), 258.
39 G. G. Coulton, *Fourscore Years* (Cambridge, 1943), 273.
40 E. M. Forster, *Goldsworthy Lowes Dickinson* (1934), 1962, ed., 116.
41 Holt Diary, 19 July 1914, Holt MSS.
42 MacCallum Scott Diary, 20 June 1914.
43 The much-quoted phrase came from Lloyd George's speech at Conway on 6 May 1916. See his *War Memoirs*, II (1933), 734.
44 See A. G. Gardiner, *The War Lords* (1915), 63.
45 Dillon to Scott, 25 July 1914, Scott MSS, 50908 fol. 24.
46 Churchill, *The World Crisis*, I (1923), 193; cf. Lloyd George, *War Memoirs*, I (1933), 53–4.
47 Temperley to Runciman (enc.), 1 January 1928, Runciman MSS.
48 Cf. Edward David, 'The Liberal Party during the First World War', unpub. M.Litt. dissertation (Cambridge, 1968), 73; and the same author's 'The Liberal Party Divided, 1916–18', *Historical Journal*, 13 (1970), 510.
49 *Hansard*, 3 August 1914, LXV, 1809–27, 1879–80; Hazlehurst, *op. cit.*, 47n; MacCallum Scott Diary, 3 August 1914, and entry on Pringle's death, 3 April 1928.
50 Asquith to Venetia Stanley, 2 August 1914, quoted in Hazlehurst, *op. cit.*, 33.
51 See Holt Diary, 2 August 1914, Holt MSS.
52 Lord Crewe, *Rosebery*, II (1931), 648; but see Lodman to Burns, 9 August 1914, Burns MSS, 46303 fol. 88.
53 W. Harris, *J. A. Spender* (1946), 37–8. Gilbert Murray did not feel

sure of him until December: Murray to Bryce, 26 December 1914, Bryce MSS, UB 12.

54 Hazlehurst, *Politicians at War*, 66–76.

55 Morley to Bryce, 24 November 1911, Bryce MSS, UB 12.

56 Nicholas Murray Butler, *The Faith of a Liberal* (New York, 1924), 5.

57 Warren Staebler, *The Liberal Mind of John Morley* (Princeton, 1943), 194–5.

58 Laski to Holmes, 8 September 1920, in M. Howe (ed.), *Holmes–Laski Letters, 1916–35*, I (1969), 278.

59 E.g. Morley to Montagu, 17 June 1916, Montagu MSS.

60 Staebler, *op. cit.*, 197.

61 Herbert Samuel, *Memoirs* (1945), 90.

62 E.g. Morley to McKenna, 18 March 1912, McKenna MSS, 4/4 fol. 13; Morley to Gilbert Murray, 1 April 1914, Murray MSS, Box 39; Morley to FitzRoy, 21 January 1916 in A. FitzRoy, *Memoirs*, II [n.d.], 563; Morley to Burns, 29 August 1918, Burns MSS, 46283 fol. 103.

63 Morley to Burns, ?3/9 July 1920, Burns MSS, 46283 fol. 112; transcript of Burns to Asquith, 2 August 1914, Burns MSS, 46283 fol. 158 for Burns' explanation of resignation in terms of 'Honour, Duty, Humanity'.

64 Burns Diary, 28 September 1917: 'Morley was delighted and full of wonder at the character number and quality of our books.' Burns MSS, 46339 fol. 159.

65 Burns Diary, 4 May 1918, Burns MSS, 46340 fol. 88.

66 He liked to believe that Asquith thought him the best-read man in the House: MacCallum Scott Diary, 20 March 1918.

67 Burns Diary, 29 November 1917, Burns MSS, 46339 fol. 191.

68 Scott Diary, 3/4 September 1914, in Wilson (ed.), *Political Diaries*, 103; cf. Burns Diary, 13 May 1915, Burns MSS, 46337 fol. 93.

69 See Sandhurst Diary, 26 May 1915, in *From Day to Day*, I (1928), 215; Esher to M. V. Brett, 3 January 1916, *Journals and Letters*, IV (1938), 1.

70 FitzRoy Diary, 4 March 1915, *op. cit.*, II, 586.

71 Memo. by Sutherland, 7 December 1915, Lloyd George MSS, D/1/1/10.

72 Scott Diary, 3 September 1915, in Wilson (ed.), *Political Diaries*, 134; Montagu to Chamberlain (copy), 30 October 1918, Montagu MSS.

73 See Swartz, *op. cit.*, 85–104.

74 Henry to Gladstone, 5 September 1914, Gladstone MSS, 46038 fol. 99.

75 Harold Spender, 'The War and the Law', *Contemporary Review*, October 1914.

76 Beatrice Webb remarked that no one had even noticed Morley's resignation: Diary, 6 August 1914, in M. Cole (ed.), *Beatrice Webb's Diaries, 1912–24* (1952), 26; cf. Stephen McKenna, *While I Remember* (1921), 178.

77 Crewe to Hardinge (copy), 6 August 1914, Crewe MSS, C/24.
78 MacCallum Scott Diary, 3 December 1914.
79 Murray to Fisher (copy), 10 August 1914, Murray MSS, Box 19.
80 Healy to Milner, 26 December 1914, Milner MSS, 139 fol. 336. See also the letters of Law, Chamberlain and Crewe quoted in M. D. Pugh, 'Asquith, Bonar Law and the First Coalition', *Historical Journal*, 17 (1974), 821–2.
81 Healy to Milner, 26 December 1914, *loc. cit.* Asquith had recently snubbed Masterman in order to placate Conservative (and Harmsworth) opinion: Lucy Masterman, *C. F. G. Masterman* (1939), 270; Maurice Cowling, *The Impact of Labour* (Cambridge, 1971), 52; Frances Lloyd George, *The Years That Are Past* (1967), 45.
82 Hugh Cecil to Robert Cecil, 10 January 1915, Cecil MSS, 51157 fols. 34, 41.
83 The 'conspiracy' theory has been pressed by S. E. Koss in 'Britain's Last Liberal Government', *Journal of Modern History*, 40 (1968), 257–77, but effectively countered by Hazlehurst, *Politicians at War*, 235–60. For a different perspective see Pugh, *loc. cit.*
84 Burns Diary, 4 February 1915, Burns MSS, 46337 fol. 43.
85 Runciman to Chalmers, 7 February 1915, Runciman MSS.
86 Oliver to Chamberlain, 26 February 1915, Chamberlain MSS, AC 14/6/5.
87 For the ultimatum see Koss, *loc. cit.*, 268n; there is a copy of it in the Lloyd George MSS, C/5/8/5. Dr Pugh's view that the election was essentially 'an attempt to avoid a Khaki election' (*loc. cit.*, 813) is, however, unconvincing. It seems very unlikely that the Conservative leadership would have risked the opprobrium of precipitating an election during a critical phase of the war.
88 Burns Diary, 28 March 1915, Burns MSS, 46337 fol. 70.
89 MacCallum Scott Diary, 5 May 1915.
90 J. P. Hennessy, *Lord Crewe* (1955), 148–9. For Lloyd George see A. M. Gollin, *Proconsul in Politics* (1964), 258, and the cautionary remarks of Hazlehurst, *Politicians at War*, 240–54.
91 Long to Law, 16 May 1915, Law MSS, 37/2/32; Chamberlain to Milner, 20 May 1915, Milner MSS, 140 fol. 106.
92 Holt Diary, 30 May and 6 June 1915, Holt MSS; MacCallum Scott Diary, 19 May 1915. 'Great Liberal Party disappears' was Burns' comment: Diary, 19 May 1915, 46337 fol. 96.
93 Stephen McKenna, *While I Remember*, 179
94 Runciman to McKenna, 19 May 1915, quoted in Stephen McKenna, *Reginald McKenna* (1948), 223. Grey agreed: see his note to McKenna later the same day: McKenna MSS, 5/8 fol. 2.
95 For Morley see Scott Diary, 27 November 1914, in Wilson (ed.), *Political Diaries*, 115; for Simon see Christopher Addison, *Four and a Half Years*, 1 (1933), 35.
96 Cf. Burns Diary, 19 May 1915, Burns MSS, 46337 fol. 96.
97 Hazlehurst, *op. cit.*, 222.

98 Henry to Gladstone, 18/26 November 1916, Gladstone MSS, 46038 fols. 113, 17.
99 J. M. Hogge, 'Free Liberalism', *Contemporary Review*, December 1919; for Pringle, see Pringle to Gilbert Murray, 11 March 1921, Murray MSS, Box 59.
100 Koss, *Sir John Brunner*, 287.
101 Long to Law [May 1915], Law MSS, 117/1/11.
102 *Manchester Guardian*, 19 May 1915.
103 Sandhurst Diary, 26 May 1915, *loc. cit.*, I, 217.
104 MacCallum Scott Diary, 27 December 1915.
105 Masterman to Samuel, 26 May 1915, Samuel MSS, A/48/11.
106 Morley to Burns, 26 May 1915, Burns MSS, 46283 fol. 63.
107 Crewe, for example, wanted to keep Munitions and the Exchequer: Crewe to Lloyd George (copy), 24 May 1915, Crewe MSS, C/31.
108 Oliver to Chamberlain (copy), 28 May 1915, Chamberlain MSS, AC 14/6/16.
109 Chamberlain to Law, 21 May 1915, quoted in Sir Charles Petrie, *The Life and Letters of Austen Chamberlain*, 2 vols., II (1940), 28.
110 Midleton to Strachey, 21 May 1915, Strachey MSS, S/18/2/14.
111 Lloyd George to Mrs Lloyd George, 20 May and 26 May 1915, in K. O. Morgan (ed.), *Lloyd George Family Letters, 1885–1936* (Cardiff and Oxford, 1973), 177–8.
112 Oliver to Chamberlain, 4 June and 30 July 1915, Chamberlain MSS, AC 14/6/17, 43.
113 The son was W. G. C. Gladstone; see Ivor Thomas, *Gladstone of Hawarden* (1936), 195.
114 MacCallum Scott Diary, 26 August 1914.
115 Burns to Strachey, 22 September 1914, Strachey MSS, S/3/3/18. For working-class fears, see Royden Harrison, 'The War Emergency Workers' National Committee, 1914–20', in Asa Briggs and John Saville (eds.), *Essays in Labour History, 1886–1923* (1971), 239–47.
116 Chamberlain to Milner, 20 May 1915, Milner MSS, 140 fol. 106.
117 *Hansard* (Lords), XVIII, 378, 408.
118 Cross to Lloyd George, 30 May 1915, Lloyd George MSS, D/20/1/6.
119 Hirst to Scott, 21 May and 28 May 1915, in Wilson (ed.), *Political Diaries*, 124–6; Scott Diary, 3 September 1915, *ibid.*, 133.
120 MacCallum Scott Diary, 22 May 1915; the entry is printed in full in Hazlehurst, *op. cit.*, 266.
121 29 May 1915.
122 The Fellowship published its manifesto on 29 May and invited a subscription of 1/- from those interested. See *Morning Post*, 29 May 1915.
123 Burns Diary, 10 June and 16 June 1915, Burns MSS, 46337 fols. 107, 110. The proponents of the scheme were 'E.D., R.L., P. and others' – presumably E. D. Morel, Norman Angell (formerly Ralph Lane) and Arthur Ponsonby.
124 Hirst to Runciman, 4 June 1915, Runciman MSS.
125 MacCallum Scott Diary, 11 June 1915.

126 Hobhouse to Runciman, 28 May 1915, Runciman MSS.
127 Simon to Murray, 28 May 1915, Elibank MSS, 8803 fol. 162.
128 Murray to Gulland (copy), 14 June 1915, Elibank MSS, 8803 fol. 165.
129 Nicoll to Strachey, 12 June 1915, Strachey MSS, S/11/2/4.
130 Esher to M. V. Brett, 6 June 1915, *Journals and Letters*, III, 247; cf.
     Burns Diary, 3 June 1915, Burns MSS, 46337 fol. 103.
131 Hirst to Lady Courtney, 17 June 1915, Courtney MSS, 11 fol. 144.
132 See MacCallum Scott Diary, 24/25 May and 2 June 1915.
133 Holt Diary, 20 June 1915, Holt MSS. The 'Seven' had become at
     least ten by this time: Nicolson, J. W. Wilson, Walter Rea, Sir
     Thomas Whittaker, Leif Jones, Murray Macdonald, Sir Frederick
     Cawley, James Falconer, William Middlebrook and Holt himself.
134 MacCallum Scott Diary, 27 May 1915.
135 Hazlehurst, *op. cit.*, 292.
136 MacCallum Scott Diary, 12 June 1915.
137 Hazlehurst, *op. cit.*, 292.
138 Holt Diary, 20 June 1915, Holt MSS.
139 Oliver to Chamberlain, 8 June 1915, Chamberlain MSS, AC 14/6/19.
140 Amery to Milner, 2 August 1915, Milner MSS, 140 fols. 199–200,
     partially quoted in Gollin, *Pronconsul in Politics*, 276–7, where the
     crucial '*might*' is printed as '*will*'.
141 Lansdowne to Asquith (copy), 5 August 1915, Balfour MSS, 49730
     fols. 283–4; Long to Law, 8 August 1915, Law MSS, 51/2/8.
142 See Dennis Hayes, *Conscription Conflict* (1949), 158.
143 Galsworthy to Gilbert Murray, 16 June 1915, Murray MSS, Box 20.
144 MacCallum Scott Diary, 18 June 1915.
145 *While I Remember*, 178.
146 Burns Diary, 5 August 1915, Burns MSS, 46337 fol. 135.
147 Montagu to Asquith, 16 August 1915, Montagu MSS.
148 Pringle to Runciman, 27 ?August 1915, Runciman MSS; note by
     Murray sent to Cowdray for comment, dated 18 August 1915, Elibank
     MSS, 8803 fols. 178–9.
149 Holt Diary, 19 September 1915, Holt MSS.
150 Asquith to Balfour, 18 September 1915, Balfour MSS, 49692 fols.
     158–9.
151 MacCallum Scott Diary, 14 September 1915. The M.P. concerned
     was Walter Rooh, though no refleotion of such fears appeared in his
     Mr. Lloyd George and the War (1920).
152 Murray to wife, 23 September 1915, Elibank MSS, 8803 fols. 188–9.
153 For Lloyd George's links with Milner and Northcliffe, see Gollin,
     op. cit., 295ff, and a note by Lady Violet Milner (dated 1928) in
     Northcliffe to Milner, 6 October 1915, Milner MSS, 141 fol. 300.
154 Margot Asquith to Murray, 15 October 1915, Elibank MSS, 8803 fols.
     244–5. Lloyd George was 'behaving like a maniac...'
155 Talbot to Law, 16 October 1915, Law MSS, 51/4/16.
156 Stevenson Diary, 19 October 1915, in A. J. P. Taylor (ed.), *Lloyd
     George: A Diary by Frances Stevenson* (1971), 69.

157 Margot Asquith to Murray, 20 October 1915, Elibank MSS, 8803 fol. 251.
158 Montagu to Asquith (copy), 22 October 1915, Montagu MSS.
159 MacCallum Scott Diary, 21 and 23 October 1915.
160 *Ibid.*, 22 November 1915.
161 Burns Diary, 2 December 1915, Burns MSS, 46337 fol. 196.
162 Law to Asquith, 18 November 1915, Asquith MSS, 15 fol. 150.
163 Harcourt to Sidney Buxton (copy), 1 December 1915, Harcourt MSS.
164 MacCallum Scott Diary, 15 and 22 December 1915; cf. Herbert Gladstone to Henry Gladstone, 7 January 1916, Glynne–Gladstone MSS.
165 *Hansard*, 21 December 1915, LXXVII, 338.
166 *Hansard*, 22 December 1915, LXXVII, 544.
167 MacCallum Scott Diary, 3 January 1916.
168 *Hansard*, 5 January 1916, LXXVII, 988.
169 *Hansard*, 6 January 1916, LXXVII, 1182.
170 Sandhurst Diary, 8 January 1916, *op. cit.*, II, 5.
171 MacCallum Scott Diary, 4 January 1916; Scott Diary, 10/11 January 1916, in Wilson (ed.), *Political Diaries*, 174; Holt Diary, 9 January 1916, Holt MSS.
172 MacCallum Scott Diary, 6 January 1916.
173 Whitehouse to Lloyd George, 16 September 1915, Lloyd George MSS, D/1/2/20.
174 MacCallum Scott Diary, 29 December 1915.
175 Asquith to Montagu, 28 December 1915, Montagu MSS.
176 Samuel to Runciman, 28 December 1915, Samuel MSS, A/46/2.
177 Montagu to Grey, 30 December 1915, Montagu MSS; cf. Margot Asquith to Hankey, 31 December 1915, quoted in Stephen Roskill, *Hankey: Man of Secrets*, I (1970), 240.
178 Margot Asquith to McKenna, 28 December 1915, quoted in Stephen McKenna, *Reginald McKenna*, 257.
179 MacCallum Scott Diary, 6 January 1916.
180 See Montagu to Asquith (copy), 3 January 1916 [misdated 1915], Montagu MSS.
181 MacCallum Scott Diary, 11 January 1916.
182 Runciman to McKenna, 23 January 1916, McKenna MSS, 5/9 fol. 23. For Hirst see *The Economist*, 15 January 1916.
183 Haldane to Gosse, 2 January 1916, Gosse MSS.
184 Sandhurst Diary, 15/18 January 1916, *op. cit.*, II, 9; *Hansard*, LXXVIII, 143–5, 148–50.
185 Burns Diary, 24 January 1916, Burns MSS, 46338 fol. 37.
186 A. J. P. Taylor, *Politics in Wartime* (1964), 24.
187 Roskill, *Hankey*, 226.
188 MacCallum Scott Diary, 13 January 1916; *British Weekly*, 20 January 1916. Cf. Barry McGill, 'Asquith's Predicament', *Journal of Modern History*, 39 (1967), 290.
189 Handel Booth in *Sunday Times*, 16 January 1916.
190 Amery quoted in P. A. Lockwood, 'Milner's Entry to the War

Cabinet', *Historical Journal*, 7 (1964), 124. See also Gollin, *Proconsul in Politics*, 323–4, 329, 333.

191 Holt Diary, 4 February 1916, Holt MSS.

192 See Stevenson Diary, 3 February 1916, in Taylor (ed.), *op. cit.*, 94.

193 *Hansard*, 2 May 1916, LXXXI, 2647.

194 MacCallum Scott Diary, 15 February 1916.

195 Sandhurst Diary, 19/20 February 1916, *op. cit.*, II, 23.

196 'Some Notes on Present War Situation', 12 March 1916, Milner MSS, 142 fols. 55–61.

197 Oliver to Strachey, 14 March 1916, Strachey MSS, S/18/3/10.

198 P. A. Lockwood, *loc. cit.*, 127–8. Cf. Bonar Law's view of Lloyd George in note by Spender of conversation with Redmond and Law, 15 March 1916, Spender MSS, 46388 fol. 131, partially quoted in J. A. Spender and Cyril Asquith, *Life of Lord Oxford and Asquith*, II (1932), 246–7. See also Robert Blake, *The Unknown Prime Minister* (1955), 280.

199 Rowntree to Cross, 26 April 1916, Lloyd George MSS, D/20/2/90.

200 Carson was Law's candidate; Curzon, Strachey's. For Balfour see Bone to Scott, 22 March 1916: '...Asquith may become Lord Chancellor and Balfour the premier', Scott MSS, 50908 fol. 193. Cf. Sandhurst Diary, 28/30 March 1916, *op. cit.*, II, 38.

201 Asquith to Lady Scott, 19 April 1916, Kennet MSS, 109/1/48.

202 Sandhurst Diary, 17 April 1916, *op. cit.*, II, 46.

203 This strategy may have originated with Montagu, Crewe and Grey: see Drummond to Montagu, 20 April 1916, Montagu MSS.

204 Austen to Hilda Chamberlain (extract), 14 December 1916, Chamberlain MSS, AC 15/3/10.

205 MacCallum Scott Diary, 23 April 1916.

206 G. P. Gooch, *Life of Lord Courtney* (1920), 509.

207 Farrer to Bryce, 11 November 1915: 'The Tories are playing for Protection *or* Conscription, as they know that one will bring the other.' Bryce MSS, UB 6.

208 McKenna was afraid that Lansdowne and Long would follow: McKenna to Runciman, 26 June 1916, Runciman MSS. For Lansdowne and Long see Lansdowne to Chamberlain, 24 June 1916, Chamberlain MSS, and memo. by Long, 15 June 1916, *ibid.*, AC 14/5/6, 13.

209 Holt Diary, 6 August 1916, Holt MSS.

210 Mallet to Runciman, 8 July 1916, Runciman MSS.

211 Burns Diary, 26 October 1916, Burns MSS, 46338 fol. 176.

212 Scott to Lloyd George, 20 April 1916, Lloyd George MSS, D/18/15/11.

213 Haldane to Gosse, 2 July 1916, Gosse MSS.

214 Lloyd George to Asquith (copy), 17 June 1916, Lloyd George MSS, D/18/2/19; Riddell, *Lord Riddell's War Diary, 1914–18* (1933), 189.

215 Lloyd George to Russell (copy), 28 April 1916, Lloyd George MSS, D/18/11/5; Addison, *Four and a Half Years*, I, 197–8.

216 Frances Balfour to Asquith, 13 December 1916, Asquith MSS, 17 fols. 251–6; cf. Esher to Haig, 29 September 1916, *Journals and Letters*, IV, 55.

217 H. A. Taylor, *Robert Donald* [n.d.], 87.
218 Lloyd George, *War Memoirs*, II, 734.
219 *Hansard*, 12 December 1916, LXXXVIII, 805.
220 *Nation*, 9 December 1916.
221 Quoted in A. J. P. Taylor, *The Troublemakers* (1956), 141.
222 *Hansard*, 28 November 1916, LXXXVIII, 291–2, 300.
223 Memo. by Strachey [December 1916], Strachey MSS, S/18/3/47.
224 Nash to Runciman, 22 December 1916, Runciman MSS; for Nash see Sir James Sexton, *Sir James Sexton, Agitator* (1936), 187.
225 Christopher Addison, *Politics from Within*, I (1924), 276.
226 MacCallum Scott Diary, 6 July 1921. But of course Addison had just been dropped by Lloyd George: see Beaverbrook, *The Decline and Fall of Lloyd George* (1963), 61–81, and Cowling, *The Impact of Labour*, 121.
227 Lloyd George to Law [n.d.] (marked 'War Office'), Law MSS, 81/1/2, printed in Lord Beaverbrook, *Politicians and the War* (1960), 504–5.
228 *Northern Echo*, 4 December 1916.
229 MacCallum Scott Diary, 11 December 1916 (but cf. entry for 4 December); Burns Diary, 8 December 1916, Burns MSS, 46338 fol. 198.
230 Kerr to Lloyd George, 4 December 1917, Lloyd George MSS, F/89/1/9. Guest was later to refer to a 'Ginger Group' of 'thirty or forty' Liberals who backed Lloyd George in 1917: *Lloyd George Liberal Magazine*, February 1922.
231 McGill, *loc. cit.*, 290; MacCallum Scott Diary, 7 December 1916.
232 *Politics in Wartime*, 32.
233 *Lloyd George Liberal Magazine*, November 1920.
234 Edward David, 'The Liberal Party Divided', *Historical Journal*, 13 (1970), 531.
235 *Ibid.*
236 Holt Diary, 10 December 1916, Holt MSS.
237 Stephen E. Koss, *Lord Haldane: Scapegoat for Liberalism* (New York, 1969), 246.

CHAPTER 2. GHOSTS IN THE MACHINE

1 Sandhurst Diary, 18/25 May 1917, *From Day to Day*, II (1929), 171.
2 E.g. Davidson to Law, 13 January 1922, Law MSS, 107/2/2A.
3 E.g. Asquith to Crewe, 9 May 1922, Crewe MSS, C/40.
4 Spender to Elibank, 6 September 1918, Elibank MSS, 8804 fol. 191.
5 MacCallum Scott Diary, 30 January 1917.
6 A. H. D. Acland to Crewe, 13 December 1921, Crewe MSS, C/1.
7 Burns Diary, 13 July 1917, Burns MSS, 46339 fol. 121.
8 Sir Geoffrey Shakespeare, *Let Candles Be Brought In* (1949), 125.
9 Stephen McKenna, *While I Remember* (1921), 186.
10 Burns Diary, 2 February and 18 November 1917, Burns MSS, 46339 fols. 41, 185.

11 Esher to Williamson, 21 January 1912, in *The Journals and Letters of Reginald Viscount Esher*, III (1938), 78.
12 Stevenson to Simon, 19 June 1917, Simon MSS. It is interesting to find Asquith himself speaking of 'this planet... being out of joint': Asquith to Lady Scott, 6 December 1916 ('midnight'), Kennet MSS.
13 7 December 1916.
14 *Northern Echo*, 11 December 1916.
15 Unpublished note by Haldane, Haldane MSS, 5923.
16 Brunner to Bryce, 15 February 1895, Bryce MSS, UB 3.
17 Herbert Asquith, *Moments of Memory* (1937), 376.
18 MacCallum Scott Diary, 22 February 1928.
19 McKenna to Runciman, 15 January 1917, Runciman MSS.
20 7 June 1919.
21 Cf. A. M. Gollin, *Proconsul in Politics* (1964), 261.
22 Dickinson to Gilbert Murray (copy), 4 April 1919, Dickinson MSS, 403 fol. 140.
23 Asquith to Runciman, 24 December 1916, Runciman MSS.
24 Burns Diary, 19 December 1916 and 3 January 1917, Burns MSS, 46338 fol. 203, 46339 fol. 26.
25 Lambert to Scott, 27 December 1916, Scott MSS, 50909 fol. 107.
26 MacCallum Scott Diary, 22 September 1922.
27 L. O. Broin, *The Chief Secretary: Augustine Birrell in Ireland* (1969), 208–9; Tom Clarke Diary, 17 June 1931, *My Lloyd George Diary* (1939), 120–1.
28 V. Bonham-Carter to Murray, 24 January 1920, Murray MSS, Box 9.
29 S. D. Waley, *Edwin Montagu* (1964), 67. For the political consequences see C. Hazlehurst, *Politicians at War* (1971), 262–3.
30 E.g. Montagu to Asquith, 5 December 1916, Asquith MSS, 17 fols. 186–92.
31 Waley, *op. cit.*, 113.
32 Montagu to Asquith, 18 June 1917, Asquith MSS, 18 fol. 12.
33 Scott Diary, 9/11 August 1917, in Trevor Wilson (ed.), *The Political Diaries of C. P. Scott, 1911–28* (1970), 298.
34 McKenna to Runciman, 1 August 1917, Runciman MSS.
35 Stansgate Diary, 14 March 1922, Stansgate MSS.
36 Churchill to Clementine Churchill, 19 January 1916, quoted in Martin Gilbert, *Winston S. Churchill*, III (1974), 688.
37 Clementine Churchill to Churchill, 30 December 1915, *ibid.*, 623.
38 Runciman to Chalmers, 7 February 1915, Runciman MSS.
39 Burns Diary, 25 April 1918, Burns MSS, 46340 fol. 84.
40 E.g. Violet Asquith to Churchill, 13 November 1915, in Gilbert, *op. cit.*, 566.
41 W. S. Churchill, *The World Crisis*, III (1927), 252.
42 *Ibid.*, 255.
43 Stephen E. Koss, *Lord Haldane: Scapegoat for Liberalism* (New York, 1969), 231.
44 Hardinge to Chirol, 3 April 1917 (copy), Hardinge MSS, 31 fol. 134.

45 See Guest's reply, dated 11 May 1917, Elibank MSS, 8804 fol. 89.

46 Memo. by Asquith, 28 May 1917, Asquith MSS, 46 fols. 132–9.

47 Asquith to Crewe, 28 May 1917, Crewe MSS, C/40; Crewe to Asquith, 31 May 1917, Asquith MSS, 18 fol. 8.

48 Roy Douglas, 'The Background to the Coupon Election Arrangements', *English Historical Review*, LXXXVI (1971), 321.

49 Burns Diary, 3 May 1917, Burns MSS, 46339 fol. 86; see also entry for 18 January 1918, 46340 fol. 34.

50 Asquith to Crewe, 23 July 1915, Crewe MSS, C/40.

51 Asquith to Samuel, 10 March 1927, Samuel MSS, A/155/(vi)/51.

52 Sandhurst Diary, 4 December 1916, *op. cit.*, II, 123.

53 Fiennes to Asquith, 7 December 1916, Asquith MSS, 17 fol. 200. This may have been mere pleasantry since Fiennes was expecting a job from Lloyd George: memo. by Waldorf Astor [July 1917], Astor MSS.

54 Sandhurst Diary, 7/8 December 1916 and 21/24 February 1917, II, 125, 146. Holt likewise believed that Asquith could be 'master of the place' in a fortnight: Holt Diary, 18 February 1917, Holt MSS.

55 Hardinge to Chirol (copy), 3 April 1917, Hardinge MSS, 31 fols. 134–5.

56 Cawley to Law, 9 March 1917, Law MSS, 81/4/8.

57 Montagu to Crewe, 10 March 1917, Crewe MSS, C/34.

58 Derby to Law, 12 March 1917, Law MSS, 81/4/15.

59 E.g. Harcourt to Ferguson, 14 March 1917, Harcourt MSS.

60 Burns Diary, 14 March 1917, Burns Diary, 46339 fol. 61.

61 Bryce to Scott, 16 March 1917, Scott MSS, 50909 fol. 77.

62 E.g. Lloyd George to Derby, 15 March 1917, quoted in Randolph Churchill, *Lord Derby: King of Lancashire* (1959), 258.

63 Hardinge to Chirol (copy), 3 April 1917, Hardinge MSS, 31 fol. 134. Cf. minute by Astor, 13 March 1917, Astor MSS.

64 Grey to Crewe, 2 February 1917, Crewe MSS, C/17,

65 Dated 19 August 1909, Runciman MSS.

66 Margot Asquith to Simon, 8 April 1924, Simon MSS.

67 MacCallum Scott Diary, 19 February 1917.

68 Esher to Fisher, 11 April 1912, *Journals and Letters*, III, 87.

69 Midleton to Strachey, 27 December 1915, Strachey MSS, S/18/2/24; FitzRoy Diary, 29 March 1915, *Memoirs*, II, 590; Russell to Murray, 11 January 1914, Murray MSS, Box 46.

70 Hardinge to Spring-Rice (copy), 23 March 1917, Hardinge MSS, 30 fol. 285.

71 Montagu 'narrative', 9 December 1916, Montagu MSS.

72 Crewe to Hardinge (copy), 24 December 1914, Crewe MSS, C/24; Hardinge to Rodd (copy), 23 August 1916, Hardinge MSS, 24 fol. 312. Runciman had been passed over for Munitions in May 1915: Peter Fraser, *Lord Esher* (1973), 285.

73 See, for example, J. H. Thomas, *My Story* (1937), 261–2.

74 MacCallum Scott Diary, 15 April 1915.

75 Sandhurst Diary, 3 April 1916, *From Day to Day*, II, 39.

76 Ivor Thomas, *Gladstone of Hawarden* (1936), 223.
77 Asquith to Gladstone, 28 February 1922, Gladstone MSS, 45989 fol. 284.
78 Margot Asquith to Bryce, 17 May ?1917, Bryce MSS, UB 1.
79 Harrison to Rosebery, 24 January and 25 July 1917, Rosebery MSS.
80 Suppressed part of draft letter to Harold Fox, 9/19 April 1912, Rosebery MSS.
81 Rosebery to 'George', 19 September 1914, Rosebery MSS.
82 Esher Journal, 17 March 1912, *Journals and Letters*, III, 84.
83 Memo. by Cecil and Curzon [n.d.], Law MSS, 81/1/36. The Conservatives vetoed the suggestion.
84 MacCallum Scott Diary, 19 December 1923. The observer was J. W. Pratt.
85 E.g. Lord Kilmuir, *Political Adventure* (1964), 22.
86 Scott to Spender, 5 February 1917, Spender MSS, 46392 fol. 256.
87 MacCallum Scott Diary, 5 December 1917.
88 E.g. Russell to Lloyd George, 18 May 1917, Lloyd George MSS, F/44/6/4.
89 Samuel to mother, 19 August 1917, Samuel MSS, A/156/542.
90 Memo. on policy, 3 December 1917, Lloyd George MSS, F/168/2/3.
91 Nicoll to Deane, 23 February 1918, quoted in T. H. Darlow, *William Robertson Nicoll: Life and Letters* (1925), 271.
92 MacCallum Scott Diary, 16 October 1917.
93 Mersey to Simon, 16 October 1917, Simon MSS; MacCallum Scott Diary, 18 October 1917.
94 *Times*, 25 October 1917; Trevelyan to Simon, 26 October 1917, Simon MSS.
95 Oliver to Carson, 26 January 1917, Lloyd George MSS, F/6/2/11.
96 Long to Law, 18 September 1917, Law MSS, 82/4/17.
97 Lord Newton, *Lansdowne: A Biography* (1929), 472.
98 Kerr to Lloyd George, 4 December 1917, Lloyd George MSS, F/89/1/9. Haldane also saw 'the hand of Loreburn': Haldane to Gosse, 29 November 1917, Gosse MSS.
99 Newton, *op. cit.*, 473.
100 G. K. A. Bell, *Randall Davidson* (1952), 848.
101 Darlow, *op. cit.*, 269.
102 Simon to Samuel, 28 December 1917, Samuel MSS, A/155/(v)/6.
103 MacCallum Scott Diary, 2 December 1917.
104 F. W. Hirst (ed.), *Gordon Harvey: A Memoir* [n.d.], 129; Newton, *op. cit.*, 473.
105 Massingham to Runciman, 26 December 1916, Runciman MSS.
106 Holt Diary, 3 December 1917, Holt MSS.
107 MacCallum Scott Diary, 5 December 1917; Burns Diary, 6 December 1917, Burns MSS, 46339 fol. 194. For an example of radical parliamentary pressure, see the debate on war aims initiated by Collins at the instigation of Runciman, on 19 December 1917: *Hansard*, c, 1993–2104.
108 See Lloyd George to Mrs Lloyd George, 13 February 1918, in K.

O. Morgan (ed.), *Lloyd George Family Letters 1885–1936* (Cardiff and Oxford, 1973), 186.
109 *Times*, 6 January 1918.
110 Grey to Runciman, 5 January 1918, Runciman MSS; Lloyd George in Cabinet, 3 January 1918, CAB 23/5/12.
111 Quoted in Bell, *op. cit.*, 886–7.
112 Ponsonby to Courtney, 29 November 1917, Courtney MSS, 12 fol. 174.
113 Hirst to Gilbert Murray, 28 December 1917, Murray MSS, Box 58.
114 Hirst to Courtney, 28 January 1918, Courtney MSS, 12 fol. 196.
115 Buxton to Lady Courtney, 28 November 1917, Courtney MSS, 12 fol. 168.
116 Henry Gladstone to Herbert Gladstone, 18 April 1918, Glynne–Gladstone MSS.
117 Esher to Hankey, 13 February 1918, Lloyd George MSS, F/23/2/14.
118 Lansdowne to Balfour, 5 February 1918, Balfour MSS, 49730 fol. 300.
119 Burns Diary, 13 and 16 February 1918, Burns MSS, 46340 fols. 47, 49.
120 Koss, *Haldane*, 233.
121 See, for example, Astor's minute for Lloyd George, 16 November 1917, Astor MSS.
122 MacCallum Scott Diary, 20 February 1918.
123 Esher Journal, 15 February 1918, *Journals and Letters*, IV, 180.
124 Hankey to Lloyd George, 15 February 1918, Lloyd George MSS, F/23/2/15.
125 Strachey to ed., *Morning Post* (copy), 28 February 1918, Courtney MSS, 12 fol. 205.
126 Sandhurst Diary, 23/27 February 1918, *From Day to Day*, II, 231.
127 Courtney to Noel Buxton (copy), 28 February 1918, Courtney MSS, 12 fol. 205.
128 Holt to Simon, 9 March 1918, Simon MSS.
129 Esher to Elibank, 12 March 1918, Elibank MSS, 8804 fol. 155.
130 Holt to Asquith (copy), 5 April 1918, Runciman MSS; Holt Diary, 5 May 1918, Holt MSS. Runciman, McKenna and (probably) Grey saw the Holt letter.
131 Beauchamp to Simon, 27 January 1918, Simon MSS.
132 Jones to Simon, ?1 May 1918, Simon MSS.
133 MacCallum Scott Diary, 11 April 1918.
134 Harcourt to Runciman, 21 June 1918, Runciman MSS.
135 Haldane to Gosse, 6 May 1918, Gosse MSS.
136 Asquith to Maclean, 13 May 1919, Maclean MSS, 465 fol. 182. For a retrospective Asquithian view, see Nancy Maurice (ed.), *The Maurice Case* (1972).
137 *Daily News*, 7 March 1929, quoted in Tom Clarke, *My Lloyd George Diary*, 45–6.
138 This is the implication of Asquith to Runciman, 15 November 1918, Runciman MSS.

139 Memo. by Elibank, 2 October 1918, Elibank MSS, 8804 fols. 193–6.
140 H. H. Asquith, *Memories and Reflections*, II (1928), 172.
141 Margot Asquith to Spender, 24 November 1918, Spender MSS, 46338 fol. 153.
142 Hardinge to Wingate (copy), 28 August 1918, Hardinge MSS, 38 fol. 246; Asquith to Bryce, 1 October 1918, Bryce MSS, UB 1.
143 Memo. by Donald [October 1922], Law MSS, 108/1/25.
144 Sir Walter Runciman, *Before the Mast: And After* (1924), 279–80.
145 Sir Charles Petrie, *Life and Letters of Austen Chamberlain*, II (1940), 132.
146 Herbert Gladstone to Henry Gladstone, 1 January 1919, Glynne–Gladstone MSS.
147 F. D. Acland to Maclean, 20 January 1919, Maclean MSS, 465 fol. 139.
148 Petrie, *op. cit.*, II, 173.
149 Runciman to Crewe, 5 January 1919, Crewe MSS, C/43.
150 See Gulland to Runciman, 4 January 1919, Runciman MSS.
151 Courtney to Simon, 24 January 1918, Simon MSS.
152 Buckmaster to Murray, 11 September 1920, Murray MSS, Box 6.
153 Acton to Crewe, 8 March 1910, Crewe MSS, C/1.
154 See 'Watchman', 'Is There an Alternative Government?' *Contemporary Review*, July 1921.
155 Spencer to Crewe, 24 June 1921, Crewe MSS, C/46.
156 E.g. *Lloyd George Liberal Magazine*, December 1920.
157 Gulland to Runciman, 11 January 1919, Runciman MSS.
158 MacCallum Scott Diary, 24 January 1917.
159 Dawson to Scott, 28 April 1919, Scott MSS, 50909 fol. 171.
160 Scott Diary, 18/20 January 1922, in Wilson (ed.), *Political Diaries*, 416.
161 Arthur Murray to Reading, 2 August 1922, Elibank MSS, 8808 fols. 151–2; cf. E. T. Raymond in *Lloyd George Liberal Magazine*, November 1920.
162 Sandhurst Diary, 1 November 1920, *From Day to Day*, II, 357.
163 Fisher Diary, 6 February 1920, Fisher MSS.
164 MacCallum Scott Diary, 1 February 1921.
165 Henry Gladstone to Herbert Gladstone, 25 May 1921, Glynne–Gladstone MSS; cf. Fitzmaurice to Bryce, 25 December 1920, Bryce MSS, UB 140.
166 Hogge to Maclean, 31 August 1920, Maclean MSS, 466 fol. 16.
167 Violet Bonham-Carter to Gilbert Murray, 18 September 1920, Murray MSS, Box 59. For the original version of the book, see E. A. M. Asquith, *The Autobiography of Margot Asquith* (1920). A more subdued version appeared in 1936.
168 Holt Diary, 17 July 1921, Holt MSS.
169 Haldane to Gosse, 4 February 1919, Gosse MSS.
170 Pease to wife, 5 January 1919, Pease MSS.
171 Herbert Gladstone to Henry Gladstone, 23 December 1921, Glynne–Gladstone MSS.

172 Michael Bentley, 'Liberal Politics and the Grey Conspiracy of 1921', *Historical Journal* (forthcoming).
173 Herbert Gladstone to Henry Gladstone, 29 November 1921, Glynne–Gladstone MSS.
174 Fitzmaurice to Bryce, 25 December 1920, Bryce MSS, UB 140; Herbert Gladstone to Henry Gladstone, 2 October 1921, Glynne–Gladstone MSS.
175 Gosse to Haldane, 5 January 1922, Haldane MSS, 5915 fol. 125.
176 Buckmaster to Crewe, 21 June 1921, Crewe MSS, C/3.
177 Lucy Masterman, *C. F. G. Masterman* (1939), 322.
178 Herbert Gladstone to Henry Gladstone, 2 March 1922, Glynne–Gladstone MSS.
179 Hudson to Gladstone, 20 December 1921, Gladstone MSS, 46475 fol. 22.
180 Stansgate Diary, 23 January 1922, Stansgate MSS. (MS partially burned.)
181 Herbert Gladstone Diary, 2 August 1922, Gladstone MSS, 46486 fol. 16.
182 Stansgate Diary, 6 February 1922, Stansgate MSS.
183 Asquith to Burns, 31 May 1922, Burns MSS, 46282 fol. 195.
184 Stansgate Diary, 22 May 1922, Stansgate MSS.
185 E.g. Stansgate Diary, 11 January 1922, Stansgate MSS.
186 Gladstone to Cecil, 1 September 1922, Cecil MSS, 51163 fol. 112.
187 Murray to Cecil, 10 October 1922, Cecil MSS, 51132 fol. 1.
188 Henry Gladstone to Herbert Gladstone, 13 October 1922, Glynne–Gladstone MSS.
189 Asquith to Cecil, 19 October 1922, Cecil MSS, 51073 fol. 35.
190 MacCallum Scott Diary, 12 October 1922.
191 Dalton Diary, 1 February 1919, Dalton MSS.
192 Laski to Holmes, 29 March 1923, in M. Howe (ed.), *Holmes–Laski Letters 1916–35*, 1 (1969), 491.
193 Memo. by Haldane [1926], Haldane MSS, 5923, fol. 17.
194 Hewins Diary, 28 May 1921, Hewins MSS.
195 Dalton Diary, 1 February 1919, Dalton MSS.
196 MacCallum Scott Diary, 15 February 1917.
197 *Ibid.*, 9 November 1915.
198 *Northern Echo*, 16 November 1918.
199 Strachey to [illegible, n.d.], Strachey MSS, S/18/4/1.
200 Bernard Mallet to Strachey, 25 August 1920, Strachey MSS, S/10/5/52.
201 Lloyd George to Law, 4 September 1920, Lloyd George MSS, F/31/1/44.
202 Burns Diary, 24 January 1919, Burns MSS, 46341 fol. 37.
203 MacCallum Scott Diary, 22 October 1917.
204 Kellaway to Lloyd George, 4 December 1916, Lloyd George MSS, E/2/19/16.
205 Geddes to Lloyd George, 30 December 1918, Lloyd George MSS, F/17/5/23; Maurice Cowling, *The Impact of Labour* (Cambridge, 1971), 57.

206 Lloyd George to Scott, 12 December 1916, Scott MSS, 50909 fol. 54.
207 Haldane to Gosse, 7 December 1916, Gosse MSS.
208 Sir Henry Robinson, *Memories: Wise and Otherwise* (1923), 264.
209 MacCallum Scott Diary, 1 February 1916.
210 FitzRoy Diary, 26 April 1920, *Memoirs*, II, 727; Scott Diary, 5 December 1916, in Wilson (ed.), *Political Diaries*, 411.
211 Burns Diary, 15 February 1917, Burns MSS, 46339 fol. 47.
212 Scott to Hobhouse, 7 May 1915, in Wilson (ed.), *Political Diaries*, 123.
213 *Journals and Letters*, IV, 71–2.
214 Riddell, *Lord Riddell's Intimate Diary of the Peace Conference and After, 1918–23* (1933), 166.
215 Rowntree to Cross, 26 April 1916. Lloyd George MSS, D/20/2/90.
216 Hobhouse to Scott, 9 December 1916, Scott MSS, 50909 fol. 46.
217 Cf. J. P. Mackintosh, *The British Cabinet* (1962), 350.
218 Harcourt to Ferguson, 14 March 1917, Harcourt MSS.
219 Hardinge to Buchanan (copy), 26 April 1917, Hardinge MSS, 31 fol. 312.
220 Henry Gladstone to Herbert Gladstone, 31 March 1917, Glynne–Gladstone MSS.
221 MacCallum Scott has 23 and 79: Diary, 11 August 1917.
222 Bryce to Murray, 3 February 1917, Murray MSS, Box 7.
223 Hardinge to Chirol (copy), 28 March 1917, Hardinge MSS, 30 fol. 263.
224 Bryce to Dickinson, 2 October 1917, Dickinson MSS, 403 fols. 207–8.
225 Scott Diary, 20 October 1917, in Wilson (ed.), *Political Diaries*, 308.
226 Montagu to Lloyd George (copy), 24 February 1917, Montagu MSS.
227 E.g. Hardinge to Hill, 4 October 1917, Hardinge MSS, 34 fol. 408.
228 MacCallum Scott Diary, 1 July 1917.
229 Chamberlain to Montagu, 17 August 1917, Montagu MSS.
230 Inchcape to Runciman, 14 September 1917, Runciman MSS.
231 Strachey to Grenfell (copy), 30 November 1917, Strachey MSS, S/18/4/32.
232 Ilbert to Brunner, 17 March and 20 April 1917, quoted in Stephen E. Koss, *Sir John Brunner* (1970), 284.
233 Fisher Diary, 21 November 1917, 6 February 1918; Fisher to wife, 18 November 1918, Fisher MSS.
234 Fisher Diary, 6 March 1918, Fisher MSS.
235 Burns Diary, 23 November 1918, Burns MSS, 46340 fol. 191.
236 Fisher to wife, 22 and 26 November 1918, Fisher MSS.
237 Hilton Young to Geoffrey Young, 16 December 1918, Kennet MSS.
238 J. M. Keynes, *The Economic Consequences of the Peace* (1919), 127–8.
239 MacCallum Scott Diary, 21 January 1919.
240 K. O. Morgan, 'Twilight of Welsh Liberalism: Lloyd George and the Wee Frees 1918–35', *Bulletin of the Board of Celtic Studies*, 12 (1968), 389.

241 See J. M. McEwan, 'The Coupon Election of 1918 and Unionist Members of Parliament', *Journal of Modern History*, 34 (1962), 296–8.
242 Davidson to Law, 13 January 1922, Law MSS, 107/2/2A.
243 Barnes to Guest, 21 November 1919, Lloyd George MSS, F/21/4/21. By the end of 1921, four Coalition Liberals had defected to the Asquithians and four Asquithians had gone over to Lloyd George: unsigned memo. [December 1921], Maclean MSS, 466 fol. 122.
244 MacCallum Scott Diary, 22 June 1919.
245 *Ibid.*, 23 December 1920.
246 Grigg to Chamberlain (copy), 7 May 1922, Grigg MSS.
247 Grigg to Nancy Astor (copy), 1 October 1922, Grigg MSS.
248 See, for example, Lambert to Maclean, 23 January 1919, Maclean MSS.
249 Young to Grigg, 23 March 1922, Grigg MSS.
250 Fisher Diary, 16 February 1920, 23 July 1920, 23 February 1921, 7 March 1921, Fisher MSS.
251 See, for example, conclusions of Cabinet, 4 July 1922, CAB 23/30/260.
252 For Fisher, see contributions to Cabinet debate, 1 June 1922, CAB 23/30/135, 139, 144; for McCurdy see his Cabinet paper on unemployment benefit, CAB 24/137/556.
253 Oliver Brett, *A Defence of Liberty* (1920), 43.
254 *Nation*, 26 November 1921, 7 January 1922, 14 December 1918.
255 *Lloyd George Liberal Magazine*, January and April 1921.
256 Elliot Dodds, *Is Liberalism Dead*? (1920), 177; Harold Storey, *The Case against the Lloyd George Coalition* (1920), 35–6.
257 Sandhurst Diary, 9 June and 31 August 1919, *From Day to Day*, II, 321.
258 Esher to L. B., 4 August 1920, *Journals and Letters*, IV, 264.
259 Henry Gladstone to Herbert Gladstone, 30 August 1919, Glynne–Gladstone MSS.
260 MacCallum Scott Diary, 25 March 1920.
261 Fisher Diary, 8 May 1920, Fisher MSS.
262 Richard Morris, M.P., in *The Times*, 17 May 1920.
263 *Lloyd George Liberal Magazine*, February 1922.
264 Strachey to Lady Buxton (copy), 5 August 1919, Strachey MSS, S/19/1/9. For another diatribe against the 'International Jew', see Maxse to Page Croft, 13 January 1916, Croft MSS.
265 MacCallum Scott Diary, 12 July 1920.
266 Guest to Lloyd George, 29 September 1920, Lloyd George MSS, F/22/2/15.
267 Fisher Diary, 18 January 1922, Fisher MSS. Cf. Hewart at National Liberal Conference, January 1922, reported in *Lloyd George Liberal Magazine*, February 1922.
268 Stansgate Diary, 16 March 1922, Stansgate MSS.
269 Fisher Diary, 4 and 8 October 1922, Fisher MSS.
270 Fisher Diary, 16 October 1922, Fisher MSS.
271 See these and other reflections in Grigg MSS.
272 Speech at Blackburn, 21 March 1921, *Liberal Magazine*, April 1921.

CHAPTER 3. EXORCISM

1 J. M. Robertson, *Mr. Lloyd George and Liberalism* (1923), 10.
2 Violet Bonham-Carter to Murray, 7 December 1923, Murray MSS, Box 10.
3 Spender to Simon, 3 May 1921, Simon MSS.
4 Stevenson Diary, 24 June 1921, in A. J. P. Taylor (ed.), *Lloyd George: A Diary by Frances Stevenson* (1971), 224.
5 Sir Charles Mallet, 'Liberalism and Mr. Lloyd George', *Contemporary Review*, June 1920.
6 Hill to MacDonald (printed), 14 December 1921, Murray MSS, Box 59.
7 Address to National Liberals at Hotel Victoria, 25 October 1922, *Lloyd George Liberal Magazine*, November 1922. Only fourteen Liberals decided to take both whips: *ibid.*, February 1923.
8 *Westminster Gazette*, 15 November 1922.
9 E.g. Cowdray to Beauchamp, 30 December 1922, Gladstone MSS, 46474 fol. 24.
10 Asquith to Maclean, 29 November 1922, Maclean MSS, 466 fol. 186; Margot Asquith to Law, 29 October 1922, Law MSS, 108/1/23.
11 ?[Illegible] to Simon, 18 November 1922, Simon MSS.
12 Masterman to Benn, 24 December 1922, Stansgate MSS.
13 *Morning Post*, 8 November 1927.
14 30 November 1922. The letter was 'thoroughly wise and hopeful'.
15 MacCallum Scott Diary, 1 December 1922.
16 Grigg to Bailey (copy), 4 January 1923, Grigg MSS.
17 *Northern Echo*, 1 December 1922.
18 Gladstone to Beauchamp (copy), 15 January 1923, Maclean MSS, 467 fols. 4–5.
19 Grigg to Bailey, 9 April 1923, Grigg MSS.
20 E.g. Islington to Crewe, 19 November 1922, Crewe MSS, C/28.
21 Beesly to Murray, 2 January 1923, Murray MSS, Box 59. The constituency was North Berwickshire, the candidate E. A. Lessing.
22 J. W. Ponsonby to Fildes (copy), 24 April 1923, Grigg MSS.
23 Lloyd George to Scott, 8 November 1922, Lloyd George MSS, G/17/11/1; cf. Grey to Strachey, 19 December 1922, Strachey MSS, S/7/8/37.
24 Grigg to Bailey, 17 May 1923, and to Allden, 3 May 1923, Grigg MSS.
25 Asquith to Crewe, 3 May 1923, Crewe MSS, C/40. For Beauchamp, see *Lloyd George Liberal Magazine*, February 1923.
26 MacCallum Scott to Pratt, 2 August 1923 (copied into former's diary).
27 Lloyd George to Hilton Young, 21 August 1923, Kennet MSS.
28 MacCallum Scott Diary, 13 November 1923. For Baldwin's reaction, Keith Middlemas and John Barnes, *Baldwin* (1969), 212.
29 *Lloyd George Liberal Magazine*, October 1923.
30 *Times*, 16 November 1923.

31 Curzon to Crewe, 22 and 26 November 1923, Crewe MSS, C/12.
32 Violet Bonham-Carter to Murray, 7 December 1923, Murray MSS, Box 10.
33 E.g. Beaverbrook to Borden, 16 December 1923, quoted in Kenneth Young, *Churchill and Beaverbrook* (1966), 67.
34 *Northern Echo*, 12 October 1923.
35 Hirst to Simon, 29 October 1923, Simon MSS.
36 Murray to Cecil, 13 November 1923, and reply, 16 November, Cecil MSS, 51132 fols. 6–7.
37 Jones to Simon, 17 November 1923, Simon MSS; *Northern Echo*, 14 November.
38 See correspondence in Grigg MSS, file Gen/4.
39 Grigg to Bailey (copy), 13 December 1923, Grigg MSS.
40 Violet Carutheres to Murray, 14 November 1923, Murray MSS, Box 59. Cf. memo. by R. H. Davies, 4 March 1925, Maclean MSS, 468 fol. 10.
41 Scott to Simon, 30 November 1923, Simon MSS.
42 Margot Asquith to Cecil, 2 December 1923, Cecil MSS, 51073 fol. 41.
43 E.g. Hudson to Gladstone, 4 November 1923, Gladstone MSS, 46475 fol. 67.
44 Dickinson Diary, 15 November 1923, in H. C. White (ed.), *Lord Dickinson of Painswick* (Gloucester, 1956), 158–9.
45 C. P. Cook, 'A Stranger Death of Liberal England', in A. J. P. Taylor (ed.), *Lloyd George: Twelve Essays* (1971), 311–12.
46 Cecil to Miss A. Bell, 22 February 1924, Cecil MSS, 51164 fol. 26.
47 Grey to Cecil, 14 October 1924, Cecil MSS, 51073 fol. 88.
48 J. J. Riley (*Southport Guardian*) to Simon, 12 December 1923, Simon MSS. Hirst was also in favour of the 'Leftward-bouncing ball': Hirst to Simon, 28 August 1924, Simon MSS.
49 Grigg to Bailey (copy), 20 March 1924, Grigg MSS.
50 Scott Diary, 1 July 1923, in Trevor Wilson (ed.), *The Political Diaries of C. P. Scott 1911–28* (1970), 442.
51 Haldane to Gosse, 13 August 1924, Gosse MSS; Haldane to ? (typed extract), 26 September 1924, Haldane MSS, 5916 fol. 154.
52 MacCallum Scott Diary, 17 October 1924.
53 ?Fletcher to Grigg, 25 March 1923, Grigg MSS.
54 Grigg to Bailey (copy), 6 March 1924, Grigg MSS.
55 MacCallum Scott Diary, 31 January and 6 February 1924.
56 Cf. Lloyd George to Megan Lloyd George, 25 March 1924: 'I am lying low – deliberately', in K. O. Morgan (ed.), *Lloyd George Family Letters, 1885–1936* (Cardiff and Oxford, 1973), 202.
57 Grigg to Bailey (copy), 20 March 1924, Grigg MSS.
58 Churchill to Cecil, 23 March 1924, Cecil MSS, 51073 fol. 104.
59 Grigg to Bailey (copy), 6 March 1924, Grigg MSS.
60 Grigg to Bailey (copy), 27 March 1924, Grigg MSS.
61 The party's bank balance stood at only just over £10,000 in 1925: unsigned secret memo., 4 August 1925, Maclean MSS, 468 fol. 73.

62 For Farquhar, see FitzAlan to Law, 26 January 1923, Law MSS, 108/4/8, and Maurice Cowling, *The Impact of Labour* (Cambridge, 1971), 247. There is a useful perspective about pre-war practice with regard to honours in J. Pease, 'History of H.H.A.' (1908), Pease MSS.

63 See Maclean/Gladstone correspondence, Gladstone MSS, 46474; and Maclean to Simon, 24 September 1924, Simon MSS.

64 Grey to Crewe, 20 November 1922, Crewe MSS, C/17.

65 See Beauchamp to Simon, 22 March 1924, Simon MSS.

66 Denman to Crewe, 26 September 1924, Crewe MSS, C/13.

67 Edge to Frances Stevenson [May 1924], Lloyd George MSS, G/6/10/16.

68 MacCallum Scott Diary, 2 May 1924.

69 Hewins Diary, 30 May 1924, Hewins MSS. The Asquithians supported the government.

70 Phillipps to Maclean, 5 August 1924, Asquith MSS, 34 fol. 134.

71 Lloyd George to Megan Lloyd George, 2 October 1924, in Morgan (ed.), *Family Letters*, 204.

72 Memo. by Maclean, 18 January 1924, Gladstone MSS, 46474 fol. 71; Mond to Lloyd George (copy), 10 August 1924, Melchett MSS. Cf. *Lloyd George Liberal Magazine*, October 1923, for the official line.

73 MacCallum Scott Diary, 6 October 1924.

74 Buckmaster to Murray, 14 September 1926, Murray MSS, Box 6.

75 See Simon to Mond, 1 February 1926, Melchett MSS.

76 24 October 1925.

77 Scott Diary, 27/30 November 1924, in Wilson (ed.), *Political Diaries*, 472.

78 Phillipps to Gladstone, 16 November 1926, Gladstone MSS, 46475 fol. 290.

79 Grigg to Lloyd George (copy), 19 June 1924, Grigg MSS.

80 Guest to Grigg, 8 May 1925, Grigg MSS. Webb noticed that Guest 'failed to carry with him any of his eight supporters': Webb to Beatrice Webb, 12 May 1925, Passfield MSS, II.3.(i).

81 Grigg to Hichens (copy), 6 May 1925, Grigg MSS.

82 Guest to Lloyd George, 1 June 1926, Lloyd George MSS, G/8/13/4.

83 'Lloyd George's Stage Army' in A. J. P. Taylor (ed.), *Lloyd George: Twelve Essays*, 251n.

84 Violet Bonham-Carter to Murray, 9 June 1926, Murray MSS, Box 10, for the '"Guest" Liberals' as 'old Coalition wreckage'.

85 Lucy Masterman, *C. F. G. Masterman* (1939), 345–6.

86 Tom Clarke Diary, 14 October 1926, in *My Lloyd George Diary* (1939), 22.

87 Memo. by Hudson and Maclean, 5 November 1924, Gladstone MSS, 46475 fol. 146. Pringle formed a 'Liberal and Radical Candidates Association': Trevor Wilson, *Downfall of the Liberal Party* (1966), 320; cf. MacCallum Scott Diary, 10 January 1926.

88 Grigg to Sinclair (copy), 6 November 1924, Grigg MSS.

89 Stansgate Diary, 30 January 1925, Stansgate MSS.

90 Asquith to Spender, 30 March 1925, Spender MSS, 46388 fol. 105.
91 Harold Storey, secret memo. on party situation [1925], Runciman MSS.
92 Murray to Reading (copy), 15 December 1924, Elibank MSS, 8808 fol. 166.
93 Runciman to Samuel, 19 November 1924, Samuel MSS, A/155/(v)/33.
94 McKenna to Runciman, 4 January 1919, Runciman MSS.
95 MacCallum Scott Diary, 1 February 1927; cf. Davies to Lloyd George [December 1916], Lloyd George MSS, F/83/10/1.
96 Fisher to Lettice Fisher [December 1924], Fisher MSS, Box 6.
97 Churchill at Burnley: see MacCallum Scott Diary, 6 February 1926.
98 Stansgate Diary, 28 January 1925, Stansgate MSS.
99 Sidney Webb to Beatrice Webb, 11/12 March 1925, Passfield MSS, 11.3.(i).
100 Ernest Benn to Wedgwood Benn, 29 April 1925, Stansgate MSS.
101 Fisher to Lettice Fisher, 15 January 1924, Fisher MSS, Box 6.
102 See MacCallum Scott Diary, 29 September 1926.
103 Oxford to Murray, 20 October 1925, Murray MSS, Box 3.
104 Margot Oxford to Keynes, 31 ?May 1926, Keynes MSS.
105 See Gladstone to Crewe, 9 July 1925, Crewe MSS, C/16.
106 Stansgate Diary, 6 August 1925, Stansgate MSS.
107 Grigg to Sinclair (copy), 6 November 1924, Grigg MSS.
108 Sinclair to Grigg, 12 November 1924, Grigg MSS.
109 Stansgate Diary, 25 January 1925, Stansgate MSS.
110 See the views of 'Col. Williams', reported in Sidney Webb to Beatrice Webb, 29 September 1925, Passfield MSS, 11.3.(i).
111 'I am in no hurry to get mixed up with that gang again' (27 August 1925): Morgan (ed.), *Family Letters*, 206.
112 Lloyd George to Gwynne, 19 May 1925, Lloyd George MSS, G/8/14/2.
113 Lloyd George to Garvin, 19 August 1925, Lloyd George MSS, G/8/5/1.
114 Hudson to Gladstone, 14 September 1925, Gladstone MSS, 46475 fol. 170.
115 E.g. Inchcape to Buckmaster [1926] in H. Bolitho, *Lord Inchcape* (1936), 221.
116 Hobhouse to Asquith, 3 September 1925, Asquith MSS, 34 fol. 228.
117 Asquith to Maclean, 12 September 1925, Maclean MSS, 468 fols. 76–7.
118 Memo. by Phillipps, 22 September 1925, Gladstone MSS, 46475 fol. 284; Stansgate Diary, 16 November 1925, Stansgate MSS.
119 Stansgate Diary, 3 December 1925, Stansgate MSS; Storey to Maclean, 22 October 1925, Maclean MSS, 468 fol. 89.
120 MacCallum Scott Diary, 28 January 1926.
121 Beauchamp to Lloyd George, 23 September, 29 November and 2 December 1925, Lloyd George MSS, G/3/5/14, 15, 16.
122 Stansgate Diary, 27 November 1925, Stansgate MSS.
123 Hodgson to Lloyd George, 5 January 1926, Lloyd George MSS, G/10/5/1.

124 Churchill to Mond, 29 January 1926, Melchett MSS.
125 MacCallum Scott Diary, 4 May 1926.
126 *Ibid.*, 11 May 1926.
127 *Ibid.*, 18 May 1926.
128 See Wilson, *Downfall*, 329–33.
129 See Scott to Hammond, 21 May 1926, in Wilson (ed.), *Political Diaries*, 486, and subsequent diary entries.
130 Hudson to Gladstone, 18 May 1926, Gladstone MSS, 46475 fols. 194–5.
131 Phillipps to Gladstone, 20 May 1926, Gladstone MSS, 46475 fol. 281; Margot Oxford to Keynes, 28 May 1926, Keynes MSS.
132 Margot Oxford to Clarke, 23 January 1929, in Clarke, *My Lloyd George Diary*, 43.
133 Keynes to Margot Oxford (not sent), 26 May 1926, Keynes MSS.
134 MacCallum Scott Diary, 26 May 1926.
135 Sidney Webb to Beatrice Webb, 8 June 1926, Passfield MSS, II.3.(i).
136 See Beauchamp to Lloyd George, 31 May 1926, Lloyd George MSS, G/3/5/18.
137 MacCallum Scott Diary, 12 June 1926.
138 Crosfield to Lloyd George, 9 September 1926, Lloyd George MSS, G/5/7/1. See also Crosfield's letters in *The Times*, 16 August, 30 August and 23 September 1926.
139 Crosfield to Lloyd George, 14 September 1926, Lloyd George MSS, G/5/7/3.
140 Secret memo. by Phillipps, 22 September 1926, Runciman MSS.
141 Phillipps to Runciman, 5 October 1926, Runciman MSS.
142 Simon to Asquith, 9 October 1926, Asquith MSS, 35 fol. 272. For Asquith's state of mind, see Haldane to Gosse, 21 June 1926, Gosse MSS.
143 J. A. Spender, *Cowdray* (1930), 269. For Spender's line see *Westminster Gazette*, 25 June 1926.
144 *Manchester Guardian*, 25 June 1926; *Reynolds News*, 24 October 1926.
145 *Manchester Guardian*, 29 June 1926.
146 Kenworthy in *Daily Chronicle*, 14 October 1926.
147 *Star*, 15 October 1926.
148 Sir Geoffrey Shakespeare, *Let Candles Be Brought In* (1949), 121.
149 Runciman, 'A Secret Note on the Plight of the Liberal Party', 1 November 1926, p. 6. Runciman MSS.
150 Loreburn to Scott, 13 April 1919, Scott MSS, 50909 fol. 169.
151 Maclean to Gladstone, 1 August 1928, Gladstone MSS, 46474 fol. 206.
152 Byles to Samuel, 18 March ?1928, Samuel MSS, A/155/(vii)/11.
153 Davies to Jones, 15 November 1926, Lloyd George MSS, G/5/13/1.
154 Confidential memo., 12 July 1929, Runciman MSS.
155 Byles to Samuel, 18 March ?1928, Samuel MSS, A/155/(vii)/11. [Emphasis added.]
156 F. H. Lambert to Hutchinson (copy), 12 November 1928, Runciman MSS.

157 Runciman to Samuel, 25 September 1927, Samuel MSS, A/155/(vi)/83.
158 E.g. Dalton Diary, 'end of 1927', Dalton MSS.
159 Cecil to Lang, 16 December 1927, Cecil MSS, 51154 fol. 12.
160 Margot Oxford to Baldwin, 8 February 1928, Baldwin MSS, 163 fol. 206.
161 Lloyd George to Collins, 3 November 1926, Lloyd George MSS, G/5/1/14; *Times*, 5 November 1926.
162 *Daily Chronicle*, 1 November 1926.
163 Charles Hobhouse to Samuel, 17 February 1927, Samuel MSS, A/155/(vi)/41.
164 See Hodgson to Lloyd George, 16 November 1926, Lloyd George MSS, G/10/5/2.
165 See J. A. Spender, *Sir Robert Hudson* (1930), 175.
166 MacCallum Scott Diary, 20 January and 1 February 1927.
167 *Ibid.*, 11 January 1922; Macnamara to Lloyd George, 23 February 1920, Lloyd George MSS, F/36/1/14.
168 E.g. Stansgate Diary, 20 May 1925, Stansgate MSS.
169 For McNair see Dalton Diary, 6/8 December 1919, Dalton MSS.
170 Middlemas and Barnes, *Baldwin*, 804.
171 Haldane to Gosse, 27 August 1924, Gosse MSS.
172 *My Lloyd George Diary*, 35–6.
173 Violet Bonham-Carter to Murray, 10 November 1926, Box 10.
174 He had represented Swansea West since 1924. See *South Wales News*, 19 November 1926.
175 MacCallum Scott Diary, 9 December 1926.
176 *Observer*, 19 December 1926.
177 Lady Selborne to Cecil, 31 August 1927 and 12 April 1929, Cecil MSS, 51157 fols. 149, 53.
178 MacCallum Scott Diary, 14 January 1927.
179 Margot Oxford to Rosebery, 20 February 1927, Rosebery MSS.
180 MacCallum Scott Diary, 22 February 1928.
181 *Times*, 14 December 1926.
182 Maclean to Gladstone, 18 February 1927, Gladstone MSS, 46474 fol. 196.
183 Grey to Gladstone, 3 August 1929, Gladstone MSS, 45992 fols. 159–61.
184 Emmott to Grigg, 11 November 1926, Grigg MSS.
185 Lunn to Glover (copy), 9 February 1927, Murray MSS, Box 59.
186 Grey to Crewe, 10 June 1928, Crewe MSS, C/17.
187 See Scott Diary, 22/23 July 1927, in Wilson (ed.), *Political Diaries*, 488.
188 Lloyd George to Samuel, 28 February 1928, Samuel MSS, A/71/9.
189 See correspondence of June/July 1928 in Crewe MSS, C/17.
190 Simon to Eggleston (copy), 11 February 1927, E. D. Simon MSS, M11/14/29.
191 Grey to Cecil, 31 March 1929, Cecil MSS, 51073 fol. 95.
192 Grey to Crewe, 16 February 1929, Crewe MSS, C/17.

193 Memo. by Phillipps, 7 May 1928, Gladstone MSS, 46475 fol. 302.
194 See David Butler, *The Electoral System in Great Britain* (Oxford, 1953), 14.
195 Strauss to MacCallum Scott, 7 April 1927, copied into the latter's diary. MacCallum Scott was a member of the Labour party by this time.
196 Sidney Webb to Beatrice Webb, 15, 17 and 30 March 1927, Passfield MSS, II.3.(i).
197 MacDonald to Murray, 29 October 1928, Murray MSS, Box 35.
198 MacCallum Scott Diary, 29 March 1927.
199 *Ibid.*, 13 February 1928. The same objection was to be made about Mrs Runciman's campaign at the St Ives by-election; see Samuel to Simon, 23 February 1928, Simon MSS.
200 MacDonald to Murray, 29 October 1928, Murray MSS, Box 35.
201 Violet Bonham-Carter to Murray, 10 November 1926, Murray MSS, Box 10.
202 Irwin to Fisher, 21 April 1928, Fisher MSS.
203 See R. Scott to Samuel, 8 February 1926, and Burns to Samuel, 3 February 1927, Samuel MSS, A/155/(vi)/1, 37.
204 MacCallum Scott Diary, 12 June 1928.
205 E.g. Sidney to Beatrice Webb, 16 May 1928, Passfield MSS, II.3.(i).
206 MacCallum Scott Diary, 1 June 1927.
207 *Ibid.*, 3 February 1928.
208 Bridgeman to Baldwin, 27 March 1929, Baldwin MSS, 175 fol. 51.
209 Melchett to Baldwin (copy), 26 March 1929, Melchett MSS.
210 Note by Lloyd George, 18 February 1929, Lloyd George MSS, G/4/4/23.
211 Clarke, *op. cit.*, 52–3; cf. Beaverbrook to Churchill, 12 July 1929, in Young, *Churchill and Beaverbrook*, 110.
212 Garvin to Lloyd George, 3 June 1929, Lloyd George MSS, G/8/5/18.
213 Margot Oxford to Keynes, 5 June 1929, Keynes MSS.
214 Phillipps to Gladstone, 5 June 1929, Gladstone MSS, 46475 fol. 312.
215 Beauchamp to Lloyd George, 21 January 1930, Lloyd George MSS, G/3/5/27.
216 Muir to Lloyd George, 1 December 1929, Lloyd George MSS, G/15/6/16.
217 Sharp to Lloyd George, 23 January 1930, Lloyd George MSS, G/32/1/1.
218 Laski to Holmes, 20 February 1927, in M. Howe (ed.), *Holmes–Laski Letters 1916–35*, II (1971), 1028.
219 Blanche Dugdale to Cecil, 15 September 1931, Cecil MSS, 51157 fol. 239.
220 Maclean to Gladstone, 14 June 1929, Gladstone MSS, 46474 fol. 212.

CHAPTER 4. UPPER AND NETHER MILLSTONES

1 *Let Candles Be Brought In* (1949), 125.
2 C. F. G. Masterman to Lucy Masterman, 26 August 1920, quoted in Lucy Masterman, *C. F. G. Masterman* (1939), 317.

3 Garvin to Grigg, 20 November 1922; Grigg to Bailey (copy), 21 February 1924, Grigg MSS.
4 Webster to Arthur Murray, 19 March 1920, Elibank MSS, 8808 fols. 68–9.
5 Letter from Percy Harris, *Times*, 12 March 1923.
6 Fisher Diary, 29 March 1921, Fisher MSS. The phrase acquires a hyphen in Michael Kinnear, *The Fall of Lloyd George* (1973), 95.
7 MacDonald to Strachey, 10 August 1923, Strachey MSS, S/10/1/1.
8 Letter from A. P. Herbert, *Times*, 12 January 1927.
9 Rothermere to Croft, 9 August 1925, Croft MSS.
10 Hewins Diary, 14 March 1921, Hewins MSS; Margaret Cole to Gilbert Murray, 23 July 1929, Murray MSS, Box 13.
11 Bryce to Murray, 15 July 1920, Murray MSS, Box 7.
12 See, for example, Harold Langshaw, *Socialism: And the Historic Function of Liberalism* (1925), 70.
13 Sir Alfred Pease, *Elections and Recollections* (1932), 74.
14 Cyril Asquith to Murray, 1 October 1931, Murray MSS, Box 3.
15 Sandhurst Diary, 8 January 1916, *From Day to Day*, II (1929), 5; cf. his report of Loreburn's views, *ibid.*, I (1928), 22.
16 Henry Gladstone to Herbert Gladstone, 4 December 1918, Glynne–Gladstone MSS.
17 Forster to Young, 4 March 1915, Kennet MSS, 28/8.
18 There is an illuminating report from one of them in the Lloyd George MSS: 'Leading Rebels – September 1918', marked 'SECRET', F/61/1/23.
19 Oliver Brett, *A Defence of Liberty* (1920), 178.
20 E.g. Haldane to Gosse, 11 November 1918 and 18 August 1919, Gosse MSS.
21 Beauchamp to Simon, 27 January 1918, Simon MSS.
22 Holt Diary, 31 December 1917 and 12 November 1918, Holt MSS.
23 Aneurin Williams, 'The General Election and the Future of the Liberal Party', *Contemporary Review*, February 1919.
24 Burns Diary, 29 December 1918, Burns MSS, 46340 fol. 209; Fisher to Lettice Fisher, 29 December 1918, Fisher MSS.
25 MacCallum Scott Diary, 14 January 1923.
26 Grigg to Bailey (copy), 21 February 1924, Grigg MSS.
27 *Northern Echo*, 22 October 1923.
28 Asquith to Murray, 20 October 1925, Murray MSS, Box 3.
29 Grigg to Bailey (copy), 17 January 1924, Grigg MSS.
30 H. Bolitho, *James Lyle Mackay, First Earl of Inchcape* (1936), 226.
31 Norman Angell, *After All* (1951), 239.
32 Grigg to Bailey (copy), 14 February 1924, Grigg MSS.
33 Lansbury to Beatrice Webb, 19 March 1924, Passfield MSS, II.4.(h).
34 MacDonald to Arthur Murray, 14 January 1919, Elibank MSS, 8808 fol. 3.
35 Dalton Diary, 8 December 1923, Dalton MSS.

36 Lovat-Fraser to Gilbert Murray, 19 January 1925, Murray MSS, Box 59.

37 Asquith to Murray, 30 September 1919, Murray MSS, Box 3; Violet Bonham-Carter to Murray, 9 May 1922, Murray MSS, Box 9; J. H. Thomas, *My Story* (1937), 38. For some classless rhetoric, see *ibid.*, 88.

38 J. R. Clynes, *Memoirs*, I (1937), 326. For his 'Liberal principles' see Beechman to Murray, 15 June [?1922], Murray MSS, Box 59.

39 MacCallum Scott Diary, 18 June 1927, for Burns' description of him as the last survivor of the Manchester school. Cf. Hirst to Simon, 11 October 1924, Simon MSS.

40 MacDonald to Ponsonby, 2 June 1922 and 28 September 1922, Ponsonby MSS.

41 Hewart at the National Liberal Conference, January 1922, reported in *Lloyd George Liberal Magazine*, February 1922.

42 Milner to Philip Gell, 20 August 1915, Milner MSS, 140 fol. 226.

43 MacDonald to Villard, 4 June 1923, quoted in M. S. Venkataramani, 'Ramsay MacDonald and Britain's Domestic Politics and Foreign Relations, 1919–31', *Political Studies*, I (1960), 246.

44 Hewins Diary, 20 January 1924, Hewins MSS.

45 Gwynne to Baldwin, 30 October 1924, Baldwin MSS, 36 fol. 29.

46 Grenfell to Milner, 19 November 1923, Milner MSS, 209 (unfoliated).

47 Baldwin to Birkenhead (draft), 14 November 1923, Baldwin MSS, 35 fols. 93–4. The finished letter was printed in *The Times*, 16 November 1923.

48 Lloyd George to Dame Margaret Lloyd George, 18 December 1935, in K. O. Morgan (ed.), *Lloyd George Family Letters 1885–1936* (Cardiff and Oxford, 1973), 211.

49 G. M. Young, *Stanley Baldwin* (1952), 153.

50 Esher to Williamson, 19 May 1926, in Oliver, Viscount Esher (ed.), *The Journals and Letters of Reginald Viscount Esher*, IV (1938), 300; Grey to Baldwin, 5 January 1929, Baldwin MSS, 164 fols. 80–1.

51 Maclean to Baldwin, 2 August 1926, Baldwin MSS, 161 fol. 154.

52 Runciman to Baldwin, 24 April 1923, *ibid.*, 159 fol. 114.

53 T. R. Davison to Baldwin, 26 December 1925, *ibid.*, 160 fol. 40. For similar opinions see Alexander Shaw to Inchcape, 19 November 1928, *ibid.*, 163 fol. 161, and the views of the northern Liberal quoted in Wickham Steed, *The Real Stanley Baldwin* (1930), 12.

54 See his entry in *D.N.B.* contributed by R. H. Brand, himself a distinguished Liberal economist. For Kerr's idealism see MacCallum Scott Diary, 5 January 1922.

55 Haldane to Gosse, 3 August 1923, Gosse MSS; Haldane to Baldwin, 8 December 1923, Baldwin MSS, 35 fol. 176. See Loreburn to Bryce, 1 February 1920, for Haldane's wanting to 'get into the limelight again', Bryce MSS, UB 10.

56 Grigg to Bailey (copy), 21 February 1924, Grigg MSS.

57 MacCallum Scott Diary, 19 September 1927.

28   *Notes to pp. 127–132*

58 P. F. Clarke, *Lancashire and the New Liberalism* (Cambridge, 1971), 343.
59 E. D. Simon, 'Ramsay Muir: Liberalism and Industry', dated 30 June 1942, E. D. Simon MSS, M11/16/32.
60 Creed to Strachey, 12 March 1922, Strachey MSS, S/19/4/9.
61 Curzon to Balfour, 10 February 1918, Balfour MSS, 49734 fol. 45; E. Hartington to Cecil [1921], Cecil MSS, 51163 fol. 43.
62 Oliver to Amery, 23 July 1915, quoted in A. M. Gollin, *Proconsul in Politics* (1964), 273; Hewins Diary, 18 May 1919, Hewins MSS.
63 Amery to Baldwin, 29 December 1923, Baldwin MSS, 42 fol. 159.
64 Amery to Page Croft, 14 January 1924, Croft MSS; cf. Amery to Baldwin, 21 December 1923, Baldwin MSS, 42 fols. 151–4. For the 'new' Conservatism generally, see Maurice Cowling, *The Impact of Labour* (Cambridge, 1971), *passim* and esp. 413–28.
65 Willoughby de Broke to Croft, 30 March 1912, Croft MSS.
66 Bledisloe to Baldwin, 31 January 1924, Baldwin MSS, 159 fols. 183–4.
67 Harold Williams, 'The Prime Minister's Deal with Lenin', *The Nineteenth Century and After*, May 1921; and Williams to Hoare, 17 April 1921, Templewood MSS.
68 Winterton to Hoare, 5 October 1921, Templewood MSS.
69 Salisbury to Law, 18 November 1921, Law MSS, 107/1/71. For Salisbury's views about the coalition see his letter in *The Times*, 24 June 1921.
70 Herbert Gladstone to Henry Gladstone, 2 March 1922, Glynne–Gladstone MSS.
71 Cowdray to Maclean, 19 July 1921, Maclean MSS, 466 fol. 68.
72 Hudson to Gladstone, 11 February 1922, Gladstone MSS, 46475 fol. 25.
73 Harmsworth to Runciman, 10 May 1918, Runciman MSS, Box 1.
74 Cowling, *op. cit.*, 48–9.
75 Rothermere to Elibank, 22 December 1919, Elibank MSS, 8804 fols. 225–6.
76 E.g. Rothermere to Maclean, 17 January 1922, Maclean MSS, 466 fol. 131.
77 Herbert Gladstone to Henry Gladstone, 2 March 1922, Glynne–Gladstone MSS; Stansgate Diary, 1 February 1922, Stansgate MSS.
78 Herbert Gladstone to Henry Gladstone, 31 October 1922, Glynne–Gladstone MSS.
79 Rothermere to Simon, 27 October 1922, Simon MSS.
80 Rothermere to Beaverbrook (extract), 3 November 1924, Lloyd George MSS, G/3/6/3.
81 See G. R. Searle, *The Quest for National Efficiency* (1971), 128–36.
82 Fisher Diary, 21 November 1917, Fisher MSS.
83 Curzon to Law, 25 February 1918, Law MSS, 82/9/16.
84 This was Archibald Salvidge's suggested title: Salvidge to Churchill, 21 February 1920, Lloyd George MSS, F/9/2/9.
85 Fisher to Lloyd George, 3 February 1920, Lloyd George MSS, F/16/7/50.

86 Riddell, *Lord Riddell's Intimate Diary of the Peace Conference and After, 1918–23* (1933), 169.

87 *Ibid.*, 365.

88 Fisher Diary, 9 January 1919 and 21 February 1919, Fisher MSS.

89 Guest to Lloyd George [1919], Lloyd George MSS, F/21/2/57.

90 Jones Diary, 2 July 1919, in K. Middlemas (ed.), *Whitehall Diary*, I (Oxford, 1969), 88.

91 Stevenson Diary, 5 July 1919, in A. J. P. Taylor (ed.), *Lloyd George: A Diary by Frances Stevenson* (1971), 188. See also A. J. P. Taylor (ed.), *My Darling Pussy* (1975), 26–30.

92 *Times*, 17/18 July 1919; see *ibid.*, 2 August 1919, for the group's declared aims.

93 *Times*, 16 July 1919. Churchill's speech was printed on 25 July.

94 *Ibid.*, 17 July 1919.

95 Hewins Diary, 16 July 1919, Hewins MSS.

96 E.g. *Times*, 8 August 1919.

97 Frances Lloyd George, *The Years That Are Past* (1967), 168.

98 Riddell, *op. cit.*, 126.

99 *Times*, 22 September 1919.

100 Arthur Murray to Wiseman, 28 July 1919, Elibank MSS, 8808 fol. 30.

101 Frances Lloyd George, *op. cit.*, 170.

102 Churchill to Lloyd George, 20 September 1919, Lloyd George MSS, F/9/1/19.

103 *Times*, 17 July 1919.

104 Stevenson Diary, 17 January 1920, in A. J. P. Taylor (ed.), *A Diary*, 197.

105 Stevenson Diary, 20 January 1920, *ibid.*, 198.

106 C. F. G. Masterman, 'The New Democratic Party', *Contemporary Review*, February 1920. Cf. memo. by Nicoll [February 1920], quoted in T. H. Darlow, *William Robertson Nicoll: Life and Letters* (1925), 295–6.

107 *Times*, 5 January 1920.

108 See his letter to *The Times* printed in Lord Swinton, *I Remember* (1948), 155–6.

109 Stevenson Diary, 23 January 1920, in A. J. P. Taylor (ed.), *A Diary*, 199.

110 Lloyd George to Balfour, 18 February 1920, Lloyd George MSS, F/3/5/3.

111 Robert Blake, *The Unknown Prime Minister* (1955), 416.

112 Law to Balfour, 24 March 1920, quoted in Blake, *op. cit.*, 416–17.

113 Macnamara to Lloyd George, 23 February 1920, Lloyd George MSS, F/1/6/4.

114 Addison to Lloyd George, 3 March 1920, Lloyd George MSS, F/1/6/4.

115 Stevenson Diary, 16 March 1920, in A. J. P. Taylor (ed.), *A Diary*, 205.

116 MacCallum Scott Diary, 15 March 1920.

117 Stevenson Diary, 18 March 1920, in A. J. P. Taylor (ed.), *A Diary*, 206.
118 *Times*, 19 March 1920.
119 Memo. by Arthur Murray, 18 March 1920, Elibank MSS, 8808 fol. 72.
120 FitzRoy Diary, 22 March 1920, *Memoirs*, II (1925), 726.
121 MacCallum Scott Diary, 17 April 1920.
122 *The Case against the Lloyd George Coalition* (1920).
123 *Ibid.*, 91.
124 MacCallum Scott Diary, 15 March 1920; Esher to L.B., 4 August 1920, *Journals and Letters*, IV, 264.
125 E.g. MacCallum Scott Diary, 30 March 1921; but cf. Samuel Storey to Law, 8 July 1921, Law MSS, 107/1/45.
126 E.g. Derby to Lloyd George, 18 November 1921, Lloyd George MSS, F/14/5/33.
127 Guest to Lloyd George, 16 January 1922, Lloyd George MSS, F/22/3/37.
128 MacCallum Scott Diary, 23 January 1922.
129 *Ibid.*, 6 February 1922.
130 Sassoon to Lloyd George, 13 February 1922, Lloyd George MSS, F/45/1/8; Beaverbrook to Lloyd George, 25 March 1922, Lloyd George MSS, F/4/6/8. It may be relevant that Beaverbrook had stayed with Sassoon at Trent during February.
131 See Cowling, *Impact of Labour*, 150–73. But cf. Lloyd George to Dame Margaret Lloyd George [1922], in Morgan (ed.), *Family Letters*, 200.
132 Jones Diary, 9 March 1923, in Middlemas (ed.), *op. cit.*, I, 234; Hewins Diary, 12 February 1924, Hewins MSS.
133 Chamberlain to Hoare, 28 January 1924, Templewood MSS.
134 Gretton to Baldwin, 1 November 1924, Baldwin MSS, 36 fol. 22.
135 Murray to Reading (copy), 15 December 1924, Elibank MSS, 8808 fol. 166. For Horne, see MacCallum Scott Diary, 13 November 1923.
136 Chamberlain to Baldwin, 18 July 1924, Baldwin MSS, 159, fol. 195.
137 Spender to Maclean, 2 October 1924, Maclean MSS, 467 fol. 135; Gwynne to Bolton, 30 October 1924, Baldwin MSS, 36 fol. 30.
138 Tyrell to Baldwin, 30 October 1924, Baldwin MSS, 159 fols. 265–6.
139 Younger to Grigg, 27 May 1926, Grigg MSS.
140 See Hope to Baldwin, 13 April 1927, Baldwin MSS, 162 fols. 146–7.
141 Sassoon to Baldwin [1929], Baldwin MSS, 36 fol. 205; Gwynne to Baldwin, 31 May 1929, *ibid.*, 36 fol. 192; Ralph Parker to Sir Geoffrey Butler, 1 March 1929, Templewood MSS; Lord Eustace Percy reported in *The Times*, 9 September 1929.
142 Churchill to Grigg, 6 March 1924, and Grigg to Bailey (copy), 8 May 1924, Grigg MSS.
143 Churchill to Baldwin, 29 June 1929, Baldwin MSS, 164 fol. 37.
144 See Michael Bentley, 'The Liberal Response to Socialism, 1918–29', in K. D. Brown (ed.), *Essays in Anti-Labour History* (1974), 42–73.
145 Russell to Murray, 14 October 1919, Murray MSS, Box 46.

146 Watkin Davies in *Lloyd George Liberal Magazine*, October 1921.
147 R. R. Lang to Ponsonby, 5 December 1917, Ponsonby MSS. Cf.
Lowes Dickinson to Ponsonby, 20 December 1917, and C. P.
Trevelyan to Ponsonby, 30 December 1918, Ponsonby MSS.
148 See, for example, T. N. Graham, *Willie Graham* [n.d.], 87–8.
149 Mary Stocks, *Ernest Simon of Manchester* (1963), 61.
150 *Nation*, 20 March 1920.
151 Goulding to Law, 23 September 1919, Law MSS, 98/5/11; Graham,
op. cit., 88. The partnership later foundered over Liberal reunion:
e.g. Howard to Maclean, 16 February 1923, Maclean MSS, 467 fol.
18.
152 Minute for Lloyd George by Waldorf Astor, 19 June 1917, Astor
MSS.
153 ?Hamby to Runciman, 26 October 1919, Runciman MSS.
154 For brief biographical information about such men, see C. A. Cline,
Recruits to Labour (Syracuse, N.Y., 1963), 149–78.
155 *Times*, 30 October 1920.
156 Elibank to Maclean (copy), 26 June 1919, Elibank MSS, 8804 fol.
214.
157 Dalton Diary, 1 January 1919, Dalton MSS.
158 Henderson to Webb, 17 May 1919, Passfield MSS, II.4.(g); cf. Dalton
Diary, 29 December 1918, Dalton MSS.
159 G. MacAllister, *James Maxton: Portrait of a Rebel* (1935), 165–6.
160 Esher to O.S.B., 12 September 1919, *Journals and Letters*, IV, 243.
161 Memo. by Beddington Behrens, 25 May 1919, Murray MSS, Box 59.
162 8 August 1919.
163 Esher to L.B., 1 January 1920, *Journals and Letters*, IV, 254–5;
Margot Asquith to Keynes, 26 January 1920, Keynes MSS.
164 Fisher Diary, 21 November 1918, Fisher MSS.
165 Contrast, for example, Lloyd George reported in *The Times*, 11 July
1919, with Maclean reported in *Hansard*, 7 August 1919, CXIX, 647.
166 E. T. Raymond in *Lloyd George Liberal Magazine*, November 1920.
For propaganda about an Asquithian/Labour alliance, see *ibid.*,
October and November 1920.
167 Lloyd George at Cardiganshire by-election victory dinner, 11 March
1921, reported in *Lloyd George Liberal Magazine*, April 1921.
168 Labour News Service, reported in *The Times*, 22 March 1920.
169 Lloyd George reported in *The Times*, 30 April 1923.
170 Lloyd George to Dame Margaret Lloyd George, 14 February and 26
September 1919, in Morgan (ed.), *Family Letters*, 190; Riddell Diary,
8 February 1919, *op. cit.*, 21; Jones to Hankey, 27 February 1919,
in Middlemas (ed.), *Whitehall Diary*, I, 80.
171 Lloyd George to Law (copy), 4 September 1920, Lloyd George MSS,
F/31/1/44; Lloyd George to Balfour (copy), 18 February 1920,
F/3/5/3.
172 Jones, in Middlemas (ed.), *Whitehall Diary*, I, 103.
173 Hankey to Jones, 17 January 1920, *ibid.*, I, 97; Kerr to Lloyd George,
18 May 1921, Lloyd George MSS, F/34/2/1.

174 E.g. Webb reported in Dalton Diary, 29 December 1922, Dalton MSS.
175 Quoted in Harold Spender, *The Fire of Life* (1926), 277.
176 Asquith to Crewe, 10 April 1924, Crewe MSS, C/40.
177 E.g. Henderson in the House of Commons, 2 May 1924. *Hansard*, CLXXII, 2056.
178 Dalton Diary, 19 January 1924, Dalton MSS.
179 Massingham to Strachey, 16 February and 14 March 1924, Strachey MSS, S/10/6/1; Fry to Murray, 23 June 1924, Murray MSS, Box 59.
180 James Wood to Maclean, 26 April 1924, Gladstone MSS, 46474 fol. 88.
181 Hilton Young to Geoffrey Young, 6 February 1924, Kennet MSS.
182 Notes by Lloyd George sent to Asquith, 20 August 1924, Asquith MSS, 34 fol. 141.
183 Laski to Beatrice Webb, 6 June 1924, Passfield MSS, II.4.(h).
184 Asquith to Crewe, 10 April 1924, Crewe MSS, C/40.
185 MacDonald to Murray, 10 October 1924, Murray MSS, Box 35.
186 N.U.C.A. handbill: copy in Astor MSS.
187 Sinclair to Grigg, 7 November 1924, Grigg MSS.
188 Parmoor to Murray, 28 October 1925, Murray MSS, Box 14; Stansgate Diary, 3 December 1925, Stansgate MSS.
189 Stansgate Diary, 25 November 1925, Stansgate MSS.
190 See P. Snowden, *An Autobiography*, II (1934), 743–4, where predating of the relevant incident may be significant. Cf. *Hansard*, 5 February 1926, CXCI, 573.
191 *Daily News*, 11 October 1926; Lloyd George to Hutchinson, 3 June 1926, Lloyd George MSS, G/8/13/7.
192 Margot Asquith to Keynes [1926, postmarked 21 June], Keynes MSS.
193 Mond reported in *The Times*, 19 September 1925; Hilton Young at meeting of N.L.F., 18 February 1926 (copy of speech in Kennet MSS); Kilbracken to Inchcape, October 1926, quoted in Bolitho, *James Lyle Mackay*, 222. For Inchcape, see Inchcape to Beauchamp, 1 September 1926, Lloyd George MSS, G/3/5/19.
194 Oxford to Hilton Young, 20 February 1926, Kennet MSS, 78/8.
195 Oxford to Wedgwood Benn, 11 February 1927, Stansgate MSS.
196 Grey reported in *The Times*, 15 December 1927.
197 Kerr to Keynes (copy), 25 August 1927, Lothian MSS, GD40/17/229/309–10.
198 Liberal Publications Dept, *Liberalism: What It Is. What It Has Done. What It Will Do* (1927), 16, 2.
199 Liberal Publications Dept, *Liberal Principles and Aims* (1925), 3.
200 Herbert Samuel, *Full Steam Ahead: A Clear Call to the Liberal Party* (1927), 16.
201 *Liberal Principles and Aims*, 4.
202 C. F. G. Masterman, *The New Liberalism* (1920), 34, 53; Samuel, *loc. cit.*, 15; *Liberal Principles and Aims*, 3.
203 Murray to Fisher (copy), 26 August 1924, Murray MSS, Box 19; Noel-Baker to Murray, 4 February 1927, *ibid.*, Box 4. Parmoor thought the hostility mutual: Parmoor to Murray, 1 July 1925, *ibid.*, Box 14.

204 Herbert Gladstone to Henry Gladstone, 20 July 1920, Glynne– Gladstone MSS.
205 Riddell, *op. cit.*, 255; report of Lloyd George's speech to Empire Parliamentary Association, *Times*, 23 December 1920.
206 Asquith to Strachey, 6 May 1918, Strachey MSS, S/11/6/20. Cf. Asquith to Crewe, 3 May 1923, Crewe MSS, C/40.
207 Grey to Murray, 3 February 1921, Murray MSS, Box 21; Wallas to Murray, 14 April 1922, *ibid.*, Box 53.
208 Fisher Diary, 3 May 1920, Fisher MSS.
209 Asquith to Murray (postcard), 2 February 1919, Murray MSS, Box 3.
210 Asquith to Cecil, 19 October 1922, Cecil MSS, 51073 fols. 34–5.
211 Harrison to Rosebery, 17 July 1916, Rosebery MSS.
212 G. Cope Morgan, *Cambridge Liberal Policy* (Cambridge, 1920), 8.
213 For one example, see the letter signed by Asquith, Maclean, Wedgwood and others enclosed in Cecil to Lloyd George, 22 July 1920, Lloyd George MSS, F/6/6/61.
214 H. A. L. Fisher, *Unfinished Autobiography* (Oxford, 1940), 126–7; Fisher to Lloyd George, 11 September 1920, Lloyd George MSS, F/16/7/59; Spender to Scott, 23 August 1919 in Trevor Wilson (ed.), *The Political Diaries of C. P. Scott, 1911–28* (1970), 377.
215 'R.P-H' to 'a Coalition Liberal', 17 February 1920, Asquith MSS, 45 fol. 71; Joseph Henry to Herbert Gladstone, 20 November 1920, Gladstone MSS, 46038 fols. 132–3.
216 Rosebery to Fisher, 11 October 1921, Fisher MSS.
217 J. M. Hogge, 'Free Liberalism', *Contemporary Review*, December 1919.
218 See Harold Fayle (ed.), *Harold Wright: A Memoir* (1934), 32–3. Cf. Burns' outburst: 'Oh Tariff what jobbery is committed in thy name', Diary, 29 September 1915, Burns MSS, 46337 fol. 163.
219 Scott Diary, 26–30 January 1917, in Wilson (ed.), *Political Diaries*, 257.
220 Kerr to Garvin, 30 July 1928, quoted in J. R. M. Butler, *Lord Lothian* (1960), 162.
221 Tom Clarke, *My Lloyd George Diary* (1939), 7.
222 Horne, introducing the second reading of the Dyes Bill 'to regulate the importation of Dyestuffs': *Hansard*, 7 December 1920, CXXXV, 1950.
223 For an Asquithian broadside, see National Liberal Federation, *A Tale of Folly and Failure* (1921), 22, 26.
224 Law to Lloyd George [December 1920], Lloyd George MSS, F/31/1/49; note by McCurdy, 11 May 1921, F/34/4/8.
225 Worthington Evans reported in Hewins Diary, 11 February and 30 March 1921, Hewins MSS. Cf. Hewart's comments on the Act, *Lloyd George Liberal Magazine*, February 1922.
226 Stansgate Diary, 14 February 1922, Stansgate MSS. For Wedgwood Benn's speech and the division, see *Hansard*, 14 February 1922, CL, 823–8.

227 Asquith to Lady Scott, 2 August 1916, Kennet MSS, 109/2/82; Hirst to Hammond, 28 October 1923, Hammond MSS, 19 fol. 196.

228 Emmott to Grigg, 1 January 1924, Grigg MSS.

229 Elibank to Maclean, 10 June 1919, Maclean MSS, 465 fol. 184.

230 Grigg to Milner (copy), 20 November 1923, Grigg MSS.

231 Darbyshire to Grigg, 1 May 1924, Grigg MSS.

232 Liberal Publications Dept, *Free Trade* (1925) and *Free Trade: A Post-war Statement of the Central Facts upon Which the Policy of Free Trade Rests* (1928). Cf. Godfrey Collins, 'The Present State of Free Trade', *Contemporary Review*, August 1921.

233 Inchcape to Asquith, [1923], quoted in Bolitho, *James Lyle Makay*, 224–5.

234 Thornborough to Runciman, 19 October 1928, Runciman MSS.

235 F. W. Hirst, *Economic Freedom and Private Property* (1935), 23.

236 Lloyd George to Churchill (copy), 1 October 1921, Lloyd George MSS, F/10/1/1.

237 Kerr to Lloyd George, 18 May 1921, Lloyd George MSS, F/34/2/1; Kerr, 'The Fundamental Obstacle to Socialism' (draft) [n.d.], Lothian MSS, GD40/17/418/637.

238 Riddell Diary, 23 October 1920, *op. cit.*, 242.

239 Lloyd George in Commons, 13 May 1921: *Hansard*, CXLI, 2392.

240 Lloyd George to Hilton Young (copy), 26 September 1921, Lloyd George MSS, F/28/8/1. An 'Asquithian' view of sound currency pervades D. M. Mason, *Monetary Policy, 1914–28* (1928).

241 Runciman reported in the *Liberal Magazine*, May 1919.

242 Mond in the notorious parliamentary debate about the desirability of abolishing capitalism: *Hansard*, 20 March 1923, CLXI, 2498, 2505. The National Liberal Organization printed the speech in a pamphlet called *Socialism: What It Really Is* (1923).

243 Lloyd George reported in *The Times*, 8 November 1922; cf. Sir John Simon, *Socialism Examined* (1923), 15.

244 *Liberal Magazine*, February 1921.

245 *Britain's Industrial Future: Being the Report of the Liberal Industrial Inquiry* (1928), 75.

246 Layton at the Summer School, 1922: *Liberal Magazine*, September 1922.

247 Holt Diary, 12 December 1926, Holt MSS.

248 E. D. Simon, by-election address at Dundee, December 1924, E. D. Simon MSS, M11/16/9.

249 Morgan, *Cambridge Liberal Policy*, 25.

250 *Nation*, 9 August 1919. For Liberal fears about the 'tyrannical powers' of trade unions, see Elizabeth Bibesco to Murray, 29 May 1920, Murray MSS, Box 3; and E. D. Simon to Webb, 26 July 1920, Passfield MSS, II.4.(g). Cf. Hardinge to Butler (copy), 11 October 1920: 'the working classes don't work', Hardinge MSS, 43 fol. 108.

251 Brett, *A Defence of Liberty*, 211.

252 *Britain's Industrial Future*, 180.

253 Brassey to Crewe, ?6 August 1919, writing about Geddes' proposed Transport Bill. Crewe MSS, C/3.
254 Kerr to Eagar (copy), 29 March 1927, Lothian MSS, GD40/17/223/212.
255 Brand to Grigg, 24 September 1921, and Grigg to Brand (copy), 29 September 1921, Grigg MSS.
256 Maclean to Murray, 4 September 1921, Murray MSS, Box 59. For the public face of the policy, see Liberal Publications Dept, *Through Retrenchment to Peace and Reform: A Speech Delivered at Waddesdon Manor, Buckinghamshire, on July 14th 1928 by the Right Hon. D. Lloyd George, O.M., M.P.* (1928).
257 Sidney Webb to Beatrice Webb, 10 February 1923, Passfield MSS, II.3.(i).
258 Henry Clay, 'Liberalism, Laissez-Faire and Present Industrial Conditions', *Hibbert Journal*, July 1926 (reprint in the E. D. Simon MSS, M11/16/22); Massingham to Haldane, 12 April ?1919, Haldane MSS, 5917 fol. 193.
259 E.g. Lowes Dickinson to Bryce, 25 March 1921, Bryce MSS, UB 5.
260 Haldane to Gosse, 8 August 1926, Gosse MSS.
261 MacCallum Scott Diary, 12 January 1925.
262 Churchill to Baldwin, 2 September 1928, Baldwin MSS, 36 fol. 111.
263 *Lloyd George Liberal Magazine*, June 1922; Kerr to Lloyd George (copy), 23 July 1926, Lothian MSS, GD40/17/223/231.

CHAPTER 5. THE LIBERAL INTELLIGENTSIA

1 'Intelligentsia, -tzia. 1920. [Russian, f. L. *intelligentia* INTELLIGENCE.] The class consisting of the educated part of the population and regarded as capable of forming public opinion.' *The Shorter Oxford English Dictionary*.
2 MacCallum Scott Diary, 31 March 1914.
3 Burns Diary, 13 April 1916 and 10 February 1917, Burns MSS, 46338 fol. 278, 46339 fol. 45.
4 Maclean to Gladstone, 3 August 1924, Gladstone MSS, 46474 fol. 108.
5 MacCallum Scott Diary, 15 January 1923.
6 Margot Oxford to Keynes, 6 August 1928, Keynes MSS.
7 N. G. Annan, 'The Intellectual Aristocracy', in J. H. Plumb (ed.), *Studies in Social History: A Tribute to G. M. Trevelyan* (1955), 241–87.
8 Murray to Fisher (copy), 25 September 1915, Murray MSS, Box 19.
9 See David Ayerst, *Guardian: Biography of a Newspaper* (1971), 397.
10 Quentin Bell, *Bloomsbury* (1968), 23–66.
11 For Oxford Hegelianism, see H. A. L. Fisher, *Unfinished Autobiography* (Oxford, 1940), 50.
12 The author is indebted to Mr Roger Starkey for the loan of Lowes Dickinson's personal copy of this book.
13 Henry Pelling, *Popular Politics and Society in Late Victorian Britain* (1968), 118.

14 See Annan, *loc. cit.*, 253.

15 Maurice Reckitt, *As It Happened* (1941), 112.

16 Ryland Adkins, 'The War and the National Temper', *Contemporary Review*, February 1915.

17 Fisher to Murray, 7 August 1914, Fisher MSS; Fisher to Rosebery, 24 December 1914, Rosebery MSS; Bryce to Eliot, 25 June 1915, quoted in H. A. L. Fisher, *James Bryce* (1927), II, 155; Lowes Dickinson to Wedd, 4 May 1916, King's College MSS.

18 H. A. L. Fisher, *Bryce*, II, 203. For a hint of Bryce's views about compulsion, see Bryce to Lowell, 28 February 1915, quoted in Keith Robbins, 'Lord Bryce and the First World War', *Historical Journal*, 10 (1967), 260.

19 Receipt dated 21 February 1916, Keynes MSS.

20 Nicoll to Moffat, 31 March 1917, quoted in T. H. Darlow, *William Robertson Nicoll: Life and Letters* (1925), 262.

21 Fisher to Murray, 12 December 1916, Fisher MSS.

22 Lowes Dickinson to Wedd, 4 November 1916, King's College MSS.

23 Lunn to Bryce, 22 November 1915, Bryce MSS, UB 10.

24 Arnold Toynbee, 'The Unity of Gilbert Murray's Life and Work', in Jean Smith and Arnold Toynbee (eds.), *Gilbert Murray: An Unfinished Autobiography* (1960), 215.

25 'An Estimate of Our Own Age', *Contemporary Review*, August 1919.

26 Norman Angell's own observations about the movement can be seen in Angell to Murray, 2 January 1922, Murray MSS, Box 1, and his *After All* (1951), 164–71. Cf. Edna Nixon, *John Hilton* (1946), 53–4, and, for a recent study, Howard Weinroth, 'Norman Angell and *The Great Illusion*', *Historical Journal*, 17 (1974), 551–74.

27 Howard to Bryce, 2 September 1914, Bryce MSS, UB 8.

28 Lowes Dickinson to Bryce (and enc.), 20 October 1914, Bryce MSS, UB 5.

29 E. M. Forster, *Goldsworthy Lowes Dickinson* (1934), 1962 ed., 164.

30 See Mrs Claremont (Hon. Sec.) to W. H. Dickinson, 26 January 1926, Dickinson MSS, 404 fol. 7.

31 See Morel's comments on 'Party Liberalism' in Marvin Swartz, *The Union of Democratic Control in British Politics during the First World War* (Oxford, 1971), 211.

32 Nixon, *John Hilton*, 62.

33 Lowes Dickinson to Murray, 11 July 1920, Murray MSS, Box 21.

34 Hirst to Courtney, 5 July 1916, Courtney MSS, 12 fol. 60.

35 Wallas to Murray, 22 June 1915, Murray MSS, Box 53.

36 Hobhouse to Scott, 2 December 1916, Scott MSS, 50909 fol. 38.

37 Fisher Williams to Murray, 14 July 1920, Murray MSS, Box 53.

38 Spender to Elibank, 6 September 1918, Elibank MSS, 8804 fol. 191.

39 Dalton Diary, 4/6 February 1919, Dalton MSS.

40 Bryce to Spender, 15 December 1918, Spender MSS, 46392 fol. 280.

41 Scott to Bryce, 6 April 1919, Bryce MSS, UB 15; cf. Harold Nicolson to father, 8 June 1919, quoted in Nicolson, *Peacemaking, 1919* (1934), 359.

42 See Asquith to Bryce, 21 May 1919, Bryce MSS, UB 1.
43 Keynes to Sheppard, 18 May 1919, King's College MSS.
44 Spender to Bryce, 15 June 1919, Bryce MSS, UB 17.
45 Keynes to Webb, 22 June 1919, Passfield MSS, 11.4.(g).
46 Margot Asquith reported in W. R. Inge Diary, 17 May 1920: *Diary of a Dean: St. Paul's 1911–34* (1949), 56.
47 J. M. Keynes, *The Economic Consequences of the Peace* (1919), 211.
48 Bryce to Scott, 20 January 1920, Scott MSS, 50909 fol. 215.
49 Scott to Cecil, 20 March 1921, Cecil MSS, 51162 fol. 147; Lowes Dickinson to Scott, 27 January 1920, Scott MSS, 50909 fol. 216.
50 Fisher Diary, 16 February 1920, Fisher MSS.
51 Murray to Balfour (copy), 25 March 1918, Murray MSS, Box 5.
52 MacCallum Scott Diary, 20 September 1927.
53 Murray to Runciman, 26 December 1919, Runciman MSS.
54 Murray to Fisher (copy), 26 August 1924, Murray MSS, Box 19. Cecil also believed that Liberals bulked large among supporters of the League: *All the Way* (1949), 159.
55 Cecil to Lady Selborne, 19 April 1926, Cecil MSS, 51157 fol. 153; Angell to Murray, 9 July 1926, Murray MSS, Box 1.
56 Stephen Gladstone to Bryce, 13 October 1918, Bryce MSS, UB 7.
57 Bryce to Murray, 14 March 1921, Murray MSS, Box 7.
58 Hardinge to Graham (copy), 12 February 1920, Hardinge MSS, 42 fols. 148–9.
59 'Is There an Alternative Government?' *Contemporary Review*, July 1921.
60 Holt Diary, 17 July 1921, Holt MSS.
61 Murray to Fisher (copy), 8 June 1921, Murray MSS, Box 19; Lyon to Murray, 10 May 1922, *ibid.*, Box 59.
62 F. W. S. Craig, *British Parliamentary Election Results, 1918–45* (Glasgow, 1969), 665–75.
63 See, for example, D. E. Butler, *The Electoral System in Britain, 1918–51* (Oxford, 1953), 149.
64 James Johnston, *A Hundred Commoners* (1931), 260.
65 Bryce to Murray, 23 December 1918, Murray MSS, Box 7.
66 Murray to Bryce, 15 March 1919, Bryce MSS, UB 12.
67 Noel-Baker to Murray, 4 January 1924, Murray MSS, Box 4.
68 Violet Bonham-Carter to Murray, 24 January 1920, *ibid.*, Box 10.
69 Beechman to Murray, 25 April [no year], Murray MSS, Box 59. The Lloyd Georgians did in fact form an 'Oxford University New Reform Association': *Lloyd George Liberal Magazine*, March 1921.
70 Haldane to Gosse, 14 May 1925, Gosse MSS.
71 Sargent to Simon, 18 June 1925, Simon MSS. For a repudiation of this charge, see *The Times*, 24 June.
72 List of supporters (n.d.) in the Simon MSS.
73 Asquith to Strachey, 24 July 1925, Strachey MSS, S/11/6/28; Haldane to Gosse, 23 June 1925, Gosse MSS.
74 Haldane to Gosse, 3 July 1925, Gosse MSS.
75 Note in Murray MSS, Box 59. Asquith's expenses amounted to £142.

76 J. R. M. Butler to author, 7 February 1973.
77 *Cambridge Review*, 23 November 1923.
78 Fisher Diary, 13 March 1920, Fisher MSS.
79 Spens to Horne, 21 March 1922, Lloyd George MSS, F/27/6/60.
80 G. Cope Morgan, *Cambridge Liberal Policy* (Cambridge, 1920), 4.
81 *Ibid.*, 7.
82 *Gownsman*, 27 October 1923.
83 *Cambridge Daily News*, 4 May 1923.
84 Murray to Oxford, 25 January 1925, Asquith MSS, 35 fol. 18.
85 Hammond to Lady Murray, 17 July 1924, Murray MSS, Box 23a.
86 Muir to Fisher, 9 February 1923, Fisher MSS.
87 Undated note by Phillipps, Runciman MSS.
88 See Trevor Wilson, *Downfall of the Liberal Party* (1966), 215.
89 Mary Stocks, *Ernest Simon of Manchester* (1963), 69.
90 Charles to Lucy Masterman [August 1922], quoted in Lucy Masterman, *C. F. G. Masterman* (1939), 323.
91 Keynes to Margot Oxford (not sent), 26 May 1926, Keynes MSS.
92 There is a list in the Murray MSS, Box 59.
93 Toynbee to Hammond, 23 December 1922, Hammond MSS, 18 fol. 204.
94 Muir to Lloyd George, 17 March [1926], Lloyd George MSS, G/15/6/5.
95 Muir to Lloyd George, 20 November 1927; Lloyd George to Muir (copy), 3 December 1927, *ibid.*, G/15/6/7–8.
96 Coombe-Tennant to Lloyd George, 31 March 1921, *ibid.*, F/96/1/15.
97 Stansgate Diary, 26 January 1925, Stansgate MSS.
98 Sutherland to Lloyd George, 5 January 1920, Lloyd George MSS, F/93/2/19.
99 Jackson to Murray, 24 August 1920, Murray MSS, Box 59.
100 Glover to Lunn (copy), 9 February 1927, *ibid.*, Box 59.
101 Stansgate Diary, 26 January 1925, Stansgate MSS.
102 Albert Mansbridge, *The Trodden Road* (1940), 103. For Haldane's involvement see Haldane to Gosse, 11 October 1921, Gosse MSS.
103 Lord Camrose, *British Newspapers and Their Controllers* (1947), 108.
104 Keynes to Lloyd George, 13 January 1931, Lloyd George MSS, G/10/5/4; Francis Birrell to Clive Bell [1931], King's College MSS.
105 H. V. Emy, *Liberals, Radicals and Social Politics, 1892–1914* (Cambridge, 1973), 113; Parsons to Ponsonby (enc.), 8 December 1914, Ponsonby MSS. Cf. Spender to Bryce, 30 April 1918, Bryce MSS, UB 17.
106 For Sacher see Josiah Wedgwood, *Memoirs of a Fighting Life* (1941), 194.
107 Spender to Bryce, 30 April 1918, Bryce MSS, UB 17.
108 Unwin to Courtney (copy), 6 May 1916, Courtney MSS, 11 fol. 292.
109 Ayerst, *Guardian*, 383.
110 See Hobhouse to Scott, 7 November 1924, and Scott to Hobhouse, 19 November 1924 (extracts), in T. Wilson (ed.), *The Political Diaries of C. P. Scott, 1911–28* (1970), 468–9.

111 W. Harris, *J. A. Spender* (1946), 88.
112 See, for example, Esher's remarks after dining with him: Esher to L.B., 25 April 1913, *The Journals and Letters of Reginald Viscount Esher*, III (1938), 123.
113 Harris, *op. cit.*, 82; secret memo. by Elibank, 2 October 1918, Elibank MSS, 8804 fol. 194.
114 Margot Asquith to Spender, 2 March 1922, Spender MSS, 46388 fol. 165.
115 See, for example, Donald's position over the Mansion House speech: Ayerst, *Guardian*, 367.
116 Sidney Webb to Beatrice Webb, 25 November 1925, Passfield MSS, II.3.(i).
117 Sir Geoffrey Shakespeare, *Let Candles Be Brought In* (1949), 116.
118 MacCallum Scott Diary, 10 January 1927.
119 *Ibid.*, 29 January 1921.
120 Bryce to Murray, 16 September 1920, Murray MSS, Box 7.
121 MacCallum Scott Diary, 22 May 1926 and 26 September 1927.
122 Keynes to Lloyd George, 13 January 1931, Lloyd George MSS, G/10/15/4.
123 Beatrice Webb to Haldane, 14 August 1928, Haldane MSS, 5917 fol. 124.
124 Dalton Diary, 16 June 1920, Dalton MSS.
125 Strachey to Runciman (copy), 16 May 1922; Runciman to Strachey, 11 June 1922, Strachey MSS, S/12/8/4.
126 Grigg to Mrs Spender-Clay (copy), 21 October 1922, Grigg MSS.
127 Riddell Diary, 23 October 1921, *Lord Riddell's Intimate Diary of the Peace Conference and After, 1918–23* (1933), 330.
128 Massingham to Strachey, 1 February [1924], Strachey MSS, S/10/6/1.
129 Mary Hamilton to Murray, 24 January 1921, Murray MSS, Box 59.
130 Examples in Laski to Holmes, 14 July 1923, in M. Howe (ed.), *Holmes–Laski Letters, 1916–35*, I (1953), 516; and MacCallum Scott Diary, 4 February 1927.
131 Strachey to Mitchell Innes (copy), 16 January 1917, Strachey MSS, S/18/4/4.
132 Hirst to Hammond, 4 March 1924, Hammond MSS, 20 fol. 25.
133 MacCallum Scott Diary, 15 January 1916.
134 Sidney Webb to Beatrice Webb, 12 October 1916, Passfield MSS, II.3.(i).
135 Holt Diary, 23 July 1920 and 21 February 1921, Holt MSS.
136 The opinion is Clifford Sharp's: Sidney Webb to Beatrice Webb, 7 November 1916, Passfield MSS, II.3.(i).
137 Margot Asquith to Murray, 17 August 1918, Murray MSS, Box 3.
138 Hammond to Murray, 15 April 1922, *ibid.*, Box 23a.
139 E. D. Simon, 're purchase of Nation', 3 April 1923; and Rowntree to Hobson (copy), 16 April 1923. For these letters and further correspondence about the *New Statesman* deal, see E. D. Simon MSS, M11/16/33.

140 Lucy Masterman, *C. F. G. Masterman*, 331.
141 Massingham to Strachey, 17 May 1924, Strachey MSS, S/10/6/1.
142 Haldane to Beatrice Webb, 11 July 1915, Passfield MSS, II.4.(g).
143 For comment on regional differences, see Donald to Elibank, 12 March 1912, Elibank MSS, 8803 fol. 27; and Ayerst, *Guardian*, 292–3, for peculiarities of distribution.
144 Henry Gladstone to Herbert Gladstone, 8 December 1916, Glynne–Gladstone MSS.
145 MacCallum Scott Diary, 3 January 1914.
146 Llewellyn Williams to McKenna, 29 December 1915, McKenna MSS, 5/9 fol. 15.
147 Massingham to McKenna, 1 January 1915 [*sic*], *ibid.*, 5/9 fol. 21.
148 Long to Law, 13 December 1915, Law MSS, 52/1/28.
149 *Hansard*, 11 March 1918, CIV, 114.
150 Asquith to Elibank, 22 April 1922, Elibank MSS, 8803 fol. 45.
151 Memo. by Asquith, 4 August 1921, Asquith MSS, 34 fol. 29.
152 Asquith in Cabinet, reported by Pease in his diary, 16 July 1912, Pease MSS.
153 Margot Asquith to Gosse, 15 October 1920, Gosse MSS.
154 Esher to Haig, 10 December 1917, *Journals and Letters*, IV, 167.
155 See, for example, Grigg to Kerr (copy), 23 September 1921, Grigg MSS.
156 Burns Diary, 5 October 1918, Burns MSS, 46340 fol. 166.
157 Ayerst, *Guardian*, 354; MacCallum Scott Diary, 2 February 1917.
158 G. Glenton and W. Pattinson, *The Last Chronicle of Bouverie Street* (1963), 44, 49. For Cadbury, see Tom Clarke, *My Lloyd George Diary* (1939), 7–8.
159 Lloyd George to McCurdy, 16 January 1926, Lloyd George MSS, G/13/1/34.
160 Spender to Maclean, 4 November 1921, Maclean MSS, 466 fol. 107.
161 Sandhurst Diary, 8 November 1915, *From Day to Day*, I (1928), 322.
162 Esher to Balfour, 22 June 1917, Balfour MSS, 49719 fol. 284.
163 Simon to Scott, 14 May 1915, Scott MSS, 50908 fol. 87.
164 Dawson to Grigg, 27 April 1922, Grigg MSS.
165 E.g. speech at Carnarvon reported in *Lloyd George Liberal Magazine*, November 1920.
166 Asquith in the House of Commons, 11 March 1918: *Hansard*, CIV, 115.
167 See *Report of the Royal Commission on the Press* (1947–9), Cmd. 7700, XX, I, 188, 193. Cf. discussion of Westminster trust in Camrose, *British Newspapers and Their Controllers*, 94.
168 Burns Diary, 23 May 1915 and 31 January 1916, Burns MSS, 46337 fol. 98 and 46338 fol. 44.
169 A. H. D. Acland to Spender, 7 April 1916, Spender MSS, 46392 fol. 236.
170 Spender to Bryce, 16 September 1917, Bryce MSS, UB 140.
171 Strachey to Herbert Asquith (copy), 5 January 1917, Strachey MSS, S/11/6/29.

172 Esher to Haig, 2 December 1917, *Journals and Letters*, IV, 166.
173 Buckmaster to Murray, 11 September 1920, Murray MSS, Box 6.
174 Guest to Lloyd George [1919], Lloyd George MSS, F/21/2/57.
175 C. F. G. Masterman, *The Condition of England* (1909), 266.
176 'The Calling of the Preacher', delivered 18 October 1910, Haldane MSS, 5922 fol. 3. The address was later printed in R. B. Haldane, *Selected Essays and Addresses* (1928).
177 Pelling, *Popular Politics*, 25–30; E. T. Davies, *Religion and the Industrial Revolution in South Wales* (Cardiff, 1965), 152.
178 R. Currie, *Methodism Divided* (1968), 249.
179 Lord Elton, *Among Others* (1938), 158.
180 Chris Cook, *The Age of Alignment* (1975), 79.
181 E.g. Hirst to Runciman, 4 June 1915, Runciman MSS.
182 E.g. Herbert Gladstone to Henry Gladstone, 6 January 1919, Glynne–Gladstone MSS.
183 *British Weekly*, 29 November 1923. [Emphasis added.] Cf. *ibid.*, 2 May 1929.
184 *Ibid.*, 13 December 1923.
185 *Ibid.*, 2 January 1919, 23 October 1924, 6 November 1924.
186 *Ibid.*, 16 May 1929.
187 *Ibid.*, 30 May 1929.
188 *Ibid.*, 20 June 1929.
189 Brailsford to Murray, 28 March 1917, Murray MSS, Box 6.
190 Full list of names in Dickinson MSS, vol. 403.
191 *British Weekly*, 6 August 1914.
192 E.g. Haldane to Gosse, 5 August 1918 and 13 June 1919, Gosse MSS.
193 See, for example, Denney to Nicoll, 12 March 1915 and 14 January 1917, in W. R. Nicoll (ed.), *Letters of Principal James Denney to W. Robertson Nicoll, 1893–1917* (1920), 247, 260.
194 See Hirst to Scott, 28 May 1915, in Wilson (ed.), *Political Diaries*, 126. There is a copy of one of Clifford's anti-conscription pamphlets, written in collaboration with Massingham, in the Milner MSS, Box 116.
195 Darlow, *William Robertson Nicoll*, 1; Harold Spender, *The Fire of Life* (1926), 279.
196 Nicoll to Lloyd George, 4 February 1920, Lloyd George MSS, F/13/7/15
197 *Lord Riddell's Intimate Diary*, 406.
198 Strachey to Clough (copy), 31 January 1916, Strachey MSS, S/18/3/4.
199 Horton to Dicey, 22 July 1911, Bryce MSS, 3 fol. 99.
200 Shakespeare, *op. cit.*, 335; Lloyd George to Mrs Lloyd George, 28 September 1914 in K. O. Morgan (ed.), *Lloyd George Family Letters 1885–1936* (Cardiff and Oxford, 1973), 173.
201 For the war period see Currie, *op. cit.*, 250–1. There is a severe attack on Shakespeare in the *British Weekly*, 5 December 1918.
202 Spooner to Grigg, 1 January 1922, Grigg MSS.
203 A. E. Garvie, *Memories and Meanings of My Life* (1938), 171.
204 Darlow, *Nicoll*, 184.

205 Henry Lunn, *Chapters from My Life* (1918), 322; E. C. Urwin, *Henry Carter, C.B.E.* (1955), 52.
206 Roger Lloyd, *The Church of England, 1900–65* (1966), 105.
207 See Charles Fenby, *The Other Oxford: The Life and Times of Frank Gray and His Father* (1970), 74.
208 Hensley Henson, *Retrospect of an Unimportant Life*, I (1942), 273.
209 Haldane to Gosse, 5 August 1918, Gosse MSS.
210 Edward Lincoln: to Scott, 7 May 1915, Scott MSS, 50908 fol. 82.
211 Gore to Murray (postcard), 9 May 1918, Murray MSS, Box 20; Hammond to Murray (copy), 11 November 1920, *ibid.*, Box 23a. For the reprisals debates see *Hansard*, CXXXIII, 925–1036 (20 October 1920) and 1467–1508 (25 October 1920).
212 Unwin to Courtney (copy), 19 May 1916, Courtney MSS, 11 fol. 292.
213 For the Lang/Cecil correspondence see Cecil MSS, 51154.
214 2 November 1916.
215 Denney in *British Weekly*, 20 August 1914.
216 Nicoll to Taylor, 3 May 1915, quoted in Darlow, *op. cit.*, 241.
217 John Clifford, 'The War and Public Opinion', *Contemporary Review*, November 1914.
218 Unwin to Lady Courtney (copy), 24 December 1915, Courtney MSS, 11 fol. 291.
219 Unwin to Lady Courtney (copy), 6 January 1916, Courtney MSS, 11 fol. 291.
220 For discussion of Welsh disestablishment, see P. M. H. Bell, *Disestablishment in Ireland and Wales* (1969), 226–318, and K. O. Morgan, *Wales in British Politics* (Cardiff, 1963), 259–79.
221 Lloyd George to McKenna, 18 April 1914, McKenna MSS, 4/4 fol. 25.
222 See, for example, his views about the expediency of an Education Bill, reported in Pease Diary, 5 June 1913, Pease MSS.
223 Lunn, *op. cit.*, 301.
224 *British Weekly*, 7 January 1915. For the position of Welsh M.P.s see article by J. Hugh Edwards in *ibid.*, 8 April 1915.
225 Asquith to Crewe, 12 May 1917, Crewe MSS, C/40.
226 Denney to Nicoll, 8 March 1915, in Nicoll (ed.), *Letters*, 245; also 14 January 1917, *ibid.*, 260.
227 Sir James Marchant, *Dr. John Clifford* (1924), 227.
228 17 April 1915.
229 Clifford Diary, 26 October 1917, quoted in Marchant, *op. cit.*, 230–1.
230 A. G. Gardiner, *Life of George Cadbury* (1923), 279.
231 7 December 1916: the article was presumably written on about 5 December.
232 *British Weekly*, 28 November 1918.
233 Stephen Koss, 'Lloyd George and Nonconformity: The Last Rally', *English Historical Review*, LXXXIX (1974), 78.
234 Lloyd George in Cabinet, 18 July 1921, CAB 23/26/128–9.
235 J. H. Shakespeare, 'Free Churchmen and the Coalition', *Lloyd George Liberal Magazine*, February 1921.

236 *Lloyd George Liberal Magazine*, April and August 1922.
237 Rev. W. Kingscote Greenland, 'Our Moral Debt to the Coalition', *Lloyd George Liberal Magazine*, November 1920.
238 Sylvester Diary, 5 February 1933, in Colin Cross (ed.), *Life with Lloyd George: The Diary of A. J. Sylvester 1931–45* (1975), 91.
239 Herbert Gladstone Diary, 30 January 1922, Gladstone MSS, 46484 fol. 3. Cf. Lloyd George to Dame Margaret Lloyd George, 29 August 1922: 'I am off with Shakespeare *alone* to Churt', in Morgan (ed.), *Lloyd George Family Letters*, 196.
240 Herbert Gladstone to Henry Gladstone, 2 March 1922, Glynne–Gladstone MSS; Herbert Gladstone Diary, 28 February 1922, Gladstone MSS, 46486 fol. 10.
241 Esher to L.B., 25 June 1923, *Journals and Letters*, IV, 289.
242 22 November 1923.
243 E.g. Strachey to Lady Astor (copy), 27 September 1923, Strachey MSS, S/1/13/2.
244 *Hansard*, 22 July 1921, CXLIV, 2614.
245 Sidney Webb to Beatrice Webb, 18 March 1925, Passfield MSS, II.3.(i).
246 Hewins Diary, 14 June 1919, Hewins MSS.
247 Violet Bonham-Carter to Murray, ?25 June 1923, Murray MSS, Box 10.
248 2 May 1929.
249 Sidney Webb to Beatrice Webb, 26 June 1922, Passfield MSS, II.3.(i).
250 C. P. Cook, 'The Destruction of the Liberal Party', unpub. D.Phil. dissertation (Oxford, 1971), 143.
251 Hewins Diary, 31 December 1923, Hewins MSS.
252 Dalton Diary, 14 June 1928, Dalton MSS.
253 Jones to Simon, 19 May 1928, Simon MSS.
254 These took place on 15 December 1927 and 14 June 1928. In both cases the revised book was rejected: in the first case by 230–205, in the second by 260–220. *Hansard*, CCXI, 2651–6; CCXVIII, 1319–24.
255 Strachey to Massingham, 13 February 1924, Strachey MSS, S/10/6/1. For Asquith's views see a note of July 1923 quoted in H. H. Asquith, *Memories and Reflections*, I (1928), 273.
256 Mitchell Banks reported in MacCallum Scott Diary, 5 June 1927.

COLLECT

1 Buckmaster to Murray, 20 March 1920, Murray MSS, Box 6.
2 Runciman to Murray, 28 April 1920, *ibid.*, Box 59.
3 Margot Asquith to Murray, 2 January 1919, *ibid.*, Box 3.
4 Muir to Murray, 25 February 1932, *ibid.*, Box 59.
5 Minute by Astor, 10 October 1917, Astor MSS.
6 Sir Alfred Pease, *Elections and Recollections* (1932), 40, 301.
7 Dicey to Bryce, 24 July 1911, Bryce MSS, 3 fols. 93–5.
8 Esher to Mallet, 4 December 1913, *The Journals and Letters of Reginald Viscount Esher*, III (1938), 146.

9 MacCallum Scott Diary, 17 September 1915.

10 Joseph Henry to Gladstone, 26 November 1916, Gladstone MSS, 46038 fol. 118; Harvey to Ponsonby, 29 December 1917, Ponsonby MSS.

11 Morley to Crewe, 5 February 1919, Crewe MSS, C/37.

12 Henry Gladstone to Herbert Gladstone, 10 September 1918, Glynne–Gladstone MSS.

13 Margot Asquith to Keynes, 20 June 1926, Keynes MSS.

14 MacCallum Scott Diary, 31 October 1915 and 12 March 1921. Cf. Bryce to Lowell, 5 September 1918, quoted in H. A. L. Fisher, *James Bryce*, II (1927), 195.

15 McKinnon Wood to Runciman, 4 January 1919, Runciman MSS.

16 Hammond to Murray (copy), 15 April 1922, Murray MSS, Box 23a.

17 Memo. by Behrens, 25 May 1919, *ibid.*, Box 59.

18 For examples see *Nation*, 11 March 1922 and 9 April 1927. For a Conservative view see Sir Charles Petrie, *Life and Letters of Sir Austen Chamberlain*, II (1940), 210; and for a Labour one, C. P. Trevelyan's preface to Harold Langshaw, *Socialism: And the Historic Function of Liberalism* (1925), viii.

19 Runciman to Cecil (not sent), 13 November 1919, Runciman MSS.

20 Loreburn to Bryce, 1 February 1920, Bryce MSS, UB 10.

21 Gosse to Haldane, 5 January 1922, Haldane MSS, 5915 fol. 126.

22 Esher to Stamfordham, 2 March 1917, *Journals and Letters*, IV, 91; Sandhurst Diary, 11 January 1921, *From Day to Day*, II (1929), 362; Haldane to Gosse, 4 January 1922, Gosse MSS.

23 MacCallum Scott Diary, 29 December 1917.

24 'An Alfred Mond Notebook', Melchett MSS.

25 Lambert to Runciman, 21 December 1920, Runciman MSS.

26 Morley to Crewe, 8 January 1920, Crewe MSS, C/37.

27 A. H. D. Acland to Bryce, 28 February 1919, Bryce MSS, UB 1.

28 Spencer to Rosebery, 3 November 1923, Rosebery MSS.

29 Rosebery to Strachey, 19 October 1921, Strachey MSS, S/12/7/37. Cf. a pre-war attitude in Alfred Hopkinson's preface to G. B. Hertz, *The Manchester Politician, 1750–1912* (1912), 6.

30 Crewe to Spender (copy), 30 March 1923, Crewe MSS, C/46.

31 Loreburn to Ponsonby, 23 April 1920, Ponsonby MSS; cf. Loreburn to Ponsonby, 3 July 1918.

32 Spender to Rosebery, 29 March 1925, Rosebery MSS.

33 R. Rhodes James, *Rosebery* (1963), 485.

34 Loreburn to Scott, 13 April 1919, Scott MSS, 50909 fol. 169.

35 Dalton Diary, 24 January 1923, Dalton MSS.

36 MacCallum Scott Diary, 29 November 1923; Grigg to Bailey (copy), 9 April 1923, Grigg MSS.

37 Coote to Murray, 22 April 1922, Murray MSS, Box 59.

38 MacCallum Scott Diary, 29 November 1923.

39 Haldane to Gosse, 7 January 1927, Gosse MSS.

40 Guest to Lloyd George, 17 October 1918, Lloyd George MSS, F/21/2/43; memo. by Guest [December 1920], *ibid.*, F/22/2/24; memo.

by ?Guest [n.d.], *ibid.*, F/167/2; Dalton Diary, 1 March 1920, Dalton MSS; Henry Gladstone to Herbert Gladstone, 30 August 1919, Glynne–Gladstone MSS.

41 Barlow to Asquith, 26 January 1925, Asquith MSS, 35 fol. 32.

42 Murray to Simon, 21 November 1922, Simon MSS.

43 Lowes Dickinson to Wedd, 4 November 1916, King's College MSS.

44 Rev. J. K. Mosley, quoted in C. E. Fayle (ed.), *Harold Wright* (1934), 74.

45 Butler to Asquith, 18 June 1918, Asquith MSS, 32 fol. 238.

46 MacCallum Scott Diary, 24 December 1923.

47 *Ibid.*, 22 July 1919.

48 *Ibid.*, 25 January 1922.

49 Hudson to Gladstone, 30 September 1921, Gladstone MSS, 46475 fols. 16–17.

50 Violet Bonham-Carter to Murray, 17 February 1920, Murray MSS, Box 10. Cf. Margot Asquith to Keynes, 26 January 1920, Keynes MSS.

51 Hilson to Brown, 4 October 1922, Simon MSS. For a Lloyd Georgian example, see Winifred Coombe-Tennant to Lloyd George, 31 March 1921, Lloyd George MSS, F/96/1/15.

52 J. M. Robertson, *Mr. Lloyd George and Liberalism* (1923), 23.

53 Butler to Strachey, 25 January 1918, Strachey MSS, S/3/4/9.

54 Fry to Murray, 16 June 1924, Murray MSS, Box 59.

55 Gladstone Diary, 17 March 1922, Gladstone MSS, 46486 fols. 11–12.

56 F. W. Hirst in *Westminster Gazette*, 28 June 1926.

57 Hudson to Gladstone, 30 September 1921, Gladstone MSS, 46475 fols. 16–17.

58 Memo. by Cecil, 1 July 1921 [dated by Asquith], Asquith MSS, 34 fol. 7.

59 Draft manifesto for Liberal Council [n.d.], Runciman MSS.

60 Spender to Bryce, 9 April 1921, Bryce MSS, UB 17; Manfield to Simon 19 January 1921, Simon MSS.

61 Cf. Law's remark: 'Perhaps it is true that in our Party we have most of the fools. But the Liberals have most of the cranks and I would rather have the fools.' Lord Swinton, *I Remember* (1948), 28.

62 MacCallum Scott Diary, 30 July 1926.

63 George to Murray, 28 October 1925, Murray MSS, Box 59.

Bibliography

The volume of secondary literature relating to the modern history of Liberalism is vast, and reducing it to a convenient list would be too arbitrary an exercise to be valuable; it will be apparent from the foregoing endnotes which monographs, biographies, theses and articles have been found most useful. Included in this bibliography, therefore, is only such primary material as was used in the preparation of the study.

UNPRINTED SOURCES

Asquith MSS	Bodleian Library, Oxford
Astor MSS	Reading University Library
Baldwin MSS	Cambridge University Library
Balfour MSS	British Library, London
Bonham-Carter Diary	Library of Churchill College, Cambridge
Bryce MSS	Bodleian Library, Oxford
Burns MSS and Diary	British Library, London
Cabinet Office MSS	Public Record Office, London
Cecil MSS	British Library, London
Chamberlain (Austen) MSS	Birmingham University Library
Courtney MSS	British Library of Political and Economic Science, London
Croft MSS	Library of Churchill College, Cambridge
Dalton MSS	British Library of Political and Economic Science, London
Dickinson MSS	Bodleian Library, Oxford
Elibank MSS	National Library of Scotland, Edinburgh
Fisher MSS	Bodleian Library, Oxford
Fowler MSS	Library of St John's College, Cambridge
Gladstone MSS	British Library, London
Glynne–Gladstone MSS	Flintshire County Record Office
Gosse MSS	Brotherton Collection, Leeds University Library
Grigg MSS	In the possession of Mr John Grigg
Haldane MSS	National Library of Scotland, Edinburgh
Hammond MSS	Bodleian Library, Oxford
Harcourt MSS	In the possession of Viscount Harcourt
Hardinge MSS	Cambridge University Library
Hewins MSS	Sheffield University Library
Holt MSS	Liverpool Central Library
Kennet MSS	Cambridge University Library
Keynes MSS	Library of King's College, Cambridge

King's College MSS	Library of King's College, Cambridge
Law MSS	House of Lords Record Office, London
Lloyd George MSS	House of Lords Record Office, London
Lothian MSS	Scottish Record Office, Edinburgh
MacCallum Scott Diary	In the possession of Mr John MacCallum Scott
McKenna MSS	Library of Churchill College, Cambridge
Maclean MSS	Bodleian Library, Oxford
Melchett MSS	Library of the British Steel Corporation, London
Milner MSS	Bodleian Library, Oxford
Montagu MSS	Library of Trinity College, Cambridge
Murray MSS	Bodleian Library, Oxford
Passfield MSS	British Library of Political and Economic Science, London
Pease MSS	Transcripts made available by Dr Cameron Hazlehurst
Ponsonby MSS	Bodleian Library, Oxford
Rosebery MSS	National Library of Scotland, Edinburgh
Runciman MSS	Newcastle University Library
Samuel MSS	House of Lords Record Office, London
Scott MSS	British Library, London
Sheppard MSS	Library of King's College, Cambridge
Simon (E. D.) MSS	Manchester Central Library
Simon (J. A.) MSS [cited as Simon MSS]	Institute of Historical Research, London
Spender MSS	British Library, London
Stansgate MSS	Fragments made available by Dr Cameron Hazlehurst
Strachey MSS	House of Lords Record Office, London
Templewood MSS	Cambridge University Library
Zimmern MSS	Bodleian Library, Oxford

PRINTED SOURCES

Contemporary publications containing useful material

Asquith, H. H., *Studies and Sketches* (1924)

Belloc, H., *The Servile State* (1912)

Beveridge, W., *Unemployment* (1909)

Bosanquet, B., *The Value and Destiny of the Individual* (1913)

Brett, Oliver, *A Defence of Liberty* (1920)

Bunsen, Victoria de, *The War and Men's Minds* (1919)

Butler, Nicholas Murray, *The Faith of a Liberal* (New York, 1924)

Bryce, J. (ed.), *The League of Nations* (Oxford, 1919)

Cavendish-Bentinck, H., *Tory Democracy* (1918)

Churchill, W. S., *The World Crisis* (6 vols., 1923–31)

Dodds, Elliot, *Is Liberalism Dead?* (1920)

Fisher, H. A. L., *The Common Weal* (Oxford, 1924)

Gardiner, A. G., *The War Lords* (1915)
Hirst, F. W., *Economic Freedom and Private Property* (1935)
Hobson, J. A., *The Crisis of Liberalism* (1909)
  The New Protectionism (1916)
Keynes, J. M., *The Economic Consequences of the Peace* (1919)
Keynes, J. M. and Henderson, H. D., *Can Lloyd George Do It?*
  (1929)
Langshaw, Harold, *Socialism: And the Historic Function of Liberalism*
  (1925)
Liberal Industrial Inquiry, *Britain's Industrial Future* (1928)
Mason, D. M., *Monetary Policy, 1914–28* (1928)
Masterman, C. F. G., *The New Liberalism* (1920)
  England After War (1922)
Maxse, L. J., *Politicians on the War-Path* (1920)
Mitchell Banks, Reginald, *The Conservative Outlook* (1929)
Morgan, G. Cope, *Cambridge Liberal Policy* (Cambridge, 1920)
Muir, Ramsay, *The Liberal Way* (1934)
Nathan, H. L. and Williams, H. H. (eds.), *Liberal Points of View* (1927)
Rea, Russell, *The Triumph of Free Trade* (1920)
Robertson, J. M., *The Meaning of Liberalism* (1912; 2nd ed., 1925)
  Mr. Lloyd George and Liberalism (1923)
Roch, Walter, *Mr. Lloyd George and the War* (1920)
Storey, Harold, *The Case against the Lloyd George Coalition* (1920)

                Some useful editions of letters and diaries
Braley, E. F. (ed.), *Letters of Bishop Henson* (2 vols., 1950–4)
Clarke, Tom, *My Northcliffe Diary* (1931)
  My Lloyd George Diary (1939)
Cole, M. (ed.), *Beatrice Webb's Diaries, 1912–32* (2 vols., 1952–6)
Esher, Oliver (ed.), *The Journals and Letters of Reginald Viscount Esher*
  (4 vols., 1934–8)
Howe, M. (ed.), *Holmes–Laski Letters, 1916–35* (2 vols., Oxford, 1969–71)
Inge, W. R., *Diary of a Dean: St. Paul's 1911–34* (1949)
MacCarthy, D. (ed.), *Letters of the Earl of Oxford and Asquith to a Friend*
  (2 vols., 1933–4)
Middlemas, K. (ed.), *Whitehall Diary* (3 vols., Oxford, 1969–71)
Massingham, H. J. (ed.), *H. W. M.: A Selection from the Writings of
  H. W. Massingham* [n.d.]
Morgan, K. O. (ed.), *Lloyd George Family Letters, 1885–1936* (Cardiff
  and Oxford, 1973)
Nicoll, W. R. (ed.), *Letters of Principal James Denney to W. Robertson
  Nicoll, 1893–1917* (1920)
Raleigh, Lady (ed.), *The Letters of Sir Walter Raleigh, 1879–1922* (2 vols.,
  1926–8)
Riddell, Lord, *Lord Riddell's War Diary, 1914–18* (1933)
  Lord Riddell's Intimate Diary of the Peace Conference and After, 1918–23
  (1933)

A. J. P. Taylor (ed.), *Lloyd George: A Diary by Frances Stevenson* (1971)
  My Darling Pussy: The Letters of Lloyd George and Frances Stevenson,
  1913–41 (1975)
Wilson, Trevor (ed.), *The Political Diaries of C. P. Scott, 1911–28* (1970)

Some autobiographies

Addison, Christopher, *Politics from Within* (2 vols., 1924)
  Four and a Half Years (2 vols., 1933–4)
Angell, Norman, *After All* (1951)
Asquith, E. A. M., *The Autobiography of Margot Asquith* (1920; 2nd ed.,
  1936)
Asquith, H. H., *Memories and Reflections* (2 vols., 1928)
Asquith, Herbert, *Moments of Memory* (1937)
Benn, E., *Happier Days* (1949)
Buckmaster, Viscount, *Roundabout* (1969)
Cecil, Viscount, *All the Way* (1949)
Chesterton, G. K., *Autobiography* (1936)
Clynes, J. R., *Memoirs* (2 vols., 1937)
Coulton, G. G., *Fourscore Years* (Cambridge, 1943)
Elton, Lord, *Among Others* (1938)
Ernle, Lord, *Whippingham to Westminster* (1938)
Fisher, H. A. L., *Unfinished Autobiography* (Oxford, 1940)
FitzRoy, A., *Memoirs* (2 vols., 1925)
Garvie, A. E., *Memories and Meanings of My Life* (1938)
Glover, T. R., *Cambridge Retrospect* (Cambridge, 1943)
Grey, Viscount, *Twenty-five Years* (2 vols., 1925)
Griffiths, James, *Pages from Memory* (1969)
Haldane, Elizabeth, *From One Century to Another* (1937)
Haldane, R. B., *Autobiography* (1929)
Hamilton, M. A., *Remembering My Good Friends* (1944)
Henson, Hensley, *Retrospect of an Unimportant Life* (3 vols., 1942–50)
Kilmuir, Lord, *Political Adventure* (1964)
Lloyd George, David, *War Memoirs* (6 vols., 1933–6)
Lloyd George, Frances, *The Years That Are Past* (1967)
Lunn, H., *Chapters from My Life* (1918)
McKenna, Stephen, *While I Remember* (1921)
Macmillan, H., *Winds of Change* (1966)
Mansbridge, Albert, *The Trodden Road* (1940)
Marriot, J., *Memories of Fourscore Years* (1946)
Midleton, Lord, *Records and Recollections* (1939)
Muir, Ramsay, *An Autobiography and Some Essays*, ed. Stuart Hodgson
  (1943)
Murray, G., *Gilbert Murray: An Unfinished Autobiography*, ed. Jean
  Smith and Arnold Toynbee (1960)
Pease, Alfred E., *Elections and Recollections* (1932)
Reckitt, Maurice, *As It Happened* (1941)
Robinson, Henry, *Memories: Wise and Otherwise* (1923)

Runciman, Sir Walter, *Before the Mast: And After* (1924)
Samuel, Herbert, *Memoirs* (1945)
Sandhurst, Viscount, *From Day to Day* (2 vols., 1928–9)
Sexton, Sir J., *Sir James Sexton, Agitator* (1936)
Shakespeare, Geoffrey, *Let Candles Be Brought In* (1949)
Spender, J. A., *Life, Journalism and Politics* (1927)
Steed, H. Wickham, *Through Thirty Years, 1892–1922* (1924)
Swinton, Lord, *I Remember* (1948)
Thomas, J. H., *My Story* (1937)
Trevelyan, G. M., *An Autobiography and Other Essays* (1949)
Wedgwood, Josiah, *Memories of a Fighting Life* (1941)

Works of reference

Craig, F. W. S., *British Parliamentary Election Results, 1918–45* (Glasgow, 1969)
Butler, D. and Freeman, J., *British Political Facts* (1968 ed.)
    Dictionary of National Biography
    Burke's Peerage
    Debrett's Peerage
    Who Was Who?
    Dod's Parliamentary Companion
    Whitaker's Almanac
    Annual Register

Periodicals

The Times	*Nation*
Manchester Guardian	*Contemporary Review*
Westminster Gazette	*Nineteenth Century and After*
Daily News	*Liberal Magazine*
Daily Chronicle	*Lloyd George Liberal Magazine*

Archive collections often contain substantial press cuttings. The Liberal Publications Department and National Liberal Organization also published a great number of pamphlets and fly-sheets.

Index

Asquith and Lloyd George are abbreviated to HHA and LG throughout.

Ilbert, Sir Courtney, 163
Inchcape, J. L. Mackay, Earl of, 76, 148
Independent Review, 164
industry, 9, 74, 89, 108, 121–2, 142–3, 154–6, 195–7, 217
Inge, W. R., 12
Ireland, 9–10, 13, 70, 74, 183, 197, 203; and war, 16, 41 and n.; and Coalition Liberals, 80; and Conservative party, 138; post-war Liberal policy, 151–2
Irwin, E. Wood, Viscount (later Earl of Halifax), 113

John, E. T., 143
Jones, J. D., 204
Jones, Joseph, 179
Jones, Leif, 64, 89, 178
Jones, Thomas, 145, 179

Kellaway, F. G., 73, 82, 89
Kenworthy, J. M., 67, 101, 132, 147
Kerr, Philip (later Marquess of Lothian), 43, 60, 76, 126, 145, 152, 168, 183; on Socialism and Liberalism, 149
Keynes, J. M., 77, 102, 108, 157, 163, 169–72, 176; an Asquithian? 177; in LG camp, 178; and Liberal press, 180
Kilbracken, Sir J. A. Godley, baron, 148
King, Joseph, 19, 143
Kitchener, General H. H., 1st Earl, 41, 195

Labour party, 31, 61, 85, 86, 90, 97–8, 106, 134, 164, 181; and Liberal party, 141–9; and conscription, 26–7; and a centre party, 132; LG's relations with, 59, 100–1; first government (1924), 90–5, 141, 146–7; 'Labour v. the rest', 121; HHA on, 123; attitude to Liberals, 112–13; relations with Nonconformity, 192, and temperance movement, 202
Lambert, George, 50, 67, 85, 136
Lambert, R. L., 31
land and Liberal policy, 10, 39, 93, 98–9, 101, 217; and Convention, 100; Land and Nation League, 107; alleged Socialism, 140–1
Lang, Cosmo, 197
Lansbury, George, 124

Lansdowne, H. C. K. Petty-Fitzmaurice, Marquess of, 25, 30, 60–1, 62–3
Laski, H. J., 18, 72, 115
Law, A. Bonar, 20, 25, 42, 65, 75, 132, 136, 145
Layton, W. T., 108
League of Nations, 89, 152, 166–72, 193, 202; and Grey, 69; as feature of Liberal policy, 150–1
Leamington meeting (1920), 81–2, 137
Lee, Arthur, 39
Lees Smith, H. B., 42, 143
Liberal Administrative Committee, 107
Liberal Anti-Nationalization Committee, 143
Liberal Candidates' Association, 103
Liberal Central Association, 107
Liberal Council, 94, 109–11, 218
Liberal Foreign Affairs Committee, 17
Liberal Industrial Inquiry, 108; see also *Britain's Industrial Future*, industry
Liberal Magazine, 81
Liberal party
  pre-war character, 13; pacifist content, 11, 16–17, 27, 61–4; splitting of, 37–45, 213; Asquithian wing (1916–22), 48–71, 80–3; Lloyd Georgian wing (1916–22), 71–83; attempts at reunion (1923/24), 84–90, 91, 146; struggle for control (1924–6), 84–98, 99–100, 101–4, and the General Strike, 101–3; revival and relapse (1927–9), 104–16
  party finance: Asquithian, 70–1, 87, (Million Fund) 99, (till empty) 103, 105–6; Lloyd George fund, (and 1924 election) 92–3, 96, 100, 105, 109, 110, (and 1929 election) 115, ('a mercenary force') 140
Liberal Summer School, 108, 177–8
Liberal War Committee, 37–8, 43
Lidgett, J. Scott, 194–5, 199
Lincolnshire, C. R. Wynn-Carrington, Marquess of, 67, 85
Lindemann, F. A. (later Lord Cherwell), 175
Lloyd George, David (later Earl Lloyd-George of Dwyfor)
  and Liberal party: Runciman finds him 'down' (1914), 13; relations with Churchill, 11, 32; wartime rift with HHA, 32; threatens resigna-

Lloyd George (*cont.*)

tion, 32–3; unpopular, 37; opposed by a 'clique', 38; growing estrangement from HHA, 39–40; likely to succeed as P.M., 41; moves to War Office, 41–2; offers resignation again, 41; 'conspiracy' and office, 43–5; secures Montagu and Churchill, 50–2; fails to secure HHA, 52–3; some Liberals sorry for him, 55; alienates House of Commons, 58–9; opposition from negotiated peace faction, 60–4; consults HHA and Grey over 'war aims', 61; and the Maurice debate (1918), 64; Asquithian attacks at coupon election, 65–6

character of his mind, 72; his genius, 72–3; his government, 73–6; no clear policy emerges, 76–7; at his peak, 77–8; his post-war appeal, 78–9; and Paisley by-election, 134; attacks HHA, 137; declares Liberalism 'done for', 82

attempts at Liberal reunion, 84ff; in 'suspended animation' (1923), 86; shares platform with HHA, 89; 'cartwheeling round the country', 89; recommends working with Labour (1924), 90; broody, 91; begins to move left, 91–2, 146–7; winds up his party organization, 92; decides to take over Liberal machine, 92ff; his money, 92; collaborates with Churchill, 93

inquiries and Labour, 94; Asquithian aversions to him, 95; acquires Masterman, 95; fails to become leader, 96; moves towards Labour, 98; moves towards Conservatives, 98; dominates Liberal party, 99; consolidates grip on the machine, 103; another reunion plan, 103; post-Asquithian arrangements, 107; acquires Simon, 108; on crimes of Liberal Council, 110; and Yellow Book, 113; and 1929 campaign, 114; in the market for a coalition, 114; election a disappointment, 114; 'a sort of Wee Free!' 121; corrupter or crusader, 127; 'a national disaster and calamity', 140

and Conservative party: talks with Law in 1915, 22; relations with Milner, 40; paradox of his impact after 1922, 131; plans for a centre party, 131–9; describes Coalition colleagues as 'Liberal minded men', 120; compared with Baldwin, 125–6; thoughts about a Horne government, 139; relationship commented on, 26, 28, 30, 33, 43, 48, 87, 128

and Labour party: rumours of alliance with Thomas, 100; did he intend 'going Labour' in 1926? 100–1; Lansbury compares MacDonald with him, 124; language of resistance to Labour, 136, but 'the poor our common comrade', 137, 155; conditions all Liberal relations with Labour, 141; and MacDonald, 146; believes Labour to be 'forging ahead', 147

other relationships: universities, 179; Nonconformity, 194, 198, 199–200, 201–2, 204; press, 181, 183, 185, 188

miscellaneous judgements: does not understand Liberal attachment to free trade, 152; economic ideas, 155

Lloyd George, Dame Margaret, 98
Lloyd George Liberal Magazine, 81, 88, 201
Lloyd Graeme, P. (later Cunliffe-Lister), 135
London School of Economics, 177, 180
Long, W., 24, 25, 30, 59
Loreburn, R. T. Reid, Earl, 60, 62, 63, 167, 184, 212
Lowes Dickinson, G., 15, 72, 142, 163–4, 167–8, 181, 193
Lucas, A. T. Herbert, baron, 24
Lucas, E. V., 165
Lunn, Sir Henry, 195, 198–9

Macara, Sir C., 199
MacCallum Scott, A., 26, 30, 33–4, 58, 78–9, 81, 82, 88, 91, 93, 112–13, 127, 137, 161–2, 184, 186, 207, 209, 211, 214–15; diary, 25, 48, 73, 101
McCurdy, C., 80, 87, 95, 96, 107, 132, 167